Political Pedagogies

Series Editors
Jamie Frueh, Bridgewater College, Bridgewater, VA, USA
David J. Hornsby, The Norman Paterson School of International Affairs, Carleton University, Ottawa, Canada

Political Pedagogies is a collection of scholarly texts on methods of teaching and learning politics. The series seeks to be the premier assemblage of book-length contributions that explores all aspects of political pedagogy, from philosophical considerations about the role and purpose of pedagogy to practical guides and strategies for teaching political science and international relations. The proliferation of journals, conferences, workshops and institutional centers devoted to teaching attest to the accelerating interest in the pedagogy of Political Science and International Relations. The challenges of teaching in the twenty-first century span sub-disciplines and connect scholars from a wide variety of institutions in a common mission critical to the health of modern democracies. Indeed, teaching may be the only focus that scholars in these disciplines truly share, and the series seeks to elevate the importance of teaching in disciplinary and social advancement. *Political Pedagogies* strives to create an inclusive and expansive space where scholars can explore what it means to teach and foster learning and provides a much-needed platform for longer, deeper, creative and more engaged scholarship that melds the teaching and research responsibilities of Political Science and International Relations faculty.

Charity Butcher · Tavishi Bhasin ·
Elizabeth Gordon · Maia Carter Hallward
Editors

The Palgrave Handbook of Teaching and Research in Political Science

palgrave
macmillan

Editors
Charity Butcher
School of Conflict Management,
Peacebuilding and Development
Kennesaw State University
Kennesaw, GA, USA

Tavishi Bhasin
School of Government
and International Affairs
Kennesaw State University
Kennesaw, GA, USA

Elizabeth Gordon
School of Government
and International Affairs
Kennesaw State University
Kennesaw, GA, USA

Maia Carter Hallward
School of Conflict Management,
Peacebuilding and Development
Kennesaw State University
Kennesaw, GA, USA

ISSN 2662-7809   ISSN 2662-7817   (electronic)
Political Pedagogies
ISBN 978-3-031-42886-9   ISBN 978-3-031-42887-6   (eBook)
https://doi.org/10.1007/978-3-031-42887-6

© The Editor(s) (if applicable) and The Author(s), under exclusive license to Springer Nature Switzerland AG 2023

This work is subject to copyright. All rights are solely and exclusively licensed by the Publisher, whether the whole or part of the material is concerned, specifically the rights of translation, reprinting, reuse of illustrations, recitation, broadcasting, reproduction on microfilms or in any other physical way, and transmission or information storage and retrieval, electronic adaptation, computer software, or by similar or dissimilar methodology now known or hereafter developed.
The use of general descriptive names, registered names, trademarks, service marks, etc. in this publication does not imply, even in the absence of a specific statement, that such names are exempt from the relevant protective laws and regulations and therefore free for general use.
The publisher, the authors, and the editors are safe to assume that the advice and information in this book are believed to be true and accurate at the date of publication. Neither the publisher nor the authors or the editors give a warranty, expressed or implied, with respect to the material contained herein or for any errors or omissions that may have been made. The publisher remains neutral with regard to jurisdictional claims in published maps and institutional affiliations.

Cover credit: Dimitri Otis/Getty Images

This Palgrave Macmillan imprint is published by the registered company Springer Nature Switzerland AG
The registered company address is: Gewerbestrasse 11, 6330 Cham, Switzerland

Paper in this product is recyclable.

Acknowledgments

The editors would like to thank Frederick "Walt" Tillman, Adam Swart, and Sushant Naidu for their editorial assistance on this book. Additionally, we would like to thank Jamie Frueh and David Hornsby, editors of the Political Pedagogies book series, as well as Anca Pusca, Editor for the series at Palgrave Macmillan, for their support and the inclusion of this book in the Political Pedagogies book series. Finally, we would like to thank the reviewers for the various chapters in the book and the contributing authors for their fantastic contributions to this volume.

Contents

1 Introduction 1
Maia Carter Hallward, Tavishi Bhasin, Charity Butcher, and Elizabeth Gordon

Part I Scholarship of Teaching and Learning and Pedagogical Research

2 Taking Teaching Philosophies Seriously: Pedagogical Identity, Philosophy of Education, and New Opportunities for Publication 13
Michael P. A. Murphy

3 Researching While Teaching and Mentoring: A Reflection on Collaboration 23
Daniel J. Mallinson

4 Metacognitive Exercises in the Political Science Classroom: Reflections and Research on Student Investment in Learning 35
Buket Oztas

Part II Leveraging Scholarship to Enhance the Pedagogy of Simulations, Games, and Role Play Exercises

5 Collaboration and Independent Study: Working with Undergraduate Students to Design, Implement, and Assess a Simulation 49
   Michelle Allendoerfer

6 Facilitating Student Learning Through Games on Human Rights 61
   Charity Butcher, Maia Carter Hallward, and Frederick Walter Tillman II

7 'I'm Gonna Make Them an Offer They Can't Refuse': Teaching Politics and Mafia Through a Role-Play to Improve Student Learning and Understanding 75
   Felia Allum and Geraldine Jones

Part III Writing Textbooks

8 Writing a Textbook Is Good for You 91
   Alasdair Blair

9 Taking Innovative Teaching to the Next Level: Writing and Publishing Instructional Materials and Textbooks 101
   J. Cherie Strachan

Part IV Conducting Research with Students

10 The Benefits and Challenges of Faculty–Student Research Partnerships 115
    Patrick Bijsmans

11 Working Smarter by Engaging Students in Political Science Research 127
    Shauna Reilly

12 The Extra-Curricular Teacher-Scholar: Funding Undergraduates to Be Research Assistants 137
    Michael T. Rogers

13	Increasing Access to Undergraduate Research Opportunities at Small Teaching Institutions Kelly Bauer	149
14	Teamwork Makes the (Research) Dream Work: Lessons in Working with a Student Research Team Julia Marin Hellwege, Cohl Turnquist, Aaron Vlasman, and Bess Seaman	161
15	Making Contingency Work: Conducting Student-Engaged Research Off the Tenure Track Alexis Henshaw	171
16	Using Survey Research as an Educational Tool: Cross-Cultural Lessons on How to Balance Research and Teaching Alfred Marleku, Ridvan Peshkopia, and D. Stephen Voss	181
17	Partnering with Master's Students on Policy Research and Practice Laila Sorurbakhsh	195
18	Graduate Students and Learning How to Get Published John Ishiyama	207

Part V Research with Students: Experiential Learning and Civic Engagement

19	Taking Community-Based Research Online: Benefits and Drawbacks for Researchers and Students Rebecca A. Glazier	219
20	Combining Project-Based Learning and Service-Learning in Teaching Global Issues Audrey Ruark Redmond	231
21	Living Our Learning: Transformative Impacts of Study Abroad and Field Studies for Students and Faculty Mark Hamilton and Katherine Almeida	245

22 Using Exit Polls to Teach Students and Sustain
    a Scholarly Agenda   259
    Matthew P. Thornburg and Robert E. Botsch

23 An Experiential Approach to Teaching the Importance
    of the Iowa Caucuses   273
    Jay Wendland

24 Triple the Benefits Without Tripling the Work:
    Combining Teaching and Research in Service
    to the Community   285
    Elizabeth A. Bennion

25 Thriving Together: Connecting Civic Engagement,
    International Relations Pedagogy, and Undergraduate
    Research as Workload   301
    Alison Rios Millett McCartney

26 Connection Over Content: How Civically Engaged
    Research Can Improve Teaching, Research, and Service   317
    Kirstie Lynn Dobbs

27 Campus & Community Engagement of Student
    Research: The Evolution of a Senior Capstone Project   327
    Carrie Humphreys

Part VI   Embedding Research in Teaching and Generating
          Research Ideas from Teaching

28 In Unity There Is Strength: How to Incorporate Your
    Research into Teaching   339
    Wei-Ting Yen

29 Creating Positive Feedback Cycles Between Teaching
    and Research   349
    Eric Loepp

30 Using Review Sessions to Jumpstart Research Projects
    in Methods Coursework   361
    Wesley Wehde

31 "Doing" Political Theory in the Classroom   373
    E. Stefan Kehlenbach

32 Picturing Connections Between Hunger
    and International Relations: Using Images
    to Improve Learning and Research   385
    Thiago Lima

33 Knowledge Production and Student Learning
    in Political Science: Bhutan and The Politics
    of Happiness   393
    Sarina Theys

Part VII Conclusion

34 Conclusion   403
    Elizabeth Gordon, Tavishi Bhasin, Maia Carter Hallward,
    and Charity Butcher

Index   413

NOTES ON CONTRIBUTORS

Michelle Allendoerfer is the Senior Director of Teaching and Learning at the American Political Science Association. Prior to joining APSA, Michelle was the faculty coordinator for the International Politics cohort of the Women's Leadership Program at the George Washington University where she taught political science courses. In addition to her research on human rights, Michelle has published on pedagogy. She received her B.A. in Political Science at Carleton College and her Ph.D. in Political Science from the University of Michigan.

Felia Allum is Professor of comparative organized crime and corruption at the University of Bath and a Senior fellow at the Higher Education Academy. Her research interests are organized crime, mafias, criminal mobility, politics-mafia links, and gender. In 2016, she was awarded *The Innovation in Teaching and Learning Award* from the University of Bath and in 2019, *The Jennie Lee Prize for Outstanding Teaching*, by the Political Studies Association.

Katherine Almeida is alumna and former assistant faculty member at the IADC and currently serves as Academic Specialist for the William J. Perry Center at National Defense University. She is a graduate of the University of Salamanca in Spain and the University of Beira Interior in Portugal. Her reflections on teaching draw on field study experiences within the Americas and Europe as well as diplomatic service for the Dominican

Republic and research and teaching in areas of development, security, social innovation, leadership, and organizational resilience.

Kelly Bauer is an Associate Professor of Political Science at George Washington University. Her research and teaching explore identity and development politics in Latin America, recently focusing on policy responses to and rhetoric about Indigenous rights, irregular migration, and human security regimes. Her writing on higher education politics and scholarship of teaching and learning recently appeared in Iberoamericana, Political Science Educator, and Strategies for Navigating Graduate School and Beyond.

Elizabeth A. Bennion is Chancellor's Professor of Political Science and Director of Community Engagement at Indiana University South Bend. As Director of IU South Bend's American Democracy Project, Bennion promotes informed and engaged citizenship as a teacher, mentor, event organizer, TV host, civic leader, media consultant, and debate moderator. She has received numerous campus, local, state, and national awards for her work as a civic educator. Her 75+ published works include large-scale, voter mobilization field experiments, best practice guides to promoting and assessing civic learning, critical reflections on race and gender politics, and three co-edited books on teaching civic engagement.

Tavishi Bhasin is a Professor in the School of Government and International Affairs at Kennesaw State University. She is an Associate Editor of the APSA *Journal of Political Science Education*. She received her Ph.D. in Political Science from Emory University. She studies the politics of identity (gender, ethnicity, religion, and language), political dissent, state repression, and democratic institutional design. She also conducts research in the area of teaching and learning. Her publications have appeared in multiple peer-reviewed journals including *Journal of Conflict Resolution* and the *British Journal of Political Science, Terrorism and Political Violence, Electoral Studies, European Political Research*, and *Journal of Turkish Studies*. She also has a book chapter on teaching research methods. She was awarded the Radow College of Humanities and Social Sciences 2021 Diversity and Inclusion Award and served as co-organizer of the 2021 TLC at the APSA conference in Seattle, Washington.

Patrick Bijsmans is an Associate Professor in Teaching & Learning European Studies and Associate Dean for Education at Maastricht University's Faculty of Arts and Social Sciences. His research interests include issues pertaining to teaching and learning in problem-based learning and to curriculum design and alignment, as well as media and Euroscepticism. Patrick is teaching courses in European Studies at B.A. and M.A. levels. He is former program director of the university's B.A. in European Studies, and has previously been involved in its teaching staff professionalization program. Website: https://patrickbijsmans.weebly.com.

Alasdair Blair is Associate PVC Academic and Jean Monnet Professor at De Montfort University. He is a member of the editorial team of *Journal of Political Science Education* and served as co-editor of *European Political Science* (2005–2023). His textbooks include *The European Union Since 1945* (2023), *Britain and the World Since 1945* (2014), *The European Union* (2012), *International Politics* (2009), and *Companion to the European Union* (2006). He is co-editor of *Teaching Civic Engagement Globally* (2021) and co-editor with Darrell Evans, Christina Hughes, and Malcolm Tight on *International Perspectives on Leadership in Higher Education* (2022).

Robert E. Botsch is a Distinguished Professor Emeritus of Political Science, USC Aiken Ph.D., UNC-CH, 1977; USCA professor, 1978–2015; Carolina Trustee Professor, Grew Endowed Chair, founded Survey Research Services; Professor of Year awards: twice USCA, USC System, Carnegie Foundation for SC and top ten national; campus awards: scholarly activity, service; authored three books, four online texts, numerous articles, book chapters, and applied research reports.

Charity Butcher is Director of the School of Conflict Management, Peacebuilding and Development and a Professor of Political Science at Kennesaw State University. She received her Ph.D. in Political Science from Indiana University. She conducts research on conflict and human rights, as well as on the Scholarship of Teaching and Learning. She is currently the Editor-in-Chief of the *Journal of Political Science Education* and is author, co-author, or co-editor of three books, including *NGOs and Human Rights* (University of Georgia Press, 2021), *Understanding International Conflict Management* (Routledge,

2020), and *The Handbook of Cross-border Ethnic and Religious Affinities* (Rowman & Littlefield, 2019). She has published numerous peer-reviewed articles in a variety of journals, including the *Journal of Political Science Education, Journal of Human Rights, International Studies Perspectives, Terrorism and Political Violence, Democratization, European Political Science,* and *International Journal of Politics, Culture, and Society.*

Kirstie Lynn Dobbs is an Assistant Professor of Practice in the Department of Political Science and Public Policy and the Early College Program at Merrimack College. Working at the intersection of comparative and international politics, she teaches courses, conducts research, and provides consulting expertise on topics related to democracy, democratization, and youth civic engagement. Dr. Dobbs also serves as the director of Merrimack's Together for Community Action initiative that connects faculty across campus through community-engaged projects.

Rebecca A. Glazier is a political science professor in the School of Public Affairs at the University of Arkansas at Little Rock. She is the Director of the Little Rock Congregations Study, a longitudinal, community-based research project on religion and community engagement. She is the author of "Faith and Community: How Engagement Strengthens Members, Places of Worship, and Society" (Temple University Press, forthcoming, 2024). Dr. Glazier is active in the scholarship of teaching and learning and is the author of "Connecting in the Online Classroom: Building Rapport between Teachers and Students" (Johns Hopkins University Press, 2021).

Elizabeth Gordon is a Professor in the School of Government and International Affairs at Kennesaw State University. Her Ph.D. is in Political Science from the University of North Carolina at Chapel Hill, where she also worked as a researcher at UNC's Institute of Government. She has published peer-reviewed articles in multiple academic journals including *Politics & Gender, Politics and Religion, Justice System Journal, Judicature, Mediation Quarterly,* and *International Journal of Sociology and Social Policy,* as well as a chapter on misogyny in American politics in *Misogyny in American Culture: Causes, Trends, Solutions* (one of Library Journal's best reference books of 2018). She currently serves as an Associate Editor of the APSA *Journal of Political Science Education.*

Maia Carter Hallward is a Professor of Middle East Politics in the School of Conflict Management, Peacebuilding and Development at Kennesaw State University. She holds a Ph.D. in International Relations from American University's School of International Service. She is the author or co-author of seven books, including *NGOs and Human Rights: Comparing Faith-Based and Secular Approaches* (University of Georgia Press, 2021) and *Struggling for a Just Peace: Israeli and Palestinian Activism in the Second Intifada* (University of Florida Press, 2011) and over two dozen peer-reviewed articles in journals including *Journal of Peace Research, International Political Sociology, Journal of Human Rights, Research in Social Movements Conflict, and Change.* Current projects include co-editing a Handbook of Peace and Conflict Studies and the role of male allyship in Middle Eastern women's rights movements. Maia served as Executive Editor of the *Journal of Peacebuilding and Development* from 2015 to 2023 and currently serves as Associate Editor of the *Journal of Political Science Education.*

Mark Hamilton is a long-term faculty member at the Inter-American Defense College (IADC), which operates across multiple languages and engages students from diverse countries, operating under the auspices of the Organization of American States. He is a graduate of Taylor University and American University's School of International Service. Mark's teaching reflections build on experiences at diverse academic institutions, workshops conducted in the Americas, Middle East, Europe, and South Asia, and consultations as a scholar-practitioner and researcher at the nexus of security studies, development, and peacebuilding.

Julia Marin Hellwege is an Associate Professor of Political Science and Director of the Government Research Bureau at the University of South Dakota. She is co-editor of *The Palgrave Handbook of Political Research Pedagogy* (2021) and *Strategies for Navigating Graduate School and Beyond* (APSA, 2022). In 2021, she won the Belbas Larson Award for teaching excellence, the university's premier teaching award. Her work has been published in outlets such as *American Politics Research, Legislative Studies Quarterly, Journal of Political Science Education,* and *Social Science Quarterly.*

Alexis Henshaw is an Associate Professor in the Political Science department at Troy University. She was previously a visiting faculty member at Duke University, Miami University, Bucknell University, and

Sweet Briar College. She is the author of *Why Women Rebel: Understanding Women's Participation in Armed Rebel Groups* (Routledge, 2017), *Digital Frontiers in Gender and Security* (Bristol University Press, 2023), and co-author of *Insurgent Women: Female Combatants in Civil Wars* (Georgetown University Press, 2019).

Carrie Humphreys is an Associate Professor of Political Science at the University of Tennessee at Martin. She teaches courses in comparative politics, international relations, and international studies. Moreover, Carrie is a proponent of experiential learning. She has led travel studies, is the Model UN advisor, and has supervised internships for her students. Her research interests focus on European politics, particularly niche parties, international organizations, and SoTL.

John Ishiyama is University Distinguished Research Professor of Political Science at the University of North Texas. He is also the former Editor-in-Chief of the *American Political Science Review* and was the founding editor-in-chief of the *APSA Journal of Political Science Education*. He is currently President of the American Political Science Association and Piper Professor of Texas. He has published extensively, producing nine books and over 150 journal articles and book chapters (in journals such as the *American Political Science Review*, *Political Research Quarterly*, *Political Science Quarterly*, *Comparative Political Studies*, *Comparative Politics*, *Social Science Quarterly*, *Party Politics*, *Europe-Asia Studies*, and *Democratization*).

Geraldine Jones was e-learning development officer at the University of Bath between 2010 and 2018 and a lecturer in Education at the University of Bath between 2018 and 2023 before she retired in 2023.

E. Stefan Kehlenbach is an Assistant Professor of political science at the University of Albany. His research develops a critical theory of technology, examining the political impacts of data and other digital technologies. His work has appeared in *Theory & Event, The Journal of Military Ethics,* and *The Journal of Political Science Education*.

Thiago Lima is an Associate Professor in the Department of International Relations and at the Graduate Program of Public Management and International Cooperation at the Federal University of Paraíba—UFPB (Brazil). He has 12 years of teaching experience in higher education institutions in Brazil and 3 years of experience teaching Food Security in undergraduate programs. He coordinates the Research Group on Hunger and International Relations at UFPB.

Eric Loepp is an Associate Professor in the Department of Politics, Government, and Law and Director of Learning Technology at the University of Wisconsin-Whitewater. His disciplinary research focuses on candidate evaluations, and his pedagogy research centers on using technology to enhance instruction. This work has been published in such journals as the *Journal of Political Science Education*, *Electoral Studies*, and the *Journal of Elections, Public Opinion, & Parties*, as well as other outlets such as *The Chronicle of Higher Education* and *Inside Higher Ed*. He is the recipient of *American Political Science Association*'s 2018 CQ Press Award for Teaching Innovation.

Daniel J. Mallinson is an Associate Professor of Public Policy and Administration at Penn State Harrisburg. His main research focus is on policy process theory, particularly policy innovation diffusion, with policy-focused research on cannabis, energy, the environment, and mental health. He also has published pedagogical and science of teaching and learning research in multiple outlets.

Alfred Marleku is Lecturer of Political Science at the University for Business and Technology, Kosovo. He received his Ph.D. in International Relations from Southeast European University, North Macedonia, but also focuses on teaching methods and pedagogy in Political Science.

Alison Rios Millett McCartney (Ph.D. University of Virginia) is Professor of Political Science and Faculty Director of the Honors College at Towson University, Towson, Maryland, USA. She is co-editor of three books published by the *American Political Science Association (APSA)*, *Teaching Civic Engagement Globally* (2021), *Teaching Civic Engagement Across the Disciplines* (2017), and *Teaching Civic Engagement: From Student to Active Citizen* (2013), several book chapters, journal articles, conference presentations, and webinars on civic engagement education and pedagogy, international relations pedagogy, and Honors pedagogy. She has received several awards, including the University System of Maryland Award for Mentoring of Undergraduates.

Michael P. A. Murphy is a Banting Postdoctoral Fellow in the Department of Political Studies at Queen's University, and an associate member of the University of Ottawa's Scholarship of Teaching and Learning

Research Unit. He is the author of *Quantum Social Theory for Critical International Relations Theorists* (Palgrave, 2021), over thirty peer-reviewed articles, and numerous book reviews and chapters. He serves as Editorial Assistant at *Security Dialogue* and Past President of the Education and Learning in International Affairs Section of the ISA. His work can be found at: http://bit.ly/37NJMkZ.

Buket Oztas is an Assistant Professor of Politics and International Affairs at Furman University, where she teaches courses on comparative politics and co-directs the Middle East and Islamic Studies program. Her research focuses on the changing institutional dynamics in predominantly Muslim countries, with a particular interest in post-Islamism and transnational identities. It also includes an ongoing research initiative on the agenda-setting powers of the European Commission. Originally from Izmir (Turkey), she holds B.A. and B.S. degrees from Bilkent University and Binghamton University (2010) and a Ph.D. from the University of Florida (2016).

Ridvan Peshkopia is a Lecturer of Political Science at the University for Business and Technology, Kosovo. He received his Ph.D. in Political Science from the University of Kentucky; he also spent a year as a postdoctoral fellow at the George Washington University. His main research areas are international relations, political behavior, and migration studies.

Audrey Ruark Redmond Ph.D., works at Georgia College & State University in Milledgeville, GA and engages students in recognizing and seeking out global points of view through intercultural competence education and resources. She is experienced in teaching courses on Comparative Politics, Global Issues, American Government, and First-Year Experience. Her courses frequently utilize active learning, innovative technology, collaborative research, and Community-Based Engaged Learning Projects.

Shauna Reilly is a Regents' professor of political science and director of the Institute for Student Research and Creative Activity at Northern Kentucky University. She has worked with students on more than 125 research projects. She is also a prolific scholar herself with seven books and numerous articles looking at ballot access and barriers through the lens of political science.

Michael T. Rogers is a Professor at Arkansas Tech University and earned his B.S. at Wabash College and Ph.D. at the University at Albany—SUNY. Scholarly achievements include co-editing *Civic Education in the 21st Century* (Lexington Books, 2015), a chapter in *Teaching Civic Engagement Across the Disciplines*, and an article in *PS: Perspectives on Politics* on organizing the political science curriculum into career tracks. Currently, he researches Anti-Federalist critiques of the Electoral College, work funded by a Student Undergraduate Research Fellowship and an NEH Summer Stipend and serves on the Political Science Education board and APSA Committee on Professional Ethics, Rights, and Freedoms.

Bess Seaman is a 2nd year MPA graduate student at the University of South Dakota and will graduate in May of 2024. Currently, she is the Planning and Development Services intern with the City of Sioux Falls.

Laila Sorurbakhsh holds a Ph.D. in Political Science from the University of Houston (2012) with specializations in Comparative Politics, American Politics, and Quantitative Methods. Her research focuses on NGOs, particularly the integration of risk, research, innovation, and uncertainty in policymaking. Laila is currently the Assistant Dean of Academic Programs, Director of Online Education, and an Assistant Professor at the Elliott School of International Affairs at the George Washington University.

J. Cherie Strachan is a Professor of Political Science and Director of the Ray C. Bliss Institute of Applied Politics at The University of Akron. Her recent publications include the co-authored textbook *Why Don't Women Rule the World*, along with articles and chapters about polarization, civility, and civic engagement pedagogy. She recently served as review editor for the *Journal of Political Science Education* and is the co-director of a consortium that facilitates multi-campus data collection for campus civic engagement initiatives and political science pedagogy.

Sarina Theys is a Lecturer in Diplomacy and International Affairs at the University of the South Pacific in Suva, Fiji Islands. Sarina is a highly experienced researcher and versatile university lecturer. She has developed, and been involved, in more than 15 research projects, collected data in 10 countries, and conducted more than 200 semi-structured and focus-group interviews with state and non-state actors. Sarina has also taught undergraduate and postgraduate students in the UK and Fiji Islands.

Some of her work was published in *International Affairs*, *Comparative Law Journal of the Pacific*, *Politics*, and *Journal of International Affairs*.

Dr. Matthew P. Thornburg is an Associate Professor of Political Science, USC Aiken. Dr. Thornburg received his Ph.D. from George Mason University in 2013 and has taught at USC Aiken since 2015. He directs the Social Sciences and Business Research Lab and co-coaches the USCA Mock Trial team. Dr. Thornburg's research interests include the effects of electoral institutions on political behavior as well as public opinion.

Frederick Walter Tillman II is a Ph.D. candidate in the School of Conflict Management, Peacebuilding, and Development at Kennesaw State University. His research focuses on the effects of nationalism, national identity, political identity, and ethno-territoriality on state, non-state, and global institutions. His past work includes contributions to the *Journal of Peacebuilding and Development* as a Resource and Interim Managing Editor. His current work involves an adjunct professorship at Kennesaw State University, collaboration on studying how values intersect with identity, and research into various pedagogical approaches.

Cohl Turnquist currently serves as the City Administrator in Flandreau, South Dakota. Turnquist is a graduate of the University of South Dakota's Master of Public Administration program.

Aaron Vlasman graduated from the University of South Dakota with bachelor's degrees in Political Science and Criminal Justice. He most recently worked as the Statewide Political Director for the South Dakota Democratic Party.

D. Stephen Voss is an Associate Professor of Political Science at the University of Kentucky. He earned his Ph.D., and studied political methodology, at Harvard University with Gary King and James Alt. His main research area is elections and voting behavior, with a focus on political methodology and on race, ethnicity, and cultural politics.

Wesley Wehde Ph.D., is an Assistant Professor of Public Administration in the Department of Political Science at Texas Tech University where he teaches courses in public policy, administration, and research methods. His research interests include emergency management, disaster policy, and public opinion related to federalism.

Jay Wendland is an Associate Professor of Political Science and Department Chair of History & Political Science at Daemen University. His research and teaching interests include the presidential nominating process, American political behavior, election reform, and the intersection of politics and popular culture. His book, *Campaigns That Matter*, explores the importance of campaign visits in the presidential nominating contests of 2008–2016.

Wei-Ting Yen is an Assistant Professor of the Government Department at Franklin and Marshall College. She has experience teaching at different liberal arts colleges and a research-intensive university. Yen researches and teaches comparative politics and political economy issues in Asia.

List of Figures

Fig. 6.1	Human rights game scenarios	67
Fig. 7.1	Conceptualization of active learning process	78
Fig. 7.2	Results from the survey question: "Choose the adjectives that described your experience of the role-play games"	84
Fig. 7.3	Results from survey question: "I spent more time researching the topic than I usually do for other units"	84
Fig. 7.4	Results from survey question: "I spent more time working with my peers outside class than I usually do for other units"	85
Fig. 17.1	Part I: Teaching policy as scientific inquiry	197
Fig. 17.2	Part II: Blending research into deliverables	200
Fig. 17.3	Parts I and II combined: Training and scoping for optimal collaboration	203
Fig. 20.1	Team placement inventory	235
Fig. 20.2	Team role proposal	236
Fig. 20.3	Front page of service-learning pre-event handout for community partner	240
Fig. 20.4	Back Page of service-learning pre-event handout for community partner	241
Fig. 23.1	Photo of students in front of the Capitol building in Des Moines, IA (From left to right: Tysai Washington, Ricardo Marquez, Sam Williams, Lindsey Hornung, Carlos McKnight. *Source* Jay Wendland)	281
Fig. 24.1	The integration of teaching, research, and service	289
Fig. 29.1	Modifying research activities for classroom use	352

xxv

Fig. 29.2   Results of media source cue experiment shared in class   355
Fig. 29.3   Truncated and non-truncated variants of welfare
             expansion data   357
Fig. 29.4   The positive feedback cycle between teaching and research 358

List of Tables

Table 2.1	Advice for teaching philosophy statements	15
Table 2.2	Reflective stages for teaching philosophy statements	18
Table 15.1	Types of student-engaged research work	173
Table 16.1	Comparing perceptions of political science students from UBT with other Western Balkan students	189
Table 19.1	Comparative data from the Little Rock congregations study, 2012, 2016, and 2020	221
Table 23.1	Iowa visits from major party candidates	278
Table 25.1	Enrollment in fall course (n = 238) 2004–2008; 2009–2015; 2017–2021	307
Table 25.2	Enrollment in spring independent study (n = 89) 2004–2022	307
Table 25.3	Graduate school outcomes	307
Table 25.4	Trackable career outcomes	308

CHAPTER 1

Introduction

Maia Carter Hallward, Tavishi Bhasin, Charity Butcher, and Elizabeth Gordon

Maria is a new professor at a regional comprehensive university. While she is excited about her new position, she is struggling to meet the various demands of her job. She is teaching four classes a semester, many of which are new preparations for her. In addition to her departmental service, she has been asked to sit on a college-wide committee on diversity, equity, and inclusion. She embraces this service opportunity, as it complements her

M. C. Hallward · C. Butcher (✉)
School of Conflict Management, Peacebuilding and Development, Kennesaw State University, Kennesaw, GA, USA
e-mail: cbutche2@kennesaw.edu

M. C. Hallward
e-mail: mhallwar@kennesaw.edu

T. Bhasin · E. Gordon
School of Government and International Affairs, Kennesaw State University, Kennesaw, GA, USA
e-mail: tbhasin@kennesaw.edu

© The Author(s), under exclusive license to Springer Nature Switzerland AG 2023
C. Butcher et al. (eds.), *The Palgrave Handbook of Teaching and Research in Political Science*, Political Pedagogies,
https://doi.org/10.1007/978-3-031-42887-6_1

teaching and research interests, but the committee meets frequently, and she is having a hard time juggling these service and teaching commitments with growing research expectations at her institution.

Marcus just received tenure at his research-intensive university. Now that he has tenure, he really wants to create new and innovative assignments for his classes and focus more on his teaching. However, he also plans to eventually apply for Full Professor, and finds it difficult to maintain his active research agenda while also spending a lot of time experimenting with new assignments in his classes. In addition, now that he has tenure, he has been asked to increase his service at the university, creating additional workload challenges.

These scenarios are likely familiar to many political scientists. Within academia, professors often face increased pressure to publish within the context of limited time and resources for research and writing, while also excelling at teaching. Although some political scientists have low teaching loads and ample research funds, the vast majority of instructors are at institutions with heavy teaching and service loads and increasing research requirements, but with very limited resources for funding this research. At the same time, faculty with heavy research expectations may struggle to find time for course preparation and innovation amid high research demands.

This book aims to be a resource for political science faculty wanting to increase their research productivity and/or teaching effectiveness with time and resource-efficient strategies. The book includes examples from faculty across various subfields and types of institutions that illustrate how instructors are aligning their research and teaching activities to "get more bang for their buck." While research related to the Scholarship of Teaching and Learning (SoTL) has become increasingly popular within the political science discipline, it represents only one way that professors can align their teaching and research. While this volume includes a section on SoTL, it also considers multiple other ways in which political scientists can integrate teaching and research, thereby improving scholarly productivity, grounding teaching in pedagogical literature, and improving student outcomes.

E. Gordon
e-mail: egordon@kennesaw.edu

We (the four editors) all work at a large, public regional university that started as a teaching college and continues to highlight teaching as the primary focus of faculty members. In 2022, we took over editorship of the *Journal of Political Science Education* along with colleagues at other institutions. We have published with undergraduate and/or graduate students, and have experienced first-hand the need to be efficient with our teaching, research, and service strategies to meet the demands of a heavy teaching load, while also achieving the research expectations and service demands of a growing R2. This project came out of conversations we have had and been privy to at conferences over the years on how to best integrate these different areas of our professional lives, each essential to the academic mission. It was clear from these conversations that our colleagues at teaching-focused institutions had also developed diverse and creative strategies to work more efficiently and find ways to integrate their teaching, research, and service. The result is a plethora of approaches, strategies, and practical examples across a varied range of subdisciplines within political science. We hope these inspire and aid you in integrating your research, teaching, and service in innovative ways.

Finding Balance

Colleges and universities are diverse entities, with varied workload expectations and resources for faculty. Public institutions may have significant limitations on their budgets and spending, externally imposed by state legislatures and dependent upon the economic and political climate within the state. While some private institutions enjoy significant funding, they face their own sets of challenges, including lower levels of endowments for smaller schools and sensitivity to economic downturns. Colleges and universities also vary widely in their missions and approaches to education. Small liberal arts colleges, for example, are likely to prioritize different things than larger comprehensive universities. While faculty at some institutions enjoy access to on-campus centers for teaching support, student research assistance, professional development opportunities, teaching assistants, etc., others do not. To further complicate the matter, faculty often do not receive training on how to navigate these varied professional spaces. Such vagaries make the job of a new faculty member even more difficult as they seek to navigate unclear rules with limited time. This volume provides political science faculty with illustrative strategies to work smarter—not harder—by linking teaching, research, and (sometimes) service in a range of educational contexts.

In addition to variation in the types of colleges and universities, different positions within academia come with disparate expectations and workload demands. For example, some faculty are tenured or on the tenure-track, while others hold full-time positions that are not tenurable. Consider too that some faculty hold temporary full-time appointments while others are contingent, with the latter possibly teaching at multiple universities in the same academic term. Some faculty may have heavy research expectations as part of their position, which may often (though not always) be accompanied by lower teaching loads. Other faculty, while having no formal research expectations, may wish to conduct research to enhance future employment opportunities. Still others may have low or moderate research expectations along with heavy teaching and/or service loads. In all these scenarios, faculty may find it difficult to balance competing demands in a way that meets the faculty member's ultimate goals.

Another challenge to consider is how research is defined and recognized within a particular institution. Some universities define research quite broadly, so that many types of scholarly activity might be included for tenure or promotion purposes, including pedagogical work, often termed the "scholarship of teaching and learning" (SoTL). However, some universities, particularly those with high research expectations, may not recognize pedagogical research within political science as equivalent to traditional research in other substantive political science disciplines. Faculty, therefore, must assess the expectations of their respective institutions and tailor their teaching, research, and service efforts accordingly. We also argue, however, that faculty in more secure positions (such as tenured faculty) should work to encourage their institutions to recognize and value many different types of research, including research focused on teaching. Such an approach helps to promote a teacher-scholar model of higher education (discussed in the next section), one we believe helps to create an environment where all the different aspects of faculty life are valued, creating faculty who see their own work across these areas as related and contributing to each other, and eventually contributing to a richer, more engaging university experience for students.

Importance of the "Teacher-Scholar" Model in Higher Education

Who is a teacher-scholar? We see teacher-scholars as individuals who find innovative and creative ways to bring their substantive research into the classroom to improve their teaching and opportunities for student learning. Relatedly, teacher-scholars may also utilize their research and methodological training to assess the effectiveness of their teaching, to consider more fully how their teaching interventions may impact student learning, rather than taking such learning as fact. By nurturing active scholars and reflective teachers, institutions of higher education improve the quality of student learning. This book considers a variety of ways to combine teaching and scholarly endeavors, with a myriad of examples to help faculty better harness this teacher-scholar model in their own professional lives.

Outline of the Book

This book is divided into six substantive parts, each focused on a different theme related to aligning research and teaching, along with a conclusion. Part I begins with a chapter that explains how the Scholarship of Teaching and Learning (SoTL) can broadly ground teaching philosophies and intentional and informed pedagogy and then discusses how professors might incorporate SoTL into their own pedagogical approaches. Murphy's chapter on teaching philosophies suggests that critical reflection on one's philosophy of teaching can help a faculty member to more organically integrate the scholarship of teaching and learning into their classes. Mallinson offers multiple ways to collaborate with stakeholders across the university community to incorporate research in the classroom. Finally, Oztas shares how she uses metacognitive exercises in the classroom to help students intentionally craft their own learning objectives as a means of practicing self-reflective learning. The data generated through such practices not only improves student engagement but also provides the basis for faculty research on student learning and curricular impact. Throughout this first section, authors reflect philosophically on the pedagogical and research impact of engaging in the scholarship of teaching and learning and provide specific strategies they have used along with tips for success.

Part II focuses more explicitly on scholarship related to the use of simulations, games, and role play exercises. Specifically, the chapters explore the creation of such teaching devices and how to incorporate them into the classroom to enhance student learning. Chapters by Allendoerfer and by Butcher, Hallward, and Tillman provide case study examples in which faculty worked with undergraduate students to develop active learning products such as simulations and games, including descriptions of the challenges such efforts entail. Faculty–student partnerships such as these allow for teaching at multiple levels—not only teaching those student participants who will benefit from the activities, but also teaching those faculty and students who develop the learning intervention. Allum and Jones detail another path for role play development. In this case, the authors use their own research on Italian mafias to create student-centered role-playing activities. In this way, their research generates opportunities for students to learn real-life skills such as teamwork and managing uncertainty, in addition to course-specific content. All authors in this section offer recommendations regarding what works (and what does not) in the crafting of simulations, role plays and games, and how to intentionally use such tools to enhance student learning and advance the goals of the teacher-scholar.

Part III includes two chapters discussing how faculty utilize textbook writing to improve their teaching, increase knowledge of the field, and enhance their research productivity. The first chapter, by Blair, asserts that the practice of textbook writing provides teacher-scholars not only with more space for sharing their own contributions, but also the opportunity to serve as ambassadors of the discipline. A good textbook can generate interest in political science topics by reaching wider (student) audiences than scholarly articles and can thereby potentially assist in future course recruitment. In the second chapter, Strachan provides advice for those concerned that textbook writing may not "count" toward promotion and tenure. She suggests that teacher-scholars document gaps they must routinely fill when developing course materials and encourages faculty to pay attention to marginalized voices. Furthermore, she walks faculty through the process of drafting a prospectus and marketing the book to potential publishers, highlighting proactive strategies. The chapters in this section not only provide practical tips for writing textbooks (key teaching tools) but also include ideas for framing the significance of textbook publications to gain more value and recognition for this hard work in tenure and promotion materials.

Part IV discusses a variety of strategies professors have used to incorporate undergraduate or graduate students into their research. The nine chapters in this section address strategies for balancing teaching and research at a wide range of institutions, from small teaching colleges to larger universities, and by faculty in various career stages, including junior faculty and contingent faculty. Several chapters discuss ways to engage students in the faculty's own research projects. For example, Bijsmans outlines challenges and opportunities for political science faculty members wishing to engage in research with students, highlighting the importance of motivation, expectations, time investment, and ethical reward structures. Reilly documents her use of course-based undergraduate research experiences (CURES) to integrate research with students into her teaching-heavy workload. Reilly shares strategies such as bringing her own anonymized research into the classroom for discussion and critique and creating a research lab with student teams developing data sets relevant to her own scholarship. Rogers emphasizes the value of the teacher-scholar model, and how employing extra-curricular research assistants can boost faculty capacity in an era of shrinking resources. He also provides practical suggestions for finding institutional, state, and other funding to pay for undergraduate researchers. Bauer provides recommendations for dealing with challenges likely faced by faculty at small teaching-focused institutions. Sharing her experience with creating a student lab-type research experience outside of the classroom, Bauer identifies take away lessons for teachers and administrators related to the learning benefits of such research opportunities. Hellweg, Turnquist, Vlasman, and Seaman expand on lessons offered by other authors in this section, sharing tips for building successful student research teams by selecting reliable students who are good communicators and prioritizing strong team dynamics and manageable tasks. The chapter includes faculty, graduate, and undergraduate student perspectives on the research team process. Henshaw brings in an additional perspective on student research experiences, that of the contingent faculty member who may work at multiple institutions or leave an institution before a project is completed. Henshaw provides useful questions faculty can ask themselves when designing projects, as well as a chart for conceptualizing the type of work involved for faculty and student researchers in various types of projects. Markelu, Peshkopia, and Voss offer an alternative method for integrating students in research and describe their research-oriented teaching strategy in which students participate in survey research. Specifically, they document innovation across the curriculum of a Kosovo-based political science department that provided students with the necessary skills and motivation to undertake such empirical inquiry. Sorurbakhsh also emphasizes the skills-based, practical focus of developing policy research capacities for master's students. Importantly, Sorurbakhsh outlines different types of projects for master's students based on different career projections and identifies the need for faculty as well as students to be trained regarding successful research partnerships. Rounding out this section is Ishiyama's chapter that looks more specifically at PhD students and ways to embed learning about the publication process into scope and methods courses. Ishiyama documents the importance of peer-peer feedback as well as a scaffolded path to publication based on an apprenticeship model. Overall, this section provides a range of examples targeting faculty working with different types of students (undergraduate, master's, doctoral) at different types of institutions (small teaching focused, regional, international) in different contexts (embedded in courses, co-curricular, independent from course structure).

Part V considers additional ways that instructors conduct research with students, such as using experiential learning within the classroom to bridge teaching and research. This section also includes examples of how faculty have connected teaching, research, and civic engagement, thereby enhancing community connections while also facilitating student learning and faculty productivity. Glazier begins the section by sharing challenges and opportunities of conducting community-based research online. Forced to move a community-based research practicum course online due to the COVID-19 pandemic, Glazier documents the ways in which this pivot opened up doors for students typically unable to participate in such projects, as well as ways that online tools can be useful complements to face-to-face projects. Redmond describes a group project in which teams were assigned types of women leaders to research, resulting in a book of vignettes about these leaders as well as service-learning activities designed for a local middle school. In addition to providing detailed instructions and templates for carrying out this high-impact learning activity, Redmond also explicitly outlines the link between the learning activities and students' own life goals. Hamilton and Almeida focus on academic field studies and study abroad opportunities, particularly cultural exchange programs, as a way to catalyze critical thinking among students and stimulate research collaboration among faculty. The authors emphasize the importance of relationship building and long-term engagement for maximizing the potential of such programs. The next two chapters illustrate how real-world political processes can be used as teaching tools and research opportunities simultaneously. Thornburg and Botsch describe a project in which students conducted exit polls at a local election, thereby creating a data set for public scholarship and peer-reviewed publication. Wendland discusses an experiential course observing the Iowa caucuses that connected and contributed directly to the author's research on campaign strategy.

Other chapters in Part V focus less on the experiential learning activity itself and more on critical strategies for implementing and tracking civic engagement efforts on campus as well as reflecting on how faculty can efficiently and effectively integrate such activities into their heavy workloads. Bennion shares her strategy for integrating teaching and research through civic engagement activities with her students, including nonpartisan voter registration drives that serve not only as learning opportunities for students but also contribute to new research projects for the author. McCartney guides readers through ways she has built university support structures for the civic engagement research she conducts with students, including the creation of an undergraduate research club. Dobbs further attests to the importance of civically engaged research within the political science discipline and the challenges in translating the significance of this type of research to university leaders. Dobbs discusses the case study of the Youth Voice program that she led in Summer 2021 as an example of a community-focused activity that provided learning opportunities for undergraduate students, research outputs in the form of conference papers and grant funding, and material for use in future political science classes. Completing this section is a chapter by Humphreys, who translated her findings on alternative modes of delivering her senior capstone presentations into a research project. She includes recommendations for turning teaching experiences into fuel for research, even when we do not know at the outset how our classroom innovation may unfold.

Part VI contains six chapters, providing a plethora of innovative and practical examples of faculty members integrating their research and teaching in the classroom to increase student engagement and improve student learning outcomes. Yen's chapter provides broad strategies for incorporating faculty research into teaching and then walks readers through a practical example of a Comparative Politics course, demonstrating how these strategies may be put into practice. Loepp describes research and teaching as mutually reinforcing, positive feedback loops, providing personal examples of how research may be featured in syllabi, be used as teaching assignments, and in turn how teaching could inform scholarship through SoTL publications. Wehde takes a different approach, using data from a working paper to spark student collaboration during a review session in a research methods course. This process allows the instructor to create exercises that serve a dual purpose. For example, the section on operationalization and measurement is used to create visualizations for working research manuscripts. Kehlenbach advocates using a collaborative approach in the classroom where students are assigned larger portions of text, including one by the author, and then discuss these critically as part of "doing theory" with the students, ultimately leading to new interpretations and ideas for research. Lima's chapter demonstrates how using images in a thoughtful and intentional manner can both engage students in classes discussing critical global issues such as hunger and poverty, but also lead to rich co-authored projects. Theys's chapter provides us with an illustrative example of a course built around the author's research. The author was able to use images and examples from their own work on Bhutan and gross national happiness, supplemented with guest speakers, to efficiently integrate their teaching and research while increasing student engagement and learning.

Finally, the book concludes in Part VII by drawing important themes from the various chapters and sections, highlighting ethical considerations related to undertaking the approaches described herein, and providing an overview of how professors can better align their teaching and research activities to improve the quality and impact of both.

PART I

Scholarship of Teaching and Learning and Pedagogical Research

CHAPTER 2

Taking Teaching Philosophies Seriously: Pedagogical Identity, Philosophy of Education, and New Opportunities for Publication

Michael P. A. Murphy

INTRODUCTION

Teaching philosophy statements gained traction in the educational development literature in the 1990s, and are now widespread, frequently appearing in job applications and tenure/promotion files. Early advocates saw the growing role of these documents as an important signal of institutional support for pedagogical development (Goodyear & Allchin, 1998). Individually, these statements serve as representations of an academic's outlook on how learning happens and what their roles are in relation to that process (Coppola, 2002; Laundon et al., 2020). While advice books on graduate school often highlight key features of marketable teaching

---

M. P. A. Murphy (✉)
Department of Political Science, Queen's University, Kingston, ON, Canada
e-mail: michael.murphy@queensu.ca

© The Author(s), under exclusive license to Springer Nature Switzerland AG 2023
C. Butcher et al. (eds.), *The Palgrave Handbook of Teaching and Research in Political Science*, Political Pedagogies, https://doi.org/10.1007/978-3-031-42887-6_2

philosophy statements, my focus in this chapter is broader. In line with the theme of this edited collection, I argue that reflecting on one's teaching philosophy presents an opportunity to work smarter, not harder, by aligning the preparation of crucial job market documents with opportunities for research and publication. While this discussion is informed by my own forays into philosophy of education and the scholarship of teaching and learning, I also draw on educational development literature that speaks to the professional and pedagogical benefits of reflection on practice in higher education pedagogy.

Teaching Philosophy Statements: Recommendations and Research

Teaching philosophy statements are written expressions of an academic's approach to teaching. In an oft-cited article, Goodyear and Allchin (1998) suggest that teaching philosophy statements represent a response to the question "Why do I teach?" (p. 110). As a document of central importance to the academic job market, the advice genre has picked up on trends of so-called "successful" teaching philosophy statements. Three sets of advice are summarized in Table 2.1. Common to all is a focus on the empirical, suggesting that teaching philosophy statements should clearly demonstrate how one's pedagogical commitments have been put into practice in different course contexts. This does not mean that the theoretical commitments are not important, but instead that they become believable and powerful when supported by examples.

Teaching philosophy statements are frequently components of teaching portfolios,[1] and a small but provocative literature provides evidence regarding the benefits that developing teaching portfolios offer higher education faculty. Of particular importance to this chapter are two benefits: first, the development of teaching confidence and capacity through reflection on practice; and second, the opportunity to engage in the scholarship of teaching and learning. The remainder of this section reviews key literature in educational development on this topic.

In a study of teaching portfolio development among new geography teachers, Joanna Bullard and Monica McLean explored the impact of this reflective opportunity on pedagogical development. They found that the

---

[1] Sometimes called "teaching dossiers."

Table 2.1 Advice for teaching philosophy statements

Reference Work	Kelsky (2015)	Calarco (2020)	Kaplan et al. (2008)
Recommendations	• Hold to one page • Support statements with specific evidence • Replace generic or obvious statements with vivid and memorable examples • Speak to the mission of the institution • Avoid excessive humility or emotion • Link research and teaching to one consistent whole • Finish with a strong conclusion	• Summarize key details in the first paragraph • Link your qualifications to the job requirements • Provide an overview of past experience, including any awards and SoTL work • Identify what motivates you as a teacher and share evidence of how you reach that goal in your courses • Point to progress that you have made as a teacher • Consider mentioning active learning	• Offer specific examples as evidence of teaching practice • Center the student perspective and recognize different learner profiles (ability, level, preferences) • Provide evidence that the writer reflects and changes teaching practices • Convey enthusiasm for teaching • Ensure that the text is well-written, clear, and readable

new instructors were able to identify concrete barriers in putting their pedagogy into practice, perceived improvement in teaching practice, and a shift toward incorporating more active learning strategies (Bullard & McLean, 2000; McLean & Bullard, 2000). The authors suggest that this reflective process may be especially beneficial in early career stages because graduate students do not typically receive as much pedagogical training as disciplinary training. Other attempts to provide early reflexive interventions for pedagogical practice have suggested that individual course portfolios can stand in where instructors do not have sufficient material for a broader teaching portfolio (Laverie, 2002). While this literature remains limited, its early interveners agree that instructors—particularly those early in their teaching careers—benefit in terms of confidence and competence from the reflexive exercise.

While pedagogical and personal development is an important end, the literature on teaching portfolios also points toward opportunities to engage in what Boyer (1991) called the scholarship of teaching, more frequently now known as the scholarship of teaching and learning (e.g. Weimer, 2006). In a study exploring the impact of teaching portfolio development on practice, Susanne Pelger and Maria Larsson (2018) report that educators had a higher level of (self-)awareness of their role as educator, more clearly understood successful practices in their classroom, drew inspiration from literature on teaching, and saw a higher value in scholarship of teaching and learning work. By clarifying what happens and what is important in their own classroom, the different elements to be adjusted, manipulated, and tested become clearer, and reference to the scholarly literature on teaching and learning builds the familiarity necessary for future entry into its debates. Part of this is a process of what Miriam Hamilton describes as building awareness of the assumptions and habits of the classroom. By first identifying and then unpacking those tacit elements, instructors are better prepared to engage in the scholarship of teaching and learning. While no study has tracked engagement in scholarship of teaching and learning research in relation to completion of a teaching dossier as of 2022, indicators of interest and preparedness lend face validity to the hypothesis.

A final point regarding the relationship between the teaching philosophy and scholarly productivity is perhaps too pragmatic (and obvious) to merit consideration in an empirical study. Once a teaching philosophy statement is written, there are words on the page. As the academic writing advice books remind us, getting words on the page is often the most difficult part (Becker, 2008; Silvia, 2018), and the mere accomplishment of writing the words means that this statement of pedagogical purpose can be put to use. Whether the words travel into a portfolio submitted for hiring, tenure, or promotion, or outwardly into the introduction of an article, chapter, or book, the written text has an existential advantage over the unwritten idea.

A New Perspective

While the literature discussed above offers specific guides for the writing of teaching philosophy statements and an interesting set of potential benefits to be gleaned from reflecting on practice, in this section, I offer a new perspective on taking teaching philosophy statements seriously. While the literature reviewed in the previous section indicates the potential benefits of taking teaching philosophy seriously, my focus here is to consider how we may think about teaching philosophies in a professionally and practically productive manner. To this end, I will draw on my own experiences in academic writing in the scholarship of teaching and learning and philosophy of education that grew out of serious reflection on my teaching philosophy.

This new perspective on teaching philosophy statements is really about examining both the document and our pedagogical selves in relation to the broader context of teaching and learning debates. It is still important to consider how examples from pedagogical practice connect to our core theoretical commitments, but by engaging systematically with educational literatures, we gain new opportunities to engage with both scholarship of teaching and learning as well as philosophy of education. This includes three reflective stages outlined in Table 2.2: asking why, finding your SoTL, and thinking about theory.

As the discussion in Table 2.2 makes clear, this process linking practice, reflection, engagement in scholarly literatures and theoretical debates far exceeds the context of writing a single document fixed in time. Closing the circle, we find that there are multiple points of interaction. Asking why helps identify core commitments that may then motivate philosophical reflection. A new theoretical insight may inspire experimentation with a teaching technique that leads to a SoTL research project, conversing with but also contributing to scholarly literature (disciplinary or transdisciplinary). While a single output—the teaching philosophy statement—may be the primary aim of this process, taking teaching philosophies seriously means exploring how these identified connections can feed into teaching practice, identify opportunities for improvement and innovation, catalyze research projects and self-studies in the scholarship of teaching and learning, and open space for reflection in applied philosophy of education. And it is important to remember that the closed circle is not a fixed endpoint—continual exploration and reflection continue.

To illustrate the steps of taking teaching philosophies seriously, I will offer a brief example of my own reflective journey through graduate school. As a teaching assistant leading discussion groups, one of my priorities was to help students work with assigned readings to help build their understanding of how key concepts could be connected to one another and applied to other concepts. To some extent, this was my own teaching by homology, repeating experiences in courses on globalization

Table 2.2 Reflective stages for teaching philosophy statements

Prompt	Steps
Asking why	At the beginning of a teaching career, it is common to reproduce the teaching practices familiar to us (Christensen & Mighty, 2010). As the first step, asking why calls on the reflective practitioner to consider what key motivations inspire the individual to teach. Two key questions at this stage are: What learning goals do you set in your courses that motivate you? Are there any particular teaching techniques, curriculum foci, assignments or assessment practices, or other course elements that are particularly meaningful to you? Making the most of this step is not merely about identifying motivations but probing deeper by continuing to ask why. We may find that the root motivations may naturally align with our pedagogical practices (whether by happy accident or intentional design). Moments of clarity will serve as particularly powerful examples for inclusion in the teaching statement, while moments of disharmony may serve either as a thought-provoking challenge to the principles or spur alternative ideas around course design. Like theoretical insights emerging from abstractions from empirical research, the process of asking why helps to open up the motivational, causal, and aspirational assumptions that structure our decision-making
Finding your SoTL	The scholarship of teaching and learning includes two types of published literature: first, transdisciplinary studies of higher education; and secondly, discipline-specific research into the signature pedagogies, threshold concepts, core debates, and other issues that connect to the content of the field.[2] While discipline-specific literature is likely to be most readily applicable, exploration of transdisciplinary research outputs can help to identify potential SoTL projects that align one's practice with established research beyond the discipline in a way that makes a novel contribution to discipline-specific debates. The process of finding your (disciplinary) SoTL completes an efficient triple-duty at this stage, insofar as it provides content to enrich a teaching philosophy statement with cutting-edge research, offers new ideas to implement in class, and familiarizes the instructor with potential venues to submit future scholarly outputs on teaching and learning

(continued)

---

[2] For a recent review of the scholarship of teaching and learning in politics and international relations, see Murphy et al. (2023).

Table 2.2 (continued)

Prompt	Steps
Thinking about theory	In the context of disciplinary research, it would hardly be fresh advice to consider what theoretical framework may be relevant to a research project. However, the connection between personal motivations and classroom practices also stands to benefit from an engagement with debates in educational theory and philosophy of education. Existing interests can be the guide here, as discussions of scaffolding can lead to Vygotsky's zone of proximal development, where play-based learning may lead to Montessori; radical empowerment of student-led learning may invoke Freire, where consideration of informal interaction may lead to Agamben's notion of study. This is not to say that all teaching philosophy statements will include theoretical framework sections. Rather, by thinking about theory, we build bridges between our own scholarly practice and ongoing theoretical and/or philosophical debates. These can offer new provocations in our pedagogy and also open up new opportunities for our lived experiences and SoTL projects to inform interventions into those debates

and international relations theory from my undergraduate experience. But a teaching development day held by our Centre for Teaching and Learning helped put me in touch with SoTL literature on active learning. Drawing on sample lessons from the literature, I was able to develop an active learning session where students worked with course readings to develop structures for essays (Murphy, 2017). In continuing to read on the topic of active learning, I began to notice an overlap in its assumptions about student agency and the political thought of Giorgio Agamben that had become the subject of my MA research. Curious about the connection, I searched the philosophy of education literature and found that there was an ongoing research community exploring precisely how Agamben's thought could be applied to questions of education (e.g. Lewis, 2013). Bringing together my disciplinary interest in Agamben's political thought, a practical experience of active learning, and a newfound engagement with Agambenian philosophy of education, I began to write on how these pedagogical, philosophical, and political ideas converge (e.g. Murphy, 2020). This philosophical interest continued (on the side) into my doctoral program, and by the time I was set to teach my first course as instructor of record, I knew my *why* when it came to active learning. However, in a larger-enrollment course, I encountered the familiar evaluation challenge in active learning. This challenge moved me from "asking why" to once again "finding my SoTL," eventually adapting a self- and peer-evaluation model to the political science classroom (Murphy, 2022). As I reached the end of my doctoral program and began preparing for the academic job market, this process formalized into the writing of a teaching philosophy statement. But by taking teaching philosophies seriously, the iterative process of reflection outlined above had already led to clarity in my pedagogical practice, exposure to thought-provoking debates in philosophy of education, and a series of peer-reviewed publications.

Conclusion

This edited volume presents a global suggestion that by aligning teaching with research, scholars can not only find satisfaction and success, but also work more efficiently in a world where work-life balance has been upended by the ever-growing demands of the neoliberal university. In the face of these time pressures, moments of efficiency are especially beneficial. I hope that this foray into teaching philosophies has provided a framework through which the multiple impacts of these statements can be appreciated. By clarifying our beliefs and assumptions about classroom practice, our pedagogical identity can find a clearer expression; by crystallizing aims, we find guides for lesson plans to be designed and teaching innovations to be studied; by engaging with philosophies and theories of education, we find whole new literatures from which to draw and to which we may contribute. Taking the time to reflect on practice can offer important benefits in terms of pedagogical development, but I have suggested that this reflection can also be understood as a powerful gateway, opening onto a new avenue of research activity.

References

Becker, H. S. (2008). *Writing for social scientists: How to start and finish your thesis, book, or article*. University of Chicago Press.
Boyer, E. L. (1991). The scholarship of teaching from: Scholarship reconsidered: Priorities of the professoriate. *College Teaching, 39*(1), 11–13.
Bullard, J. E., & McLean, M. (2000). Jumping through hoops?: Philosophy and practice expressed in geographers' teaching portfolios. *Journal of Geography in Higher Education, 24*(1), 37–52.
Calarco, J. M. (2020). *A field guide to grad school: Uncovering the hidden curriculum*. Princeton University Press.

Christensen Hughes, J., & Mighty, J. (2010). *Taking stock: Research on teaching and learning in higher education*. Queen's School of Policy Studies.

Coppola, B. P. (2002). Writing a statement of teaching philosophy. *Journal of College Science Teaching, 31*(7), 448.

Goodyear, G. E., & Allchin, D. (1998). Statements of teaching philosophy. *To Improve the Academy, 17*(1), 103–121.

Hamilton, M. (2018). Bridging the gap from teacher to teacher educator: The role of a teaching portfolio. *Studying Teacher Education, 14*(1), 88–102.

Kaplan, M., Meizlish, D. S., O'Neal, C., & Wright, M. C. (2008). 16: A research-based rubric for developing statements of teaching philosophy. *To Improve the Academy, 26*(1), 242–262.

Kelsky, K. (2015). *The professor is in: The essential guide to turning your Ph. D. into a job*. Crown.

Laundon, M., Cathcart, A., & Greer, D. A. (2020). Teaching philosophy statements. *Journal of Management Education, 44*(5), 577–587.

Laverie, D. A. (2002). Improving teaching through improving evaluation: A guide to course portfolios. *Journal of Marketing Education, 24*(2), 104–113.

Lewis, T. E. (2013). *On study: Giorgio Agamben and educational potentiality*. Routledge.

McLean, M., & Bullard, J. E. (2000). Becoming a university teacher: Evidence from teaching portfolios (how academics learn to teach). *Teacher Development, 4*(1), 79–101.

Murphy, M. P. A. (2017). Using active-learning pedagogy to develop essay-writing skills in introductory political theory tutorials. *Journal of Political Science Education, 13*(3), 346–354.

Murphy, M. P. A. (2020). Active learning as destituent potential: Agambenian philosophy of education and moderate steps towards the coming politics. *Educational Philosophy and Theory, 52*(1), 66–78.

Murphy, M. P. A. (2022). Evaluating simultaneous group activities through self-and peer-assessment: Addressing the "Evaluation Challenge" in Active Learning. *Journal of Political Science Education, 18*(4), 511–522.

Murphy, M. P. A., Heffernan, A., Dunton, C., & Arsenault, A. C. (2023). The disciplinary scholarship of teaching and learning in political science and international relations: Methods, topics, and impact. *International Politics*, 1–19.

Silvia, P. J. (2018). *How to write a lot: A practical guide to productive academic writing*. American Psychological Association.

Pelger, S., & Larsson, M. (2018). Advancement towards the scholarship of teaching and learning through the writing of teaching portfolios. *International Journal for Academic Development, 23*(3), 179–191.

Weimer, M. (2006). *Enhancing scholarly work on teaching & learning: Professional literature that makes a difference*. Jossey-Bass.

CHAPTER 3

Researching While Teaching and Mentoring: A Reflection on Collaboration

Daniel J. Mallinson

The pressure to publish continues to increase across academia, even for faculty with relatively high teaching loads. This reflection is based on my own experiences at two types of institutions, but the hope is that my experiences can be valuable to anyone facing a higher teaching load and a research expectation or wishing to continue their research in a teaching-heavy position. I have been fortunate to experience multiple different means of combining teaching, mentoring, and research. I hope my experience will spark some ideas for your own work. I will begin the reflection with a brief overview of the two academic positions that I have held so far. That context is helpful for understanding the requirements and expectations at those institutions for both teaching and research. Then I will discuss four different types of teaching-research experiences: (1) pedagogy research; (2) research on stand-alone programming; (3) substantive

D. J. Mallinson (✉)
Penn State Harrisburg, Middletown, PA, USA
e-mail: mallinson@psu.edu

© The Author(s), under exclusive license to Springer Nature Switzerland AG 2023
C. Butcher et al. (eds.), *The Palgrave Handbook of Teaching and Research in Political Science*, Political Pedagogies, https://doi.org/10.1007/978-3-031-42887-6_3

research embedded in classes; and (4) working with undergraduate and graduate students directly.

For some context, I have held two tenure-track positions. First, I was an Assistant Professor of Political Science at Stockton University (2015–2017). Now, I am an Associate Professor of Public Policy and Administration at Penn State Harrisburg. Both positions required research, but the expectations are much higher at Penn State than at Stockton. Stockton is a typical regional comprehensive. Such institutions can offer a challenging environment if they want both stellar teaching, because of their large undergraduate student bodies, and are elevating scholarship expectations as they seek to raise their profile. Plus, mid-sized institutions also demand significant service contributions from their faculty. That said, pedagogical research was far more valued at Stockton than it is at Penn State, which meant that embedding scholarship of teaching and learning (SoTL) research in my classes was well worth it for tenure and promotion. Penn State Harrisburg is a regional campus in the Penn State system, but it has an unusual profile. In many ways it is a regional comprehensive like Stockton, however, we are reviewed by the same penultimate promotion and tenure committees as those at the flagship campus (University Park). By contrast, we have a higher teaching load (3–3, versus 2–2 at UP). Unlike many faculty at regional comprehensives, however, I teach in undergraduate, master's, and Ph.D. programs, so I work with graduate students. Thus, Penn State Harrisburg is R1-ish, but with a higher teaching load. These details are relevant for understanding how I approach research and teaching, but the aim of this chapter is to offer lessons learned for faculty at a variety of institutions.

SoTL Research

This volume goes beyond discussing SoTL research alone, and rightly so, but SoTL research was my first foray into including publishable research in my classes. In fact, I had the great fortune of being exposed to SoTL research as a graduate student. Zach Baumann, now at Nebraska Wesleyan, was an instructor for Penn State's 350-seat Introduction to American Government course. I was assigned as one of his teaching assistants (TA) and Zach had the forethought to develop a survey to evaluate two pieces of teaching technology that he used in the course: lecture capture and iClickers. Zach included his TAs in evaluating the data and publishing the results, with me working on the lecture capture project

(Baumann et al., 2015; Mallinson & Baumann, 2015). Without seeing how Zach thought about this research, approached recruiting students, and dealt with the ethical challenges of studying one's own students, I am not sure that I would have thought to engage in this research as I set out on my own.

After the initial frenzy of prepping brand-new classes at my first academic position (Stockton), I started to think about how I might incorporate more active learning in my courses. As I thought about that, I took the lessons from Zach's class and considered how I might evaluate students' perceptions of those techniques and how they affected learning outcomes. In an introductory course on public administration, I decided to incorporate the California Budget Simulation into the section on public budgeting. The aim was to have students try their hand at crafting a budget and dealing with scarcity and tradeoffs. Evaluating their experiences through qualitative analysis of student surveys resulted in two publications, one on the survey results (Mallinson, 2018b) and one reviewing the simulation (Mallinson, 2018a). The analysis was admittedly rudimentary, as I undertook the project by myself. Stockton did not have a teaching and learning support center for faculty, but some institutions do.

In a second project, I collaborated with a member of career services to develop a new course in public service careers. This collaborative venture was far more enjoyable, though we were only able to teach and assess the new course once as I moved to Penn State Harrisburg after my second year. We did, however, publish one scholarly article and one trade publication from the effort (Mallinson & Burns, 2018, 2019). This project taught me the value of collaborating on SoTL research, as we brought different strengths both to the course design and its assessment.

Moving to Penn State Harrisburg offered new opportunities. Both our campus and University Park have teaching institutes that support faculty in the classroom and SoTL research. The opportunity to merge my subject matter expertise with their pedagogical and technological expertise has been invaluable. I have specifically worked with a team of instructional designers and pedagogical researchers to evaluate the effect of Nearpod, a student engagement system (kind of a grown-up iClicker), on student learning. Our work is slowly coming to fruition (Cruz et al., 2022; Mallinson & Cruz, 2022), but it has also grown into opportunities to lead a faculty learning community on student engagement, speak at events with Nearpod staff, and more. I strongly encourage anyone seeking to conduct SoTL research in their classes to collaborate on those projects not only with other subject matter experts (i.e., political scientists), but also with faculty from education departments or staff from teaching institutes. I recognize that not everyone has a teaching center on their campus but building external collaborations through attending the APSA Teaching and Learning Conference and engaging with the APSA Education section can yield more fruitful and personally satisfying outcomes (Becker et al., 2022).

STAND-ALONE PROGRAMMING

Faculty, especially at teaching-oriented institutions, often find themselves drawn into activities that bridge teaching and service, such as planning Constitution Day programming, running a Model UN, or coaching mock trial. Many of these programs are assumed to produce learning outcomes but systematic evaluation of these expectations can lead to publication (Ahmadov, 2011; Bengtson & Sifferd, 2010; Dunn, 2019; Engel et al., 2017). Such stand-alone programming with students and even the public can be an opportunity for good social science research (e.g., Siedschlag et al., 2021). One such project that I participated in was the development of a health policy simulation at Stockton. Working with our service-learning staff, we developed a simulation that walked students through different vignettes and characters that helped them understand the real barriers to accessing healthcare in the United States. Journals like *Simulation & Gaming* are interested in publishing evaluations of new simulations and other active learning techniques (Mallinson & O'Hanlon, 2017). The key for us was we not only published an article, but also made our materials available online for anyone wanting to replicate the simulation. APSA's new Educate platform is a great opportunity to pair a publication, say in the *Journal of Political Science Education*, with publicly available materials.

RESEARCH EMBEDDED IN CLASSES

This section will discuss embedding publishable research in classes and the next will discuss working with students on (undergraduate and graduate) theses and independent studies. Given that we teach political science, our students are often required to take some kind of research training course(s) during their studies (Mallinson et al., 2021). Giving students practical hands-on experience with research can be valuable to their learning and provide tangible receipts that they can include in job and graduate school application packets. In my Public Policy Analysis course, a writing intensive class all our policy majors must take, I have worked over the last four years to develop a team-based research project in collaboration with Harrisburg City Council. This started after one member of the council, Dave Madsen, reached out to our school to see if any faculty would be interested in developing research projects to support city lawmakers. We started the project allowing students to brainstorm and choose their own topics, which led to solid buy-in, but not very useful products. Starting in 2020, we transitioned to choosing a single topic that the class would sub-divide into teams. This resulted in much stronger policy analysis and valuable final products that were self-published as technical reports. The first was on underutilization of Harrisburg's Reservoir Park, the second on implementation of its new strategic plan, and the third on coping with severe weather (Mallinson, 2020, 2021, 2022). While students commonly wish that they could have chosen their own topic, they also appreciate being able to work on something that is submitted to the city. Additionally, this work prepares students for the reality that they will rarely be able to "choose their own topic" in their future jobs. Instead, they are more likely to be appointed to teams and projects by their employers. After completing these assignments, students can present this work in future employment and graduate school applications as an example of their writing and teamwork ability.

Another course that lends itself to having students conduct research is the capstone seminar. I have had mixed experiences in using the possibility of publication to increase the rigor of research done in capstones. Fortuitously, the journal *Case Studies in the Environment* launched the same year that I developed my environmental policy capstone (2018). The aim of the journal is to publish case studies that can be used in environmental science, law, and policy courses. I decided to task my students with developing their own teaching cases, with one requirement: they must represent Pennsylvania. Students again worked in teams and were required to write their final case studies using the formatting and structure guidelines of the journal. There was no guarantee of publication in the journal, nor was there a requirement to submit their work, but two out of three teams produced case studies that had potential for submission. These were also the two teams that desired to have their work published. So, for these teams, the prospect of publication pushed their work further than for the team that did not care to publish, as was evident in the final product. Of course, the papers were not ready for submission right after the semester. For the two groups who wanted to publish, I came on as an author and helped them revise and reshape the cases. Both cases were published (Bell et al., 2018; Shollenberger et al., 2019) and I was also able to publish my own piece on how I used case writing in my class (Mallinson, 2019).

The CSE opportunity was something very tangible for undergraduate and master's students (I had both in the capstone), but I had less success with a different approach. In the fall of 2020, I taught a health policy capstone and took a similar tack of requiring students to work in teams to produce case analyses. Alas, there is not "Case Studies in Health Policy," so I had to look for opportunities in more traditional journals. It may have been some confluence of the students and the pandemic teaching conditions, but no projects ended up being either of sufficient quality or of sufficient student interest to work further toward publication. Because I have only taught that class once, and it was amid the pandemic, I cannot generalize the experience, but it simply did not work out that time. Granted, I also did not have to put substantial time into revising for submission, which meant I could walk away from the class without the additional time cost.

The final model that I have used for embedding research in teaching is the Gary King model of having students conduct replication and extension projects (King, 1995, 2006). While King does this with success with undergraduate students (at Harvard), I have not had that opportunity. Instead, I have used this approach in teaching multivariate statistics to our Ph.D. in Public Administration students. They must identify a paper published in the last 10 years that either uses techniques taught in the course or could benefit from one of those techniques. They then conduct either a direct replication with the original data or a conceptual replication using the paper. Then, they must extend the original analysis, often with either a different (i.e., "better") statistical approach or the addition of new data or a new case. Many of these projects have been excellent, though only a few students have followed through in publishing their work, much to my surprise. I did work with one student to publish a replication that emerged from an idea I helped them develop (Menon & Mallinson, 2022), and I am part of a second paper that took an additional two years of work and is currently under review. It is yet to be seen if students will publish papers from my Spring 2022 course, but several of them have submitted their work to upcoming conferences. In this case, I only join a paper if the students request my help in working on it toward publication, but the prospect of publishing has motivated many of these doctoral students to produce largely excellent work in the course.

Working Directly with Students

Many of us have some opportunity to work directly with students, though which students varies substantially. Most programs have independent study options, which can be undesirable for faculty if they receive no compensation for the additional labor. That said, independent studies can be leveraged for publishable work, which is how I have typically approached them. If a student wants to do an independent study with me, I do some background work to think about what might be a publishable project that we could put together. Sometimes this works out, and sometimes it does not. I had two independent studies where the students fell short of keeping up with their study and instead rushed their work at the end. Effective scaffolding can help prevent this to an extent, but not completely. Students often set aside their independent study work when they have pressing deadlines in other courses. But in another case the student and I were able to publish the independent study work (Mallinson & Zimmerman, 2022), though with *six years* of additional off-and-on work revising it and sending it to different journals. Part of the challenge with publishing the paper was that it was on a topic outside of my specific expertise. This approach can appeal to a student's interest, but will require a great deal more time on the faculty's part to yield a publishable product. Granted, this is another area where faculty can collaborate to both increase publication potential and provide a better learning outcome for their students. I have done this recently with an honors student by collaborating with an outside expert on their topic. Doing so has enriched the student's learning and has helped us identify a potentially publishable research question and design.

Undergraduate honors, master's, and doctoral theses are also ways to merge your research with teaching and mentoring. As with independent studies, I try to help my honors students develop an idea that has the potential of being publishable. I cannot provide too much advice here yet, as I am early in working with two honors students, but they produce work that is well superior to many independent studies. Like bringing research and publishing into the classroom, pushing an honors student to think about publication, and then helping them work toward it, can be very rewarding for them (and for you!) as they can include that work in future applications to jobs or graduate school. This is particularly important for undergraduates considering an academic career, as the arms race for publication has now filtered down to undergraduate education, and many admits to top-ranked Ph.D. programs in political science already have publications.

Not all of us have graduate students in our programs, but I have been fortunate to work with solid master's and doctoral students at Penn State Harrisburg. One master's student had been my research assistant and asked to do his capstone with me. We were able to publish his study of evidence-based policymaking in the American states (Yingling & Mallinson, 2020) and we have kept in touch as he worked his way through law school. This student ended up reaching out to me when he was writing a paper for an independent study in his third year, and we are now collaborating on that piece too. Working with doctoral students is also a joy, and a ton of work and time. But it is worth it if you have the opportunity. Working with them has not only been productive, but also very personally satisfying.

Concluding Reflections

I have been very fortunate to have many different opportunities to combine my teaching, mentoring, and research. It is rewarding both professionally and personally. I have reached a point in my career where pretty much everything I write is collaborative, and I love that. Working with my students is time-consuming. In many ways, it is much slower than writing something myself. But seeing their creativity and encouraging their development as researchers is rewarding. I hope that these examples can spark your thinking about how you might incorporate research into your various teaching activities. Bear in mind that these activities do not always pay off. They may require more work than your own research since you are working with novice researchers, and you may find yourself extending yourself into topics that you do not typically work on. But the collaborative effort is rewarding, and it gives you someone else with whom to share the highs and lows of research and publishing. Further, the close mentoring that comes with collaborating on publication will help teach students important lessons that extend far beyond the content of any course.

REFERENCES

Ahmadov, A. (2011). When great minds don't think alike: Using mock trials in teaching Political thought. *PS: Political Science & Politics, 44*(3), 625–628. https://doi.org/10.1017/S1049096511000722

Baumann, Z. D., Marchetti, K., & Soltoff, B. (2015). What's the payoff?: Assessing the efficacy of student response systems. *Journal of Political Science Education, 11*(3), 249–263. https://doi.org/10.1080/15512169.2015.1047104

Becker, M., Bennion, E. A., Brown, C. M., & Loepp, E. D. (2022). Resources for teaching excellence: APSA's education section and the TLC. In K. G. Lorentz, D. J. Mallinson, J. Marin Hellwege, D. Phoenix, & J. C. Strachan (Eds.), *Strategies for navigating graduate school and beyond*. American Political Science Association.

Bell, A. N., Hernandez, M. A., Kremer, K., & Mallinson, D. J. (2018). Geologic history, hydrology, and current public policy: The case of radionuclides and water quality in Pennsylvania's Marcellus Shale Region. *Case Studies in the Environment, 2*(1), 1–11. https://doi.org/10.1525/cse.2018.001388

Bengtson, T. J., & Sifferd, K. L. (2010). The unique challenges rosed by mock trial: Evaluation and assessment of a simulation course. *Journal of Political Science Education, 6*(1), 70–86. https://doi.org/10.1080/15512160903467638

Cruz, L., Mallinson, D. J., Emery, J., Illingworth, W., & Cruz, C. (2022). Engaging engagement: A multi-disciplinary study of app-based student response technology. *Journal of Excellence in College Teaching, 33*(3), 123–146. http://celt.miamioh.edu/ject/issue.php?v=33&n=3

Dunn, J. P. (2019). A "model" for active learning and leadership development: International Model NATO. *Journal of Political Science Education, 15*(4), 528–534. https://doi.org/10.1080/15512169.2018.1544907

Engel, S., Pallas, J., & Lambert, S. (2017). Model United Nations and deep learning: Theoretical and professional learning. *Journal of Political Science Education, 13*(2), 171–184. https://doi.org/10.1080/15512169.2016.1250644

King, G. (1995). Replication, replication. *PS: Political Science & Politics, 28*(3), 444–452. https://doi.org/10.2307/420301

King, G. (2006). Publication, publication. *PS: Political Science and Politics, 39*(1), 119–125. https://doi.org/10.1017/S1049096506060252

Mallinson, D. J. (2018a). California budget simulation. *Journal of Political Science Education, 14*(3), 418–421. https://doi.org/10.1080/15512169.2017.1417861

Mallinson, D. J. (2018b). Teaching public budgeting in the age of austerity using simulations. *Teaching Public Administration, 36*(2), 110–125. https://doi.org/10.1177/0144739418769406

Mallinson, D. J. (2019). Teaching environmental policy by having students write case studies. *Case Studies in the Environment.* https://doi.org/10.1525/cse.2018.001776

Mallinson, D. J. (Ed.). (2020). *Improving community use of Harrisburg's Reservoir Park.* PUBPL 304W. https://sites.psu.edu/djmallinson/files/2020/06/Mallinson-ed.-2020-Improving-Community-Use-of-Reservoir-Park.pdf

Mallinson, D. J. (Ed.). (2021). *Implementing Harrisburg's Comprehensive Plan.* PUBPL 304W. https://sites.psu.edu/djmallinson/files/2021/06/Mallinson-2021-Implementing-Harrisburgs-Comprehensive-Plan.pdf

Mallinson, D. J. (Ed.). (2022). *Coping with severe weather in Harrisburg.* PUBPL 304W. https://sites.psu.edu/djmallinson/files/2022/06/Mallinson-ed.-2022-Coping-with-Severe-Weather-in-Harrisburg.pdf.

Mallinson, D. J., & Baumann, Z. D. (2015). Lights, camera, learn: Understanding the role of lecture capture in undergraduate education. *PS: Political Science & Politics, 48*(3), 478–482. https://doi.org/10.1017/S1049096515000281

Mallinson, D. J., & Burns, P. (2018). Increasing public service career interest and confidence. *PA Times, 3*(4), 2–3.

Mallinson, D. J., & Burns, P. (2019). Increasing career confidence through a course in public service careers. *Journal of Political Science Education, 15*(2), 161–178. https://doi.org/10.1080/15512169.2018.1443820

Mallinson, D. J., & Cruz, L. (2022). Fostering civic agency in an American Government course. *Journal of Political Science Education, 18*(4), 476–491. https://doi.org/10.1080/15512169.2022.2098137

Mallinson, D. J., Marin Hellwege, J., & Loepp, E. D. (Eds.). (2021). *The Palgrave handbook of political research pedagogy.* Palgrave Macmillan.

Mallinson, D. J., & O'Hanlon, E. (2017). Between the patient and politics—A Ready-to-use simulation for human service practitioners. *Simulation & Gaming, 48*(6), 855–870. https://doi.org/10.1177/1046878117734260

Mallinson, D. J., & Zimmerman, M. C. (2022). Judicial selection and state gay and reproductive rights decisions. *Justice System Journal,* 43(3), 302-322. https://doi.org/10.1080/0098261X.2022.2081637

Menon, A., & Mallinson, D. J. (2022). Policy diffusion speed: A replication study using the state policy innovation and diffusion database. *Political Studies Review,* 20(4), 702-716. https://doi.org/10.1177/14789299211052828

Shollenberger, H., Dressler, E., & Mallinson, D. J. (2019). Invasive snakehead and introduced sport fish illustrate an environmental health paradox of invasive species and angler demand. *Case Studies in the Environment,* 3(1), 1–10. https://doi.org/10.1525/cse.2018.001370

Siedschlag, A., Lu, T., Jerković, A., & Kensinger, W. (2021). Opioid crisis response and resilience: Results and perspectives from a multi-agency tabletop exercise at the Pennsylvania Emergency Management Agency. *Journal of*

Homeland Security and Emergency Management, 18(3), 283–316. https://doi.org/10.1515/jhsem-2020-0079

Yingling, D. L., & Mallinson, D. J. (2020). Explaining variation in evidence-based policy making in the American states. *Evidence & Policy, 16*(4), 579–596. https://doi.org/10.1332/174426419x15752577942927

CHAPTER 4

Metacognitive Exercises in the Political Science Classroom: Reflections and Research on Student Investment in Learning

Buket Oztas

Designed to encourage students to "think about thinking" and "learn about learning" (Biggs, 1985; Flavell, 1976), metacognitive exercises are activities and classroom practices that aim to enhance meta- (that is, a higher state of) cognition, or "the awareness or understanding of one's own cognitive processes or acquired knowledge" (Gassner, 2009). Such exercises encourage student participation in identifying affinities with course objectives and autonomy in articulating learning goals, both of which are essential for the development of self-motivation for future learning and careers (Ryan & Deci, 2020). Learning plans, metacognitive journals, and reflective prompts also provide faculty with valuable information about students' skills, interests, and preconceived notions,

---

B. Oztas (✉)
Department of Politics and International Affairs, Furman University, Greenville, SC, USA
e-mail: buket.oztas@furman.edu

© The Author(s), under exclusive license to Springer Nature Switzerland AG 2023
C. Butcher et al. (eds.), *The Palgrave Handbook of Teaching and Research in Political Science*, Political Pedagogies,
https://doi.org/10.1007/978-3-031-42887-6_4

which can be used to generate discussions, frame course concepts and theories, and represent diverse views on critical issues. These exercises help students construct a cycle of self-regulated learning (Zimmerman, 2002; Zimmerman & Schunk, 2004) by prompting them to (1) articulate their goals and motivations, (2) develop a plan to achieve these goals, (3) closely monitor their performance throughout the semester, and (4) evaluate their learning strategies and disciplinary knowledge at semester's end.

Building on Lusk's article on metacognitive strategies in the political science classroom (2016), this reflective essay outlines how one instructor at a small liberal arts college planned, designed, and implemented a Scholarship on Teaching and Learning (SoTL) project and came to reject the "false choice between the responsibilities of scholarship and teaching" (Frueh, 2020, p. 2). Preliminary results suggest that simply by incorporating student learning objectives into class discussions and assigning a few metacognitive tasks throughout the semester, instructors can help students understand the value of their work and become more engaged overall. This gives students the time and skills to make their own contributions to current political science conversations and pose questions that transcend the boundaries of current understanding, which in turn inspires researchers to explore uncharted territories and push the boundaries of knowledge. Furthermore, metacognitive journals, self-assessments, and reflective essays provide data on decision-making processes, biases, and assumptions, which helps scholars explore new perspectives on political discourse and generate new insights into public opinion and civic participation. The same data make it possible for political science faculty to unite their research and teaching by conducting research on the impact of their pedagogical approaches, instructive techniques, assessments, and curricular innovations on student learning and engagement. In that regard, incorporating metacognitive assignments in a political science classroom opens up new research opportunities and allows political science faculty to translate their methodological skills and disciplinary learning into evidence-based research practices, eliminating the oft-cited tension between teaching and research.

Setting Expectations

Junior faculty often teach large introductory courses that attract first-year students or non-majors with little knowledge of (or interest in) the subject matter. The mix of skills, interests, and proficiencies these students bring to the classroom presents numerous challenges, such as simultaneously engaging students who are not particularly interested and those who are more advanced. Consequently, we must ask two important questions: "How can anyone teach a topic like 'world politics' - elusive, all-encompassing, and constantly changing, to an audience so diverse?" and "What can a course like this usefully cover?"

When I started teaching Introduction to World Politics, I was blissfully unaware of many of these difficulties. I assumed that my students understood the *why*s and *how*s of the course from the syllabus, had the necessary study skills, and were approaching the course with specific goals in mind. I spent most of my time deciding what I wanted them to learn, carefully planning each class, and devising assignments to check learning. I often spent hours—if not days—preparing lectures, and gradually adopted "a sage on the stage" approach, where "the professor is the central figure..., the one who *has* the knowledge and transmits this knowledge to the students, who simply memorize the information and later reproduce it on an exam —often without even thinking about it" (King, 1993). Not surprisingly, students did not retain much information, and I had almost no time left for research.

After a semester or two, I had to acknowledge that my "one-size-fits-all" approach did not work for all students, especially in introductory classes. By investing most of my energy in course content, I was teaching the *subject matter*, not *the student*. By depriving students of the agency to explore topics on their own and process information in new and personally meaningful ways, this approach ignored the students' unique abilities and interests and placed the entire burden of teaching and learning on me, the professor. This was exhausting and time-consuming, frequently stressful, unrewarding, and, more importantly, ineffectual. I eventually realized it made more sense to adopt a learner-centered approach and help students develop a "repertoire of learning skills" (Candy et al., 1994).

A learner-centered view of teaching means meeting students where they are and finding effective learning strategies for their different backgrounds and levels. This, in turn, entails figuring out the most important lessons students should take away from the course, organizing and presenting this material in an engaging manner, and connecting the big problems of world politics *out there* with the students *in here*. In Shinko's words, the key is "to help them identify their own passions and enable them to become vested in the class" (Frueh, 2020, p. 116). My learning journey, therefore, started with two simple questions: why do students take an introductory world politics class, and how (and when) do they engage with the course material?

Planning Learning Tasks

Through no fault of their own, many students begin the semester with no clear sense of why they are taking a given course or what they hope to accomplish in it (Lusk, 2016). Pintrich, for instance, notes that "we are continually surprised at the number of students who come to college having very little metacognitive knowledge; knowledge about different strategies, different cognitive tasks, and particularly accurate knowledge about themselves" (2002, p. 23). To succeed in higher education, however, students must develop an understanding of their learning processes and "be conscious of who and where they are in relation to themselves, their peers, and society" (Garcia-Magaldi, 2010, p. 74).

Existing scholarship on teaching and learning highlights the importance of exercises that aim to develop active and higher-order processing (that is, metacognition) through planning strategies, reflection, and finally, evaluation (Veenman et al., 2006; Zohar & Barzilai, 2013). Self-reflection activities are particularly important in introductory-level courses where many students need to develop a deeper understanding of effective learning practices (Lusk, 2016) and adapt their study habits with the assistance and guidance of a professor (Biggs, 1985). Thus, my courses now begin with an assignment that combines goal-setting and strategic planning. Students are asked to think about their goals in silence, reflect on their educational choices (such as why they are interested in the course, what they hope to learn, and how they plan to connect the course's learning objectives to their personal and professional goals), and come up with realistic plans to achieve these goals by the end of the semester. After processing their ideas, they share their goals in small groups and "think-pair-share" exercises which often inspire them to revise their learning plans before they submit them.

This ungraded assignment makes students more aware of and deliberate in their choice of learning objectives and strategies before the semester starts (e.g., "I want to be an inquirer, not a follower; someone who learns and takes information from others, analyzes it, and learns how this knowledge contradicts, meshes, and blends with my current knowledge"). According to Taylor, this self-awareness empowers students to take responsibility for their educational journeys, allowing them to "gain a measure of control over their study activities, and in doing so, change the way they view themselves from passive receivers of knowledge to active makers of meaning" (1999, p. 36). By taking ownership of their learning process, they develop intrinsic motivation, i.e., "the tendency to seek out novelty and challenges, to extend and exercise [their] capacities, to explore, and to learn" (Deci & Ryan, 2000, p. 70). Consequently, the majority focus on SMART (specific, measurable, attainable, realistic, and timely) goals rather than grades. These students evaluate their progress toward those goals after each assignment, gradually incorporating metacognitive strategies into their studies, and ultimately becoming independent and self-directed learners (Biggs, 1985). "I think I met my goals for the semester and learned more than I even expected to," one student reflected during one of our in-class sessions, "even though I am not a politics major, with each politics course I take, I want to take even more!"

Learning plans help students develop a sense of autonomy and deepen their engagement with course content. Furthermore, the insight they give into student expectations, interests, goals, and concerns helps me select appropriate case studies, design relevant activities, and facilitate class discussions accordingly. Since students often demand to know how class topics relate to their personal and professional trajectories, it makes sense to have them identify content that piques their interest and create a roadmap clearly aligned with their agendas. This approach doesn't require recreating the course every semester; instead, student input is primarily used to select cases, examples, and the content of the learning activities, including questions for structured debates and topics for class discussions (which do not require any changes in the syllabus). Ultimately, this way of incorporating student interests take less time than creating or revising a content-focused course each semester.

Monitoring Cognitive Activities

The literature suggests that actual learning occurs when students ask and answer questions about new knowledge and explain it to others (McGuire, 2015; Pintrich, 2002). Professors facilitate this process by creating conditions that enhance intrinsic motivation and self-regulation and by giving students opportunities to "develop an understanding of their own knowledge and learning processes" (Colthorpe et al., 2018, p. 273). In addition to teaching and reinforcing meta-conceptual frameworks, Ryan and Deci argue, professors can provide challenges that promote "internalization and integration" of this self-regulatory behavior and help students "feel competent, related, and autonomous" (Deci & Ryan, 2000, p. 74). Teaching becomes more successful, in other words, when the instructor accompanies and guides students on their learning journeys than when the instructor single-handedly plots out one learning journey for all.

In learner-centered teaching, class discussions are organized around themes students find exciting and engaging. I have the students (rather than me, the instructor) formulate questions on the assigned readings and submit them before class. This assignment, which is worth 10–15% of the course grade, encourages students to do the readings, make connections between topics and current events, and apply their skills and interests to class discussions. It also allows me to assess their readiness for class activities, identify what they find most interesting (or confusing), and monitor their progress. Their questions set the agenda for the day and help me find topics (or "hooks") that create fun and valuable learning experiences. I design mini-lectures around these questions, which provide a shared context and vocabulary for everyone in class and lay the groundwork for discussions. These mini-lectures are supplemented by think-pair-and-share activities on course material and, from time to time, metacognitive reflective questions ("How do you feel about the quality of your work this week? Are there any lessons to be learned for the future?"). Collaborative learning exercises, where students explore and solve their own discussion questions in small groups, encourage students to embrace learning by "tak[ing] their own questions seriously and follow[ing] honestly where the answers lead" (Frueh, 2020, p. 9). As one student noted, "anyone can skim a text and search for the answer to a question, however, making the reader or student ask the question forces them to think about the topic."

This practice also turns the course into an exploration of concepts, theories, and perspectives of world politics rather than rote memorization of actors and institutions. Students read arguments, examine them to see if they can withstand scrutiny, and advance their own arguments and counterarguments. I do not "give away answers" or tell them "what to think," even though some students experience discomfort as they grapple with multiple (and often competing) explanations and demand more straightforward explanations. Instead, I assign tasks (authentic assignments, such as simulations and structured debates) designed to empower students to use their previous knowledge, come up with their own questions and critiques, make connections across different courses and disciplines, and transfer their skills from one setting to another. As students "sort through the complex mix of feelings triggered [by] new information [that] collides with unexamined knowledge" (Chick et al., 2009, p. 11), I provide support and direction through formal and informal feedback sessions and simple metacognitive exercises integrated into coursework. Ultimately, students build metacognitive skills (e.g., "I found myself [...] more aware of how I can further improve my presentation and discussion leading skills because of the reflection and feedback assignments"), learn to evaluate the merits of arguments (e.g., "[this course] pushed me outside my comfort zone and forced me to think about concepts deeper than previous classes had"), come to understand alternative points of views (e.g., "having my long-held views be challenged has inspired me to look deeper into issues that I am interested in"), and bring their own creativity and unique perspectives to discussions (e.g., "learning about different regimes taught me that I should never take democracy or my inherent rights for granted").

Even though the current events and case studies we cover change based on student interest, course expectations, main assignments, and deadlines remain consistent throughout the semester. That is why metacognitive practices integrate rather seamlessly into existing syllabi and do not take much class time. Reading (and grading) discussion questions takes less than an hour each week thanks to a simple scale measuring relevance, clarity, and originality. When students ask challenging questions or need help understanding issues better, the process takes longer but such cases often reveal alternative points of view and new research questions for me to explore. Moreover, as students begin making connections across topics, they send more critical and sophisticated questions, some of which align with my own interests or ongoing projects and inspire me to explore new directions or extend their investigations. Discussion questions, in that sense, can lead to collaborative efforts between students and researchers which results in richer and more comprehensive research outcomes.

Evaluating the Progression Toward Goals

The final aspect of this metacognitive approach is prompting students to reflect on their learning journey and assess the quality of their work throughout the semester. Reflection prompts encourage students to evaluate their progress in light of the goals they set for themselves at the beginning of the semester. Reflective sessions also remind students to be the agents of their learning process, effectively manage their time by prioritizing tasks and regularly monitoring progress, and evaluate their ability to understand and explain world politics. These skills, in turn, help them identify their successes and failures (e.g., "before World Politics, I was ignorant to the world news around me, and did not care enough to read about it. I have gotten much more interested in reading news from around the world and I often ponder how I would address problems if I were the person in charge"), learn from their mistakes (e.g., "I wish that I had spoken up more and gotten more involved in the class discussion just so that I could get much more out of the class"), and improve the quality of their work in the long run (Lusk, 2016).

These sessions culminate in a reflection essay that counts toward the final grade (Boud & Falchikov, 2006). The reflection assignment asks students to make sense of their experience by (1) linking course material to their personal and professional development, (2) illustrating their intellectual growth, and (3) demonstrating an awareness of their skills and levels of knowledge (Hosein & Rao, 2017). Grades are based not just on the students' ability to demonstrate *how much they learned*, but also on their ability to integrate the course and its objectives into their learning goals, evaluate their class performance with these goals in mind, and address the issues encountered in the learning process to improve learning outcomes in the future (Lusk, 2016).

Reflection has pedagogical value beyond performance evaluation and expectations, as it invites students to contemplate their assumptions and rethink their role among the actors and institutions of world politics. The reflection process helps students articulate their amorphous ideas and feelings with some level of precision and avoid oversimplification and dualistic thinking (Chick et al., 2009). It also increases student satisfaction with the course. When comparing their final exam essays to their learning plans, most students, including general education students, indicate they are proud that they have the vocabulary to understand and analyze global events. These preliminary findings suggest that the process of reflection empowers students as agents and lifelong learners who explore the intricacies of world politics by building personal relationships with the subject matter and course material.

Incidentally, far from inflating their success in the class for self-esteem reasons or "impression management", most students indicate that they became "more humble in their goals" but "more effective in producing outcomes." After all, this learning model does not give students the "comfort" of knowing everything; rather, it helps them become more comfortable with ambiguity and uncertainty, which is a valuable transferable skill. In fact, so many students were willing to acknowledge the limits of their knowledge and come up with plans to successfully attain their goals that last year, I launched a research project to see if there was actually any effect of their metacognitive exercises. This project examines students' learning plans, identifies the metacognitive skills and habits they developed, and measures the longitudinal changes in their self-reported patterns of learning, attitudes toward the course, and levels of knowledge and interest. Learning plans and reflection essays provided the qualitative data for generating theories using the principles of grounded theory and made it easier to gauge the impact of mini-lectures, class discussions, and assignments on teaching and learning. Thus, in addition to improving student learning, these metacognitive strategies also provide excellent material for pedagogical research. They also show that student responses to activities and teaching methods could challenge instructors to think creatively and explore novel pedagogical approaches, innovative methodologies, and previously overlooked subjects. By doing so, instructors can create ground-breaking research projects that make significant contributions to scholarship on teaching and learning in all disciplines.

Closing the Loop

Recent scholarship on pedagogy in political science demonstrates that practitioners are well-positioned to contribute to conversations about teaching and learning within the discipline. The discipline's focus on political learning and socialization, combined with signature pedagogies and years of training in quantitative and qualitative methods, prepare political science faculty to conduct evidence-based research measuring student learning and to design and evaluate innovative pedagogies to further motivate and support students and improve their performance (Bernstein, 2012).

Political science offers a wealth of opportunities to strengthen students' transferrable cognitive skills, such as designing and conducting research on how our students learn. Since the discipline continues to "embrace the principles of the SoTL movement" and value evidence-based work on teaching and learning, it is easier to align these practices with research expectations and conduct research that is more closely connected to practice (Bernstein, 2012). Metacognitive assignments can be designed to help instructors understand student interests, motivations, and approaches to learning, identify factors that help or hinder student engagement, establish the effectiveness of teaching strategies, and improve the overall teaching and learning experience, which creates a basis for future research projects. And when metacognitive assignments are integrated into existing coursework (e.g., asking students to produce reading questions or reflect on their debate performance), they require little additional time or energy from the professor. Such projects thus fit the teacher-scholar model nicely, as they demonstrate how research-informed pedagogical interventions can raise new research questions and contribute to the scholarship of teaching and learning (SoTL) literature without creating significant additional work.

The metacognitive model also provides opportunities for students to give meaningful input into faculty research. As students using this model tend to be more motivated and engaged with the material, they are more likely to make valuable contributions to the field. Moreover, student questions frequently reflect emerging societal concerns or current issues, bringing attention to topics that may have been overlooked or underexplored in the literature. With their fresh perspectives and sensitivity to contemporary challenges, students can introduce and shed light on areas of research that have direct implications for society. By investigating these questions, researchers can help address real-world problems and make their research more relevant and impactful.

This reflective essay itself is a metacognitive exercise that aims to demonstrate that effective teaching does not have to come at the expense of research productivity. Teaching world politics using metacognitive strategies can be a research focus, thus allowing instructors to better understand the processes that facilitate learning while maintaining fresh perspectives on teaching and content. It also creates fertile ground for the discovery of new research topics, new approaches to current research, and opportunities for collaboration between students and researchers. Moreover, when students take greater ownership of their learning, instructors spend less time on traditional lecture-style preparations, freeing up time for research. Thus, the metacognitive approach not only has the power to transform student learning; it can also transform faculty research by making students and classes active sources of inspiration and data and narrowing the gap between teaching, learning, and researching.

REFERENCES

Bernstein, J. L. (2012). Signature pedagogies in political science. *Exploring More Signature Pedagogies: Approaches to Teaching Disciplinary Habits of Mind*, 85–96.

Biggs, J. B. (1985). The role of metalearning in study processes. *British Journal of Educational Psychology, 55*(3), 185–212.

Boud, D., & Falchikov, N. (2006). Aligning assessment with long-term learning. *Assessment & Evaluation in Higher Education, 31*(4), 399–413.

Candy, P. C., Crebert, R. G., & O'leary, J. (1994). *Developing lifelong learners through undergraduate education* (Vol. 28). Australian Government Public Service.

Chick, N., Karis, T., & Kernahan, C. (2009). Learning from their own learning: How metacognitive and meta-affective reflections enhance learning in race-related courses. *International Journal for the Scholarship of Teaching and Learning, 3*(1), 1–28.

Colthorpe, K., Sharifirad, T., Ainscough, L., Anderson, S., & Zimbardi, K. (2018). Prompting undergraduate students' metacognition of learning: Implementing 'meta-learning' assessment tasks in the biomedical sciences. *Assessment & Evaluation in Higher Education, 43*(2), 272–285.

Deci, E. L., & Ryan, R. M. (2000). The "what" and "why" of goal pursuits: Human needs and the self-determination of behavior. *Psychological Inquiry, 11*(4), 227–268.

Flavell, J. H. (1976). Metacognitive aspects of problem solving. *The nature of intelligence* (pp. 231–235). Erlbaum.

Frueh, J. (Ed.). (2020). *Pedagogical journeys through world politics*. Palgrave Macmillan.

Garcia Magaldi, L. (2010). Metacognitive strategies based instruction to support learner autonomy in language learning. *Rev. Canar. Estud. Ingleses 61*, 73–86. https://riull.ull.es/xmlui/handle/915/13367

Gassner, L. (2009). *Developing metacognitive awareness-a modified model of a PBL-tutorial*. Retrieved September19, 2020, from http://hdl.handle.net/2043/10880

Hosein, A., & Rao, N. (2017). Students' reflective essays as insights into student centered-pedagogies within the undergraduate research methods curriculum. *Teaching in Higher Education, 22*(1), 109–125.

King, A. (1993). From sage on the stage to guide on the side. *College Teaching, 41*(1), 30–35.

McGuire, S. Y. (2015). *Teach students how to learn: Strategies you can incorporate into any course to improve student metacognition, study skills, and motivation*. Stylus Publishing, LLC.

Lusk, A. (2016). Metacognitive strategies in the introduction to political science classroom. *Journal of Political Science Education, 12*(2), 141–150.

Pintrich, P. R. (2002). The role of metacognitive knowledge in learning, teaching, and assessing. *Theory into Practice, 41*(4), 219–225.

Taylor, S. (1999). Better learning through better thinking: Developing students' metacognitive abilities. *Journal of College Reading and Learning, 30*(1), 34–45.

Veenman, M. V., Hout-Wolters, V., Bernadette, H. A. M., & Afflerbach, P. (2006). Metacognition and learning: Conceptual and methodological considerations. *Metacognition and Learning, 1*(1), 3–14.

Zimmerman, B. J. (2002). Becoming a self-regulated learner: An overview. *Theory into Practice, 41*(2), 64–70.

Zimmerman, B. J., & Schunk, D. H. (2004). Self-regulating intellectual processes and outcomes: A social cognitive perspective. In *Motivation, emotion, and cognition* (pp. 337–364). Routledge.

Zohar, A., & Barzilai, S. (2013). A review of research on metacognition in science education: Current and future directions. *Studies in Science Education, 49*(2), 121–169.

PART II

Leveraging Scholarship to Enhance the Pedagogy of Simulations, Games, and Role Play Exercises

CHAPTER 5

Collaboration and Independent Study: Working with Undergraduate Students to Design, Implement, and Assess a Simulation

Michelle Allendoerfer

This chapter is a reflection on a collaboration with two undergraduate students, Tianshan Fullop and Jacob Warwick, that resulted in a paper presented at the 2016 APSA Teaching and Learning Conference in Portland, Oregon. I'd like to acknowledge and thank Tianshan and Jacob for their hard work in creating and implementing the simulation and to the students in my Introduction to Comparative Politics sections in the Fall 2015 semester for their participation and feedback.

M. Allendoerfer (✉)
American Political Science Association, Washington, DC, USA
e-mail: mallendoerfer@apsanet.org

© The Author(s), under exclusive license to Springer Nature Switzerland AG 2023
C. Butcher et al. (eds.), *The Palgrave Handbook of Teaching and Research in Political Science*, Political Pedagogies,
https://doi.org/10.1007/978-3-031-42887-6_5

49

Introduction

Instructors and students have found value in using simulations in international relations classes for decades. There are a variety of in-depth "off-the-shelf" simulations available to political science educators, especially for those specializing in international relations, including Statecraft, International Relations in Action, and ICONS. Multi-day simulations such as these can better mirror real world complexity and demonstrate interactions between class concepts than shorter simulations. When I struggled to find an in-depth comparative politics simulation that would engage students with multiple concepts at once, the idea of creating my own was daunting. Thus, I involved two upper-level undergraduate students in the development process through an independent study (IS) course.

In this chapter, I discuss how I worked with these students to develop a simulation for an Introduction to Comparative Politics course, how this effort aligned teaching and research, and share some valuable lessons learned. The experience resulted in learning opportunities for two groups of students: the advanced undergraduate students who developed the simulation and engaged in the scholarship of teaching and learning around the simulation, and the first-year students enrolled in the introductory course. I hope this discussion will encourage other instructors to integrate advanced undergraduates or graduate students in the scholarship of teaching and learning in ways that are advantageous for the instructor and multiple groups of students.

Why Simulations?

While it is outside the scope of this chapter to provide a comprehensive review of the scholarship on simulations and active learning, I want to briefly situate the goals of the collaboration in literature on the use of simulations. This is useful to frame why this experience was beneficial for me, the independent study (IS) students, and the introductory class students.

Simulations are expected to increase student knowledge (see, for example: Dorn, 1989; Frederking, 2005; Pettenger et al., 2014), increase civic engagement (Bernstein & Meizlish, 2003), and enhance higher order levels of learning (Wheeler, 2006). When designed and implemented well, simulations "create situations in which students are more actively engaged with the learning process" (Pettenger et al., 2014, p. 5). Simulations engage students and provide opportunities for them to construct knowledge (Asal, 2005). By providing students with opportunities to "do" political science, simulations give students a tool through which they will better understand the material. In essence, simulations allow political science classrooms to become lab-like learning environments common in the physical sciences (Asal, 2005). Students can, within the confines of the simulation rules, manipulate variables, observe outcomes, and (if all goes according to plan) observe theories in action. Introduction to Comparative Politics classes are tasked with teaching many abstract concepts to students with little experience in political science. Simulations, then, "can be a valuable tool to help students finally grasp abstract theoretical concepts and recognize fundamental challenges in conducting global politics" (Taylor, 2013, p. 134).

Empirically, most of the literature on the effectiveness of simulations focuses on content knowledge as a measure of effectiveness. This literature itself is divided into two broad strands: student perceptions of their learning (e.g., student reflections, questionnaires, and student evaluations) and objective measures (e.g., test questions). In the case of the former, students typically report that simulations had positive effects on their learning (Caruson, 2005; Shellman & Turan, 2006; Krain & Shadle, 2006; van der Meulen, 1996). Beyond content knowledge, students also tend to report that simulations improved their critical thinking and/or decision-making skills (Caruson, 2005; Shellman & Turan, 2006).

Other scholars have introduced objective measures to capture the effectiveness of simulations. Some studies use a pre-test/post-test model; others use quasi-experimental designs to compare the simulation class (i.e., treatment) to a traditionally taught class (i.e., control group). Among the studies that use objective measures of student knowledge acquisition, the findings are mixed (see, for example, Ishiyama, 2013, for a comprehensive review). On the one hand, Frederking (2005) finds that students in American Government courses that included a Senate simulation performed better on six of eight measures of student learning, and Shaw (2004) finds positive student learning outcomes following different international relations role-play activities. On the other hand, other scholars find no statistically significant difference in learning outcomes in students who have participated in simulations and those in traditionally taught classrooms (see Raymond, 2010, for a comprehensive review of the literature). Using an experimental design with pre-tests and post-tests,

Krain and Lantis (2006) find that both their Global Problems Summit simulation and traditional lecture/discussion techniques are effective. It is important to note, however, that studies have not found simulations to *worsen* student learning outcomes.

Designing the Simulation: A "Win-Win-Win" Collaboration

While myriad instructor-created simulations are shared in journals and on websites, "off-the-shelf" simulations may not always match course objectives. As Glazier (2011) notes, "When instructors attempt to wedge into a course available simulations that may not fit the curriculum or learning goals, the potential benefits of these activities diminish" (pp. 378–379). Creating a simulation specifically for a course ensures that it targets the desired learning objectives; however, this takes significant time and may serve as a deterring factor (Glazier, 2011).

The Independent Study Course

Although others (Shaw & Rosen, 2010) have shared strategies for creating simulations efficiently, I explored a different approach to this problem and collaborated with advanced undergraduate students through an independent study (IS) course. Their "product" for the course was the development and implementation of a three-day simulation for an Introduction to Comparative Politics course. We structured the IS course around a syllabus that included learning goals for the simulation, focusing on identifying the key skills and knowledge-building the simulation would support, and comparative politics readings. The readings for the IS students reinforced and extended material from the students' prior coursework to provide the relevant background knowledge to develop the simulation. Although both students had completed comparative politics courses, it was valuable to spend the first few weeks of the independent study going into more depth on certain concepts that were central to the simulation. Next, the students developed the simulation with my feedback throughout the process. The students were both members of the Executive Board of a student organization that developed and ran international politics simulations. Their experience meant that I did not have to give a lot of feedback on the mechanics of the simulation (e.g., the online tool they used to manage the activity). My feedback focused on how I thought the simulation would support the learning objectives. The students facilitated the multi-day simulation during the Introduction to Comparative Politics class, which ran during the same semester. This included providing the introductory class students with work to do in advance of the simulation, introducing and managing the simulation, and leading the debriefing discussion at the end of the three days.

The IS students continued their involvement by working closely with me to write a conference paper that introduced the simulation and presented assessment data. The co-authored paper gave the IS students an opportunity to engage in the scholarship of teaching and learning. They were involved in the entire paper process, but worked most deeply on the simulation description and the data analysis. With their input, I embedded questions in a quiz prior to the simulation (pre-test) and after the simulation (post-test). As part of the process, the IS students completed the university's required IRB training and helped write the IRB application. The students—one of whom was a statistics major—analyzed the pre-test/post-test assessment data and wrote the analysis section of the paper.

Description of the "Precious Balance" Simulation

As part of the independent study course, the students learned about key concepts in the Introduction to Comparative Politics course such as: what factors lead states to choose different government structures and political frameworks; what are the consequences of various types of political systems; how do factors like gender, race, ethnicity, religion, and socio-economic status influence how individuals behave and what political systems they prefer; and, how do economic issues like foreign investment and the availability of natural resources influence political structures and behavior. These elements of the course's core curriculum were factored into the design of both the structure and plotlines of the simulation.

The simulation, called "Precious Balance," asked students in the Introduction to Comparative Politics course to work in small groups of about 4–6 students each, as founding members of a fictitious country in a region with a history of conflict. The students were assigned demographic characteristics and political backgrounds. The simulation first prompted participants to develop a constitution for their new country, with the students' assigned identities leading to different preferences and goals.

The simulation did not predetermine regime type; teams had the flexibility to decide to be democracies or autocracies, decide on different electoral systems, and ways to select executives. Based on their constitutional design, teams elected or appointed political positions for group members. These two stages—constitutional design and assigning political positions—filled the first half of the simulation, generally running 1.5 class periods (of 75 minutes) to accomplish. Once teams finalized their constitutions and roles, the rest of the simulation—the second half of day two and the first half of day three—tasked the teams with managing political crises (both student-initiated crises and plotlines developed as part of the simulation). To informally assess student learning, the second part of the third class ended with a debriefing session led by the IS students. The debriefing session was crucial to guide the students in drawing out lessons of the simulation. Students first focused on why they made the constitutional decisions they made; this allowed for a rich discussion and application of various class readings. Another important theme was comparisons across groups based on constitutional design decisions. For example, were democracies better equipped to handle crises? Were parliamentary systems more effective than presidential systems?

Benefits of the Collaboration

In this section, I elaborate on the various benefits of this simulation development model for three groups: the instructor, the IS students, and the students enrolled in the course. As the instructor, this collaboration helped me in at least three ways. The independent study students developed a robust and detailed simulation that directly considered the course's learning objectives that I would not have had the time to develop. Additionally, another key component of the independent study was the process of co-authoring a conference paper. Although we did not pursue publication—for a variety of reasons—it is possible that a collaboration like this could lead to a co-authored publication for the faculty member. Finally, as a professor, the opportunity to work closely with two enthusiastic students all semester was certainly a benefit.

Second, developing a simulation for an introductory course and co-authoring a paper provided a unique learning opportunity for the IS students. Creating a simulation required a deep understanding of the material, as the students created a "world," designed scenarios to illustrate particular concepts and theories, and had to work "on the spot" implementing the simulation in class. Specifically, the IS course was structured to achieve three key learning objectives for the students:

- Apply a deep understanding of key comparative politics concepts to the simulation.
- Create and facilitate a multi-day simulation in an intro-level course.
- Evaluate the effectiveness of the simulation using pre-test/post-test assessment data and student evaluation data.

Third, the students in the Introduction to Comparative Politics course benefited from this collaboration. Not only were the specific learning objectives for the course at the center of the simulation, but the IS students designed the simulation to account for the unique characteristics of this class, which was part of a first-year Women's Leadership living-and-learning program. The students all identified as women, lived together, and took two classes together per term. This unique class structure has presented challenges for some "off-the-shelf" simulations in prior years. Because the students live together and take other courses together, I found that overly competitive simulations did not work well. I have used the Statecraft simulation in the past and found that the level of competition in the simulation created negative intrapersonal dynamics inside and outside of the classroom. In the "Precious Balance" simulation, students were divided into groups to represent countries with the first objective being to cooperate with their group members to develop a constitution. In the second stage, there were transnational crises to address; but there was nothing in the structure of the simulation that predisposed the students to cooperation. This simulation was designed knowing the characteristics of the students and the context of the course. And, lastly, the students benefited from working with facilitators who were near-peers. At least one of the students in the course went on to join the Executive Board of the same simulation student organization to which the two IS students belonged and continued to be actively involved in simulations for the rest of her undergraduate study. Since the students in the course were all first-year students, this experience gave them insight into opportunities at the university for upper-level students.

Overall, the collaboration was a "win-win-win": the instructor had a three-day simulation developed and implemented; the independent study students had a deep learning opportunity and chance to co-author a conference paper; and the students in the course benefited from a simulation designed specifically to meet their unique learning needs.

Lessons Learned
Finding Independent Study Students

Perhaps the most important determinant of the success of this collaboration was the background and motivation of the IS students. The students were members of a student organization that created and ran international politics and conflict simulations. Members of the student organization initially reached out to me to volunteer to run a simulation for my students in the Introduction to International Politics class. After this simulation and conversations with two of these students, we developed this idea for this collaboration. This meant the students started the project with the necessary background and experience with simulation design—much more than I had. Although this might not be a common student organization at other institutions, Model UN experience might be an alternative. If I was working with students without that experience, I would have had to spend some additional time getting them up to speed on simulation design, which may have negated the "time saved" part of the collaboration. If working with students less familiar with designing simulations, one could assign a couple of articles about simulation design, such as Glazier (2011), Boyer and Smith (2015), Smith and Boyer (1996), Wedig (2010).

Although the independent study was a fall course, the IS students were eager and willing to start the relevant reading during the summer. If we had to wait until the semester started to do the necessary background work before creating the simulation, it may have been a challenge to introduce the content to the independent study students and provide time for them to design the simulation. An alternative would be to have the IS course and the introductory course in different semesters. Many variables are at play here. Students who are more knowledgeable about the course content may not need as much background preparation during the term;

shorter simulations would not require as much time to prepare and implement; and students with experience with simulations might need less time to develop the simulation.

Set Clear Timelines and Expectations

While finding motivated and experienced IS students is important, managing a complex collaboration also requires setting clear expectations. Independent study courses in general require a different relationship with students to ensure they are completing agreed-upon tasks with a certain degree of autonomy and independence. Since the outcome of this IS was part of another course, there was less room for error such as the IS students not meeting deadlines. I had to rely on the IS students to work efficiently. I was fortunate that these two students did not deviate from our timeline; but we did set a timeline and expectations at the beginning of the semester and regularly communicated. I reviewed outlines and early drafts of the simulation and provided feedback, in addition to bi-weekly meetings with the IS students.

A second type of expectation-management I would advise concerns the instructor's expectations of the final product and anticipating how to react if the outcome does not meet the instructor's objectives. While this was not a significant issue in my case, the simulation did have more of an international politics component than I anticipated. We addressed this in a future iteration of the simulation and the students still learned a lot. However, giving control over to students might be scary and it is possible the product will not meet expectations. Anyone who has done simulations and active learning knows that sometimes activities fall flat or outright fail; I find that using the debriefing period to talk about why and how can still create valuable learning opportunities for the students.

CONCLUSION

One frequently cited disadvantage of simulations is the time it takes to properly develop a simulation that enhances learning, especially one that meets your course's particular learning objectives. By collaborating with upper-level undergraduate students, faculty members can outsource the development of simulation materials while at the same time creating significant learning opportunities for two groups of students: the students participating in the simulation and those creating it. Student feedback in debriefing memos and course evaluations were positive, with one student summarizing the experience as: "… a great experience and a wonderful culmination of the semester's learning and effort" (Anonymous Student, 2015). There is a time investment on the faculty member's part as the advisor for the independent study; in this case, the time spent was well worth it for the simulation product which can be used with minimal assistance in the future.

References

Anonymous Student. (2015). Introduction to comparative politics course evaluation. George Washington University.

Asal, V. (2005). Playing games with international relations. *International Studies Perspectives, 6*(3), 359–373.

Bernstein, J. L., & Meizlish, D. S. (2003). Becoming congress: A longitudinal study of the civic engagement implications of a classroom simulation. *Simulation & Gaming, 34*(2), 198–219.

Boyer, M. A., & Smith, E. T. (2015). Developing your own in-class simulations: Design advice and a 'commons' simulation example. In *Handbook on teaching and learning in political science and international relations*. Edward Elgar Publishing.

Caruson, K. (2005). So, you want to run for elected office? How to engage students in the campaign process without leaving the classroom. *PS: Political Science and Politics, 38*(2), 305–310.

Dorn, D. S. (1989). Simulation games: One more tool on the pedagogical shelf. *Teaching Sociology*, 1–18.

Frederking, B. (2005). Simulations and student learning. *Journal of Political Science Education, 1*(3), 385–393.

Glazier, R. A. (2011). Running simulations without ruining your life: Simple ways to incorporate active learning into your teaching. *Journal of Political Science Education, 7*(4), 375–393.

Ishiyama, J. (2013). Frequently used active learning techniques and their impact: A critical review of existing journal literature in the United States. *European Political Science, 12*(1), 116–126.

Krain, M., & Lantis, J. S. (2006). Building knowledge? Evaluating the effectiveness of the global problems summit simulation. *International Studies Perspectives, 7*(4), 395–407.

Krain, M., & Shadle, C. J. (2006). Starving for knowledge: An active learning approach to teaching about world hunger. *International Studies Perspectives, 7*(1), 51–66.

Pettenger, M., West, D., & Young, N. (2014). Assessing the impact of role play simulations on learning in Canadian and US classrooms. *International Studies Perspectives, 15*(4), 491–508.

Raymond, C. (2010). Do role-playing simulations generate measurable and meaningful outcomes? A simulation's effect on exam scores and teaching evaluations. *International Studies Perspectives, 11*(1), 51–60.

Shaw, C. M. (2004). Using role-play scenarios in the IR classroom: An examination of exercises on peacekeeping operations and foreign policy decision making. *International Studies Perspectives, 5*(1), 1–22.

Shaw, C. M., & Rosen, A. (2010). Designing and using simulations and games. In *Oxford research Encyclopedia of International Studies*.

Shellman, S. M., & Turan, K. (2006). Do simulations enhance student learning? An empirical evaluation of an IR simulation. *Journal of Political Science Education, 2*(1), 19–32.

Smith, E. T., & Boyer, M. A. (1996). Designing in-class simulations. *PS: Political Science & Politics, 29*(4), 690–694.

Taylor, K. (2013). Simulations inside and outside the IR classroom: A comparative analysis. *International Studies Perspectives, 14*(2), 134–149.

van der Meulen, Y. (1996). A role-playing exercise for development and international economics courses. *The Journal of Economic Education, 27*(3), 217–223.

Wedig, T. (2010). Getting the most from classroom simulations: Strategies for maximizing learning outcomes. *PS: Political Science & Politics, 43*(3), 547–555.

Wheeler, S. M. (2006). Role-playing games and simulations for international issues courses. *Journal of Political Science Education, 2*(3), 331–347.

CHAPTER 6

Facilitating Student Learning Through Games on Human Rights

Charity Butcher, Maia Carter Hallward, and Frederick Walter Tillman II

Significant research has focused on the potential benefit of using simulations and games within the classroom. These studies have shown that such activities can improve student learning, increase student engagement, and can encourage students to develop critical thinking skills and evaluate contending perspectives regarding complex real-world problems. This chapter outlines an active learning approach to the politics and practice of human rights involving both student game creation and game playing.

C. Butcher (✉) · M. C. Hallward · F. W. Tillman II
School of Conflict Management, Peacebuilding and Development, Kennesaw State University, Kennesaw, GA, USA
e-mail: cbutche2@kennesaw.edu

M. C. Hallward
e-mail: mhallwar@kennesaw.edu

F. W. Tillman II
e-mail: ftillma1@kennesaw.edu

© The Author(s), under exclusive license to Springer Nature Switzerland AG 2023
C. Butcher et al. (eds.), *The Palgrave Handbook of Teaching and Research in Political Science*, Political Pedagogies,
https://doi.org/10.1007/978-3-031-42887-6_6

Through a directed research experience, undergraduate students created a series of games based on the theory and practice of human rights, particular cases of human rights violations, and/or human rights-based advocacy campaigns. Students also considered ways to assess learning through their games. The sections that follow outline the authors' experience with this SoTL-based project, including a discussion of student learning, reflections on challenges, and recommendations for how professors might improve on our attempt in future game-related projects and research with undergraduate students.[1]

SIMULATIONS AND GAMES AS A PEDAGOGICAL TOOL

International relations courses often focus on abstract concepts that can be difficult for students to grasp; therefore, it is important to utilize various pedagogical techniques when teaching such topics, including active learning and student-centered approaches (Bean & Melzer, 2021; Bickman, 2003; Fox & Ronkowski, 1997). Active learning displaces (or supplements) passive information delivery and focuses instead on encouraging students to engage the course material through application, debate, and participation within the discipline itself. The benefits of student-centered discovery-based learning are numerous, including increased knowledge retention (Hertel & Millis, 2002; Krain & Nurse, 2004). When instructors use these approaches, students are not merely passive receivers of information, but help shape the content and pace of the learning process, taking ownership of their education as active participants with opportunities to learn independently (Collins & O'Brien, 2003). Such learner-centered teaching prioritizes student learning through partaking in information sharing or contributing to individual or collective problem-solving. These opportunities provide students with experiences to learn along multiple levels of Bloom's taxonomy (Armstrong, 2010), as students must think critically and creatively in a problem-solving manner as they apply and evaluate concepts rather than simply remembering them; they also engage more directly with a range of learning styles (i.e. visual, auditory, kinesthetic, and reading). Ideally, such active engagement in the material helps students develop a positive relationship with

---

[1] This project was approved by the Kennesaw State University Institutional Review Board, Study # IRB-FY21-663.

the subject matter and provides additional motivation to learn (Lumpkin et al., 2015).

Simulations and games are two experiential learning strategies that bring the abstract to life (Asal, 2005; Butcher, 2012). In international relations courses, games can help cover basic concepts while also being fun; learning material is covered through competitive (and sometimes cooperative) play among students with defined criteria for success (Glazier, 2015; McCarthy, 2014). Games can include anything from board games to online simulation competitions (Epley, 2016; Mattlin, 2018). Simulations give students a scenario or situation to make choices as real world or fictitious actors using course material for guidance. For example, students might be assigned roles as members of the UN Security Council faced with a contentious decision, or as members of different ethnic groups competing over power and resources in a divided country. Simulations are often more open-ended and less formally structured than games, but both can provide competitive and/or cooperative opportunities for students.

Professors in political science have used simulations and games to improve student engagement in a variety of areas, including foreign policy, elections, protracted conflict, political theory, and human rights (Allendoerfer, 2021; Handby, 2021; Kirschner, 2020; Powner & Allendoerfer, 2008; Robinson & Goodridge, 2021; Taylor, 2013). Cohen et al. (2021) emphasize that game playing can increase student engagement and satisfaction with a course.

Recent research recommends aligning simulations with specific course objectives to enhance, not substitute for, other course material, such as lectures, discussions, etc. (Butcher & Njonguo, 2021). Without proper scaffolding for applying theory and methods, students can struggle to articulate and apply what they learned through traditional instruction methods (Horn et al., 2016). The literature identifies problems related to time, resources, consistency in application, and integration of simulations and games (Moizer et al., 2009; Powner & Allendoerfer, 2008; Raymond, 2010).

Difficulties in application prompt a debate on the types of simulations that can impact student experience as well as desired outcomes (Beers et al., 2017; Taylor, 2013; Powner & Allendoerfer, 2008; Krain & Lantis, 2006). Some scholars have found that simulations did not positively enhance student performance compared to traditional learning methods (Powner & Allendoerfer, 2008, p. 75; Raymond, 2010). One study of quantitative and qualitative data shows a decrease in overall interest in course material after simulations (Schnurr et al., 2014). However, other research demonstrates increased student interest as well as skill development as a result of classroom simulation, as well as making students more receptive to other role-playing games as the course progresses into complex topics (Asal, 2005; Belloni, 2008; Butcher & Njonguo, 2021; Shellman & Kürşad, 2006). As such, we consider simulations and games useful pedagogical tools.

Student-Centered Learning and Game/Simulation Creation

Significant research has considered how games and simulations impact student learning, but only a few scholars, such as Kent (2021), have focused on how students might benefit from participating in the creation of games for the classroom. In a directed research experience with four undergraduate students, we built on Kent's innovative assignment to encourage students to think further on the pedagogical impact of games and simulations in the classroom. The goal was to help students learn and apply course material in an engaging, fun manner, and for instructors to gain active learning tools to use in future courses. We also hoped for a collaborative paper co-authored with students reflecting on the experience. By designing games/simulations, students learn to apply the information they have learned and to develop new skills (use of material learned, resourcefulness, communication, collaboration, and managing their resources effectively). Successful implementation of student-created simulations and games can offer insights into the educational value of such high-impact practices outlined in past research (Kilgo et al., 2015). In addition, by having students participate in creating the games and simulations they would use in class, we could potentially counter some of the previous findings of the literature, where participating in simulations and games decreased student interest in course materials (Schnurr et al., 2014).

For this project, we asked students to create games on the theory and practice of human rights, particular cases of human rights violations, and/or human rights-based advocacy campaigns. In addition, students were asked to create tools to assess the learning achieved from playing their games. The section below outlines this directed research project, focusing on the games and assessment tools students were asked to create. We reflect on the process and challenges we faced, along with recommendations on how others might successfully implement similar projects in the classroom.

Student Creation of Human Rights Games and Assessments

Typically, undergraduate students are used as subjects in SoTL research, but in this directed study, which happened during the COVID-19 pandemic, we recruited interested undergraduate students to create human rights games and/or simulations through a posting on a university web page devoted to undergraduate research. We recruited students that had previously taken introduction to international relations and had a basic level of understanding of human rights and international law. In addition, all of the students who contacted us expressed interest in human rights, and signed up for a directed study course during summer term that began with readings focused on international human rights law and international humanitarian law. Once students had a general introduction to these topics, they read research on the use of simulations and games in international relations, including how to assess student learning from such activities; we met virtually periodically to discuss student reactions to the readings and answer any questions. After students had an idea of how games and simulations were used in international relations courses, they began creating their own games to teach about their selected human rights concepts along with an assessment tool to measure student learning for their game (such as pre-and post-tests). Students presented (virtually) the initial versions of their games and assessment tools to each other and the professors, received feedback, and revised their games before final submission. In addition, students wrote critical reflection papers where they deliberated on what they learned by participating in this project, including concepts related to human rights, skills they gained and challenges they faced, and how games might be a useful way for students to learn about international relations.

The goals of this project were twofold. First, we hoped that the students directly involved in the project would increase their knowledge about human rights and could articulate ways that games and simulations might be able to help students learn about this topic. Second, we wanted usable games/simulations and related assessment tools that we could use in standard undergraduate courses to help teach human rights concepts. We anticipated that the student game developers would then help administer the games, assessment tools, and be co-authors for a SoTL conference presentation or journal article. Thus, this project was meant to involve students in a broader research project.

Reflections and Challenges

The success of the project, based on our goals, was mixed. Related to the first goal, students did exhibit increased knowledge about human rights—which was shown through their discussion board contributions, the concepts they attempted to present in their games, and in their reflection papers. For example, one student noted that the course was different than ones she had previously had at the university because, "it made me think past simple 'What are human rights' questions" and "brought me to search what they are, what treaties protect them, how to teach others about them and why they matter so much for everyone."

We found the project partially successful in meeting our second goal. Students created a variety of games to help teach and review human rights concepts, and two of the four students developed games with the potential to be used outside of this initial classroom setting. One student created a game in which students gain points by answering questions about human rights correctly. Students spin a spinner and choose from a stack of cards (worth 100–500 points) and then attempt to correctly answer the question. The team with the most points wins.

Another student created an online game in which students move through a series of scenarios related to international humanitarian law and are asked how to handle each scenario. The game begins with the prompt: "You are at war with the enemy state. You are a soldier given specific instructions: complete the mission BUT DO NOT BREAK THE GENEVA CONVENTION. How will you complete the game in order to capture the target but not make any violations?" Students are then faced with a variety of situations that require them to make a decision (see Fig. 6.1). When students made decisions, a brief write-up would appear alerting them to the appropriate humanitarian laws that pertained to the scenario and giving additional information about these laws.

These two games could be utilized in a course to help students either review human rights-related concepts or to practice applying human rights law in real-world situations. Thus, the project was successful in generating potential games for classroom use, although the assessment

1. You are in the midst of a war. As a soldier, you are to follow rules set by the Geneva Convention, the body of public International Law that provides humane treatment. When you first step onto the battlefield you are greeted with a wounded child of the enemy state. What do you do?

2. The wounded child is taken to medical personnel. You ensure that the child has made it there safely. However, when you reach the hospital you notice that there are light individual weapons housed in it. You also notice many enemy combatants are being treated in the hospital. What do you do?

3. You leave the hospital and continue on your way. On the way, you notice an enemy. You are about to pull for your weapon but realize that they are surrendering to you and have thrown their weapon away. What do you do?

4. You finally capture the enemy target that you had been searching for. When you take him into custody, you notice he is wounded but you have orders to interrogate them. What do you do?

5. Once the enemy is treated you begin the interrogation. In order to finish your task, you must gain any and every piece of information you can get. They are a difficult person to interrogate and sometimes refuse to answer you. What do you do?

Fig. 6.1 Human rights game scenarios

tools developed by the students were weak and would need to be overhauled if we wanted to use them to evaluate the success of these games in teaching human rights concepts. Because only fifty percent of the games were potentially useful and even those needed additional work, our second goal was not entirely met.

Lessons Learned and Recommendations

Perhaps the biggest challenge we faced in this project was with student creation of assessment tools. Students had difficulty identifying specific learning outcomes for their games and providing instructions for how instructors could use their products in a classroom setting. The student-created assessments tended to be overly general and not specific enough to test whether the games they created impacted student learning. As such, the assessment tools need to be rewritten before we can evaluate their impact on student learning. This, combined with various challenges related to meeting as a virtual class meant we were not able to test any of the games in the classroom, therefore we were unable to co-author a paper with these directed study students as originally envisaged. Given the difficulty of creating solid assessment tools even among faculty members, it is not surprising that undergraduate students did not succeed at this high-level skill on their first attempt; in the future we will provide more scaffolded learning on this area of the course so that students can have more examples seeing and practicing with assessment tools. We will also partner with campus actors, such as our Center for Excellence in Teaching and Learning, to help provide students with better resources. Additionally, rather than having this directed study open to students having only a minimum level of international relations background, we would target invitations to known students with a background in the subject area, such as upper division international affairs majors.

A second significant challenge was that the course was conducted entirely virtually, and there was no face-to-face contact between students and faculty. Additionally, students joined the directed study based on their interest in human rights, but they did not all have the same level of background in international affairs and were at different points in their study. This impacted the course not only because we did not have a common basis of knowledge to draw from, but the virtual course environment impacted our ability to have students practice the games together and engage in collective trouble-shooting sessions. While we attempted to do this online, we were hampered by our inability to physically touch game components for some of the designs, and students could not even pass these off to faculty for future course usage since many students moved home during the pandemic and did not live near campus. Communication with students was challenging, perhaps due to the online and summer-term nature of the course, but also compounded by COVID fatigue more generally. This had significant implications for our ability to use even the two promising games in other courses. For example, the online human rights game isn't easy to transfer from the website utilized by the student to one that could be used in class. Further, the professors would have to make their own cards and gather additional playing materials to utilize the quiz-style game in class. Both of these problems might have been more readily prevented in a face-to-face class where students and professors met regularly as we would have access to the physical materials and more opportunities for guiding students in their selections of hosting sites. In addition, this face-to-face interaction could have allowed us to provide stronger feedback to students to improve their games between iterations.

We continue to believe that there is value in having students develop and play games as a means of learning both course content and critical thinking skills. We also think this is an innovative and valuable way to incorporate undergraduate students into a research project. However, based on our experience, we have developed a set of recommendations for moving forward with courses that engage students in the design component of classroom games.

First, the project would have been better suited to a face-to-face 15-week semester course rather than a virtual eight-week summer course. In a face-to-face setting, we would have the capacity to play the games together in real time, which would give the game creators more valuable feedback on the strengths and weaknesses of their products and a greater likelihood of strong games for future use. Further, a face-to-face, 15-week format would allow more opportunities for student-faculty dialogue and discussion over the strengths and weaknesses of their games, assistance with the challenges they face, and also more devoted time to learning about assessment strategies and protocols.

Second, the project may also work better embedded in a relevant upper-division course where students are more incentivized to see their projects through to the end rather than a directed study course. Given that students would already have some relevant topical background knowledge and the course would impact their major GPA, embedding might enhance the quality of the games.

Third, if the goal is to go beyond conceptual learning through game creation for enrolled students and to test the learning of other students through game playing, we would recommend spending significantly more time discussing the theory and practice of assessment and student learning outcomes. Students struggled to grasp how to create and measure learning outcomes, and as a result faced challenges creating assessments for their games. More content about learning through games should be provided to answer the question: how do games help you learn? What do you want students to learn from playing this particular game? Perhaps integrating some think/pair/share activities in class related to these questions might encourage students to think more deeply about their games beyond the practicalities of play. It might also be useful to invite someone from the Center for Excellence in Teaching and Learning to lead a lesson specifically focused on assessment strategies as an additional resource.

Fourth, it would be useful to have students work in teams rather than as individuals in order to provide additional scope for creativity and effort-hours in game creation. Given the small number of students enrolled in the directed study and its online nature, students opted to create their own games, although we provided the option of working in pairs. In a regular course with higher enrollment and face-to-face class sessions, we could require teams and provide space for group work in class. Having groups could help create more polished, complex, and diverse final products and provide additional student-student learning opportunities throughout the game development process. In addition, higher enrollment would provide more opportunities to play-test the games that students create.

Fifth, although we only had time for students to submit two versions of their game in the 8-week course (a rough draft for group feedback and a final draft), we think having students create more than two drafts of the games is essential. One additional draft of each game would have made them more polished at the end of the semester and readier for implementation in the classroom. Allowing time for playing each game in small groups in class between drafts will also help students identify and troubleshoot problem areas.

Finally, if possible, we would also encourage using class time to discuss game design in conjunction with a discussion of learning objectives. A guest lecturer could be invited to teach about game design, the students could study more on metacognitive literature, and could benefit from the resource of Stanford Design Thinking: 5 Staged Process of Creativity (https://dschool.stanford.edu/).

While this project affirmed the benefits of active learning through games for learning course content related to human rights, it underscored the importance of scaffolding such activities, affirming the SoTL literature that emphasizes *how* such activities are implemented and debriefed is directly related to the amount of learning that occurs. Different from simulations, where the pre-simulation role preparation and post-simulation debriefing are critical faculty intervention points for student learning, faculty feedback is needed on a more iterative basis with the student-led game course. Opportunities for student learning and reflection occurred at multiple stages rather than just at the beginning and end, including identifying learning objectives, aligning learning objectives with the game design, developing and testing the game, and then revising the game based on player feedback. Thus, in a course where students are active designers, we needed to provide more structure and instruction related to the project, logistics, and game design than we would in a course where students are merely playing the game. At the same time, we had to keep a keen eye on the course objectives and learning outcomes. By more explicitly focusing on these multiple feedback loops in future course iterations, we can better engage students in the process of SoTL knowledge creation and instructors in their pedagogical choices.

References

Allendoerfer, M. (2021). Teaching human rights with active learning. In *Oxford research encyclopedia of international studies*. Retrieved January 9, 2023, from https://doi.org/10.1093/acrefore/9780190846626.013.605

Armstrong, P. (2010). *Bloom's taxonomy*. Vanderbilt University Center for Teaching. Retrieved January 9, 2023, from https://cft.vanderbilt.edu/guides-sub-pages/blooms-taxonomy/.

Asal, V. (2005). Playing games with international relations. *International Studies Perspectives, 6*(3), 359–373.

Bean, J., & Melzer, D. (2021). *Engaging ideas: The professor's guide to integrating writing, critical thinking, and active learning in the classroom*. Wiley.

Beers, D. J., Raymond, C., & Zappile, T. (2017). Promoting global empathy and engagement through real-time problem-based simulations. *International Studies Perspectives, 18*(2), 194–210.

Belloni, R. (2008). Role-playing international intervention in conflict areas: Lessons from Bosnia for Northern Ireland education. *International Studies Perspectives, 9*, 220–234.

Bickman, M. (2003). *Minding American education: Reclaiming the tradition of active learning*. Teachers College Press.

Butcher, C. (2012). Teaching foreign policy decision-making processes using role-playing simulations: The case of US-Iranian relations. *International Studies Perspectives, 13*(2), 176–194.

Butcher, C., & Njonguo, E. (2021). Simulating diplomacy: Learning aid or business as usual? *Journal of Political Science Education, 17*, 185–203.

Cohen, A., Alden, J., & Ring, J. (2021). Using a 'gateway game' to stimulate student interest and build roundational knowledge. *Journal of Political Science Education, 17*(1), 104–115. https://doi.org/10.1080/15512169.2021.1921588

Collins, J. W., & O'Brien N. P. (2003). *The Greenwood dictionary of education*. Greenwood Press.

Epley, J. (2016). Learning by doing: Using an online simulation game in an international relations course. *Journal of Interactive Learning Research, 27*(3), 201–218.

Fox, R. L., & Ronkowski, S. A. (1997). Learning styles of political science students. *PS: Political Science & Politics, 30*(4), 732–737

Glazier, R. (2015). Teaching international relations. In J. Ishiyama, E. Simon, & W. Miller (Eds.), *The handbook of teaching and learning in political science and international relations* (pp. 265–276).

Handby, E. (2021). Classroom games to teach contemporary political theory. *Journal of Political Science Education, 17*(1), 23–31. https://doi.org/10.1080/15512169.2021.1914640

Hertel, J., & Millis, B. J. (2002). *Using simulations to promote learning in higher education: An introduction.* Stylus Publishing

Horn, L., Rubin, O., & Schouenborg, L. (2016). Undead pedagogy: How a zombie simulation can contribute to teaching international relations. *International Studies Perspectives, 17*(2), 187–201.

Kent, A. (2021). The power of play: Enhancing learning through game creation assignments. *Presented at the 2021 Annual Midwest Political Science Association Conference.*

Kilgo, C. A., Ezell Sheets, J. K., & Pascarella, E. T. (2015). The link between high-impact practices and student learning: Some longitudinal evidence. *Higher Education, 69*(4), 509–525.

Kirschner, S. (2020). Simulating negotiation in protracted conflicts. *Journal of Political Science Education, 16*(4), 430–440.

Krain, M., & Lantis, J. S. (2006). Building knowledge? Evaluating the effectiveness of the global problems summit simulation. *International Studies Perspectives, 7*(4), 395–407.

Krain, M., & Nurse, A. M. (2004). Teaching human rights through service learning. *Human Rights Quarterly, 26,* 189–207.

Krain, M., & Shadle, C. J. (2006). Starving for knowledge: An active learning approach to teaching about world hunger. *International Studies Perspectives, 7*(1), 51–66.

Lumpkin, A., Achen, R. M., & Dodd, R. K. (2015). Student perceptions of active learning. *College Student Journal, 49*(1), 121–133.

Mattlin, M. (2018). Adapting the diplomacy board game concept for 21st century international relations teaching. *Simulation & Gaming, 49*(6), 735–750.

McCarthy, M. (2014). The role of games and simulations to teach abstract concepts of anarchy, cooperation, and conflict in world politics. *Journal of Political Science Education, 10*(4), 400–413.

Morgan, A. L. (2003). Toward a global theory of mind: The potential benefits of presenting a range of IR theories through active learning. *International Studies Perspectives, 4*(4), 351–370.

Moizer, J., Lean, J., Towler, M., & Abbey, C. (2009). Simulations and games: Overcoming the barriers to their use in higher education. *Active Learning in Higher Education, 10*(3), 207–224.

Powner, L., & Allendoerfer, M. G. (2008). Evaluating hypotheses about active learning. *International Studies Perspectives, 9*(1), 75–89.

Raymond, C. (2010). Do role-playing simulations generate measurable and meaningful outcomes? A simulation's effect on exam scores and teaching evaluations. *International Studies Perspectives, 11*(1), 51–60.

Robinson, A., & Goodridge, M. (2021). Objective assessment of pedagogical effectiveness and the human rights foreign policy simulation game. *Journal of Political Science Education, 17*(2), 213–233.

Schnurr, M. A., De Santo, E. M., & Green, A. D. (2014). What do students learn from a role-play simulation of an international negotiation? *Journal of Geography in Higher Education, 38*(3), 401–414.

Shellman, S. M., & Kürşad, T. (2006). Do simulations enhance student learning? An empirical evaluation of an IR simulation. *Journal of Political Science Education, 2*(1), 19–32.

Taylor, K. (2013). Simulations inside and outside the IR classroom: A comparative analysis. *International Studies Perspectives, 14*(2), 134–149.

CHAPTER 7

'I'm Gonna Make Them an Offer They Can't Refuse': Teaching Politics and Mafia Through a Role-Play to Improve Student Learning and Understanding

Felia Allum and Geraldine Jones

Introduction

Although organized crime and the Italian mafia are very fashionable and sexy topics, it is easy to be influenced by stereotypes and fictionalized accounts portrayed in film and television. There are many people who write about mafias, but few who do real research about their multifaceted and complex existence and relationships. 'We decided for a vendetta after my brother's death' once said Neapolitan Camorra boss, Pasquale Galasso (Procura della Repubblica di Salerno, 1995: 44) to explain why he went from being a law-abiding citizen to a powerful mafia leader. How do you explain this notion of 'revenge' to students? Can we communicate our

F. Allum (✉) · G. Jones
University of Bath, Bath, UK
e-mail: f.s.allum@bath.ac.uk

research findings to our students in an efficient, engaging, and innovative way?

Our universities are encouraging us to develop a practice that integrates research into teaching as this has been shown to have wide-ranging benefits including enhancing students critical thinking skills, independence of thought, and self-belief (Elken & Wollscheid, 2016). Being both an outstanding researcher and an inspiring teacher is not a given, although as academics we are expected to be both. Teaching can often become the poor relation due to challenging workloads and risks of failure (as measured by unit evaluations) inhibiting innovation (Brew & Mantai, 2017). This leads to traditional lectures and seminars being the fall-back option for teaching despite not always providing an optimal learning environment and encouraging students to adopt more passive approaches to learning.

Integrating research into teaching typically involves adopting more student-centered approaches where learning takes place through active involvement and immersion in key concepts. However, there is little research regarding how lecturers achieve this in practice. Joseph-Richard et al. (2021) suggest a design process shaped by lecturers' individual (and varied) conceptions of integrating research into teaching and characterized by a 'research into teaching mindset that drives [them] to voluntarily engage in pragmatic research-teaching integrations to liberate students into real learning' (Joseph-Richard et al., 2021, p. 1).

In this chapter we contribute a case study showing how one such integrated project took place in a fourth-year optional unit in the department of Politics, Languages, and International Studies at the University of Bath (UK) thanks to the collaboration between a researcher and education expert.[1]

We wanted to link the researcher's findings on Italian Mafias with student-centered teaching. The unit was structured around four research themes that the researcher had been working on: (1) cultural norms of mafia groups, (2) drug trafficking business and rules, (3) extortion and control of the territory, and (4) political relationships and electoral campaigns. This new approach involved an ambitious redesign of a whole unit of study where traditional teaching was transformed into a

---

[1] This was a University of Bath Teaching Development Fund project that was approved by the University and did not require separate ethics approval from IRB. Student feedback was collected with informed consent headers on surveys etc.

series of role-play games. Here, we recount and reflect upon this experience in terms of how—by embedding research into innovative teaching methods—we improved the students' knowledge, understanding of mafia dynamics, and their general life skills.

Embedding Research in Student-Centered Teaching

The unit '*Organized Crime and Democracy in Italy*' had been taught as ten one-hour lectures and ten one-hour seminars. This format followed the typical teaching pattern offered by the department: information and theories were given to students via lectures in big lecture theaters while seminars provided space and time for students to present understanding to their peers and ask questions. The problem here was that student engagement was poor in the seminars, and attendance gradually tailed off over the semester.

The new format was centered on four key two-hour role-play games based on the lecturer's research. These 'games' were fictionalized scenarios designed by the students around given themes that emerged from the researcher's work. The researcher gave students lectures and assigned articles. The aim was to place the students at the center of their learning experience and empower them to role-play the academic concepts and theories they had learnt. The teacher took a backseat role as an enabler, guide, and advisor accompanying the students as they were recruited into a mafia family and had to make decisions about inter-clan politics, drug trafficking, extortion, and political-mafia relations. Students were immersed in important themes arising from the lecturer's research and were asked to adopt roles typical of the research participants. The empathy they developed with these roles could potentially give students an insight into the challenges of researching these contexts.

The Pedagogical Rationale

Based on empirical evidence, Chickering and Gamson (1987) highlight active learning as key in their seven principles of good academic practice. Healey et al. (2014) conceptualize active learning processes as shown in Fig. 7.1.

Role-play is an active learning strategy that leads students to take considerable responsibility for their own actions and learning and thereby

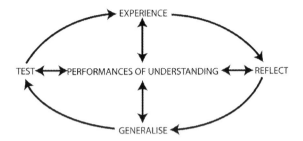

Fig. 7.1 Conceptualization of active learning process

become directly involved in the teaching process. Role-play has been used in many disciplines to achieve learning gains in the cognitive, affective, and psychomotor domains (Rao & Stupans, 2012). For example, it may be used to solve problems in public policy where a variety of stakeholder viewpoints are represented or to apply and develop professional skills (legal, clinical, social care, etc.) in a low-risk environment or to explore values and assumptions and develop empathy with minority or marginal groups. Broadly, a simulated context provides the immersive learning environment where complex social/cultural dynamics can be experienced in the first person.

Role-play as a teaching strategy in the humanities—where outcomes are more cognitively orientated—is less common, although there has been a resurgence in this approach to learning with the ease of generating computer simulated virtual environments in political science, environmental science, economics, etc. In the humanities, students are situated typically within a simulated scenario and may be actively engaged in shaping it while encountering constraints, tensions, and dilemmas of the context in question. Students adopt roles and play out their actions and reactions in character as a scenario evolves in real time. Learning opportunities occur through researching a role, playing the role, and reflecting on actions taken during and after the scenario has played out (Moon, 2004). McCarthy (2014) makes the distinction between role-play simulations which attempt to mirror real-life scenarios and games where the scenarios are plausible fictional constructs that capture the essence of real contexts.

What Are the Benefits of Role-Play?

In contrast to the traditional lecture-based approach to learning often found in Higher Education (HE), role-play has been shown to be particularly effective in motivating student engagement (Stevens, 2015). This may be explained from a theoretical perspective with reference to Self Determination Theory (SDT) (Ryan & Deci, 2000). SDT views motivation as a continuum (from intrinsic to extrinsic sources) reflecting the degree of autonomy afforded to the individual to undertake an activity. One of the core hypotheses of SDT is that more autonomous forms of motivation will lead to greater engagement in learning activities (Jang et al., 2010). Arguably, role-play activities afford high levels of autonomy to students.

When role-play involves enacting a scenario as a group, it develops communication skills through negotiation with other 'players' adopting roles with different perspectives. A sense of communal involvement is created through building a shared understanding of complex social domains (Westrup & Planander, 2013). Role-play as a learning experience requires students to actively apply and synthesize theoretical concepts in real time which arguably supports more effective learning through increased knowledge retention (Westrup & Planander, 2013). Immersion in a role can also build a strong sense of empathy and stimulate (self) reflection, an essential component of effective learning (Moon, 2004). The benefits of learning through role-play are summed up succinctly by Pavey and Donoghue (2003): "to get students to apply their knowledge to a given problem, to reflect on issues and the views of others, to illustrate the relevance of theoretical ideas by placing them in a real-world context, and to illustrate the complexity of decision-making" (p. 7).

What Challenges Do Role-Play Teaching Strategies Pose?

Lean et al.'s (2006) survey of academic staff across several HE Institutions indicate a number of perceived drawbacks to implementing role-play as a teaching strategy. These include a lack of resources to support the design and increased time demands (perhaps as much as a fifty percent increase in workload over and above a standard lecture). Unfamiliarity of staff and students in conducting learning through role-play can potentially lead to unpredictable results and anxious students. Some of these challenges can be mitigated by providing resources to staff new to this way of facilitating learning, freeing up academics' time, and providing access to networks to enable informal learning (Moizer, 2009). Asal and Blake (2006) advise focusing attention on three equally important phases of a role-play intervention, namely preparation, interaction, and debriefing. Assessing learning through role-play can also be challenging as the learning outcomes are often diverse and spread across cognitive and affective domains and skills development. Often assessment is added on as an afterthought. According to Raymond and Usherwood (2013), there are missed opportunities, "if the full potential of [role-play] simulations is to be realized, then assessment has to be integrated from the start, informed by learning objectives chosen by the instructor, and incorporated into simulation design" (p. 164).

Students may also find this teaching approach challenging to engage with because the norms of interactions in lectures and seminars have been replaced with a new set of 'rules.'

Acting a role in front of your peers may be particularly stressful for some shy students, a real concern since stress has been shown to negatively impact learning (Cornelisse et al., 2011).

Role-Playing Organized Crime in Mafia Clans

Designing the Intervention

We arranged meetings and workshops with experts identified via our networks to understand the key issues and potential pitfalls of role-plays. The unit was therefore structured in such a way that preparatory classes built up to four two-hour games designed by the students around specific questions aiming to stimulate critical thinking and relating to key issues arising from new research. These included sexuality, violence, political corruption, criminal mobility, alliances, and civic resistance within a mafia context.

We felt it was important to induct the students into the role-play approach, so the unit began with icebreaker role-play activities with time for discussion and questions. As background for developing their role and designing their role-play game, students were offered five lectures introducing topics and readings relating to organized crime and the Mafia.

The Role-Play Games

Students were assigned roles and divided into small groups to form mafia clans via a recruitment game. They worked together in their 'clans' to develop scenarios around given themes. In playing out their individual roles in the context of their clan and in interaction with other gangs, students were able to learn about the hierarchies, bonds, and culture driving inter and intra-gang relationships.

The first two games were led by the lecturer and required very general readings. Space within the room where the games took place became central to our games because the territory is key to mafias and their power. The room had to be large so that mafia clans could all exist in this space, a feature of paramount importance to help students comprehend the notion of territory.

1. **Recruitment game**: This game sought to make students think about motivations for joining criminal organizations and what skills are necessary for an efficient criminal organization. Students pulled their roles out of a hat, including leaders (male and female), foot soldiers, advisors, associates, and killers. Each student had to prepare for interviews as the leaders would recruit their clans. This game worked at two levels: the leaders had to decide what kind of members and skills they wanted whereas the members had to make sure they had the best skills set. So, a whole series of job interviews took place during the game: leaders sought to recruit members to their clan in order to have the strongest clan. If a foot soldier was wanted by two clans, they made the decision. Each person had to justify their decisions and choices. This game produced four clans that existed in a set territory which was the seminar room.
2. **Business activity game:** This game was to make students reflect about the economics of mafia groups. The newly formed clans had to: (1) decide their main activities, (2) present their business plans to the other clans, and (3) think about their priorities and how they would function based on feedback from the lecturer. This process led students to think about the illegal and legal activities of crime groups.

Next, students had two weeks to prepare for their games by researching and writing a game plan based on two or three key issues they would have to deal with as a clan. Each clan group was randomly given an envelope containing a topic with questions, concepts, and issues which the students would have to develop 'in role.' Because each clan had to involve the other clans during their designated seminar time, the whole group undertook a thought process about how to behave and make decisions.

Each clan prepared one of the following games:

1. **Inter-clan relations**; which included research on motivations for joining crime groups, mafia affiliation rituals, criminal values, and how to deal with traitors.
2. **Drug trafficking;** covering research such as routes, funds and organizations of drug trafficking, importation and local distribution and money laundering techniques.
3. **Extortion;** covering research on the importance of extortion and racket strategies, intimidation, violence and the notion of 'territory.'
4. **Political-mafia relations;** covering research on violence, corruption, political-vote exchanges, and corrupt officials.

The role-plays developed in real time shaped by student interactions which caused them to think on their feet and make decisions applying their knowledge gained through academic reading. While forcing students beyond their comfort zones, it also empowered them. For example, in Game 1, the son of the local boss unexpectedly declared his homosexuality in front of the whole community and rival clans. The reactions of all the different clan members and alliances had to be developed on the fly by assimilating issues of homosexuality, the Catholic Church, and the mafia. Game 4 provides another example. When the election of the local mayor was taking place, rival gangs had come to an agreement to rig the elections. Students were all shocked when another candidate unexpectedly won because one of the election officials had been bribed.

Making Sense of the Games

To consolidate their learning, it was key for the students to reflect on each game, the choices, and actions they took. This debrief, seeking explanations from research findings and importantly the lecturer's analysis and feedback, became an essential part of the learning process. Indeed, the lecturer's capacity to explain their research and answer students' questions was central to students' further developing their knowledge. Much learning would have been lost without a debriefing session after each game.

Assessing the Outcomes

The learning outcomes of this unit were for students to: (1) gain in-depth knowledge of the phenomenon of organized crime gangs in Italy, including a detailed understanding of their political, economic, and social features as well as their relationships with politicians and businessmen; (2) become familiar with theories of organized crime and its political significance; (3) become familiar with the major debates about organized crime in Italy; (4) be able to respond in an informed manner to questions about the existence and persistence of organized crime in Italy and the threat it poses to Italian democracy; and (5) design and write a role-play on an aspect of organized crime in Italy which demonstrates the empirical and theoretical knowledge detailed above.

We chose a variety of forms of assessment in order to mark different aspects of students' learning process:

1. Weekly e-journal (and individual in-role reflective account of recent events).
2. Game plan (a group essay explaining the plan of action for their game).
3. Critical Reflection (an individual essay synthesizing their roles' experiences over the four games in relation to important mafia values).

These three forms of assessment were chosen to assess students' skills and competences, student substantive knowledge, and group work.

Evaluation

We were keen to develop and improve this role-play intervention to offer the best possible learning experience for students. To this end, we adopted a process of continuous evaluation including student surveys, focus groups, and lecturer and independent observer reflections. This snapshot from the student survey gives an overview of the student experience of participating in the role-play games (see Fig. 7.2).

Despite the experience being chaotic and stressful for some, learning was experienced as motivating and fun for many. Student attendance was above 90% for all the sessions which indicated a high level of student engagement. The survey showed high levels of intellectual engagement outside the sessions as well, as indicated in the responses in Figs. 7.3 and 7.4.

One notable issue of engagement was the reluctance of a few shy students to buy into the role-play approach. They felt it forced them to take on a voice when they would prefer to hide. Overall, the role-play approach adopted in the unit can be considered a valuable and engaging learning experience for students.

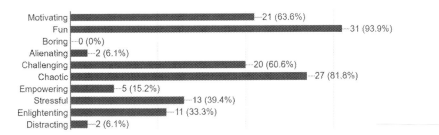

Fig. 7.2 Results from the survey question: "Choose the adjectives that described your experience of the role-play games"

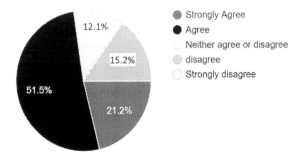

Fig. 7.3 Results from survey question: "I spent more time researching the topic than I usually do for other units"

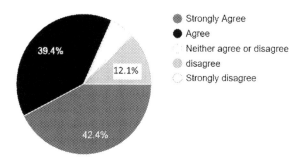

Fig. 7.4 Results from survey question: "I spent more time working with my peers outside class than I usually do for other units"

Conclusion

Role-plays are labor-intensive for both the students and the lecturers designing and organizing them. During the game play, the lecturer must respond to an unpredictable learning environment, keep order, and guide interactions, which can be stressful. The learning process is full-on for students who must apply their knowledge in real time, requiring full immersion in the academic literature and lecturer's research. However, connecting with the lecturer's research in this way resulted in unprecedented levels of engagement.

For students to gain the most value from the role-play, a debriefing session allowing students to ask questions and reflect back on the game is essential. Here, the presence of a knowledgeable lecturer/researcher as a guide and advisor is key to consolidating learning. Clearly not every unit can be taught in this innovative way. But, a role-play lends itself to creatively embedding research into the teaching of social and political sciences (in our case, the Italian Mafia) as well as developing wider life skills such as teamwork, managing uncertainty, and decision-making in complex environments.

References

Asal, V., & Blake, E. L. (2006). Creating simulations for political science education. *Journal of Political Science Education, 2*(1), 21–28.

Brew, A., & Mantai, L. (2017). Academics' perceptions of the challenges and barriers to implementing research-based experiences for undergraduates. *Teaching in Higher Education, 22*(5), 551–568.

Chickering, A. W., & Gamson, Z. F. (1987). Seven principles for good practice. *AAHE Bulletin, 39*, 3–7.

Cornelisse, S., van Stegeren, A. H., & Joëls, M. (2011). Implications of psychosocial stress on memory formation in a typical male versus female student sample. *Psychoneuroendocrinology, 36*(4), 569–578.

Elken, M., & Wollscheid, S. (2016). *The relationship between research and education: Typologies and indicators: A literature review* (Publication No. 8). Nordic Institute for Studies in Innovation, Research and Education. https://www.researchgate.net/publication/307477715_The_relationship_between_research_and_education_typologies_and_indicators_A_literature_review/link/57f3b7b408ae280dd0b72db3/download

Healey, M., Flint, A., & Harrington, K. (2014). *Engagement through partnership: Students as partners in learning and teaching in higher education.* Higher Education Academy.

Procura della Repubblica di Salerno. (1995). Ufficio del PM Dr Ennio Bonadies, Trascrizione del confronto registrato il 6.5.1995 tra P. Galasso e A. Rosanova Ferrara relative al pro. pen. N. 961/93/21.

Jang, H., Reeve, J., & Deci, E. L. (2010). Engaging students in learning activities: It is not autonomy support or structure but autonomy support and structure. *Journal of Educational Psychology, 102*(3), 588–600.

Joseph-Richard, P., Almpanis, T., Wu, Q., & Jamil, M. (2021). Does research-informed teaching transform academic practice? Revealing a RIT mindset through impact analysis. *British Educational Research Journal, 47*(1), 226–245.

Lean, J., Moizer, J., Towler, M., & Abbey, C. (2006). Simulations and games. *Active Learning in Higher Education, 7*(3), 227–242.

McCarthy, M. (2014). The role of games and simulations to teach abstract concepts of anarchy, cooperation, and conflict in world politics. *Journal of Political Science Education, 10*, 400–413.

Moizer, J. (2009). Simulations and games: Overcoming the barriers to their use in higher education. *Active Learning in Higher Education, 10*(3), 207–224.

Moon, J. A. (2004). *A handbook of reflective and experiential learning: Theory and practice.* Routledge.

Pavey, J., & Donoghue, D. (2003). The use of role play and VLEs in teaching environmental management. *Planet, 10*(1), 7–10.

Raymond, C., & Usherwood, S. (2013). Assessment in simulations. *Journal of Political Science Education, 9*(2), 157–167.

Rao, D., & Stupans, I. (2012). Exploring the potential of role play in higher education: Development of a typology and teacher guidelines. *Innovations in Education and Teaching International, 49*(4), 427–436.

Ryan, R. M., & Deci, E. L. (2000). Intrinsic and extrinsic motivations: Classic definitions and new directions. *Contemporary Educational Psychology, 25*, 54–67.

Stevens, R. (2015). Role-play and student engagement: Reflections from the classroom. *Teaching in Higher Education, 20*(5), 481–492.

Westrup, U., & Planander, A. (2013). Role-play as a pedagogical method to prepare students for practice: The students' voice. *Högre utbildning, 3*(3), 199–210.

PART III

Writing Textbooks

CHAPTER 8

Writing a Textbook Is Good for You

Alasdair Blair

Introduction

The study of political science has never been more relevant. From the rise of populism to the impact of the COVID-19 pandemic, a defining global trend of the twenty-first century is the retreat from democracy and the rise of authoritarian leadership (Freedom House, 2022). Even within so-called 'democratic' states, there are uncomfortable and unacceptable challenges to democratic rules. Whilst the United Kingdom (UK) is often regarded as 'the mother of parliaments,' this did not stop Prime Minister Boris Johnson's unlawful prorogation of Parliament for five weeks in August 2019 at the height of the UK's Brexit discussions (Supreme Court, 2019), nor did it prevent his intentional misleading of Parliament over illegal COVID-19 lockdown parties with government ministers and officials at Number 10 Downing Street (UK Parliament, 2023).

Scholarship investigating many of these issues will likely lead to publications in academic journals, not only because these topics are contemporary, relevant, and worthy of investigation but also because there has

A. Blair (✉)
De Montfort University, Leicester, UK
e-mail: ablair@dmu.ac.uk

© The Author(s), under exclusive license to Springer Nature Switzerland AG 2023
C. Butcher et al. (eds.), *The Palgrave Handbook of Teaching and Research in Political Science*, Political Pedagogies,
https://doi.org/10.1007/978-3-031-42887-6_8

been a significant expansion in the number of academic journal publishing outlets for political scientists. Established political science associations, such as the UK Political Studies Association (PSA), the American Political Science Association (APSA), and the European Consortium for Political Research (ECPR), have established new academic journals over recent decades. There has also been an increase in the number of journals that are specifically focused on open access, such as Political Research Exchange (PRX). There is a plethora of online blogs that include the ECPR's 'The Loop' and 'APSA Educate.' Political science scholars are also publishing research in what were once regarded as 'out of area' disciplines, ranging from healthcare to education, since the problems that we seek answers for often involve collaboration with multidisciplinary research teams.

This trend of working in areas once deemed less relevant is shaped by changes in the access and handling of data, such as the opening-up of archives and the use of statistical surveys. But it is also a reflection of the way that the study of political science has changed over the last two to three decades. Whereas a political science curriculum in the 1990s was dominated by a focus on the study of party systems, in the 2020s it is dominated by the study of issue politics, such as austerity and populism. These issues challenge political science academics to ensure that they can discuss and communicate matters to the wider public and show they are relevant to students sharing these concerns. Many of these issues cut across disciplinary boundaries, with research centres focusing on austerity and urban politics likely to involve collaborators from business studies, economics, accountancy, architecture, and health. Collaborations have been aided by improvements in technology platforms, the opening of publishing opportunities, and strategies pursued by research funding councils to focus on multidisciplinary grand challenges.

This expansion in opportunities to publish, combined with an internationalisation of the discipline, has been met by guidance on political science journal publishing (Blair et al., 2020; Breuning & Ishiyama, 2021). A focus on academic journal publishing has been influenced by the significance that is attached to citations for faculty obtaining their first foot on the career ladder and maintaining their academic progress through what is commonly referred to as the 'publish or perish' approach (Rond & Miller, 2005). This approach is different from that of three decades ago, when many faculty published little, and those who did would publish at best an article or two a year and a book every 3–4 years. Today

Google Scholar citation metrics are an important feature of academic life and the impact factor attached to academic journals is a key determinant of their standing. Yet, whilst measurement through metrics is a key factor of academic life, this publishing approach does not always reflect the breadth and nature of our discipline where a sizeable proportion of political science teaching takes place in Community Colleges and less research-intensive universities, where faculty often have significant teaching loads that involve the whole breadth of the discipline (Bowman, 2020: 123–128). It is also the case that journal articles provide a limited amount of scope to say something new about the issue under consideration. As Richard Rose noted over a decade ago, 'after reviewing the literature and describing the methods, there is only limited space in an article for saying something fresh. By contrast, a book provides ample space for dealing with both context and concepts' (Rose, 2010: 417).

Yet, despite Rose's arguments, far less focus has been attached to the writing of books in political science. One of the reasons for this silence is that textbook writing is often deemed less important by professional associations and university promotion committees. This is both a paradoxical and ironical situation given that teaching income in all but the most exclusive institutions subsidises research income and yet, despite this situation, teaching is often the poor second cousin of the profession. Whilst it is possible to understand the importance of research in terms of advancing knowledge, very few universities would survive if they did not have any students. Perhaps most importantly, these students, particularly in the large revenue-generating lecture classrooms, are introduced to new subjects through textbooks.

Why Textbook Writing Matters

Textbook writing should be regarded as an important feature of the health of the political science discipline and the relevance and content of textbooks is especially important for introductory courses, where they serve as an important marker for the health of the discipline (Atchison, 2017). In his reflections on writing economics textbooks, N. Gregory Mankiw noted that instructors in introductory courses are 'like ambassadors for the economics profession' (2020: 216). This is a particularly telling phrase as it signifies the importance of communication in these gateway courses and also conveys a sense of the selling of the discipline to the student audience. For political science, this is an important concern given that many academic departments are facing recruitment challenges, a point which was at the forefront of the APSA Task Force on Rethinking Political Science Education (Ishiyama, 2022). And whilst the Task Force did not extend itself into making pronouncements on the importance of writing textbooks, I would argue that writing textbooks should be viewed as an important part of a political science academic's contribution in terms of educating the future generation of students and the wider public regarding the critical relevance of the field to the world at large. Writing a good textbook has the potential not only to demonstrate the importance of political science as a discipline but an accessible and compelling textbook may also engage and captivate students who are left craving more and thus enrol in additional courses.

This raises the question as to where textbooks fit into the panoply of work that a modern-day academic might undertake. Our discipline faces significant challenges in terms of demonstrating its relevance and responding to challenges from populism, anti-intellectualism, as well as a focus by policymakers (and students) on degrees in the hard sciences over the social sciences. Textbooks play a vital role in helping to address this challenge by bringing to the fore a focus on a subject area that really matters for the health of global governance. They also address important issues that are all too often overlooked, including ethnic diversity and gender (Atchison, 2017; Scola et al., 2021). Writing textbooks should be viewed as part of a holistic publishing strategy that includes a range of research outputs, including short blogs of 500–1,000 words, briefings for policymakers, peer-reviewed journal articles, and book projects. Whilst sub-1,000-word articles can be useful for establishing what is increasingly viewed as a 'media presence,' this is quite different from the scholarly efforts required to write a book. Today even journal articles are becoming quite short, with many journals having strict word lengths that often do not exceed 7,000 words. Given that such pieces leave little room for a significant contribution to be made, a relevant question that might (or should) be asked is what does all this effort really amount to and who is it for?

For the teacher-scholar, textbooks offer a compelling complement to journal publications for a number of reasons. First, a good deal of work that is published in academic journals is at best an extension of the existing body of scholarship. Once that scholarship has been cited and noted, there is little time and space to demonstrate the author's own unique contribution. Further, journals also have a high rejection rate, which varies from

30 to 80% of articles submitted. And whilst all academics expect the possibility of rejection, revising and resubmitting work to other journals is a time-consuming process with little guarantee that the final product, even if accepted and published, will be read by more than a small number of individuals, and rarely read by policymakers and practitioners in government. As a young academic I remember discussing the work of the eminent Political Scientist Andrew Moravcsik with a senior official in the European Council, who knew only of the Slovakian footballer Ľubomír Moravčík. In contrast, textbooks may be read by scores of students every semester, reaching a much broader audience. Such anecdotal reflections are of course, not empirically rigorous, but they serve a point in jolting the reader to consider the significance and relevance of our work in terms of its reach outside of the traditional academic communities and its impact on our students.

What Type of Textbook Should You Write?

In broad terms, authors of textbooks need to think about not only why they want to write a textbook but also really think carefully about the audience for the book. In some instances, the decision is straightforward in that the textbook forms part of an established series and therefore your textbook is going to fit into a recognised structure and format. Series textbooks, for example, take away the need to think about the overall word length as well as the structure and layout in terms of the use of images, tables, figures, and graphs. All these points are likely to be taken care of in terms of the approach already taken. A book series will also have an overall editor in charge and therefore your task as a potential author is to think about the gap that exists in the series, such as in terms of a country study, an institutional study, or a focus on an issue, theme, or theory. The challenge here is, however, to think about the balance between writing a general textbook and writing a more niche book that is likely to have fewer course adoptions and thereby less potential readership.

For this reason, the pre-planning for writing a textbook should be viewed as a serious endeavour that takes time as you want to ensure that your work gets noticed and read. Given that a primary aim of textbook writing is to inform students and to assist the faculty who teach them, a good starting point is to think about the type and level of course that you would expect the textbook to be pitched at as well as what would be new and different about your particular approach to the topic at hand.

Whilst some more advanced textbooks might straddle between upper-level undergraduate courses and Master's level courses, most textbooks need to think about the level of prior knowledge that a student would bring to the subject. This is helpful in framing your understanding of the boundaries that are likely to frame the writing, such as in relation to the depth of scholarship, the need for case studies and supporting materials, the use of exemplar questions and reference points. Most importantly, you also need to think about the structuring of the book in terms of the flow of information and the relationship between individual chapters as well as the way in which chapters are often structured into themes or parts. This also reflects the changing nature of textbook publication where individual chapters can be digitally downloaded and where content can be repackaged by publishers, authors, and instructors. For example, publishers offer opportunities for faculty to create their own course book that brings together a range of work, which is further evidence of the changes that digital technology has brought to the publishing industry. As an author, you might want to consider whether your book will only be available electronically. And even if it is available in printed form, the reality is that most libraries (and students) will only purchase the digital copy.

An Individual or Collaborative Project?

When considering whether to author a textbook on your own or to invite partners to collaborate, remember that as with any writing project, the pace is likely to be dictated by the slowest member of the team. At a personal level, I have authored books on my own, jointly with a co-author, and also been part of editorial teams. For each collaborative project, someone must drive the work and be the 'sole' voice that helps to get the work over the line. Collaborative writing projects in this sense are rarely democratic exercises where everyone shares the load equally. Thus, whilst writing a textbook might seem a great idea, still having the writing commitment 3 or 5 years later is likely to be a wearing experience. Some textbooks are likely to require a team effort and if you are lucky to have a successful book that goes into multiple editions, it is likely that your book will develop 'legs' and 'arms' and evolve further than the original idea. It is also possible that members of the writing team might come and go because of other commitments. It is therefore important to think about the colleagues that you are going to be doing all this work with because, unlike an academic journal article where you might be inclined to add a colleague to the list of authors because they were your supervisor or provided some useful information, writing a book is not a place for casual passengers. Instead, think about co-pilots and engineers who can help build and navigate when the terrain changes and new developments arise.

Once you have decided who (if anyone) you are going to be undertaking the work with, you also need to think further about the idea that you want to pitch either to a series editor or directly to a publisher. Here, it is important to think about your time commitments in terms of when you can deliver the book. This might seem an obvious point, but it is important to think about when the final copy of the book is going to go to 'print.' Timing does matter in terms of the alignment with academic publishing trends such as the start of teaching terms and the publicity attached to the book. Timing is particularly important in the case of edited books where it is likely that one of the contributing authors will either be late or never deliver. Other contributors might go over word length. This requires the need for diplomacy and a firm hand to enforce a deadline and to keep the work within the overall word limit.

What Makes a Good Textbook?

A successful textbook is not solely determined by whether it goes into multiple editions. But if it does, well done. You have clearly done something right! Most textbooks are going to take time to write, and you should ideally test your ideas on your colleagues and on your own students. Whilst it might seem obvious that textbooks should be written by individuals who enjoy writing and who are prepared to take on feedback from editors and publishers, it can be surprising that this is not always understood. A good editor is likely to vastly improve the quality of your work and getting clarity from a publisher on the editing process should be an important part of your contract discussions. For seasoned academics, the feedback from editors can be direct and at times brutal. Taking on board this feedback will make your work better and because the textbook market is highly competitive, this will also ensure that your work is likely to be more successful. Success can be determined by many factors, including endorsements where quotes at the back of the book can be helpful. It is also important to think about marketing, which goes beyond the role of the publisher. Where are you going to disseminate your ideas? In a blog, via twitter, at a conference? Or all of them? Given that you will have spent many hours (and years) on your work, you want to ensure that it is noticed. In this sense, a key feature of success should be that your book is read widely and used by students that you teach. This requires you to think about what your students need (and want) and not just what you think is good for them. Textbook writing is therefore not a process where you are writing for an audience of one. A good textbook should be accessible and offer some challenge to those who read it. There should be a sense of progression in the text, with the chapters structured in a logical manner. Given that chapters are often digitally downloaded and read as individual works on their own, you should consider how each chapter tells a story on its own. Remember that an experienced journal author does not necessarily make a good textbook writer. The audiences are different, and the style of writing is not the same. Finally, you should not overlook the fact that textbooks are there to aid students' understanding and make life easier for the faculty doing the teaching. If you find your students stretching for the dictionary, thesaurus, or another textbook, you might wish you had solicited more feedback. If, on the other hand, your students can understand your points and be engaged with your writing, then you are onto a winner.

References

Atchison, A. L. (2017). Where are the women? An analysis of gender mainstreaming in introductory political science textbooks. *Journal of Political Science Education, 13*(2), 185–199.

Blair, A., Buckley, F., Rashkova, E., & Stockemer, D. (2020). Publishing in political science journals. *European Political Science, 19*(4), 641–652.

Bowman, P. J. (2020). The contingency professor, the tenured professor, and the generalist: Life as a Community College political scientist. *Journal of Political Science Education, 16*(1), 123–128.

Breuning, M., & Ishiyama, J. (2021). *How to get published in the best political science and international relations journals*. Edward Elgar.

De Rond, M., & Miller, A. N. (2005). Publish or perish: Bane or boon of academic life? *Journal of Management Inquiry, 14*(4), 321–329.

Freedom House. (2022). *Freedom on the world 2022: The global expansion of authoritarian rule*. https://freedomhouse.org/sites/default/files/2022-02/FIW_2022_PDF_Booklet_Digital_Final_Web.pdf. Accessed 26 June 2023.

Ishiyama, J. (2022). An introduction to the "rethinking political science education" task force. *Political Science Today, 2*(1), 3–5.

Mankiw, N. G. (2020). Reflections of a textbook author. *Journal of Economic Literature, 58*(1), 215–228.
Rose, R. (2010). Writing a book is good for you. *European Political Science, 9*(3), 417–419.
Scola, B., Bucci, L. C., & Baglione, L. (2021). "Pale, male and stale"? An analysis of introductory readers in political science. *Journal of Political Science Education, 17*(S1), 770–793.
Supreme Court. (2019, September 24). *Judgment R (on the application of Miller) (Appellant) v The Prime Minister (Respondent) Cherry and others (Respondents) v Advocate General for Scotland (Appellant) (Scotland).* https://www.supremecourt.uk/cases/docs/uksc-2019-0192-judgment.pdf. Accessed 26 June 2023.
UK Parliament. (2023, June 15). *Matter referred on 21 April 2022 (conduct of Rt Hon Boris Johnson): Final Report.* https://publications.parliament.uk/pa/cm5803/cmselect/cmprivi/564/report.html. Accessed 26 June 2023.

CHAPTER 9

Taking Innovative Teaching to the Next Level: Writing and Publishing Instructional Materials and Textbooks

J. Cherie Strachan

INTRODUCTION

Given academia's heightened focus on the scholarship of discovery and publication metrics, political scientists—especially tenure-track political scientists who have not been fully promoted and fixed-term faculty who are not rewarded for publishing in general—are often reluctant to invest time in writing a textbook. Such reluctance is unfortunate, as it stymies the development of innovative instructional material and contributes to inertia in our broader discipline's approach to teaching and learning. This chapter seeks to address this dilemma by providing advice for teacher-scholars who would like to write a textbook but worry that doing

---

J. C. Strachan (✉)
Ray C. Bliss Institute of Applied Politics, The University of Akron, Akron, OH, USA
e-mail: Jcw39@uakron.edu

© The Author(s), under exclusive license to Springer Nature Switzerland AG 2023
C. Butcher et al. (eds.), *The Palgrave Handbook of Teaching and Research in Political Science*, Political Pedagogies,
https://doi.org/10.1007/978-3-031-42887-6_9

so will not count toward scholarly publications, retention, tenure, and promotion.

Why Your Textbook Project Matters

A quick scan of prominent political science textbooks reveals a common trend in our discipline. Popular textbooks have traditionally been written by established scholars in our field. After these teaching resources become well-established, ensuing editions are often updated by adding former students or junior colleagues who work at similar elite institutions to the coauthor list. Another tactic is to rely on ghostwriters who are paid a fee to update topics and chapters, who may never be publicly recognized as contributors. Senior colleagues willing to undertake the work of organizing and summarizing a semester's worth of knowledge in their areas of expertise undeniably provide an invaluable resource to the discipline. Further, scholarly prominence can help establish a textbook's credibility as a trusted teaching resource. This credibility can be reassuring, especially when we are required to prep a new class in an unfamiliar area. Almost all of us have faced this situation early in our teaching careers, and our mentors likely gave us the same piece of advice: Assign your students the second-best textbook in the field, while mining the most detailed and up-to-date textbook for lecture material. Dedicated teacher-scholars, especially those of us required to teach a wide array of courses beyond our research specialization, know from firsthand experience just how important the resource of a good textbook can be.

Yet the production of knowledge by a small number of scholars largely affiliated with elite institutions in the Global North could also be problematic. As our mentors' common advice about finding good teaching resources clearly indicates, textbooks achieve a symbolic status as official "repositories knowledge" for the discipline (Ferree & Hall, 1996). They are used to frame and organize the substantive content of what *should* be taught. Moreover, they often reflect implicit assumptions about pedagogy and influence *how* materials will be taught. When teaching resources are produced by a narrow subset of elite political scientists, the materials created will inevitably reflect their similarly limited worldviews and lived experience, as well as the materials best suited to the type of students they teach. A recent *PS* symposium on writing textbooks underscores this concern, as all 12 contributing authors were affiliated with US institutions; only four worked on campuses without a doctoral program (The Teacher Symposium, 2022).

Further, content analyses of political science textbooks consistently reveal egregiously limited representation of women and members of minoritized groups in both substantive content and images (Allen & Wallace, 2010; Atchison, 2017; Brandle, 2020; Cassese & Bos, 2013; Cassese et al., 2012; Clawson & Kegler, 2000; Nemerever et al., 2021; Olivo, 2012; Scala et al., 2021; Wallace & Allen, 2008). This oversight persists, at least in part, because at the types of elite institutions where scholars have time to write textbooks, tenured professors have been predominantly white and male. Notably, only one of the contributors to the PS symposium described above was a woman (The Teacher Symposium, 2022).

Even as our discipline has become more diverse, women and minoritized faculty are more likely to fill adjunct and fixed-term roles or to earn tenure at regional public universities, minority-serving institutions, small liberal arts colleges, and community colleges, all of which require heavy teaching loads that leave less time for research and writing (Flaherty, 2016). Political science's embrace of traditional scholarship (or the scholarship of discovery) over pedagogy research (or the scholarship of teaching and learning) means even colleagues at teaching institutions believe they must expend precious research time publishing in peer-reviewed journals rather than writing textbooks. Yet teacher-scholars at these types of institutions have much different teaching experiences than those at elite research-intensive universities. They are more apt to teach first-generation, minoritized, or at-risk students—and hence to develop and incorporate engaged learning activities and innovative pedagogies out of sheer necessity. Similarly, the fact that textbook authors tend to work at elite institutions in the Global North means that the pedagogy embedded in political science textbooks is often not designed to meet the needs of students in the Global South.

Recent evidence of these teacher-scholars' burgeoning efforts to advance innovative pedagogy can be found in articles published in the *Journal of Political Science Education, International Studies Perspectives, European Political Science*, and *PS: Political Science and Politics*, and in the American Political Science Association's (APSA) teaching-focused website *Educate*. Our teacher-scholar colleagues' deep commitment to active learning can be found in edited collections dedicated to teaching international relations and political science (Frueh, 2020; Lantis, 2021; Mallinson et al., 2022; Murray et al., 2022; Smith & Hornsby, 2022; Szarejko, 2022) and in APSA's three edited volumes dedicated to civic engagement pedagogy (Matto et al., 2017, 2021; McCartney et al., 2013). Yet even a quick glance will confirm that few of these approaches make an appearance in traditional textbooks. For example, none of the authors of the most prominent Intro to American Government textbooks have published pedagogy research about ways to most effectively convey the knowledge that they summarize. Hence the lack of political science instructional materials published by scholars who prioritize innovative teaching alongside disciplinary knowledge is unfortunate for another reason. It stymies easy access to cutting-edge resources and contributes to inertia in our broader discipline's approach to teaching and learning.[1]

With these concerns in mind, this chapter provides advice about how to write a textbook and concludes with suggestions for ensuring this work counts toward retention, tenure, and promotion. My hope is that a more diverse array of political scientists will be inspired to incorporate their lived experience and teaching expertise to produce the innovative, representative, and engaging instructional materials that our colleagues and our students deserve.

IDENTIFY A NEED

Perhaps the most important first step in writing a textbook is to identify a need for updated materials or a new approach to traditional subject matter. Who among us has not been frustrated by the limited or outdated array of texts available for a core class in our rotation? Who hasn't spent

---

[1] Other social sciences more quickly embraced and elevated the status of the Scholarship of Teaching and Learning (SoTL), signaling our discipline's belated embrace of teaching innovation. While political science allotted a small portion of *PS, Political Science & Politics* to teaching-related articles, SoTL-dedicated journals such as *The Journal of Political Science Education* and *International Studies Perspective* were not launched until 2005 and 2000 respectively. Further, JPSE did not become an APSA-wide publication until 2017. In comparison, history launched pedagogy outlets in the 1940s (*The History Teacher*) and in 1976 (*Teaching History, A Journal of Methods*). The disciplines of Communication (with the National Communication Association's *Communication Education* in 1952), economics (with *The Journal of Economic Education* in 1969), and Sociology (with the American Sociology Association's *Teaching Sociology* in 1973) also preceded political science in embracing and elevating pedagogy research as a distinct disciplinary subfield.

hours cobbling together materials to compensate for overlooked content or lackluster aspects of the primary texts we resigned ourselves to assign? Take note when you experience these frustrations, because if you are unhappy with available instructional materials, chances are that others are similarly frustrated. Give labels to the substantive content and learning experiences you believe are missing. Keep track of the ways you have compensated for the gaps in readily available teaching resources. Are you assigning supplementary reading or developing classroom exercises that are not included in available textbooks? If the readings and activities you cobble together are substantial, they may provide the basis for an innovative new textbook.

For example, I had become dissatisfied with women and politics textbooks several years prior to coauthoring my recent textbook, *Why Don't Women Rule the World?* (CQ Press 2019). I was concerned that the textbooks on the market did not address the deep history of patriarchy or its long-term consequences on women's ability to participate in public life. I also thought they paid inadequate attention to the experiences of US women with intersectional identities, with even less effort made to extend the concept of intersectionality to minoritized women in other countries. Finally, I was determined to include civic engagement pedagogy in all my classes, yet no existing resources incorporated learning activities specifically designed to bolster women students' anticipation of participating in politics or running for office. Ironically, I did not fully realize these materials provided much of what I needed to pitch and write a textbook until I described what I wanted in an ideal textbook to a CQ acquisitions editor, who responded that if a book like this one was going to be published, I would probably have to write it myself!

Recruit Compatible Coauthors

Writing a textbook can feel like a daunting undertaking, especially if you plan to develop in-class activities and assignments. One path forward may be to identify coauthors to share the work. While I was flattered and intrigued by the suggestion that I should write my ideal textbook, I knew that I did not have the bandwidth, in terms of expertise or time, to write the women and politics text I envisioned as a solo author. I immediately reached out to colleagues who I thought would be equally excited about the project. If you consider collaboration, prioritize identifying scholars whose substantive areas or pedagogy expertise complements your own.

For example, I reached out to two comparativists to balance my expertise in American politics. Compatible work habits are also important. Be sure to have clear agreement on how writing and organizational tasks will be divided in advance, to avoid confusion or disagreements throughout the project.

Consider Publishers and Meet with Acquisition Editors

Rather than rely on serendipity, as in my case, if you are convinced that you have an idea for instructional materials that fill an important gap in what is available, be proactive. Consider potential publishers. Do you envision a primary text, a supplemental reader, or an activities book? Is the intended course a general education requirement with high enrolment? Is it an upper-level course in a class that is regularly taught in most political science programs? Or is the resource you have in mind tailored to a narrow topic that fewer institutions will cover? Large private publishers will be most interested in textbooks for required courses or popular electives, while small private or university presses will be more interested in instructional materials that serve a niche in the discipline. Take note of who is publishing instructional materials for the class you have in mind and consider targeting those with no or out-of-date materials.

You might begin by discussing your idea with a publisher's sales representative—but you will eventually need to schedule a meeting with an acquisition editor. Large publishers have more than one, each dedicated to various disciplines and subfields, so make sure to identify the appropriate person to contact. Acquisition editors often attend major conferences, and they are more than happy to schedule meetings in advance. Pending conference schedules, a virtual meeting or phone call might be easier. Prior to this conversation, make sure that you can readily, but also briefly, articulate why your textbook would be unique and how it addresses a need that available options are not currently meeting.

If an acquisition editor would like to pursue the project further, they will ask for a prospectus. If the answer you receive is no thanks, simply ask for input, be prepared to incorporate any worthwhile advice, and move on. Just because your project is not a good fit with one press does not preclude finding a good match. On the other hand, you may generate interest from more than one press. If this is the case, you might want to ask questions that will help you decide which is the best fit for you.

Topics of potential inquiry should include royalty structures and advances; copyright concerns; advertising and promotion strategies; budgeting for cover art; limits on images, figures, and tables; and access to copy editing and indexing services.

Draft a Prospectus and Sample Chapter

Before your acquisition editor can pitch your project to their press, you will need to provide them with a prospectus and, most likely, at least one sample chapter. A textbook prospectus should include standard sections such as the basic approach and need for the book, a proposed table of contents, and abstracts of proposed chapters. If active learning or engaging classroom activities are highlighted as an important feature, be prepared to provide several examples of these materials as well. Finally, while most presses will undertake their own in-depth market analysis further along in the process, you should include a section on the strengths and weaknesses of competing textbooks already on the market, as well as why your approach is better or unique.

Frankly, I learned how to write a prospectus by asking a mentor who had successfully published several textbooks if I could see an example. If you have similarly situated mentors or colleagues, consider reaching out. Sharing examples should not be an issue if your project does not directly compete with one of theirs. Finally, you should also feel comfortable asking your acquisitions editor about content they would like to see included.

You should also be prepared to provide a list of potential reviewers, as well as their relationship to you and to your project—as most publishers will rely on external reviewers. Insights from this process will be used to refine and improve your project—and external reviewers who see their suggestions incorporated into the final project are often happy to provide blurbs for promotional materials and back covers.

Be Proactive During the Publication Process

The publication process for a textbook will feel familiar to anyone who has published book chapters or journal articles. Your contract will outline a schedule for submitting chapter drafts, as well as when copy edited and final proofs should be due. Publishers typically prefer launching new textbooks in the late summer in time for fall course adoptions. Yet it is just as important to be realistic and negotiate extra time if you need it, as promotional strategies are tied to anticipated publication dates. If you are unhappy with some aspect of your book throughout this process—placement of figures or tables, proposed cover art, color scheme and aesthetics, or copy edits that change substantive meaning—address the issue directly with your team. My coauthors and I, for example, were unhappy with all the initial options presented for our book's cover art. We wound up describing the image, color scheme, and font we envisioned—and after several iterations with an in-house designer, we wound up with a cover that we all loved because we felt it better reflected the overarching themes of our text.

Help Your Publisher Promote Your Book

Your publisher should implement an agreed-upon strategy for promoting your textbook. Steps they will likely undertake include ensuring sales representatives are familiar with your book and suggest it as an option to their contacts, providing a certain number of desk and review copies to interested colleagues, featuring your book on their website and printed promotional materials, and prominently displaying the text in exhibit halls at important conferences.

You, however, can supplement these efforts. You can give your publisher the information they need to suggest reviews in pedagogy journals that regularly assess new teaching resources, like the *Journal of Political Science Education* and *European Political Science*, or for an interview on podcasts like *New Books in Political Science*. If your textbook includes an innovative pedagogy, consider writing blog posts for outlets like APSA *Educate*, sponsoring faculty development workshops at APSA-TLC, coordinating short courses for APSA's annual meeting, or presenting your work at the International Studies Association's Innovative Pedagogy Conference or the European Conference on Teaching and Learning. When current events highlight the importance of substantive content covered in your textbook, consider writing an editorial for a blog that reaches a broader audience. Even if you don't mention the textbook directly, you will be able to include a link in your author bio. If you are willing to Zoom in as a guest classroom speaker for colleagues who adopt the book, be sure to let your publisher know. Make sure your own university communication office is aware you have published a textbook, so that they can use it to pitch you as an expert for media interviews.

Other simpler self-promotion tactics include adding a link to your email signature, along with tweets and social media posts. My coauthors and I were able to divide and conquer, as we incorporated all these approaches into our efforts to help promote *Why Don't Women Rule the World?*

Making It Count for Retention, Promotion, and Tenure

Of course, all this advice is for naught if political scientists do not believe their efforts to author textbooks will count toward retention, promotion, and tenure. Before committing to a textbook project, I strongly suggest junior faculty consult their department and university guidelines, which describe how the production of instructional materials is counted. In addition, consider the department culture and, when in doubt, have a frank conversation with those responsible for handling these processes at your institution. Some colleagues and institutional cultures are happy to count textbooks toward scholarship, while others are only willing to count the production of instructional materials toward excellence in teaching or disciplinary service. If the latter description applies to your department, make sure you have adequate peer-reviewed publications or monographs to check off boxes for excellence in scholarship before tackling a textbook. I was a tenured, full professor by the time I considered writing a textbook. My department by-laws provided explicit details about how the book would count toward scholarship, which precluded the need to negotiate support from colleagues.

There are ways, however, to bolster the claim, in promotion and tenure packages, that a textbook project should count toward scholarship. One simple tactic is to incorporate original research throughout relevant chapters of the book, perhaps by embedding these findings in sidebars where appropriate. My coauthors and I incorporated our own germane original research findings into several sidebars of our textbook. Making sure that your publisher sends the prospectus and draft chapters out for external review can also bolster the overall credibility of your project. Another possibility, especially if the book incorporates an innovative pedagogy, is to use student activities or learning experiences as the treatment in a classroom-based experimental design, publishing the findings in a peer-reviewed pedagogy outlet. This provides greater support for the efficacy of innovative pedagogy.

Regardless of whether you count the textbook toward research, teaching, or service, make sure your narrative fully explains its value and contribution, as well as how it fulfills criteria outlined in your own institution's guidelines. A final piece of advice, if your institution relies on an external review process, is to provide a list of potential external reviewers who understand that pedagogy research is now a well-established and well-regarded area of substantive research and who will be willing to consider your institution's criteria (rather than their own) in evaluating your case. An ideal external reviewer would also be familiar with the substantive content of your textbook project, enabling them to speak to the contribution your work makes to the field.

Conclusion

With this advice in hand, my hope is that more of you—especially those of you dedicated to active learning and intersectional civic engagement pedagogy or who are concerned with meeting the needs of women and minoritized political science students not only in the US but across the globe—will seriously consider becoming textbook authors. Together, we can collectively produce more innovative instructional materials to meet the needs of an increasingly diverse student body.

References

Allen, M. D., & Wallace, S. L. (2010). Teaching introduction to American government/politics: What we learn from the visual images in textbooks. *Journal of Political Science Education, 6*(1), 1–18.

Atchison, A. L. (2017). Where are the women? An analysis of gender mainstreaming in introductory political science textbooks. *Journal of Political Science Education, 13*(2), 185–199.

Brandle, S. (2020). It's (not) in the reading: American government textbooks' limited representation of historically marginalized groups. *PS: Political Science & Politics, 53*(4), 734–740.

Cassese, E. C., & Bos, A. L. (2013). A hidden curriculum? Examining the gender content in introductory-level political science textbooks. *Politics & Gender, 9*(2), 214–223.

Cassese, E. C., Bos, A. L., & Duncan, L. (2012). Integrating gender in the political science core curriculum. *PS: Political Science & Politics, 45*(2), 238–243.

Clawson, R. A., & Kegler, E. R. (2000). The 'race coding' of poverty in American government college textbooks. *The Howard Journal of Communications, 11*(3), 179–188.

Ferree, M. M., & Hall, E. J. (1996). Rethinking stratification from a feminist perspective: Gender, race, and class in mainstream textbooks. *American Sociological Review, 61*(6), 929–950.

Flaherty, C. (2016, August 22). Colleges hire more minority and female professors, but most jobs are adjunct, not tenure track, study finds. *Inside Higher Education*. https://www.insidehighered.com/news/2016/08/22/study-finds-gains-faculty-diversity-not-tenure-track

Frueh, J. (Ed.). (2020). *Pedagogical journeys through world politics*. Palgrave Macmillan.

Lantis, J. S. (Ed.). (2021). *Active learning in political science for a post-pandemic world, from triage to transformation*. Palgrave Macmillan.

Mallinson, D. J., Hellwege, J. M., & Loepp, E. (Eds.). (2022). *The Palgrave handbook of political research pedagogy*. Palgrave Macmillan.

Matto, E. C., McCartney, A. R. M., Bennion, E. A., Blair, A., Sun, T. & Whitehead, D. (Eds.). (2021). *Teaching civic engagement globally*. American Political Science Association.

Matto, E. C., McCartney, A. R. M., Bennion, E. A., & Simpson, D. (Eds.). (2017). *Teaching civic engagement: From student to active citizen* (2nd ed.). American Political Science Association.

McCartney, A. R. M., Bennion, E. A., & Simpson, D. (Eds.). (2013). *Teaching civic engagement: From student to active citizen*. American Political Science Association.

Murray, B., Brill-Carlat, M., & Höhn, M. (2022). *Migration, displacement, and higher education, Now what?* Palgrave Macmillan.

Nemerever, Z., Piazza, K., & Hill, S. (2021). Incorporating gender politics into introduction to US government curriculum. *College Teaching, 70*(3), 358–363.

Olivo, C. (2012). Bringing women in: Gender and American government and politics textbooks. *Journal of Political Science Education, 8*(2), 131–146.

Scola, B., Bucci, L. C., & Baglione, L. (2021). Pale, male and stale? An analysis of introductory readers in political science. *Journal of Political Science Education, 17*(1), 770–793.

Smith, H. A., & Hornsby, D. J. (2022). *Teaching international relations in a time of disruption*. Palgrave Macmillan.

Szarejko, A. A. (Ed.). (2022). *Pandemic pedagogy, teaching international relations amid COVID-19*. Palgrave Macmillan.

The Teacher Symposium. (2022). Lessons learned from political science textbook authors. *PS, Political Science & Politics*. https://www.cambridge.org/core/journals/ps-political-science-and-politics/firstview

Wallace, S. L., & Allen, M. D. (2008). Survey of African American portrayal in introductory textbooks in American government/politics: A report of the APSA standing committee on the status of Blacks in the profession. *PS: Political Science & Politics, 41*(1), 153–160.

PART IV

Conducting Research with Students

CHAPTER 10

The Benefits and Challenges of Faculty–Student Research Partnerships

Patrick Bijsmans

Academics are continuously confronted with conflicting demands to publish excellent research, do fabulous teaching, and engage in related (and sometimes not so related) administrative tasks. We are not always able to teach subjects that exactly fit our research expertise, for instance, due to constraints that follow from curriculum design or the ever-changing objects of study in political science and related fields (Bijsmans & Versluis, 2020). At the same time, research is often seen as academics' principal activity (see Shin et al., 2014).

One possible way of handling these conflicting demands is to connect teaching and research in alternative ways, for instance, through research partnerships between faculty and students. Even though explicit data appears to be missing, anecdotal evidence suggests that such partnerships are relatively rare in political science. For instance, Page (2015) writes

P. Bijsmans (✉)
Department of Political Science, Maastricht University, Maastricht, The Netherlands
e-mail: patrick.bijsmans@maastrichtuniversity.nl

© The Author(s), under exclusive license to Springer Nature Switzerland AG 2023
C. Butcher et al. (eds.), *The Palgrave Handbook of Teaching and Research in Political Science*, Political Pedagogies, https://doi.org/10.1007/978-3-031-42887-6_10

that they are "more common in the STEM subjects (Science, Technology, Engineering and Mathematics), where students can join a professor's research team. It is less common in political science" (p. 341). I have also noticed this at my home institution. In January 2022, I co-organised a workshop on teaching-research integration with my colleague Sally Wyatt. Only half of the twenty colleagues attending the workshop indicated that teaching influenced their research beyond regular coursework or supervision. These colleagues referred to, for instance, drafting bibliographies together with students or new research ideas that followed from teaching experience. Only one colleague had actually engaged in faculty–student research partnerships resulting in joint research output.

Faculty–student research partnerships are quite common in disciplines such as engineering, psychology, and the sciences. Consequently, there is also an abundant literature in those fields that engages with the design of such partnerships and the accompanying benefits and challenges. What can political science learn from this literature? This chapter outlines the main benefits and challenges of faculty–student partnerships. While discussing the literature, I will also reflect on my own experience with such partnerships. This chapter concludes by offering advice that might inspire you to engage in faculty–student partnerships yourself.

Why Consider Engaging in Faculty–Student Research Partnerships?

In disciplines such as engineering, psychology, and the sciences, faculty–student research partnerships are quite common. Faculty and students' positive experience has resulted in specific courses aimed at establishing such partnerships (Page, 2015; Tweed & Boast, 2011), but also in, for instance, dedicated sections for student contributions on online platforms such as *EuropeNow*[1] and even dedicated journals such as *Reinvention: An International Journal of Undergraduate Research*.[2] The literature on faculty–student partnerships mentions several benefits for both students and faculty.

---

[1] https://www.europenowjournal.org.
[2] https://reinventionjournal.org/.

Perhaps the most obvious benefit for faculty concerns research efficiency and output (Jalbert, 2008; Payne & Monk-Turner, 2005). Assistance in retrieving literature and collecting data can, for instance, be extremely helpful when embarking on a new project. Yet, the literature also refers to acquiring new research insights through regular exchange with students, who may ask different, new questions in comparison to colleagues, or who might introduce new literature helping us to stay up-to-date (Fenn et al., 2010; Hartley, 2014). In addition to these more tangible results, joint faculty–student research output can also be viewed as an example of teaching excellence, which is gaining importance in discussions about diversifying academic careers and valuing scholarship and teaching. For instance, reporting on an example from the field of psychology, Wagge et al. (2019) write that faculty–student research partnerships offer "a rare opportunity for instructors to have a documentable experience blending teaching, scholarship, and close mentoring" (p. 4, see also Jalbert, 2008, p. 114).

For students, benefits range from acquiring a deeper understanding of research to more general rewards in relation to future careers and personal development. Working on a collaborative research project can help train people skills but also competences such as time management. In an article co-authored by undergraduate students and academics, Jones et al. (2012) report on a project that brought together students and researchers from different disciplines. The students found that, among other benefits, doing research with academics helped them in their studies more broadly through acquiring more insights into questions and methodologies that were important in their own discipline. Yet, the benefits of these new insights extend beyond students' current studies. For instance, reporting on experience from the field of economics, Fenn et al. (2010) write that "a student who has acquired such skills sends a strong signal to employers and graduate selection committees" (p. 260).

While some of the literature on faculty–student research partnerships focuses exclusively on either undergraduate or graduate students, the benefits and challenges listed largely overlap. But there is a more important distinction that emerges from this literature, namely that we should distinguish between two forms of faculty–student research partnerships: (1) cooperation following from *research supervised by* academics and (2) doing *joint research with* students (Payne & Monk Turner, 2005). The former can refer to thesis supervision, but also to supervision of other coursework. This may not lead to joint faculty–student research products but can certainly have a positive effect on our research. As a matter of fact, from reading literature together to teaching courses on research skills and methods, being confronted with different insights brought in by students can help refresh and expand conceptual, theoretical, and methodological horizons. A thesis conference during which students present their research is just one example of an activity in which such a fruitful exchange may take place (Douglas et al., 2018).

In contrast, doing joint research with students entails that they will be co-producers of new data and/or knowledge. Beyond the obvious possibility of doing research together with student assistants, there is also the option of having students do a research internship or research placement. The latter can help students get a better insight into research, while it offers us new input and insights regarding our research (Tweed & Boast, 2011). While students may not always have similar insights into what research is all about, when they engage in actual research, they often find it a more rewarding exercise than expected.

Personally, I have engaged in doing *research with* students, as well as in attempting to turn *supervised student research* into something worth publishing. As I will explain below, the latter arguably comes with more challenges. Yet, at the same time, my most successful attempt of a faculty–student research partnership was a supervised Master's thesis resulting in a collaborative peer-reviewed article. The article was published by a good journal *and* was awarded with the journal's best article prize (Barth & Bijsmans, 2018)! My experience with doing *research with* students has resulted in more research output—with some projects still ongoing. In one case, the eventual publication concerned an article that two of our students first contributed to by means of aiding in data collection and analysis. Gradually they also read more and more literature, and we had several discussions on where to take the research. The students also presented our joint project to colleagues within our home institution and wrote a first draft. It took my colleague and me many more versions to end up with a publishable manuscript, but we succeeded. We acknowledged the students' hard work by listing them as co-authors (Bijsmans et al., 2022).

In both examples, it was students' commitment that made a difference. In the first case, the student was already very organised and motivated. Despite new obligations, she showed extraordinary commitment to making our partnership a success, ensuring an effective and ultimately successful process of rewriting (and substantially shortening) the thesis, adding new literature, and even additional data. In the second case, both students were not just very committed, but they had also expressed ambitions to continue doing research. One has moved on to become a PhD student, whereas the other currently works as a research consultant. Hence, this example shows how working together has benefits for both faculty and students.

THE CHALLENGES OF FACULTY–STUDENT RESEARCH PARTNERSHIPS

Notwithstanding the benefits outlined above, the literature also mentions several challenges for academics and students who engage in joint research projects. One set of challenges concerns the *type of students* to work with. Ishiyama and Breuning (2003), Page (2015), and Tweed and Boast (2011) report on initiatives that relied on voluntary participation by students and, hence, students' intrinsic motivation. The examples of my own experience discussed above are illustrative of this point. Whereas research is one of our primary tasks, it is likely that this is not the case for students. For many, doing research is not even their most favourite pastime (Adriaensen et al., 2015). They may find it useful, but unsurprisingly their main objective usually is to pass the course (Griffiths, 2015; Payne & Monk-Turner, 2005). Still, some students may be enticed by the prospective of publishing. This means that it is important to identify potential student research partners at an early stage. In this context, Fenn et al. (2010) suggest "seeking students with raw ability and self-discipline rather than existing skills: Although skills can be taught, the ability to learn and to self-direct is much harder to instill" (p. 272).

A second set of challenges and drawbacks is related to *expectations*. Realistic expectations are important to avoid disappointment on both sides. This includes accepting that students' main objective may be to pass the course. In addition, while students may have taken several research courses and may have also written several papers, engaging in an actual research project is often a completely different challenge (Jalbert, 2008; Jones et al., 2012). Hence, it is important to show students what doing research actually entails. This includes being transparent about what it takes to commit to a research project (Griffiths, 2015). For instance, the process towards publication is likely to extend beyond the timeframe of students' formal involvement.

Consequently, a third challenge of faculty–student research partnerships concerns the *time investment* required on both sides. Students will not do all the work for you. Furthermore, it is likely that they need to be supervised during the research process (Fenn et al., 2010; Jones et al., 2012; Payne & Monk-Turner, 2005). Things that may come naturally to us are often quite new to even the better, more research-savvy students. They may have less insight into the research process and normally will have no idea of what it takes to turn a good paper or thesis into something publishable. In addition, on both sides, other obligations might derail joint research efforts (other courses or research, personal circumstances, life).

I have encountered these three challenges before, particularly when attempting to turn *supervised student research* into something worth publishing. First, this option concerns students who are usually at the end of their studies. They are about to move on to a new challenge such as a Master's programme or a job and may quickly find out that their new obligations must come first. Second, many of these students do not have research ambitions. For them it may be an attractive opportunity, but one among many. We cannot force them to continue working on the paper, even when we have already put work into it—and we can certainly not take their work and use it for our own purposes. Similar challenges can occur when doing *research with* students, often due to the depth and engagement resulting in a longer than anticipated project. One project got off to a flying start in 2018. We all knew that writing a full article would take more time, but were convinced that we could do this. The student and I even presented our work at an international conference. Yet shortly afterwards, our efforts came to a standstill due to familiar and understandable reasons. First, my colleague in the project left for a new job outside of academia, next the student moved on to other studies and eventually beyond. Only recently did we manage to send the paper to a journal.

This last experience has meant that in other projects colleagues and I have been reassessing the aims of collaborative research efforts with students. In one case the focus of the partnership has therefore been on creating a dataset and accompanying codebook,[3] whereas in a linked

---

[3] https://www.researchgate.net/publication/342437796_Codebook_Curriculum_Dataset.

project we have worked on several blogs instead of (only) aiming for peer-reviewed articles (Schilder et al., 2022). This relates to a fourth set of challenges identified in the literature, namely challenges concerning *type of output*. From the perspective of faculty, a peer-reviewed article or a book chapter may be the ultimate form of output. At the same time, this may not always be realistic. Several authors therefore suggest considering other forms of output, such as blogs, datasets, or policy papers (Griffiths, 2015; Wagge et al., 2019).

Whatever the form of output, the issue of authorship needs to be considered. This is related to a final set of challenges connected to *ethical issues*. Hartley (2014) suggests that it is acceptable that academics are the first authors of papers co-authored with undergraduate students. Yet, the question is whether this sufficiently reflects a research partnership (Bliss, 2002; Fenn et al., 2010; Griffiths, 2011). In most of the research partnerships that I have engaged in, students have been acknowledged as co-authors. But in other cases, they only played a small role in projects and were only thanked for their work in the eventual publication. We also discussed the question of authorship during the aforementioned 2022 workshop. Among the issues raised were the need to acknowledge students' work and the conviction that in a mutually beneficial relationship work should not be outsourced to students. Nevertheless, students may still perceive a hierarchical relationship (Page, 2015; Payne & Monk-Turner, 2005).

Guidelines towards faculty–student research partnerships may be absent or might not always help address these issues. For instance, the APSA's 2022 ethical guide mentions that "advisors are not entitled to claim joint authorship with a student on a thesis or dissertation or work submitted per an assignment for one of the student's classes" (p. 19) and that faculty "acknowledge significant academic or scholarly assistance from" students (p. 2). While the former may be obvious, the latter does not clearly state how to acknowledge students' contributions. This makes it even more important that research partnerships rest on clear expectations and agreements (Griffiths, 2011; Payne & Monk-Turner, 2005).

Advice

Doing research with students or even working with a student to convert their supervised research into something publishable is less common in political science and related fields. But experience in other fields shows that it is worth considering embarking on such a cooperative process. While a productive research partnership may be easier to achieve when doing research with students, the same factors that may complicate *working on supervised research*, can also come into play when *doing research with students*. So, considering the literature and my own experience, what could you do to ensure that faculty–student research partnerships stand a higher chance of success?

1. *Sit down with your potential student research partner(s) to discuss each other's expectations.*

Be transparent about each other's expectations and make sure they are realistic, also when it comes to deliverables. If you have previously embarked on faculty–student research partnerships, use examples of both the opportunities *and* the challenges. Discuss with students what they want to take away from the experience—perhaps have them write down a few concrete learning objectives outlining what they would like to learn?

2. *Be realistic about the required time investment on both sides.*

Jointly drafting intended learning outcomes and agreeing about deliverables might also clarify what training students require (cf. Tweed & Boast, 2011, p. 602). They won't do the work for you; you will have to guide them, train them, and will probably have to do additional work to make something publishable. At the same time, students should know that productive research is likely to take more time than set aside for the course, thesis, or research internship.

3. *Consider working together with more than one student at the same time.*

Some authors warn against working with several students, as this requires additional coordination and may raise problems of consistency

(Jalbert, 2008; Payne & Monk-Turner, 2005). Yet, my own experience is positive. Students can support each other by discussing literature together, but also by exploring the challenges of analysing data and possible solutions for those challenges. New ideas for the project might arise from this.

4. *Suggest other deliverables as concrete achievement.*

Blogs, datasets, and other research products will also benefit ongoing research and can still be an exciting, but at the same time more manageable, opportunity for students. Jalbert (2008) notes that the quality of such publications may be lower, which may be tricky bearing in mind promotions. Yet, by no means do they close the door to a peer-reviewed article—many of us will have experienced how a small idea became the start of a research project.

5. *Consider what you have on offer to reward students for their work.*

Financial resources to pay for students' work may not always be available but students should also benefit (Fenn et al., 2010; Ishiyama & Breuning, 2003). Students will, of course, learn about doing research, might earn study credits, and may even co-author a piece of academic writing. But perhaps you can also pay for students' participation in an international conference where you can present your research together?

Despite this advice, you may still ask whether given the challenges discussed above, it is worth engaging in a research partnership with students. For instance, the time saved by students helping you with your work may be spent on supervising them to ensure that they execute tasks well. But perhaps this is a too narrow way of looking at this. In particular, shouldn't academics in fields such as political science be engaging with non-experts to learn more about how others perceive the societal issues that we study in depth? Even when nothing concrete came out of my research partnerships with students, in each case I learned something new, read new literature, and expanded my horizon. Students came up with great ideas and suggestions, which helped me see different perspectives on the topics that I was working on, and, in my view, this alone makes it worth doing.

References

Adriaensen, J., Kerremans, B., & Slootmaeckers, K. (2015). Editors' introduction to the thematic issue: Mad about methods? Teaching research methods in political science. *Journal of Political Science Education, 11*(1), 1–10. https://doi.org/10.1080/15512169.2014.985017

American Political Science Association. (2022). *A guide to professional ethics in political science* (3rd ed.). https://apsanet.org/Portals/54/diversity%20and%20inclusion%20prgms/Ethics/APSA%20Ethics%20Guide%20-%20Final%20-%20February2022_Council%20Approved.pdf?ver=5mQAFYQz3xLhbd4OkQWg6Q%3d%3d

Barth, C., & Bijsmans, P. (2018). The Maastricht Treaty and public debates about European integration: The emergence of a European public sphere? *Journal of Contemporary European Studies, 26*(2), 215–231. https://doi.org/10.1080/14782804.2018.1427558

Bijsmans, P., Schakel, A. H., Baykal, A., & Hegewald, S. (2022). Internationalisation and study success: Class attendance and the delicate balance between collaborative learning and being lost in translation. *European Journal of Higher Education, 12*(3), 314–331. https://doi.org/10.1080/21568235.2021.1971099

Bijsmans, P., & Versluis, E. (2020). Problem-based learning and the relevance of teaching and learning European studies in times of crises. *European Political Science, 19*(4), 668–686. https://doi.org/10.1057/s41304-020-00263-0

Bliss, D. Z. (2002). Publishing with students—An uncontrolled variable. *Nursing Research, 51*(6), 345–346.

Douglas, C., Yearsley, J., Scott, G. W., & Hubbard, K. E. (2018). The student thesis conference as a model for authentic and inclusive student research dissemination. *Higher Education Pedagogies, 3*(1), 319–341. https://doi.org/10.1080/23752696.2018.1478675

Fenn, A. J., Johnson, D. K. N., Griffin Smith, M., & Stimpert, J. L. (2010). Doing publishable research with undergraduate students. *The Journal of Economic Education, 41*(3), 259–274. https://doi.org/10.1080/00220485.2010.486728

Griffiths, M. (2011). Publishing undergraduate and postgraduate student work: Some guidelines and protocols. *Psychology Teaching Review, 27*(1), 78–80.

Griffiths, M. (2015). Publishing with undergraduates: Some further observations. *Psychology Teaching Review, 21*(1), 76–80.

Hartley, J. (2014). Publishing with undergraduates. *Psychology Teaching Review, 20*(2), 158–160.

Ishiyama, J., & Breuning, M. (2003). Does participation in undergraduate research affect political science students? *Politics & Policy, 31*(1), 163–180. https://doi.org/10.1111/j.1747-1346.2003.tb00892.x

Jalbert, T. (2008). Experiences in publishing peer-reviewed research with undergraduate accounting and finance students. *Journal of Accounting Education, 26*(3), 104–117. https://doi.org/10.1016/j.jaccedu.2008.08.003

Jones, R., Race, L., Sawyer, C., Slater, E., Simpson, D., Mathews, I., & Crawford, K. (2012). Being a student as producer—Reflections on students co-researching with academic staff. *Enhancing Learning in the Social Sciences, 4*(3), 1–7. https://doi.org/10.11120/elss.2012.04030020

Page, E. (2015). Undergraduate research: An apprenticeship approach to teaching political science methods. *European Political Science, 14*(3), 340–354. https://doi.org/10.1057/eps.2015.17

Payne, B. K., & Monk-Turner, E. (2005). Collaborating with undergraduates: Obstacles and tips. *Journal of Criminal Justice Education, 16*(2), 292–299. https://doi.org/10.1080/10511250500082153

Schilder, T., Adriaensen, J., & Bijsmans, P. (2022). How much choice should students have over their curriculum? *Wonkhe*. https://wonkhe.com/blogs/how-much-choice-should-students-have-over-their-curriculum/

Shin, J. C., Arimoto, A., Cummings, W. K., & Teichler, U. (Eds.). (2014). *Teaching and research in contemporary higher education: Systems, activities and rewards*. Springer.

Tweed, F., & Boast, R. (2011). Reviewing the 'research placement' as a means of enhancing student learning and stimulating research activity. *Journal of Geography in Higher Education, 35*(4), 599–615. https://doi.org/10.1080/03098265.2011.559579

Wagge, J. R., Brandt, M. J., Lazarevic, L. B., Legate, N., Christopherson, C., Wigeons, B., & Grahe, J. E. (2019). Publishing research with undergraduate students via replication work: The collaborative replications and education project. *Frontiers in Psychology, 10*(247). https://doi.org/10.3389/fpsyg.2019.00247

CHAPTER 11

Working Smarter by Engaging Students in Political Science Research

Shauna Reilly

Earning tenure, being promoted, and even the day-to-day activities of a faculty member can be overwhelming. Thus, finding a way to tie activities together is key to finding balance and being successful. My path to success is research both from a research mentoring perspective and from a personal publication perspective. In this chapter, I demonstrate how I was able to leverage my involvement in undergraduate research mentoring into a successful research agenda and how this activity can serve the entire academic mission of teaching, research, and service.

Being on the tenure-track is not something anyone can prepare you for nor can others relate to outside of academia. When starting my tenure-track job at a regional comprehensive university directly out of graduate school, I felt the enormous pressure of balancing a 4-4 teaching load with an active research agenda and service responsibilities. Frankly, I called my dissertation advisor and apologized for taking so much of his time

S. Reilly (✉)
Northern Kentucky University, Highland Heights, KY, USA
e-mail: Reillys3@nku.edu

© The Author(s), under exclusive license to Springer Nature Switzerland AG 2023
C. Butcher et al. (eds.), *The Palgrave Handbook of Teaching and Research in Political Science*, Political Pedagogies,
https://doi.org/10.1007/978-3-031-42887-6_11

during the dissertation process (albeit taking up even more time by doing so). The pressure to do it all, impress tenure committees, and have some semblance of balance is often discussed in higher education circles—but few concrete examples exist of how to achieve it. This leaves junior faculty in a particularly challenging place having to decide on the merits of every professional opportunity. The answer for me has been to find your place, your connection, and your passion—creating a way to connect everything and work smarter, not harder.

In this chapter, I share my insights and experiences with others who find themselves facing similar academic pressures. I found my footing on the tenure-track by engaging students in undergraduate research, which made me unique in my department. This focus also showcased what our students were capable of, which in turn engaged other faculty in similar student research activities. I involved undergraduate students in political science research in three ways: developing course-based research, mentoring independent projects, and collaborating with students on publications. I would argue that my success in gaining tenure, full promotion, a Regents' professorship, and an administrative career is due in large part to my involvement of undergraduate students in political science research. This not only furthered my own research but it enabled curriculum development and innovative teaching aspects, as well as connected service activities to create a fully interconnected portfolio. In the section that follows, I provide examples of how I integrated these efforts in my journey to tenure and promotion.

Developing Course-Based Research

I developed course-based undergraduate research experiences (CURES) in multiple classes early in my career as a way to demonstrate to students how they can write the equivalent of a research article (complete with data collection and analysis) and create work that could eventually be presented at conferences.[1] I often worked on a project alongside my students and would provide updates along the way to demonstrate the challenges and successes of the research process. This not only created a relationship with my students but also motivated them, helping them relate to academic work in a different way by celebrating their work and seeing

---

[1] I later used this model to develop a rubric that is used to evaluate courses at my university for scholarship intensive courses combining service and teaching together.

how they fit into the greater academic conversation. When they design surveys for my public opinion class, I also design a survey for a research project (this does require some advance planning) and we competed in a joking manner about who had more respondents (I win every time). By timing the courses and assignments strategically, I further integrate teaching and scholarship. Students do the data analysis and present their work in the spring (as do I), which lines up nicely with deadlines for Midwest or Southwestern conferences. Similarly, when teaching in the fall, we take advantage of a statewide conference that was welcoming to student presenters. Such events provide students with presentation opportunities and helps hold me accountable by providing external deadlines for my own scholarship. CURES can seem intimidating but when you look at how it can dovetail with your own research, they are a seamless way to advance your teaching and scholarship at the same time—while benefiting your students.

Research, Teaching, and Service Impacts

Beyond the deadlines and limited competitiveness on deadlines and response numbers, how did this affect my scholarship? I often provide pieces of my research to demonstrate academic work to students. For example, in my methods class, I present students with my own works in progress (anonymized—no one wants to criticize their professors) as well as published work by other scholars and teach students how to perform their own substantial review of academic articles. This not only pushed me to create good work that I would not be embarrassed to show my students (tougher critics than any academic reviewer) but also gave them hands-on experiences evaluating research. At the end of this section, I would share a recent review of my work to provide them with an opportunity to compare their own reviews to those done by other academics. Students all enjoyed the Reviewer 2 conversations and memes that arose and witnessed that my work, just like theirs, has room for improvement. This process not only demonstrates higher academic standards but also creates some lighthearted moments and student–faculty connections around getting negative feedback. Developing such innovative research-focused courses often ties into university plans to incorporate high-impact practices into the curriculum, and often pays dividends in performance evaluations and future enrollments, all of which can strengthen one's teaching portfolio come review time.

The service benefits of research-infused teaching may be less clear, but I have found multiple ways of integrating my student research experiences into service activities, including the university curriculum committee, student research institute, and the political science program. Imagine the conversations you can have with prospective parents and students about the applied nature of your classes, the activities students have participated in, and their eventual career outcomes. When I served as political science program coordinator between earning tenure and being promoted, I was able to use the results of my student research techniques in recruitment activities to emphasize the number of our graduating students who participated in experiential learning (a key buzzword for parents)—we reached a high of 80% one year. There are also many opportunities for linking student research in the classroom to broader professional networks, including through discipline-specific organizations like the American Political Science Association, or with groups such as the Council for Undergraduate Research. Thus, your work in student research can benefit not only your teaching and research portfolios but also your university (in terms of recruitment and service) and your own professional development.

Mentoring Students Outside of Class

In addition to integrating research in the face-to-face classroom, a number of my students work on projects outside of class on topics that interest them—these are proposed and implemented by the students themselves. However, before taking this approach to student research, faculty should make a cost-benefit calculation. While some students work well on their own, others require constant contact, taking time away from other projects/classes/activities. When I first started working on these independent projects, our college offered a single course release for every 12 independent projects you mentored; however, this benefit has disappeared with budget cuts. Consequently, the dedicated folks who want to explore this approach to student research may consider doing so a bit later in their career once they have tenure and/or promotion. Honors Capstones and other independent projects can contribute to the larger academic literature (on a small scale) and working with students through these processes is rewarding but the symbiotic relationship I mentioned earlier (and the theme of this book) indicates that these projects should not be on the forefront of your plan of working with student researchers.[2] Alternatively, if they are in your plan, please consider the challenges and pitfalls of doing so.

Research, Teaching, and Service Impacts

Accompanying students to professional conferences and guiding them through the process from abstract submission to formal presentation provides another valuable opportunity for linking teaching and research. In Kentucky where I teach, some of the university's performance-based funding is based on the number of students who participate in student research prior to graduation. This definition of student research includes an external presentation of said research; thus, conference presentations and even student publications are strongly encouraged by the university. An additional benefit of taking students to professional conferences is that it required me to have something worthy of presentation at the same time. This has had a tremendous impact on my scholarship, as over twelve years I have presented at 22 additional conferences due to student presentations—many of which resulted in publications or finding new co-authors. Such presentations also had additional teaching benefits, as the students garnered encouragement and lowered their own anxieties by watching my presentation panel and learning strategies they could use for their own presentations at the conference. Further, conference attendance leaves a lasting impression on students; not only does it provide a demonstrated example of academic professionalism beyond the scope of class but they see the inner workings of how academic literature is developed, it also gives them confidence that they were presenting work at the same place as political science scholars.

An added benefit of presenting with students at smaller statewide conferences is the opportunity to cultivate professional relationships that can lead to additional opportunities for you as a faculty member. These can include additional conference funding, and opportunities for external service, such as serving on executive boards for conferences and journals and finding co-authors and even external letter writers for the tenure and promotion process. For example, our university is located in a tristate

---

[2] I fell into this trap early in my career before understanding how to navigate this process more effectively. Please consider this advice as "do not as I do" to work smarter not harder.

area with convenient access to other states, so I joined the Ohio association—where I quickly moved through the ranks of the executive and served as the conference program chair (bringing the annual conference to our university), president and associate editor of their journal. This enabled me to network with colleagues who served as references for me, and I served as external tenure reviewer for others. I would never have considered attending these smaller conferences if I had not emphasized this opportunity to present as a focal point for my students; however, the intrinsic professional benefits of such conferences have served my career well. An additional benefit of student conference presentations is publication in undergraduate journals at the university or state level. If a student journal does not exist at your university, creating one can count in both teaching and service areas depending on your role. Thus, while facilitating student learning and development, the effort also benefits your own career portfolio.

Collaborating with Students on Publications

Publishing with students is a requirement for tenure in some disciplines at our university, although not political science, and thus did not occur to me until later in my academic career. I always felt that student work is their own and thus they ought to own it entirely; however, co-authoring with students is a symbiotic endeavor that has directly impacted my publishing record while also advancing student learning. For example, a few years ago a student of mine who was an economics/political science double major was assisting with some data analysis and uncovered some major issues with the data for my book. He was able to collect additional data, check the sources, and refine the analysis as part of his work with me. As a result of his contribution, I felt that he deserved authorship credit and listed him as a contributing author on one of my books. Without his help, the book would have lost a source of credibility; at the same time, combined with his record of solo publications, the co-authorship gave him a foot-up on graduate applications and direct entry into a PhD program. I can only hope he pays the opportunity forward when he becomes a professor in a few short years.

Research, Teaching, and Service Impacts

More recently, I have created a research lab to incorporate students into my research projects. My lab was started during the summer of 2020 to recruit and retain students who may not have returned in the Fall of 2020 without some additional incentives (this was seen as an innovative way by our university to address retention at the university) and served as a research, teaching, and service activity for me. For the structure of the lab, I set up two teams of five students (one to work on each of my current projects), with folks rotating in and out of the teams as their schedules and interests allowed. These projects require developing original datasets and with team leads, we have been moving through the systematic elections data collection successfully for two years.

In terms of my scholarship, the data collection will result in two book manuscripts and comprehensive datasets for use in other projects as well. I could not have even dreamed of tackling either of these projects without my students' exemplary ability in collecting data. Both of these projects were on my "when I have the time" list of research projects and I can now foresee completion of the books in the next couple of years due to the research assistance of my lab students. The successes of the research lab have now pushed me to think about other projects that I did not think were possible with my teaching and administrative load. The students have even been working on specific projects related to the larger project on their own (some of these are co-authored with me and some are co-authored between students themselves). They challenge the assumptions of the projects; they are tenacious, and they bring a unique perspective that is far better than the feedback I could get at a conference from someone briefly reading a chapter or section of the manuscript. These lab assistants will ultimately push my publications and my contributions to the field far more than if I had worked on these projects alone.

The lab has had a significant impact on my teaching too, as in the first year, each of the 12 students involved either applied to a graduate program or had a job offer upon graduation. The process demonstrated the value of having research experience on their resume and contributed to their future success. Those who served as lab "leads" were also able to emphasize their roles as leaders on their resumes, which provided an extra benefit. As for service, being able to demonstrate the success of this lab to new faculty or faculty unfamiliar with this kind of structure created mentoring opportunities on campus. Ultimately, I would argue that this was the most successful form of involving students in that it hit on all three areas of faculty evaluation, and parallels one that faculty in the sciences have implemented for years.

Working Smarter

The undergraduate research activities discussed in this chapter help faculty enhance their contributions in the areas of teaching, research, and service and to attain significant outcomes in all three areas from the same activity. Using these various approaches helped me create a meaningful and successful publication record, build a network of students who went on to graduate programs or successful careers, and led to my role as founding director of our university's Institute for Student Research and Creative Activity. In this most recent position, I conduct research on student research and creativity in a more comprehensive manner, thereby coming full circle to help other faculty and students participate in the same activities.

In some ways, writing this chapter feels like a love letter to my students and my career. Certainly, the activities described reflect my own path but recognize that you can find an interconnected path that serves your individual teaching, research, and service goals in other areas (another great example could be in the area of service learning). The pressures of the tenure track sometimes obfuscate the benefits we provide to our students and ourselves in the process; I hope I have provided a way to see the connections and ease of which things like student research can work to support your career. Some key lessons from this chapter:

- Well-designed student research activities can help you fill each category of the academic mission with consolidated effort.
- Teaching can be used to inform your career—what innovation do you enjoy the most? How can it serve you in different areas? What can you incorporate into your classes to further service?
- When asked to take on new responsibilities, ask: how does it fit into your goals/vision for your career?
- Cultivating professional networks at the state and local level can really have lasting impacts on your career—across teaching, research, and service?
- Have realistic expectations regarding how many students you can take on. Supervising 10 students in your lab is too many when

you first start out. Remember student–faculty research is a learning process for us all.

Unquestionably, the involvement of undergraduate students in research is what has driven my career thus far, and I look forward to the new directions it takes me as I move throughout the next stages of my professional journey. I hope you also come to see student research not as an added task or substantial time commitment, but rather to further your career.

CHAPTER 12

The Extra-Curricular Teacher-Scholar: Funding Undergraduates to Be Research Assistants

Michael T. Rogers

In 2015, Roger Smith—future American Political Science Association (APSA) president—argued "political scientists particularly need to resist the pressure to move further away from the researcher/teacher model of academic life and towards disciplinary segregation into those who are almost exclusively researchers and those who almost exclusively teach." His reason, "combining teaching and research, difficult as it can be to do, ultimately strengthens both" and makes "*both* our research and our teaching... more valuable to more people" (2015, p. 374). Smith's call, coming well after the 1998 Boyer Commission called for "integration of research and teaching," is just as needed today (Bauer & Bennett, 2003).

While Smith examines forces pulling the teacher-scholar model apart, he lacks strong cases for how the two can come together positively. As

M. T. Rogers (✉)
Arkansas Tech University, Russellville, AR, USA
e-mail: Mrogers6@atu.edu

one example, the "extra-curricular teacher-scholar" is presented here. This model is particularly relevant given the resources gap Smith identifies as fueling the teacher-scholar split. It explains how the "Great Contraction" is only amplifying the resources gap, while the extra-curricular teacher-scholar model can shrink the resources gap challenge felt particularly at teaching institutions. Drawing on ten years of experience as an extra-curricular teacher-scholar, I then discuss some lessons learned about how to effectively employ undergraduates as research assistants and how to fund them.

The Great Contraction and the Resources Gap

Over the last half century, higher education has undergone profound changes as the unprecedented growth of the mid to late twentieth century has given way to the "Great Contraction" today (Gardner, 2021). At the center of the Great Contraction is decreasing enrollment, as over the last two years there has been a 7.4% or 1.3 million decline in students at both the undergraduate and graduate levels. Worse, the decline is persisting beyond the pandemic (Nietzel, 2022). This Great Contraction is amplifying the competition for limited resources and exacerbating the resources gap Smith argues plagues academia (Gardner, 2021; Smith, 2015). While privileged research institutions are the most shielded from the Great Contraction, faculty working at institutions driven by teaching and student enrollments are being challenged to do more, to help recruit and retain students all while continuing their heavy teaching loads, seeking grants and funding, and advancing their research agendas for tenure and promotion.

Of course, the resource gap is not simply between faculty at research universities versus teaching ones. There are also cross-disciplinary resource gaps, particularly between faculty in STEM and those in the liberal arts. As Rosowsky (2020) notes, the National Institutes of Health (NIH) has a budget of $42 billion and the National Science Foundation has a budget of $8 billion, while the National Endowment for the Arts (NEA) and National Endowment for the Humanities (NEH)—constant targets for congressional cuts—have budgets of only $160 million apiece. A key factor underlying this disciplinary resource discrepancy is, as Smith (2015) observes, declining public support and approval of disciplines outside STEM.

Likewise, there can also be intra-disciplinary resources gaps. For example, as a social *science* discipline, political science has been particularly prone to overemphasizing research at the expense of teaching (Rogers, 2017; Smith, 2015). Thus, political science has reproduced within its discipline the segregation and resource gap typical of higher education generally (Katz & Eagles, 1996; Lowry & Silver, 1996). Even as political science desires to be seen as a rigorous, scientific discipline it has not escaped the public disapproval typical of the liberal arts. In fact, the public's distrust of political science is worse given political polarization and the controversy of the subjects it covers, as well as the discipline's production of graduates seeking professions with low public approval like lawyers, bureaucrats, and politicians (Rogers, 2021).

As the Great Contraction intensifies the resources gaps and public disapproval presents added challenges for political science, all hope need not be lost. The extra-curricular teacher-scholar model can positively help faculty, particularly at teaching universities, meet such challenges. Securing funding to hire undergraduates as research assistants offers faculty a workforce to advance their research agendas while also giving students invaluable practical work experience that counters the public perception the discipline is just another impractical liberal arts program. Even more, undergraduate research (UR) is known to help retain current students and can be an invaluable marketing tool to recruit new ones (Craney et al., 2011; Lopatto, 2009).

THE EXTRA-CURRICULAR TEACHER-SCHOLAR

Capitalizing on the educational best practice of UR, the extra-curricular teacher-scholar model involves faculty advancing their scholarship by hiring undergraduates as research assistants (Linn Marcia, 2015). Murray (2017, pp. 5–6) identifies three general ways UR is pursued. First is the student-centered version done within the curriculum. This is when a faculty member oversees the research projects of students, something political scientists routinely do particularly in research design/methods and/or senior seminar projects if not other courses. The extra-curricular teacher-scholar model, however, is realized in the other two forms. For, the second is a faculty-directed approach, where the student is a research assistant, doing assigned research jobs beside and for the faculty member. Similarly, the third involves a more collaborative approach, where the research project has intellectual contributions from both the student and faculty member that culminate in co-authorship work.

While political scientists often employ graduate students as research assistants or collaborators, it is our STEM colleagues who have more actively employed undergraduates in their lab research (Reisberg, 1998). There are some political scientists who engage undergraduates in research, as demonstrated by awards like The Craig L. Brians Award for Excellence in Undergraduate Research and Mentorship (APSA). However, too many faculty see UR as an added burden, noting the benefits for students but believing it is just more work for faculty. The resource benefits to faculty, particularly at teaching universities, can outweigh the costs.

Recognized as a best practice in higher education, most scholarship on UR emphasizes the extensive benefits to students (Linn Marcia, 2015), as it produces both cognitive and affective benefits (Murray, 2017, pp. 46–57). Key cognitive benefits include students showing better problem-solving abilities, communication skills, research abilities, critical thinking skills, and working independently. On the affective side, students show increased confidence and a heightened sense of accomplishment (Bauer & Bennett, 2003; Craney et al., 2011; Lopatto, 2009). UR also promotes a "science-identity," or the ability to appreciate, adopt, and apply the scientific method and perspective in studying and understanding phenomena in the world (Lopatto, 2009; Seymour et al., 2004).

With respect to the resources gap and the challenges of the Great Contraction, UR students tend to secure more financial support, have higher graduation rates, and earn more national accolades (Craney et al., 2011; Ishiyama, 2005). The long-term benefits for UR are also quite significant, as it helps students clarify their career plans, find jobs and is routinely used for graduate school recruitment (Bauer & Bennett, 2003; Craney et al., 2011; Linn Marcia, 2015; Seymour et al., 2004). While UR often requires more than a year to show the greatest benefits, the gains—that include more funding and increased retention and graduation—found across multiple disciplines (e.g., STEM, psychology, economics, political science, etc.) can benefit more than the students themselves.

Still, UR is not without criticism. From the student perspective, the most common criticism is access, as UR opportunities go to the strongest academic students and are experienced disproportionately by Caucasian males (Murray, 2017, Ch. 8). Then, some students see their role as receivers of research knowledge not its producers, while others grumble they are simply worker bees for faculty (Evans & Witkowsky, 2004). The first criticism speaks to an unhealthy educational conditioning of students; the latter reflects what students can do is often undervalued by faculty.

While student criticisms of UR are minimal, faculty skepticism is more extensive. On the benefits side, faculty tend to vocalize only the student gains while being quick to list the significant costs it poses for them (Hunter et al., 2007). Foremost, faculty are skeptical of the abilities of undergraduates, believing they lack the academic skills necessary (Evans & Witkowsky, 2004; Hoyt & McGoldrick, 2017; Morales et al., 2017). Alternatively, Reisberg (1998) suggests some see UR as no more than "glorified homework," placing additional teaching burdens on faculty. Academics also observe that UR is typically not rewarded in tenure and promotion and such mentorship is too time consuming (Hoyt & McGoldrick, 2017). Not surprisingly, Morales et al. (2017) find faculty who are skeptical of UR or see no tenure and promotion rewards for it are the least likely to undertake such activities.

Faculty skepticism of UR discourages a more widespread use of the extra-curricular teacher-scholar model. While studies of UR note the extensive student benefits, it is much less likely to cover those for faculty. Then, the faculty benefits listed tend to be emotional satisfaction, things like enjoying overseeing students' "professional initiation" and seeing UR students go onto graduate programs (Murray, 2017, p. 62). But what substantive benefits do faculty get? One study notes that "Over time most faculty met research goals, published or presented work with student collaborators, and benefited from the contributions of their 'mini-colleagues,'" and some professors found it rewarding to collaborate with "some damn smart people," people being undergraduates (Laursen et al., 2012, p. 35). Undergraduates do not always come with the disciplinary skills that academics desire, yet this suggests they are more capable than often assumed and they can bring other skills (like being technologically hip), have perspectives faculty may benefit from, and provide a much-needed labor force that helps faculty close the resource gap and more efficiently realize their research agendas.

Lessons from a Decade of UR

With over a decade of experience with UR, it has been these substantive benefits for my research agenda along with the emotional satisfaction mentoring undergraduates that has kept me practicing the extra-curricular teacher-scholar. In that time, I have worked with over half a dozen undergraduates to find funding (almost $20,000) that paid them to be research assistants. One of the first lessons learned was that students are capable of doing much more than faculty expect.

Naively, I began using what Lopatto (2009, pp. 18–19) calls the "employee" approach, hiring undergraduates to do menial tasks like making phone calls, photocopying articles from the library, or doing web searches. Students can and should be hired to be much more than worker bees. Instead, I recommend following Lopatto's remaining two approaches, the apprentice or the collaborator, as being more in line with the extra-curricular teacher-scholar. While the employee approach allowed me to focus time on the research and not the busy work that may go into it, the latter gave students more practical research skills and experiences useful to their future careers while helping me achieve more grand research goals like producing a large N data set, conducting interviews, or collaborating on an in-depth content analysis.

For example, I recruited three undergraduates to apply for UR funding ($7,000) through our UR Center and then walked them through and involved them in multiple aspects of the research process and activities. Two students spearheaded contacting secondary schools. They built a data set of how many semesters of civics Arkansans typically experience in high school. These students also helped recruit a dozen colleges and universities across the US to participate in a study of the American Government general education course. Their help resulted in the creation of a large N (over 3,000) pre-test/post-test data set of college students, as well as a smaller data set of over 40 faculty that assesses their pedagogical approach to teaching the course. They participated in the IRB, helped recruit schools, and attended an APSA Teaching and Learning Conference where they learned about best practices in civic engagement. As for the third student, he was a business data analytics major. He was able to do an initial cleaning of the data and did some initial analysis that all three presented at ATU's research symposium. It is worth repeating these students helped produce a large N data set. This was done without needing to pay the prohibitive costs of hiring a data firm. This data has resulted in multiple manuscripts that are being developed for publication as journal articles and/or a book.

Additionally, multiple smaller grants ($2,000 to $4,000) have been secured to hire students as research assistants. One grant came from our UR Center. It funded hiring a student to assist in conducting interviews of civics teachers in Arkansas. The student helped complete the IRB and collaborated on developing the interview script. He scheduled and conducted the interviews alongside me. Being more tech savvy, he also took care of the transcriptions, finding an app for his phone that recorded and transcribed the interviews. Recently, I worked with another student through a state-funded UR grant to collaborate on a content analysis. We worked together to identify the key terms by which to search the texts; she collected the content data, helped assemble the data matrix, and even attended and co-presented the initial findings at the Midwest Political Science Association's annual meeting. She was active in all aspects of the content analysis but graduated (going onto graduate school with funding) so has not participated in the write-up of the manuscript. She represents the closest I have come to a collaborator and she is acknowledged in the manuscript for her work.

As for additional lessons learned, there are many. For one, carefully select students. The students I work with I already have a rapport with through the major; typically, they are the strongest students from the program's research design/methods and senior seminar courses. Second, one must set clear expectations of the work needed and routinely check in with students weekly or biweekly. As a general rule, I recommend not having students work more than ten hours a week. That said, I do have them identify the time during the week they will be doing the work. Likewise, I have them meet weekly with me to hold them accountable. Inevitably, there are weeks they are not able to do much on the research front given exams and other work, but the weekly check-in deadlines keep them (and me) being productive.

Then, as noted above, mentorship is central. It is important to walk students through the method of analysis and the steps it requires. Students may have read about our methods in a research class, but executing them effectively requires practice and experience. Students may have practiced them in a lower stakes class assessment, but not the high stakes of research for publication. They may have completed an IRB as a class assignment or for conducting their research, but the process is often more complex and demanding for a faculty application. Good mentorship builds their confidence; lack of guidance encourages them to flounder.

Finally, as an extra-curricular teacher-scholar arguably the most important lesson is how to find funding to hire undergraduates. The variety of professional activities (IRB submissions, conferences or symposia presentations, publications, mentorship and even extra-curricular fellowship) one can take with undergraduates that go beyond formal course work and credit is extensive (Murray, 2017, pp. 89–93). However, I am reluctant to do any extra-curricular teacher-scholar UR without funding them, as that exploits undergraduates.

I take pride in having found funding for all my research apprentices to date. As Murray (2017) observes, "Issues of affordability also affect the undergraduate experience itself, mainly by increasing the necessity of student employment" (p. 139). Linn (2015) adds "funding may be especially important at developing UR at teaching-focused institutions." Pre-COVID there was an interest in expanding UR experiences and funding to more disciplines (Murray, 2017, Ch. 9). Post-COVID funding is slowly coming back and political scientists should take advantage of it. The only scholarly discussion of the economics of and funding for UR generally is found in Murray (2017, see Ch. 5 & 10) and he notes faculty must be active fundraisers for UR. While his focus is on national organizations and the history of funding for UR by the federal government, Murray (2017, p. 145) advises to look "in-house." Many colleges and universities readily provide funding for UR. My own experiences reinforce this point. Most resources can be secured in-house, so start there and move out. If for no other reason, start in-house because the funding competition typically becomes more competitive as one moves out.

While the terrain at every college, university, and state varies, below is a roadmap for navigating UR funding. Hiring a student as a research assistant does not require a large grant; it can be covered with a few thousand dollars, an amount that likely still leaves some funds for the student to attend a conference as well. Junior scholars may not know opportunities for funded collaboration with undergraduates are often readily available. They tend to require less strenuous and time-consuming application proposals, nor do they tend to be as competitive as faculty research grant programs.

That said, start the investigation in-house with your college or university's grant office. Most have one and they are a great clearing house to learn about in-house and external funding opportunities. It was the grants office at my university where I learned about a couple of the funding sources I have used. First, it was through ATU's grant office that I learned of a large in-house funding source for UR, ATU's Student Interdisciplinary Research Grants (SIRG). It offered up to $10,000 (ATU, 2022). I secured a grant for over $7000 through this program to hire three undergraduates (and even one graduate student) to develop a large N data set of students and a small N data set of faculty across a dozen colleges and universities.

Also, the ATU grants office made me aware of another funding opportunity through the state of Arkansas. They encouraged my student and me to apply for the Student Undergraduate Research Fellowship (SURF) program through the Arkansas Department of Higher Education (ADHE). The ADHE offers up to $4000 for undergraduates in the state of Arkansas to do research with faculty and travel to conferences to present (ADHE, 2022). This program funded the student who collaborated in the content analysis. Surprisingly, an internet search of states revealed no other state education departments offer such collegiate UR funding. Given UR's popularity, lobbying state higher education agencies might get more states to do so given the Arkansas precedent.

Working with the grant office will probably also lead one to another primary source for funding, the in-house UR center. If your institution has a UR center, the grant office will know. If it does not, this should be the next entity you look for on campus. An internet search of UR funding quickly revealed every state has colleges or universities with UR centers offering funding opportunities. While COVID saw such funding opportunities shrink at many institutions, my institution's UR center is now again offering grants for up to $2000 (ATU, 2021). I have secured funds multiple times from our UR center to hire students as research assistants.

For another in-house source, many colleges and universities offer their faculty research grants and/or professional development grants. These vary in size and have stipulations on what they can be spent on but if student research assistants are allowed, one only needs a thousand or two from it to hire an undergraduate student. I used this method initially, before ATU had a UR Center. Through these various sources, I have secured approximately $20,000 in grant funds to hire students as research assistants, which has been invaluable in advancing my scholarship over the past decade.

After in-house possibilities are exhausted or if larger funds are desired, then one should refer to Murray (2017, Ch. 5 and 10) for the federal and private foundation options. While much of Murray's (2017, pp. 70–72) discussion is geared to STEM (e.g., the National Science Foundation, Department of Energy, National Institutes of Health, among others) and are highly competitive programs, there are some promising ones for political scientists like the National Endowment for the Humanities or the federal Department of Education. As for the private foundations covered, they tend toward STEM (e.g., Research Corporation for Science Advancement, Howard Hughes Medical Institute, etc.) as well, but do not preclude political science (Murray, 2017, pp. 72–74).

The Extra-Curricular Teacher-Scholar for Political Science

While there is variation among specific disciplines, over half of all STEM students are likely to experience UR, but the rates for social sciences are about one-quarter and for humanities about one-fifth (Murray, 2017, pp. 84–85). Worse, Lopatto (2006) found over half of social science and humanities students did their research solo, while only a fifth of natural science students did so. Looking specifically at political science departments, Ishiyama (2021, p. 379) found only about 23% of them had formally structured UR programs. By following the example of STEM and providing more collaborative UR experiences, political science can benefit from the higher matriculation rates associated with UR. As UR opportunities are expanded to more students, especially paid ones, retention should improve.

Combining extra-curricular teaching of funded research assistants has significantly helped advance my scholarship over the last ten years. It has been a central way I have dealt with the resource gap I have faced being at a teaching school with a heavy teaching load. Research studies of UR show it can address some of the challenges of the Great Contraction, like expecting faculty to help with retention and graduation rates. None of the students I have hired to be research apprentices have failed to graduate and one has gone onto graduate school with full funding. Given UR often has multiple funding opportunities for faculty in-house and does not necessitate large grants, political scientists particularly at teaching schools will find the extra-curricular teacher-scholar may just be the way to secure the funding and labor force to shrink the resource gap and advance their scholarship more efficiently. As an added bonus, they will forge relationships with students that are particularly rewarding and strengthen those students' career trajectories.

References

ADHE. (2022). *Student Undergraduate Research Fellowship/SURF*. www.adhe.edu. Retrieved June 30, 2022, from https://sams.adhe.edu/Scholarship/Details/SURF

APSA. *Political Science Education (Section 29)*. apsanet.org. Retrieved June 24, 2022, from https://apsanet.org/section29

ATU. (2021). *Undergraduate research*. www.atu.edu. Retrieved June 30, 2022, from https://www.atu.edu/uresearch/

ATU. (2022). *Internal grant programs*. www.atu.edu. Retrieved June 30, 2022, from https://www.atu.edu/research/index.php

Bauer, K. W., & Bennett, J. S. (2003). Alumni perceptions used to assess undergraduate research experience. *The Journal of Higher Education, 74*(2), 210–230.

Craney, C., McKay, T., Mazzeo, A., Morris, J., Prigodich, C., & de Groot, R. (2011). Cross-discipline perceptions of the undergraduate research experience. *The Journal of Higher Education, 82*(1), 92–113. http://libcatalog.atu.edu:2091/stable/29789506

Evans, R., & Witkowsky, D. (2004). Who gives a damn what they think anyway? Involving students in mentored research. *National Social Science Journal, 23*(1), 21–30.

Gardner, L. (2021). The great contraction. *Chronicle of Higher Education, 67*(12), 3.

Hoyt, G. M., & McGoldrick, K. (2017). Promoting undergraduate research in economics. *The American Economic Review, 107*(5), 655–659. http://libcatalog.atu.edu:2091/stable/44250478

Hunter, A., Laursen, S., & Seymour, E. (2007). The role of undergraduate research in students' cognitive, personal and professional development. *Science Education, 50*(4), 36–74.

IBL. (2022). *Political science*. www.pathwaystoscience.org. Retrieved June 29, 2022, from https://www.pathwaystoscience.org/Discipline.aspx?sort=SOC-PolySci_Political%20Science

Ishiyama, J. (2005). Examining the impact of the wahlke report: Surveying the structure of the political science curricula at liberal arts and sciences Colleges and universities in the midwest. *PS, Political Science & Politics, 38*(1), 71–75. https://doi.org/10.1017.S1049096505055812

Ishiyama, J. (2021). What Kinds of departments promote undergraduate research in political science? *Journal of Political Science Education, 17*(3), 371–384.

Katz, R. S., & Eagles, M. (1996). Ranking political science programs: A view from the lower half. *PS: Political Science and Politics, 29*(2), 149–154. https://doi.org/10.2307/420692

Laursen, S., Seymour, E., & Hunter, A.-B. (2012). LEARNING, TEACHING AND SCHOLARSHIP: Fundamental tensions of undergraduate research. *Change*, 44(2), 30–37. http://www.jstor.org/stable/23595155

Linn Marcia, C. (2015). Undergraduate research experiences: Impacts and opportunities. *Science*, 347(6222). https://www.science.org/doi/10.1126/science.1261757

Lopatto, D. (2006). Undergraduate research as a catalyst for liberal learning. *Peer Review*, 8(1), 22–25.

Lopatto, D. (2009). *Science in solution: The impact of undergraduate research on student learning*. Research Corporation for Science Advancement.

Lowry, R. C., & Silver, B. D. (1996). A rising tide lifts all boats: Political science department reputation and the reputation of the university. *PS: Political Science and Politics*, 29(2), 161–167. https://doi.org/10.2307/420694

Morales, D. X., Grineski, S. E., & Collins, T. W. (2017). Faculty motivation to mentor students through undergraduate research programs: A study of enabling and constraining factors. *Research in Higher Education*, 58(5), 520–544.

Murray, J. L. (2017). *Undergraduate research for student engagement and learning*. Routledge.

Nietzel, M. T. (2022, May 26). New report: The college enrollment decline worsened this spring. *Forbes*. https://www.forbes.com/sites/michaeltnietzel/2022/05/26/new-report-the-college-enrollment-decline-has-worsened-this-spring/?sh=3c21e94d24e0

Reisberg, L. (1998). Research by undergraduates proliferates but is some of it just glorified homework? *The Chronicle of Higher Education*, 44(37), A45–A47.

Rogers, M. T. (2017). The history of civic education in political science: The story of a discipline's failure to lead. In E. C. Matto, A. R. M. McCartney, E. A. Bennion, & D. Simpson (Eds.), *Teaching civic engagement across the disciplines* (pp. 73–96). The American Political Science Association.

Rogers, M. T. (2021). A career-oriented approach to structuring the political science major. *PS, Political Science & Politics*, 54(2), 387–393. https://doi.org/10.1017/S1049096520001791

Rosowsky, D. (2020, June 11). The teaching and research balancing act: Are universities teetering. *Forbes*. https://www.forbes.com/sites/davidrosowsky/2020/06/11/the-teaching-and-research-balancing-act-are-universities-teetering/?sh=450267152ed8

Seymour, E., Hunter, A., Laursen, S., & Deantoni, T. (2004). Establishing the benefits of research experiences for undergraduates in the sciences: First findings from a three-year study. *Science Education*, 88, 493–534.

Smith, R. M. (2015). Political science and the public sphere today. *Perspectives on Politics*, 13(2), 366–376.

UNT. (2019). *UNT nsf-reu on conflict management and peace science*. www.unt.edu. Retrieved June 29, 2022, from https://politicalscience.unt.edu/peace-studies/unt-nsf-reu-conflict-management-and-peace-science

CHAPTER 13

Increasing Access to Undergraduate Research Opportunities at Small Teaching Institutions

Kelly Bauer

Undergraduate research experiences are a high impact learning practice, but access to these opportunities is frequently limited at teaching-focused institutions, where students have fewer faculty working on their areas of interest and faculty have less research time and support. How can faculty with heavy teaching loads sustainability facilitate students' access to undergraduate research experiences? This chapter documents successes and challenges from a student-faculty collaborative research initiative on immigration politics in Nebraska started in August 2019.[1] It documents powerful student learning outcomes but concerning sustainability challenges, in hopes of assisting other faculty and administrators interested in efficiently and effectively expanding research and teaching through undergraduate research opportunities at smaller teaching institutions.

[1] Human subjects research was approved by the Nebraska Wesleyan University Institutional Review Board, NWU-IRB#202,001,251-S.

K. Bauer (✉)
George Washington University, Washington, DC, USA
e-mail: kbauer2@gwu.edu

© The Author(s), under exclusive license to Springer Nature Switzerland AG 2023
C. Butcher et al. (eds.), *The Palgrave Handbook of Teaching and Research in Political Science*, Political Pedagogies,
https://doi.org/10.1007/978-3-031-42887-6_13

Promise and Limitations of Undergraduate Research Experiences

Undergraduate research experiences are categorized as one of eleven High Impact Practices (HIPs), documented by the American Association of Colleges and Universities to produce deep learning and engagement across undergraduate student populations (Kuh, 2008). While undergraduate research experiences in the sciences are more common, until recently, conversations about these learning experiences in political science have focused on classroom research training, most often through research methodology and senior capstone courses (Ishiyama, 2019; Ishiyama & Breuning, 2003). Recent work has documented innovative efforts by faculty to import the collaborative and hierarchical laboratory model of research to the social sciences, pulling undergraduate research experiences out of the traditional class structure into a valuable scaffolded research training and mentoring model (Becker, 2019; Weinschenk, 2021). As such, labs are "both vertical and horizontal in nature: vertical because they are led by faculty who supervise research assistants (RAs), and horizontal because faculty leaders work together and RAs work together" (Zvobgo, 2022, p. 730), offering the potential to promote research, teaching, and learning beneficial to both students and faculty.

But, access to these valuable learning experiences in political science is unevenly distributed across institutions, subfields, and methodologies. If undergraduate research experiences occur through a course, the topic and methodology is often selected by the student, and it is labor-intensive work for faculty to advise outside of their areas of expertise (Buddie & Collins, 2011). If these experiences occur outside of the classroom, the work is often set up to efficiently advance the faculty's research agenda, and may not be structured with pedagogical practices that facilitate student learning. Considering research documenting how political science privileges certain forms of knowledge creation, particularly by methodology, and that these disparities are reflected in which students start and continue in the field, it is crucial for the discipline to consider how undergraduate research experiences can be more equitably distributed and accessible to students (Becker et al., 2021).

How do these trends play out at teaching-focused universities? At first glance, undergraduate research experiences might seem to be a natural fit for teaching-focused institutions, where there might be more flexible curriculum, institutional incentives to prioritize student learning opportunities, and pedagogical support for students to play active roles in their learning by co-creating knowledge (Cook-Sather et al., 2014). But, creating these experiences requires heavy lifting and long-term investment on the part of faculty (Mangum, 2022). For faculty at teaching-focused universities, can creating and running undergraduate research experiences be a way to work smarter, not harder?

Efforts to Align Research and Teaching at Nebraska Wesleyan University (NWU)

The question of how to best integrate and balance research and teaching defined much of my tenure track journey at a small undergraduate liberal arts university. I saw undergraduate research opportunities as an ideal way to explore my passions for both my research and teaching agendas while providing a valuable learning experience for students.

My early attempts to strike this balance failed. I did not have many students with the language skills to work as research assistants on grant-funded research, nor enough students to design a credit-bearing research experience course on a specific topic that would count toward my semester course load. Nebraska Wesleyan University (NWU) does have an endowed fund to support limited expenses associated with student-faculty collaborative research that occurs outside of the classroom, but to receive funds, the grant proposal must be student-initiated and written. Such requirements result in a substantial time investment from upper-level students and faculty, with no guarantee of funding. After completing one grant during my first year on the tenure track, I left frustrated by how this institutional structure, while incredibly valuable to the student, was limited to students whose methodological training, language skills, and career interests mapped onto faculty expertise and depended on faculty willingness to add an uncompensated independent study to their workload.

As a result of these various frustrations, I sought to create a different model for involving students in my research. In August 2019, I formed a student-faculty collaborative research initiative, Study of Immigration Politics in Nebraska (SIPN). I was motivated to find a structure that offered an undergraduate research experience to a broader range of students, and by recent conversations with other faculty working to import a lab model into political science. The initiative was the result of a summer of pondering, summarized in the paragraph below.

What Topic and Method?

One of the first challenges of this project was selecting a topic in which a range of students had sufficient (1) interest and (2) methodological training. For most cohorts of NWU students, my own research on identity politics and policy in Latin America has neither, particularly as most upper-level language students studying abroad and/or close to graduation have less availability for ongoing research projects. I addressed these challenges by identifying the core puzzles that motivate my research agenda, stripped from the context where I usually study those questions. Then, I reflected on how students might already be curious about those questions based on their experiences in their own lives and communities, and how a research experience could invite those students to think critically about those everyday conversations.

Which Students?

While the research initiative itself was motivated by an effort to ensure broad student access to research opportunities, I also wanted to establish a record of success ensuring future students would be joining a project with well-established expectations and outcomes. For the first semester, I focused on developing success and expertise among students, hoping this would set up future students' success. By starting with a small group of students who had excelled in classes with me, I also hoped that those students would develop their own research interests and get excited about mentoring and serving in leadership roles in future projects. For the second semester, I recruited more broadly. I emailed an application to all majors in the department, as well as a few colleagues in other departments in the humanities and social sciences who might know of other interested students. I also asked students who participated in the first semester to talk to friends who might be interested, and to be honest as students approached them to inquire about the process. Certainly, this method of diffusion is much more effective on a small campus, but it did prompt younger students to join in.

What Institutional Structure?

As an experimental project, I ran the first and second semesters independent of any institutional curricular structure and without compensation. Students had the option to enroll in independent study credit (none did because of their existing course load), and were co-authors on the project. I attempted to keep many best practices of course management despite it not being a course. We had a shared Google drive, where we kept a list of assignments and meeting agendas, shared pdfs, and uploaded and commented on each other's work.

TEACHING AND RESEARCH OUTCOMES

The first semester was particularly successful. I recruited three undergraduate students to join the research project. Each had taken classes with me, where they demonstrated their interests in local immigration politics and political science research. We met as a group for one hour per week across the semester, workshopping research, grant writing, and academic conference presentations. We also worked through grant writing, and academic conference presentations and preparations. While I set the initial list of tasks and estimated a timeline to ensure we would be ready for the planned conference at the end of the semester, the research and writing process was collaborative with each member taking on a responsibility of work to prepare for the following week. The resulting collaborative paper analyzed 100 + news articles covering immigration politics in Nebraska from September 2017-September 2019 (Bauer et al., 2021). We presented the paper at the North Central Council of Latin Americanists annual meeting in October 2019; the three student scholars were awarded a travel grant to support their participation and scholarship, and the research was recognized with the conference's Collaborative Research Award.

Students' self-reported learning outcomes are revealing of the promise of an undergraduate research experience. First, students reported that this experience brought research methodology course conversations to life. One reported:

> The actual application of research methods during this process was so helpful to understand how things operate in the real political science research world. You can read a million journals and argue about a million

theories but until you have a question and hypothesis you care about and have to find a defensible way to study it, you just can't quite understand the process.

Another described:

I learned a lot about case selection so I think through how data is collected, how we are being consistent in what we are using for data and where are we getting it, why the significance of using data from certain timelines are in comparison to another set of timelines, and how much data we were collecting. I did not know to ask these questions, and these were also the same questions I was starting to learn to ask in the research methods courses and having a direct application of what that looked like helped in understanding the importance of the research methods classes as well.

Each was enrolled in a political science methodology course while participating in the collaborative research, and each reported that their research experiences in and out of the classroom were mutually beneficial for their learning.

Second, students reported that their learning from collaborative research was very different from their learning in traditional classes. In meetings, students often asked for answers to both research decisions and outcomes. While I offered deadlines and stages of the research process, I left decisions about content and methodology of the research open to discussion. Students reflected on the underlying uncertainty of the research process by stating:

I think the fact that it was sort of an experimental process was very helpful for me because I learned how to navigate the process on my own a little bit without the usual structure and guidelines that I usually gravitate towards, which gave me a better understanding of the research process and the different choices you have to make based on the kind of research you want to do.

Students reported that this uncertainty prompted more creativity and experimentation in both their thinking and skill development. One reported:

I also gained more confidence in my writing and much of that had to do with the mentoring and in learning to share 'ugly' drafts. Personally, this was a huge improvement because I do not like sharing incomplete work and this pushed me to do something outside of my comfort zone. For classes, I am only conditioned to turn in the papers I want graded so this was a different experience particularly to have other students also see my not-so-great writing.

While a course syllabus provides a clear trajectory, assignments, assessment standards, and timelines, students found the lack of a syllabus to be initially unsettling but opened space for experimentation and growth.

Students also commented on the unexpected benefits of learning through collaborative group work. As one summarized:

The area I made the most gains was learning to work in a group. I am not a big fan of group projects and this research experience required a lot of group work even though many parts of the research were individual. Although we took on individual tasks to write different portions of the paper, without the conversations from our weekly meetings, it would have been difficult to write a cohesive paper. … This experience made me think so positively of group work. This was also the first time I have ever written anything in such length as a group, but being able to do this together was one of the best parts about the research experience as we were able to rely on each other's strengths.

Others shared similar comments about the experience of presenting at an academic conference, noting "I learned a lot from the conference that we attended through watching other presentations and listening to the feedback and questions that other intellectuals contributed to our research, which was really valuable and unexpected" and "I did not realize that I would be so intrigued by presenting our data to others and explaining why we did what we did and how it can be used." While students who joined this research project were high-achieving students who often contribute more than they benefit from group work and peer critique, this collaborative process was new, exciting, and valuable.

Finally, students reflected thoughtfully on how the experience allowed them to both experiment with and narrow their professional development plans. One shared:

Thinking about grad school as the future plan, I really wanted to understand what research would be, and it felt like a great way to learn and experience that in a non-scary way because it meant I did not have to wait until senior seminar to either confirm or rethink about my career path.

Another realized that they were better suited for a different type of politics work, reporting "... I don't think research in the academic capacity is for me. It is super interesting and I loved learning about the topic but at the end I was more interested in policy solutions." Another shared:

> I liked thinking about the 'so what' and the implications of the public opinion we analyzed. This helps me think about what I am interested in and showed me that while I enjoy the research, I want to pursue a career that takes it a step further and figures out what to do about addressing the implications that research presents.

The format of the non-structured, non-graded research experience provided a space for students to explore and clarify their professional interests.

Conclusions

Early evidence from my experience starting a student-faculty collaborative research initiative at a teaching institution highlights how an undergraduate research experience can challenge students into different layers of cognitive analysis of both content and process. While the lack of structure was initially challenging, students came to value how the structure allowed for experimentation, specialization, and individualization. By centering my research with undergraduate students around one topic, I was able to more intentionally and transparently structure research opportunities for a range of diverse students who would not have been able to participate in NWU's existing institutional structures for research, and collaboratively learned from and with students. This opened up fulfilling new teaching and research opportunities in my own professional trajectory; it was a moment of working both harder and smarter.

The powerful teaching, learning, and research outcomes reported by students who participated in this research experience have been well-documented in other contexts, and faculty and administrators should work to ensure broad student access to similar opportunities. However, my experiences highlight the challenges of sustainably creating these research initiatives at teaching institutions. While my own institution had an endowed fund to support some student research, this structure prioritized advanced upper-level students and travel and receipted expenses, and relied on student interests overlapping with faculty expertise as well as faculty's willingness to support the research with uncompensated labor. These resources, and those at similar institutions, could benefit more students if these funds supported student and faculty time, and incentivized faculty to create ongoing research opportunities that do not require repeat funding requests from students or faculty. Faculty and administrators should advocate for these small changes in funding structures to sustainably offer these experiences to a broad range of students.

As small teaching institutions face increasing financial and enrollment pressures, we risk growing gaps in which faculty might offer and which students might access undergraduate research opportunities. Considering the documented value of these learning experiences, faculty and administrators should insist on the importance of integrating faculty research and teaching to support undergraduate research at small teaching institutions. This resists more consumer models of education focused on delivering specific content in pursuit of specific profitable degrees, instead advocating for the outcomes students report here. In addition to ensuring that funding structures facilitate broad access for faculty to create and students to access undergraduate research opportunities, this could also include organizing these opportunities through existing classes (of course, with institutional support and recognition of the work this adds to faculty). It is crucial for our conversations about working smarter to align research and teaching to consider and advocate for undergraduate research experiences at teaching institutions.

References

Barnes, T. D. (2018). Strategies for improving gender diversity in the methods community: Insights from political methodologists and social science research. *PS, Political Science & Politics, 51*(3), 580–587. https://doi.org/10.1017/S1049096518000513

Bauer, K. (2021). Research design as professional development and empowerment: Equipping students to see, analyze, and intervene in political realities. In *The Palgrave handbook of political research pedagogy* (pp. 151–160): Springer. https://doi.org/10.1007/978-3-030-76955-0_12

Bauer, K., Redfern, S., Wang, H., & Woo, S. (2021). Surpassing the wall of Nebraska nice: Analysis of immigration rhetoric in Nebraska journalism. *Great Plains Research, 31*(1), 57–73. https://doi.org/10.1353/gpr.2021.0003

Becker, M. (2019). Importing the laboratory model to the social sciences: Prospects for improving mentoring of undergraduate researchers. *Journal of Political Science Education, 1–13*. https://doi.org/10.1080/15512169.2018.1505523

Becker, M., Graham, B. A., & Zvobgo, K. (2021). The stewardship model: An inclusive approach to undergraduate research. *PS: Political Science & Politics, 54*(1), 158–162. https://doi.org/10.1017/S1049096520001043

Buddie, A. M., & Collins, C. L. (2011). Faculty perceptions of undergraduate research. *PURM: Perspectives on Mentoring Undergraduate Researchers, 1*(1), 1–21. https://doi.org/10.1145/1513593.1513598

Cook-Sather, A., Bovill, C., & Felten, P. (2014). *Engaging students as partners in learning and teaching: A guide for faculty*. John Wiley & Sons.

Ferguson, K. (2016). Why does political science hate American Indians? *Perspectives on Politics, 14*(4), 1029–1038. https://doi.org/10.1017/S1537592716002905

Fujii, L. A. (2017). *The real problem with diversity in political science*. Duck of Minerva.

Ishiyama, J. (2019). What kinds of departments promote undergraduate research in political science? *Journal of Political Science Education, 1–14*. https://doi.org/10.1080/15512169.2019.1667242

Ishiyama, J., & Breuning, M. (2003). Does participation in undergraduate research affect political science students? *Politics & Policy, 31*(1), 163–180. https://doi.org/10.1111/j.1747-1346.2003.tb00892.x

Kuh, G. D. (2008). Excerpt from high-impact educational practices: What they are, who has access to them, and why they matter. *Association of American Colleges and Universities, 14*(3), 28–29.

Mangum, M. (2022). Collaborating on research with undergraduate students: A comparative institutional-racial analysis. *PS: Political Science & Politics, 1–4*. https://doi.org/10.1017/S1049096522001093

Nonnemacher, J., & Sokhey, S. W. (2022). Learning by doing: Using an undergraduate research lab to promote diversity and inclusion. *PS: Political Science & Politics, 55*(2), 413–418. https://doi.org/10.1017/S1049096521001633

Ravecca, P. (2019). *The politics of political science: Re-writing Latin American experiences*. Routledge.

Reyes-Núñez, R. L., Blanco, F., Benenson, J., Cortés-Rivera, J. J., Gomez-Aguinaga, B., Heckler, N., Jamieson, T., Mwarumba, N. (2023). Building inclusion, equity, and diversity into graduate student Coauthorship. *PS: Political Science & Politics, 56*(1), 189–192. https://doi.org/10.1017/S1049096522000919

Shames, S. L., & Wise, T. (2017). Gender, diversity, and methods in political science: A theory of selection and survival biases. *PS: Political Science & Politics, 50*(3), 811–823. https://doi.org/10.1017/S104909651700066X

Verge, T. (2016). The virtues of engendering quantitative methods courses. *PS: Political Science & Politics, 49*(3), 550–553. https://doi.org/10.1017/S1049096516000962

Weinschenk, A. C. (2021). Creating and implementing an undergraduate research lab in political science. *Journal of Political Science Education, 17*. https://doi.org/10.1080/15512169.2020.1795873

Zvobgo, K. (2022). Research labs: Concept, utility, and application. In *Handbook of research methods in international relations* (pp. 729–747). Edward Elgar Publishing.

CHAPTER 14

Teamwork Makes the (Research) Dream Work: Lessons in Working with a Student Research Team

Julia Marin Hellwege, Cohl Turnquist, Aaron Vlasman, and Bess Seaman

Working with student research assistants can be a very rewarding teaching and mentoring experience allowing faculty to make significant progress toward a successful research agenda. That said, balancing mentoring and teaching valuable skills while meeting your own research goals can prove

J. M. Hellwege (✉) · C. Turnquist · A. Vlasman · B. Seaman
University of South Dakota, Vermillion, SD, USA
e-mail: Julia.hellwege@usd.edu

C. Turnquist
e-mail: cohlturnquist@cityofflandreau.com

A. Vlasman
e-mail: vlasmanaaron@gmail.com

B. Seaman
e-mail: Bess.Seaman@coyotes.usd.edu

quite challenging, and it took the lead author several years to start figuring it out. We offer some experiences, advice, and tips for working with research assistants from the perspective of a faculty member, but we also examine the students' (both graduate and undergraduate) experience including potential challenges. In this sense, we seek to offer some reassurance that given the right tools and guidance, undergraduate students can be helpful assets for a research team. Some of the key benefits we discuss are increased opportunities for research/experience, teaching/learning, and team building. We attain these goals with a level of respect and responsibility; each member is an integral part of the team and is fully included in the projects. Some of the core limitations or challenges center around preparation and communication, particularly willingness to communicate weaknesses. Overall, we hope to offer a comprehensive view of doing research with student research assistants and how to ensure everyone gets the most out of the teamwork, in other words- how to make the dream of balancing research and teaching work.

Faculty Perspective

As I thought about how to contribute to this volume, it was not lost on me that not everyone has access to funds to build a team of paid research assistants. That said, many universities and colleges offer small internally competitive research grants and are more likely to support student opportunities than faculty directly. When new faculty are first assigned, or hire, a research assistant, they generally have two equally strong but conflicting feelings: (1) Yes! I finally have an assistant to support me the way I supported my faculty mentors and (2) I am so accustomed to working by myself that I have no idea what to delegate or what my expectations should be (particularly if they are not a Ph.D. student). Even after six years, I continue to cultivate my team culture, but I have learned that the better I am about breaking down a project into smaller, more manageable tasks, the better I can delegate and consequently the better the students perform.

Student selection is a crucial task for team success. I have found that the most important qualities for a good research assistant are reliability and communication. In fact, I've found these much more important than GPA or skill level. Because of this, I typically hire students who I already know, usually someone who has taken my class before or is my advisee. This approach creates significant selection bias, which is why I have made sure to announce in my classes and share more openly that I regularly hire students so that they will be more likely to ask me for openings. If a student expresses interest, I make sure to have a one-on-one meeting with the student prior to the start of the semester to discuss team member expectations.

One of the most important lessons I have learned is the importance of honesty. Otherwise, information and expectations gaps will widen and the team will fail, at least in the short term. Maintaining honest, regular, and professional communication is key to success. Each person (including the faculty member) must be comfortable sharing their needs, goals, and skill levels. One of the simplest, yet most important parts of a successful research team is holding regular meetings. We meet bi-weekly throughout each semester as it allows for a balance between accountability and flexibility. For my own benefit, I try to schedule these meetings on days when I'm not teaching (keeping "research days" and "teaching days" separate is another part of the balance for me). The team model also means that despite working on separate projects, we all meet at the same time. This ensures that I have fewer meetings in a week but also that I come well-prepared for our meetings and focus on the relevant projects.

Research assistants do not always result in a substantial net gain in productivity. Managing and overseeing student research assistants takes a considerable amount of work; for obvious reasons, they are not as capable or efficient as anticipated and the work is not always done correctly (for a variety of reasons). That said, the more work put into the structure and management of the team, including assigning specific tasks and responsibilities, the higher the likelihood of *mutual* benefit. It may take time to calibrate how long specific tasks should take, but regular and *specific* check-ins and oversight can help move tasks along and ensure progress is made. I learned this lesson the hard way. Early on, when working one-on-one with student assistants, we would have occasional check-ins, but they tended to be more informal, and (as became obvious later) it allowed students to shirk being specific about their progress, which resulted in a lack of progress at the end of the semester. On some occasions, this was because instructions were unclear and students were concerned about being honest with me about their inability to complete the task. On other occasions, students have had personal circumstances hindering their progress. Either way, what I had perceived as a generous and informal approach ultimately harmed us both. The students did not learn from the experience nor did I make progress on my research agenda. On rare occasion, ending students' contracts may be a mutually beneficial decision, and even welcomed by students who may have been too scared to speak up. The team approach, with regular meetings, creates a level of accountability and vulnerability, both for the students and for myself, that allows us to tackle any issues in a more productive manner.

The most rewarding part of a research team is the mentoring I am able to impart and the opportunity for a less formal teaching experience. A research team of assistants is different from a class lab model where the lab is used as a pedagogical tool to guide students through a research experience. Instead, I treat research assistants as members of a team with various goals who work together (with a team leader more than a professor) and with shared accountability (between each other and the faculty lead). Meetings should not follow a structured syllabus, but time can be used to workshop skills, such as writing (e.g., emails, grant proposals and reports, and survey questions), using software (e.g., Excel, Qualtrics, Stata and Mendeley), and administrative management (e.g., time management tools or budgeting). Incorporating workshops builds the bridge between research and teaching. Our research meetings often deal with our broader professional lives (and even personal lives) and I can offer tasks, tutelage, and deeper mentorship. Having a close, collaborative team who I can meet with, confide in, and who hold me accountable and motivated is tremendously helpful.

There are considerable practical and ethical considerations for managing a team of research assistants. Most of us faculty know about academic overwork and the general mismatch between our workload structure and the traditional reporting of logged hours. While I appreciate having a well-organized administrative assistant, I am often frustrated by her asking me to approve of the number of hours students have worked—as their "supervisor," when I see my role more as a team leader who trusts that the students are working the number of hours they have reported, but more than that I recognize that some weeks or months they may have less work or less ability to work allotted hours, and I'm happy to allow them to "bank" those hours for the future, "as long as the work gets done." This has led to numerous conversations with students about professional behavior (e.g., report your hours and do it on time), but also how to navigate bureaucratic systems that sometimes do not necessarily reflect the actual work and ethics in the workplace.

I should pause here also to note the importance of compensation for research assistants. As noted above, I make use of low-competition, internal grants to fund my undergraduate research assistants. That said, I have on occasion taken on volunteers but for very specific reasons (e.g., the student was not ready but wanted a short-term experience to try it out or because I had a desperate short-term need and made that clear). In each case that a student has decided to move from volunteer to a "full" position I have found funding for them in the following semester. The final consideration is on acknowledgments and co-authorship. On my team, and with very few exceptions, the students are primarily research assistants who contribute through administrative tasks or data or literature collection, and not analysis or writing. As such, prior to this chapter, the team had not co-authored any works. Here it should be noted too, that very few (and no team members so far) of our students go on to earn a Ph.D. That said, it's important to acknowledge them and their contributions. To this end, I am sure to acknowledge them by name in my published works and I have a dedicated space on my website (https://www.juliamarinhellwege.com/research-team), which also provides a level of legitimacy the students can point to in their resumes. I had not realized prior to hiring student research assistants that simply including them on projects, and sharing my work and my tasks, allowed them to visualize more clearly how political science works in action.

Graduate Student Perspective

Serving as the only graduate student on a majority undergraduate research team is a balance of responsibilities and opportunities. Each member of the team has specific responsibilities they are tasked with completing. However, there is always an exception to the rule and in the case of our team, the exception is the graduate research assistant. I am often assigned the "extra" research responsibilities that otherwise would fall through the cracks. I am also given more opportunities related to working in a professional environment and how to apply research to my education and future career.

I've learned that timelines do not always meet reality and additional time may need to be allocated. Along with the "extra" responsibilities comes the need for strategies that can help ensure that all deadlines are met and tasks are completed. One such beneficial strategy is implementing sound time management, including prioritizing and scheduling tasks. Starting the semester off by noting important deadlines and time needed for completion allows for greater success on both team and class responsibilities. It is very important to communicate about class assignments to make sure those are prioritized and that time is protected. Exercising sound time management is one of the main challenges, but it helps to mitigate the effects of unanticipated tasks and ensures all work is complete with ample time to spare.

One of the most beneficial aspects of taking on additional opportunities is the ability to work in a professional environment prior to entering the workforce. Working under a professor who is one of the most active researchers not only in our department, but also on our entire campus presents ample opportunities for professional interaction. Her ambition and willingness to delegate allowed me to work with other professors and professionals in the field. For example, I had the opportunity to do some formatting and preparation for an edited book that required extensive communication with other scholars. As a member of the research team, I saw first-hand the massive amount of planning, communication, and execution that it takes to successfully publish a book. The experience surrounding preparing and formatting a book for publication is an outstanding learning process, but what was even better was learning how to coordinate, interact, and work with professionals in the field. Seeing how academics work together to overcome challenges, along with watching them capitalize on opportunities, has been an experience that I could only have by being involved in a research team.

Finally, working on a research team helped me realize how to apply our research to my education and future career. During undergraduate studies, it was sometimes difficult to know how to apply what I learned or how it would apply to a future career. However, as a graduate researcher, I have been fortunate to see the link between the team's research and my future career as a city manager. The research application is especially true regarding our team's emphasis on representation, as it has supplemented my MPA education and ensured that I emphasize equity in my future work. I also appreciated having teaching opportunities with undergraduate students on the team as it will help me in managing employees in the future. Graduate students, especially, should be able to clearly see the application of the lessons and perspectives in their future careers and endeavors. Overall, working on a research team has been one of the most impactful experiences for me, both professionally and personally. The ability to assist the lead researcher, while also leading undergraduate students, is an experience that you can only have on a research team. My advice is to ensure that all team members are passionate about research, are delegated substantial tasks, and are given opportunities to work together and problem-solve; the end result is impactful research, teamwork, and professional development.

Undergraduate Perspective

Working as an undergraduate research assistant can be a rewarding experience for any college student interested in growing their research skills and overall knowledge of political science. Both of us (Bess and Aaron) started on the research team with limited experience in research. In addition, Aaron was a first-generation college student who felt navigating college was both a challenging and alienating experience. That said, Bess also noted that coming in as a new person on the team, some of the students on the team had more experience and they knew what was needed to conduct efficient and successful research, which was somewhat intimidating. Sometimes the main difficulties for student research assistants are simply not knowing where to begin the research and not knowing what resources are available. That said, both of us feel this opportunity was about much more than the research skills we learned or an appreciation of the literature. For first-generation students in particular, being part of a research team offers an opportunity to seek advice, find a stable income, and make connections in the department. Those are otherwise difficult tasks when you have no concrete perception of a college experience. Simply put, it is hard for a train to advance when there are no tracks beneath.

As first-time research assistants, we found that learning the importance of working independently and managing our time well are keys to success. We learned that, especially when we first started, it was sometimes difficult to balance school, work, and research (even more if you have another job). It was helpful to schedule time throughout the week to work on each research assignment, e.g., working for 1–2 hours on the days with less schoolwork or fewer classes. While it was important to be empowered to do tasks independently, it could be somewhat overwhelming. Bess found the university library was an excellent resource and a good starting point. With the help of our librarian, she was able to acquire research materials through the Inter-Library Loan program that she was previously unaware of. She felt fortunate to have assistance from someone who was willing to communicate with her directly. However, there were some challenges as others did not accept her as a proxy. Ultimately, a balance between independence and guidance while working within the structures of the university is important.

Despite the availability of advising, some students find it hard to reach out to and relate to their assigned advisor. Having a position on a research team allowed us to build a relationship with a professor in the department who had a deep knowledge of scheduling and academic advising. A professor–student relationship like this is a vital tool for success as this person can become a mentor and an advocate (for example, as a future job reference). This is just one of the many peripheral roles a professor with a research team can take on. While having a research team is a reliable way to meet deadlines, start new projects, and further your research interests, we also saw it as a way to extend a lifeline to students who would otherwise be without guidance. Similar to finding adequate advising, a research assistant position can be a gateway into the department for many students. It can be tough to build connections with professors outside of the normal classroom setting. As research assistants, we were able to build a connection with our professor, but also get to know and sometimes work with other professors. Such a connection can lead to other opportunities, potential internships, and advising and mentoring. Moreover, those connections can help mitigate feelings of alienation and isolation.

College is expensive for most students who choose to pursue it. Regardless of financial situation, choosing to get a college degree comes with a considerable amount of financial stress, especially for first-generation students. The day-to-day costs of college are often hidden and sometimes beyond comprehension. Working as a research assistant helped us develop research, data collection, and writing skills, but it also reduced our level of financial stress. Offering paid research assistant positions may require a lot of effort in submitting for grants and doing paperwork, but a paid position can be a difference-maker, especially for first-generation college students, regardless of the amount. Beyond financial support, the opportunity to earn money in a relevant field is invaluable. It is important that the professor acknowledges the financial aspect and makes sure paperwork is completed at the start of the semester so that there is no delay in payment; a missed or reduced paycheck can make a big difference in paying for rent or other necessities.

When considering who to bring on to your research team, it is important to evaluate their research abilities, data experience, overall work ethic, and all of the standard evaluation metrics. But don't overlook or undersell first-generation college students or those with limited prior research experience and who are less likely to know or understand this opportunity. The benefits students, especially first-generation, gain from holding a research assistant position reach much farther than just research experience. A position can be a gateway to a prosperous future and a rewarding college experience.

Conclusions and Recommendations

Overall, working on a research team presents students with opportunities to build skills, lead others, navigate a professional environment, receive mentoring and advising, earn some money, and learn how to apply research to future careers. The combination of the lessons on conducting research, working on a team, and learning about representation and equity cannot be replicated in another format and our team has given us a perspective that will propel us into the future. That said, there are some lessons we've learned and changes we plan to implement to build a stronger team. Some of these recommendations come from our experiences, while others are suggestions noted by other social scientists using research teams or labs (see Bittner, 2021 for an excellent review of her Gender Politics Lab at Memorial University).

Perhaps most importantly, we recommend team leaders to be transparent and specific with your research team about your instructions and expectations. Setting expectations around hours and budgets provides a clear outlook to all of us as we find ways to manage to find an academic, professional, and social balance. Additionally, be thoughtful about the potential needs of your students that may go unexpressed. Depending on their level of familiarity with a given program or research area, students may be reluctant to admit they have questions, especially in a team setting. In this case, we recommend one-on-one check-ins, if not in-person at least via email. These check-ins allow students to bring forth concerns that they may not feel comfortable voicing in a group setting, and they also allow you to keep track of students' mental health in comparison to their workload.

As we've built our research team, we have developed the desire to formalize our activities, even if there is no dedicated space or budget. We are finding that creating more formal structures with more informal communication is a winning strategy. It is important to review university policy related to seemingly simple things like naming the group or creating a logo. In some cases, names such as "lab" or "center" have legal meanings tied to university support. Moving forward, we plan to incorporate more formal lessons for the full team. Adding short lessons on data and project management software will expose everyone to new tools and also help formalize the meeting and keep us on track. We highly recommend getting very organized on time management, particularly timesheets, by creating spreadsheets for the number of hours worked and hours remaining, and calendar reminders for submission. Discussing timekeeping and accounting as part of the meeting is an important lesson in professionalism. We are very open in our discussion about hours and budgets. This serves as a lesson for the students and alleviates some bureaucratic stress for the faculty member.

We recommend preparing a team manual and onboarding materials, something we have yet to do ourselves. As the semesters and years go on, we end up repeating (and forgetting) a lot of information, such as how to set up university employment, track hours, team culture, communications, and expectations. A manual will be helpful for faculty to manage bureaucratic tasks and help set a professional and supportive tone and will be reassuring to students who may initially struggle to work in and adapt to an organized academic setting. Another part of onboarding is building early rapport in the first meeting to create accountability and encourage communication between the student members. It may seem like a small gesture, but having mugs with our team name and going out for coffee for at least the first meeting, and for a meal at the last meeting, goes a long way for team building.

Ultimately, having open discussions, open agendas, and including the entire research team in all facets of the research process creates opportunity for professional interaction, academic growth, and research productivity. Overall, having a research team is a rewarding experience and establishing "ground rules" and structure while maintaining open communication and appropriate expectations ensures that the team, and the dream, work.

Reference

Bitter, A. (2021). Teaching research design: The gender and politics lab and reflections on the lab model for the social sciences. In D. J. Mallinson, J. Marin Hellwege, & E. D. Loepp (Eds.), *The Palgrave handbook of political research pedagogy* (pp. 205–214). Palgrave Macmillan.

CHAPTER 15

Making Contingency Work: Conducting Student-Engaged Research Off the Tenure Track

Alexis Henshaw

Contingency will be the new reality for many early career scholars in political science. As is the case in other academic fields, tenure-track employment has generally been on the decline. Data from the American Political Science Association (APSA) show a significant decrease in overall positions during a ten-year period, with the number of advertised jobs in political science declining by about 20% between 2010 and 2020 (McGrath & Diaz, 2021a). The decline in overall employment coincides with a rise in positions off the tenure track. Scholars entering their first position post-Ph.D. are now more likely to end up in a contingent position than in a tenure-track placement—a development that upends established notions of the academic career path (McGrath & Diaz, 2021b).

A. Henshaw (✉)
Department of Political Science, Troy University, Troy, AL, USA
e-mail: ahenshaw@troy.edu

© The Author(s), under exclusive license to Springer Nature Switzerland AG 2023
C. Butcher et al. (eds.), *The Palgrave Handbook of Teaching and Research in Political Science*, Political Pedagogies,
https://doi.org/10.1007/978-3-031-42887-6_15

A more coherent approach to understanding the landscape of contingent labor—and advising new Ph.D.s on how to succeed in contingent positions—is necessary. This chapter addresses how to blend teaching, research, and mentoring in ways that benefit both students and contingent faculty. It is my hope that it also offers opportunities for broader reflection on the future of work in political science. While "contingent faculty" is a term that can encompass a range of academic titles, including adjunct positions, post-doctoral researchers, visiting professors, and lecturers, my reflections draw largely on my own experiences, which include two years as an adjunct instructor, five as a graduate teaching assistant, and five years as a visiting faculty member at institutions of varying size, character, and resources.

My Journey to the Tenure Track

In my path to academic employment, I experienced work in several distinct contingent roles. First, I spent two years as an adjunct instructor at public, teaching-focused institutions. This occurred after I completed a terminal M.A. program in Political Science, but before beginning my Ph.D. I had a full-time job in a professional field at this time, so teaching as an adjunct was something I chose to do for professional experience, rather than as a primary source of income. Upon getting accepted to a Ph.D. program, I spent five years working as a graduate assistant while completing my doctorate. Finally, after finishing my Ph.D., I spent five years in "visiting" faculty roles at four very different institutions, including two small liberal arts colleges, a regional comprehensive university, and a private R1 institution.

Spending over a decade in contingent roles was not part of my life plan. The journey to the tenure track was particularly arduous during my five years as a visiting faculty member, when the realities of the job market demanded that I stay active in my research even while teaching a full-time course load, receiving little to no institutional research support, and moving to a new state every 1–2 years. Going through this experience showed me how ill-equipped many faculty advisors are to guide graduate students through a job market that has gone through rapid and fundamental change. As is the case with many graduate students, I had advisors who expected me to place into a faculty position before my dissertation was done. Once I left the institution, they felt their job as mentors was done. As a visiting faculty member, then, I was largely left on my own to make contingency work in ways that might get me to the tenure track—a goal I ultimately accomplished. It is my hope that this chapter might help others find ways to align teaching and research to serve their own career goals.

Making Contingency Work: Choosing a Project

For contingent faculty, choosing a project to work on with students involves several considerations. On the one hand, collaborative projects should be of mutual benefit. This means you will want to consider from a pedagogical perspective how your project might serve the overall learning goals of your course (if you are indeed working with students you currently teach). Time is another important consideration. If you are in a time-delimited post, like a visiting professorship, you may only have 1 to 2 years working at the same institutions as your students. Increasingly, this timeline is not sufficient to span the life cycle of a peer-reviewed journal article. This also introduces questions about your own ability to commit to a project. As faculty in a contingent position, there's nothing wrong with reflecting on your own boundaries regarding emotional labor and time commitments outside a formal contract. Are you personally willing to continue with a project that requires intensive supervision or mentoring, even after your contract has ended?

Table 15.1 offers an overview of how time and engagement concerns map onto the types of collaboration I examine below. This mapping is largely based on my own experience; it may, for example, be possible to have longer-term data work projects where students (once trained) require less oversight. But these arrangements invite discussion about pedagogical goals. If both you and your students are devoting more time to the project, how can you maximize learning outcomes during that period?

Table 15.1 Types of student-engaged research work

	Time required	
Instructor Engagement	Less	More
Less	Data Entry (Short-Term)	Data Entry (Long-Term)
More	Research Assistance	Co-Authorship

Data Entry

Of the collaborative projects discussed in this chapter, data work can likely be done in the least amount of time and with comparatively less direct involvement from the instructor than other forms of collaboration. I incorporated data work into a semester-long course in gender and politics at a liberal arts college in a class of about 20 students. This project came about more by chance than anything else. An NGO I was working with at the time had sent me some requested data, but it came as a series of reports and digital slides. To facilitate analysis, I had to convert this data to a spreadsheet. As my class that term was covering related material, I offered them the chance to do some data entry work for extra credit. The data work was completed in about a 3-week period during the second half of a 15-week term.

This project was in fairly low demand in terms of both time and instructor engagement. I benefitted from the fact that this group consisted of upper-division students, who already had familiarity with using a spreadsheet program. It also helped that the work involved simple data *entry* (i.e., recording data that was already quantified) rather than data *coding*. The latter would have required more training in terms of establishing coding criteria, training students on how to use those criteria, and checking their work. As it was, even in this data entry project I found several errors made by the students. My decision to make this an optional project for students was guided by my own sense that the work was rote and that it offered a somewhat narrow learning experience. We did devote some time after the project to a class discussion, in which students who took part had the chance to share what they had read in their reports and how it mapped onto topics in our course. That activity allowed students who did not participate in the data entry to hear about potential real-world applications of things they had learned. However, this discussion was confined to a portion of a single class period. If a faculty member has more time or a larger data collection project, an activity such as this could be sustained in the longer term. Still, data entry on its own can be less than exciting. Some additional engagement is needed to make it an engaging learning experience.

Working with Research Assistants

Working with students as research assistants may offer an alternative that provides opportunities for more intense faculty-student engagement and deeper learning outcomes. Depending on your arrangement with your institution, research assistance can also provide paid labor for the students who choose to participate in these activities. Indeed, your views on whether students should be paid for their research assistantship may structure whether or how the working relationship takes shape.

As a visiting assistant professor at a small liberal arts college, I had access to funding and was able to hire research assistants at two different periods. As contingent faculty, having access to departmental funds for research assistants is likely the exception rather than the rule. This can be one of the many things you ask about when applying for a contingent faculty position. For many liberal arts colleges, student-engaged research may be a part of the mission and there may be a willingness to make funds available. Alternatively—as was the case in my situation—departments may have standing funds available for research assistants. They may be willing to make these funds available to contingent and visiting faculty. In the absence of departmental funds, faculty can seek to cover research assistant wages using grant funds, if they believe funding is an ethical requirement. Unpaid research assistantships also, of course, exist and are a possibility if you believe that the mentorship or experience you are providing is its own reward.

Because I was able to access departmental funds to hire research assistants (RAs), certain aspects of the relationship were structured for me. I was able to hire my assistants for one semester at a time, had to follow some minimal guidelines in the hiring process, and was discouraged from hiring current students. In terms of work, there were few constraints on what tasks I was allowed to delegate. In practice, I mostly had the students find and summarize articles for literature reviews. One assistant also helped with planning and logistics for a research workshop I co-organized. As with most things, I felt I became better at hiring, using, and mentoring RAs over time. The first RA I hired was incredibly capable, though not necessarily interested in my research topic (women and non-state armed groups). As a result, the interactions sometimes felt transactional rather than truly like mentoring. The second RA I hired was much more enthusiastic and inquisitive about the subject matter. Moreover, the fact that I was able to involve her in organizing a workshop, even using funds to help her attend the professional meeting, probably provided her with a richer experience.

Contingent faculty must, of course, also consider their own needs and potential benefits in entering into such a relationship. It is important to stress that the most meaningful experiences with research assistants involve a tradeoff: *You* as the instructor must invest some time and energy into building the relationship—and that investment becomes more intensive the more involved you want your student to be. At the highest level of time investment, research assistantships may turn into co-authoring relationships.

Co-Authoring With Students

I had the opportunity to co-author a peer-reviewed article with a group of undergraduate students during my last year as a contingent faculty member, while I was on a one-year visiting appointment at an R1 institution (see Henshaw et al., 2019). Obviously, co-authoring while on a non-renewable one-year contract involved a lot of work and more than a little luck. First, I was lucky enough to be at an institution that was supportive of student-engaged research and which offered me the chance to teach a small, semester-long seminar on a topic related to my ongoing work. Second, I was fortunate to have an exceptional group of undergraduate students who were enthusiastic about the project. Finally, our group was able to find an outlet that was soliciting articles for a special issue on a related topic just as we were designing our project. We secured an invitation to submit a full manuscript to the journal before the semester was over.

Still, even with all of this working in our favor, we encountered obstacles similar to those other contingent faculty are likely to face. The first related to the timeline. While our course lasted 15 weeks (the duration of the spring semester), it took about a year and a half from the time we agreed to work on a group project to the time the article appeared in print. In that time, I changed institutions, which complicated things logistically. In the end, while all of my students shared co-authorship, their contributions necessarily varied. I can identify three distinct phases in the project, the first of which occurred while we were in class together, the second of which occurred immediately following the course, and the last of which involved the period between then and the article's publication.

The first of these phases was the most collaborative. Given the small size of our group, the students had elected early on in the term to do one group research project that we might try to publish, rather than smaller independent projects. I presented them with several options, but the choice to write on women's leadership in armed groups was theirs. Drawing on my past experience (discussed in the previous sections), I understood the importance of having a clear vision of the end product and a realistic understanding of what students could do in the span of one semester. While we were in class together, the agreement was that they were going to engage in some coding—starting from a partial data set I already had—and that they would each work on case study research that might be included in the final article. Because we were seeing each other regularly, we also built time into our class sessions to have progress reports and to share themes and commonalities across the cases they were researching. We built many of these thematic discussions into the analytical sections of the piece. Ultimately, this first phase of the research involved participation from all co-authors and left us with important building blocks including a data set, case studies, and analytical takeaways. It did not, however, leave us with a final draft.

The second phase, which involved bringing together the piecework, necessarily involved a smaller set of co-authors. Because much of the work had to be done after the end of the term and in the months following, I told the students their active contribution was optional beyond this point. While I got ongoing permission from all of the students to use their work in exchange for co-authorship credit, only a few of the students continued to actively help bring the draft together. This worked relatively well, as the students who continued with the project self-selected and were the most interested and engaged. Once the piece was submitted, the journal's workflow required the selection of a single corresponding co-author, and I took full responsibility for dealing with the process after that.

This process overall worked well, with a few caveats. I lamented that my students were not able to be more fully engaged throughout the entire process. The fact that I had moved to another institution was a hindrance, as e-mail was the only means of contact that I had with this group after I moved. At a large research university, faculty might have similar issues keeping in touch with students after a term ends. I had somewhat idealistically hoped students might get a closer look at the peer review/editorial process, but the logistics of meeting tight deadlines meant that—although I shared reviews, drafts, and correspondence with the team—I couldn't fully engage them in the process. I know that most of the students appreciated being part of the experience and were pleased to see their work in print. I also hope that each student *did* see their contribution in the final work, even if they were not part of writing the draft article. That said, it was bittersweet to me that we were unable to debrief as a group and celebrate together at the end of the project. Now, in the post-COVID-19 era, I would be more likely to plan video meetings or maybe an "article launch" celebration via video chat. Overall, though, this experience taught me that while co-authorship with students can be worthwhile, it still requires a great deal of time and energy, especially where parts of the project have to be done while student and instructor are at different institutions.

Conclusions

This chapter has offered an overview of how to make contingent faculty arrangements "work" by way of student-engaged research. One takeaway is that it is possible for contingent faculty and students to create meaningful and mutually beneficial work arrangements. Another is that faculty must navigate time constraints, resource limitations, and limits on their own emotional bandwidth in developing such projects. The preceding examples offer insight into what questions you might ask yourself in designing such a project. These may include:

- What work do I need done?
- What aspects of this project can students feasibly do?
- How much time do I have to invest in mentoring/training these students?
- How long do I want the working relationship to last?
- What forms of support are available, in terms of funding, equipment, access to materials, etc.?
- What is the benefit of this relationship to the student(s)?
- What is the likelihood of this work contributing to publishable research?
- Do I believe it is ethically important to pay students for their work, and what constraints might my institution place on funded projects?

This last point, about ethics, looms large in questions about contingency and work. Many contingent faculty are already in work arrangements that are ethically questionable. Time and resources, therefore, are a greater constraint for contingent faculty than for their tenured or tenure-track peers. Put bluntly, many institutions do not see professional development for contingent faculty as a worthwhile investment. Many do, however, see student engagement in research as a worthy goal. Candidates for contingent positions should plan to negotiate for resources up front and in strategic ways. Asking about possibilities for student-engaged research signals a candidate's willingness to engage in active learning and/or create opportunities for students. Resources like faculty-student interaction grants (to fund collaborative projects) or funds for research assistants may also be available to contingent faculty. There is space for colleagues and Ph.D. advisers to be allies in this process. As an adviser, do you know how to prepare students to navigate the contingent job market? As a colleague, do you know of pockets of funding to which contingent colleagues might be entitled? Could you open up new opportunities for contingent faculty-student interaction by sharing departmental resources? The nature of academic labor is changing and creating a culture that is welcoming for student-engaged research will increasingly mean opening space for collaboration between contingent faculty and their students.

References

Henshaw, A., Eric-Udorie, J., Godefa, H., Howley, K., Jeon, C., Sweezy, E., & Zhao, K. (2019). Understanding women at war: A mixed-methods exploration of leadership in non-state armed groups. *Small Wars & Insurgencies, 30*(6–7), 1089–1116.

McGrath, E., & Diaz, A. (2021a). *2020–2021 APSA EJobs report: The political science job market*. American Political Science Association. https://preprints.apsanet.org/engage/apsa/article-details/617310b764e2af043b0f58c8

McGrath, E., & Diaz, A. (2021b). *APSA graduate placement report: Analysis of political science placements for 2018–2020*. American Political Science Association. https://preprints.apsanet.org/engage/apsa/article-details/61649e5d8b620d1d574c4b7f (October 25, 2021).

CHAPTER 16

Using Survey Research as an Educational Tool: Cross-Cultural Lessons on How to Balance Research and Teaching

Alfred Marleku, Ridvan Peshkopia, and D. Stephen Voss

Research professors in political science face a worsening dilemma when it comes to reconciling their scholarship with their teaching. Cutting-edge quantitative methods have become increasingly specialized and technically

---

A. Marleku · R. Peshkopia (✉) · D. S. Voss
Department of Political Sciences, University for Business and Technology, Prishtina, Kosovo
e-mail: ridvan.peshkopia@ubt-uni.net

A. Marleku
e-mail: alfred.marleku@ubt-uni.net

D. S. Voss
e-mail: dsvoss@uky.edu

D. S. Voss
Department of Political Science, University of Kentucky, Lexington, KY, United States

© The Author(s), under exclusive license to Springer Nature Switzerland AG 2023
C. Butcher et al. (eds.), *The Palgrave Handbook of Teaching and Research in Political Science*, Political Pedagogies,
https://doi.org/10.1007/978-3-031-42887-6_16

demanding, whereas undergraduate majors early in their college careers arrive no better prepared to apply mathematics than their predecessors half-a-century earlier (Bergbower, 2017; Buchler, 2009). Exposing students to disciplinary research, yet doing so in a way that is educational rather than exploitative, has never been harder.

Yet reconciling the teaching and research missions, treating them as complementary rather than discordant, may never have been more important. College students increasingly find themselves underemployed after graduation, and in the United States they often carry significant debt. Employability pressures discourage the pursuit of liberal arts (Azizi et al., 2023; Jańczak, 2022; Krauz-Mozer et al., 2015). Embedding students in the research process is one way to enhance job-market preparedness and, therefore, increase the discipline's attractiveness.

This chapter offers one solution for reconciling the dilemma: involving students in survey research, ideally within a broader curriculum spanning topical and methods instruction. Drawing on our experience teaching survey research in varied contexts—in the Balkans and the United States, embedded in both methodological and substantive offerings, using in-person interviewing as well as telephones—we describe strategies for employing survey research as a teaching tool.[1]

Our Approach's Foundations

Practical interests usually drive students toward political-science programs. By confronting students with intimidating scientific abstractions, methods courses can pose an obstacle to their progress (Bergbower, 2017). Much of the pedagogical literature, therefore, concerns overcoming math anxiety (Buchler, 2009; Daigle & Stuvland, 2021; Rozgonjuk et al., 2020). The scholarship of teaching and learning (SoTL) offers numerous ways for instructors to teach methods (Fisher & Justwan, 2018; Kollars & Rosen, 2017; Murphy, 2015; Rom, 2015), such as scaffolding—advancing in complexity (Adriaensen et al., 2014) or toward quantification (Bernstein & Allen, 2013).

---

[1] Since the university where this research was based does not have an IRB, we followed human-subject protection guidelines consistent with the best international standards and in compliance with the APSA Ethical Guidelines.

Having students conduct research gives them a practical application for the esoteric concepts of scientific inquiry. Research-oriented classroom instruction allows students to participate in a project across its major phases (Huber, 2013, p. 11). Such in-depth experience increases confidence and develops core skills pertinent to employability such as critical thinking, collaboration, and digital-media usage (Elken & Wollscheid, 2016).

Research-oriented teaching can be more demanding than traditional instruction, but Druckman (2015) proposes one way to restore balance: incorporating into a course the instructor's own research projects. That way, students not only witness ongoing efforts at discovery (Druckman, 2015, p. 53), they gain a sense of satisfaction from participating in real-life scholarly efforts (Druckman, 2015, p. 54).

Such research-based learning need not be restricted to methods offerings. Both non-methods instructors and students enrolled in topical courses gain from the integration of substantive and methodological learning. Embedding research projects into coursework helps students improve their understanding of both theory and methods, compared to when those are taught in isolation, cultivating professionally valuable competence—and it enhances the teacher's professional development too (Lunde et al., 2020).

The main challenge to research-based learning is that publishable studies may require more than a semester. One solution is to have cohorts work with data gathered by their predecessors (Murphy, 2015). A more ambitious solution is to spread quantitative training across the curriculum (Slootmaeckers et al., 2014).

In sum, when pursuing our curricular innovations, we sought to align scholarship and instruction by spreading research-based learning across a curriculum, generating real-life projects (rather than student-assessment products) that spanned different courses and different student cohorts.

SURVEY RESEARCH SURMOUNTS CONTEXTUAL BARRIERS

Research-oriented teaching may be more difficult in political science than it is in "hard" sciences. Outside of elite programs, researchers rarely possess enough grant funding to employ undergraduate teams. Nor will most projects require the sort of engaging low-skilled labor— measuring chemicals, feeding salamanders—that integrates novices into bench science.

Student-level obstacles to research-based learning depend on context (Anson, 2021; Druckman, 2015; Murphy, 2015; Rom, 2015). American undergraduates might have heard that they must do more than earn high marks if they want a good job, but they hold relatively fixed expectations about what a legitimate workload should be; the average student gives a course perhaps two hours per week outside of class (Arum & Roksa, 2011). The evolving nature of research projects and the tendency for workloads to become unequal will offend American norms of predictability and egalitarianism.

In comparison, promoting research to students in the Western Balkans can be especially difficult. Yugoslavia's violent breakdown and Albania's troublesome transition to democratization left significant scars on the region's economic institutions, not simply on its educational systems. Specifically, while it's true that students will tend to lack necessary mathematical foundations (OECD, 2020), as they may in the United States as well, student-level obstacles to pursuing political-science research in the Western Balkans often are motivational, rooted in pessimism about employability. Balkan students need to be sold on the tangible merits of research experience, a task not aided by most institutions in the region (Azizi et al., 2023; Kollars & Rosen, 2017).

Teaching students using survey research provides a way around most such difficulties. First, students rightly perceive interviewing as not requiring an unrealistic time commitment or level of training. (They may leave to other team members the thornier sampling and post-survey technical issues.) Second, survey implementation allows students to "get away from the books" and interact with others, alleviating the sense of social isolation that homework can generate. Third, even untrained students can shape portions of the research design, cultivating a sense of ownership.

To better illustrate the benefits of survey-based instruction, we introduce in the next section one approach we have taken to magnify the benefits described above, an approach that evolved after numerous other experiments in research-oriented teaching.

Building a Research-Based Curriculum

We began experimenting with using students in survey research in 2008 when Peshkopia was assigned to lead a US-based International Migration course, with Voss as mentor. Together, they devised a project in which students conducted a face-to-face survey on immigration attitudes in the Ohio River Valley (Klette & Voss, 2018). We transferred that experience to the Balkans in 2010, when implementing a Swiss-funded research project on Balkan immigration attitudes. Peshkopia and Voss trained student teams recruited in Albania, Bosnia and Herzegovina, Montenegro, North Macedonia, Serbia, and Greece to collect public-opinion data, and involved the most-ambitious students in analyzing those data (Voss & Peshkopia, 2012).

Performing this field work over several years, we encountered two main obstacles: the exorbitant expense that comes from transporting students so that they could interview respondents in person, and the unreliability of student teams after surveys have been completed and the school term ends.

We tackled the latter problem first. Peshkopia and Voss, in 2012, conceived the idea of creating a digital platform for collecting survey data that could combine the interviewing and data entry into a single step (which also eases interviewer training). Peshkopia partnered with computer-science professors and students to create the Skuthi app, developed fully as the iziSurvey app under the aegis of Gjirafa.com, a digital company in Kosovo (Peshkopia et al., 2014). We then addressed the other difficulty by switching to mobile-phone surveys in 2015 using random-digit dialing. Operating in a region dominated by cell-based telecommunications and having access to proprietary software provided a low-cost way for students to give computer-assisted interviews virtually.

Student involvement originally either needed to be extracurricular or squeezed into a single course, but we started lacing survey research throughout the curriculum. We began with research-oriented teaching in political science methodology courses—which originally began in the third semester of our bachelor program but, following the advice of Bergbower (2017), later moved to the fourth semester—and then we added courses such as Political Behavior and Foreign Policy Analysis to the research process, because they appeared late enough in the curriculum that most students would be both well acquainted with major topics in the discipline and mature enough to tackle the esotericism and complexity of methodological concepts. Moreover, by the time they reach most of our research-oriented courses, students have begun to receive information from outside the university about job-market requirements; they are more receptive to the benefits of engaging in academic activity that extends beyond the classroom walls.

We train our students in the general concepts behind measuring public opinion in an intro methods course. However, conducting mobile-phone public opinion survey requires more (1) training in how to administer telephone surveys and (2) how to navigate the intricacies of our surveying digital platform, iziSurvey. One new concept, which turns out to be grasped by students easily, is (3) random-digit dialing (RDD). A second concept, also unfamiliar to students, is (4) experimentation, so we need to familiarize them first with the survey experiment as a concept, and then move to the steps they must follow in the software to assign respondents randomly to different treatment groups. We also train students (5) to overcome technological difficulties, (6) re-call respondents if the line fails, (7) assign later hours for interviews with respondents who might be busy at the moment, to avoid bias caused by workday availability, and understand the logic of (8) randomized response order and (9) conditional questions. Finally, we carefully train students in (10) research and survey ethics—the most important, for our purposes, being respect for the respondent and respondent's sensitivities, while also giving them (11) techniques for gently pushing the respondent along to get the interview completed. Although mobile-phone surveys tend to suffer low completion rates, over the years of applying them with our students, we have managed to reach a respectable 42–45 percent response rate, well above the 10–20 percent recommended as acceptable by the AAPOR Cell Phone Task Force (2010).

The next innovation came when Marleku and Peshkopia were able to institutionalize these curricular innovations while reforming the political-science curriculum at a private institution in Kosovo, University for Business and Technology (UBT). Starting in 2013, we spread survey research across UBT's program, harmonizing topical and methods offerings. Now courses such as Political Behavior and Political Analysis look like extensions of the methods sequence; topical and methods instruction have become reciprocal.

UBT's course offerings within this program operate like research laboratories, delivering three main components. A course first develops the *theoretical* foundations of a topic. Then students undertake the *practical* task of testing those foundations empirically with previously collected data, which gives students a sense of continuity with their predecessors. Finally, students either work on a *research* paper stemming from that analysis or engage in fieldwork collecting new data for later courses. The latter choice gives students access to additional, more-personalized, instruction in the intricacies of survey design and execution.

Benefits of the Research-Based Curriculum

Our research-based learning model avoids many difficulties caused by varying student interests. Individual interviews do not take long, so even students with limited commitment can contribute to the effort. The overall arc of the research does not rely on even a single student engaging in a start-to-end project because projects span multiple courses and extracurricular opportunities. Yet the program creates the opportunity for a student to do so: collecting data in one course, replicating it in another country as part of summer practicum, analyzing it in a second course, and writing up the research either as a culminating assignment for that class or as a capstone thesis for the degree. Dedicated students also have opted to continue their research outside of the curriculum, coauthoring with mentors. Students have presented those papers at international conferences, and some have published work in peer-reviewed journals (Peshkopia et al., 2018, 2019). Most students at least get their data-collection efforts acknowledged in published work, giving a verifiable achievement to place on resumes (Fisher et al., 2022; Hale & Peshkopia, 2021; Page & Peshkopia, 2022; Peshkopia, 2020; Peshkopia & Giakoumis, 2021; Peshkopia & Trahan, 2020, 2022; Peshkopia & Voss, 2016). Moreover, since most of our students become familiar with survey methods, some of them are daring to undertake survey research on their own. We as instructors have offered them our assistance and technology to set the process in motion, and also to link students up with each other for mutually beneficial collaboration (e.g., combining their questions into a single survey).

The positive outcomes do not end when the students finish working with us. Leaving aside the many past participants who chose to pursue graduate study, participants have gone on to relevant jobs at research institutions or in state agencies requiring data analysis. These successes have inspired other faculty members at UBT to embrace computer-based applications and led administrators to organize training programs in quantitative methods.

Benefits from research-oriented learning extend beyond the surface level, a claim we have documented empirically. During the 2021–2022 academic year, we conducted a survey with political-science students in 11 universities in three countries in the region (Albania, Kosovo, and North Macedonia). That survey included both UBT students who had started the methods curriculum (39) and those who had not (34), allowing us to compare them with students from the other regional institutions at the same point in their programs.

Table 16.1 offers t-test group comparisons between UBT students and students from other Western Balkans universities. The findings are encouraging. UBT students start out less open to math, statistics, and computers. Those three ratios flip for students who are past their third semester, differences that are statistically significant. Our research-oriented teaching/learning environment seems to alleviate student resistance to technical training.

One reason students express more openness to technical skill acquisition is that they may gain confidence in the training's usefulness. As the last row in Table 1 illustrates, students were asked whether they felt their studies were delivering practical skills that could lead to a professional life in political-science-related employment. Students early in the UBT program are not especially optimistic, but time in the UBT methods program leads to a significant difference. A second question related to knowledge acquisition showed a similar, if weaker, improvement.

Research-oriented teaching/learning also carries social benefits. The students grow closer together while collaborating, especially the ones who perform fieldwork outside their native country. Socializing with professors in informal settings demystifies academia. We've shown that student collaboration in research projects leads to greater student interest in research-oriented studies in political science (Marleku et al., 2022, 2023).

Not everything has been rosy. The first major problem with implementing a research-oriented curriculum comes with faculty-member limitations. As the department has begun to hire a few faculty members able and willing to lead students in research, more courses have been designed according to some form of research-oriented teaching. Now, courses such as Political Behavior, Foreign Policy Analysis, Global Politics, U.S. Foreign Policy, Comparative Policies of the Welfare State, Government and the Market, and Governing Quality use forms of research-oriented teaching/learning. However, this requires effort from both instructors and students beyond the traditional classroom meeting. Students sometimes enroll in our program unaware of its expectations, thinking that their workload will consist of listening to instructor lectures and taking notes for an exam. Those with inflexible obligations to family or outside

Table 16.1 Comparing perceptions of political science students from UBT with other Western Balkan students

	Fewer than 4 semesters completed				More than 3 semesters completed			
	UBT	The rest	Diff	p	UBT	The rest	Diff	p
Prefer theory-oriented studies in PS	5.29	6.33	−1.05	*	6.67	6.44	0.23	
Prefer philosophy-oriented studies in PS	5.03	5.80	−78		6.03	5.67	0.36	
Prefer history-oriented studies in PS	5.15	6.09	−0.94	*	6.03	6.00	0.03	
Prefer jurisprudence-oriented studies in PS	5.00	6.24	−1.24	**	6.23	6.28	0.05	
Prefer practice-oriented studies in PS	5.55	6.89	−1.35	**	7.52	6.54	0.98	*
Prefer statistics-oriented studies in PS	4.97	5.83	−0.86		6.93	5.71	1.23	*
Prefer mathematics-oriented studies in PS	3.58	4.67	−1.09	*	6.07	4.47	1.60	**
Prefer data-oriented studies in PS	4.91	5.76	−0.85	*	6.89	5.31	1.58	**
Prefer computer appl.-oriented studies in PS	4.94	5.99	−1.05	*	7.04	5.63	1.41	**
Prefer research-oriented studies in PS	5.77	6.26	−0.49		6.86	6.00	0.86	
Gaining skills for a professional life in PS	6.27	6.08	−18		7.46	5.97	1.49	**

Note * $p < 0.05$; ** $p < 0.01$

jobs complain about the research workload. Other students, acculturated to patronage-based Balkan norms, neglect the academic portion of our courses (despite explicit syllabus policies), expecting that fidelity to a professor's project guarantees high marks. Thus, we continue to seek the right balance between satisfying students who prefer hands-on learning and serving those who prefer traditional instruction. But on balance, our initial efforts have paid off, moving research from the fringes toward the center of our curriculum.

Conclusion

In our work as political scientists, we struggle to balance teaching and research. The obvious solution is to combine those missions, yet the discipline offers no consensus on how to conduct research-oriented teaching and no training in it—so most of us who pursue that pedagogical approach must figure it out as we go. Convinced that research-based learning benefits both students and society, however, we have been experimenting with it for more than a decade, first in the United States, then in the Western Balkans.

Students in the Western Balkans share one important trait with their American peers: a tendency to enroll in political science expecting a math-free environment. Therefore, teaching quantitatively oriented research methods must surmount individual-level hurdles in both contexts. Rooting our approach in survey-based research has proved an especially valuable tool under those circumstances. The technical demands allow us to serve students with wide variation in ability and interest, and the interactive nature of such research accommodates student social needs.

Shifting our experiment to the Western Balkans did bring benefits. The innovative nature of UBT allowed us to try something extraordinary—giving us sufficient access to ranking administrators to sell curricular reform, and sufficient flexibility to reorient our political-science program toward empirical inquiry. Attempting to transfer that technology elsewhere—such as back to the U.S. context where we started our initiative—would face a different mix of challenges and opportunities. Students may bring to a program greater motivation or training, but also fixed expectations about what teachers or courses may demand. Rigid curricula or extensive extracurriculars might interfere with in-depth research. A bureaucratized institution with more remote leaders might be harder to reform.

Given the changing occupational needs of social-science graduates in the post-industrial world, however, we hope that our experience encourages leaders within other political-science programs to consider attempting a similar transition. Nonetheless, we also acknowledge that high-level programmatic reforms may not be possible in most university contexts, and individual instructors may not have research needs easily shifted into the curriculum. Research-oriented teaching could work well in just one or two courses within the framework of any curricula, led by a couple of research-active scholars—which is what we did for seven years, before expanding it throughout much of the curriculum.

References

AAPOR Cell Phone Task Force. (2010). *New considerations for survey researchers when planning and conducting RDD telephone surveys in the U.S. with respondents reached via cell phone numbers.*

Adriaensen, J., Coremans, E., & Kerremans, B. (2014). Overcoming statistics anxiety: Towards the incorporation of quantitative methods in non-methodological courses. *European Political Science, 13*(3), 251–265. https://doi.org/10.1057/eps.2014.8

Anson, I. G. (2021). Goal orientation in political science research instruction. *Journal of Political Science Education, 17*(sup1), 403–420. https://doi.org/10.1080/15512169.2020.1791144

Arum, R., & Roksa, J. (2011). *Academically adrift: Limited learning on college campuses.* University of Chicago Press.

Azizi, A., Marleku, A., & Peshkopia, R. (2023). The disruptive role of private higher education in the Western Balkans. In S. Edwards & J. Masterson (Eds.), *Government response to disruptive innovation: Perspectives and xxaminations* (pp. 36–57). IGI Global.

Bergbower, M. L. (2017). When are students ready for research methods? A curriculum mapping argument for the political science major. *Journal of Political Science Education, 13*(2), 200–210. https://doi.org/10.1080/15512169.2017.1292917

Bernstein, J. L., & Allen, B. T. (2013). Overcoming methods anxiety: Qualitative first, quantitative next, frequent feedback along the way. *Journal of Political Science Education, 9*(1), 1–15. https://doi.org/10.1080/15512169.2013.747830

Buchler, J. (2009). Teaching quantitative methodology to the math averse. *PS: Political Science & Politics, 42*(3), 527–30. https://doi.org/10.1017/S1049096509090842

Daigle, D. T., & Stuvland, A. (2021). Teaching political science research methods across delivery modalities: Comparing outcomes between face-to-face and distance-hybrid courses. *Journal of Political Science Education, 17*(sup1), 380–402. https://doi.org/10.1080/15512169.2020.1760105

Druckman, J. N. (2015). Merging research and undergraduate teaching in political behavior research. *PS: Political Science & Politics, 48*(1), 53–57. https://doi.org/10.1017/S1049096514001607

Elken, M., & Wollscheid, S. (2016). *The relationship between research and education: Typologies and indicators: A literature review.* Nordic Institute for Studies in Innovation, Research and Education.

Fisher, A., Hale, H. E., & Peshkopia, R. (2022). Foreign support does not mean sway for illiberal nationalist regimes: Putin sympathy, Russian influence, and Trump foreign policy in the Balkans. *Comparative European Politics, 21,* 152–175. https://doi.org/10.1057/s41295-022-00308-2

Fisher, S., & Justwan, F. (2018). Scaffolding assignments and activities for undergraduate research methods. *Journal of Political Science Education, 14*(1), 63–71. https://doi.org/10.1080/15512169.2017.1367301

Hale, H. E., & Peshkopia, R. (2021). Trump sympathy in the Balkans: Cross-border populist appeal. *Mediterranean Politics, 28*(3), 375–398. https://doi.org/10.1080/13629395.2021.1956775

Huber, L. (2013). Warum forschendes lernen nötig und möglich ist. In L. Huber, J. Hellmer & F. Schneider (Eds.), *Forschendes lernen im studium. Aktuelle konzepte und erfahrungen* (pp. 9–35). UVW, Univ.-Verlag Webler.

Jańczak, J. (2022). Political science research and teaching in Central and Eastern Europe: Shifting political contexts and academic interests in the 1990–2020 period. *PS: Political Science & Politics, 55*(3), 578–580. https://doi.org/10.1017/S1049096522000105

Klette, A. H., & Voss, D. S. (2018). *Why do higher levels of education lead to increased tolerance for migrants? Analyzing Kentucky survey data from the pre-Trump years.* Paper presented at the annual meeting of the Kentucky Political Science Association, Murray, KY, March 1.

Kollars, N., & Rosen, A. M. (2017). Who's afraid of the big bad methods? Methodological games and role play. *Journal of Political Science Education, 13*(3), 333–345. https://doi.org/10.1080/15512169.2017.1331137

Krauz-Mozer, B., Kułakowska, M., Ścigaj, P., & Borowiec, P. (2015). Political Science at the dawn of the 21st century. In B. Krauz-Mozer, M. Kułakowska, P. Ścigaj, & P. Borowiec (Eds.), *Political science in Europe at the beginning of the 21st century* (pp. 9–19). Jagiellonian University Press.

Lunde, G. H., Bakke, A., & Areskoug-Josefsson, K. (2020). Piloting a research-oriented teaching model in a bachelor program for social educators: A way to increase competence in research methodology and sexual health? *Uniped, 43*(3), 260–74. https://doi.org/10.18261/issn.1893-8981-2020-03-08

Marleku, A., Peshkopia, R., & Voss, D. S. (2022). Research-oriented studies in political science: How research collaboration shapes Southeast European student learning preferences. In *11th International Conference on Business, Technology and Innovation 2022* (p. 199). UBT Press.

Marleku, A., Peshkopia, R., & Voss, D. S. (2023). Research-oriented studies in political science: How research collaboration shapes Southeast European student learning preferences. *Journal of Political Science Education* Online first. https://doi.org/10.1080/15512169.2023.2196023

Murphy, C. (2015). The use of peer modeling to increase self-efficacy in research methods courses. *Journal of Political Science Education*, 11(1), 78–93. https://doi.org/10.1080/15512169.2014.985107

OECD. (2020). *Education in the Western Balkans: Insights from PISA*. OECD.

Page, D., & Peshkopia, R. (2022). Blurring lines of responsibility: How institutional context affects citizen biases regarding policy problems. *Political Studies Review*, 20(1), 148–157. https://doi.org/10.1177/1478929920982871

Peshkopia, R. (2020). An ally to the people: EU membership conditionality and Albanians' attitudes toward EU membership. *European Societies*, 22(2), 266–289. https://doi.org/10.1080/14616696.2019.1660393

Peshkopia, R., Arifi, A., & Sheqiri, G. (2019). The role of personality traits and political trust in people's attitudes toward EU membership. *European Politics and Society*, 21(4), 452–469. https://doi.org/10.1080/23745118.2019.1672357

Peshkopia, R., Cahani, M., Cahani, F., & Voss, D. S. (2014). SKUTHI: Developing a tablet-based survey technology and its application in teaching research methods in social sciences. *Applied Technologies & Innovations*, 10(3), 91–100. https://doi.org/10.15208/ati.2014.15

Peshkopia, R., & Giakoumis, K. (2021). Nationalistic education and its colorful role in intergroup prejudice reduction: Lessons from Albania. *Southeast European and Black Sea Studies*, 21(3), 457–480. https://doi.org/10.1080/14683857.2021.1932161

Peshkopia, R., Konjufca, D., Salihu, E., & Lika, J. (2018). EU membership conditionality in promoting acceptance of peremptory human rights norms: A case study in Albania considering public opinion. *The International Journal of Human Rights*, 22(10), 1355–1376. https://doi.org/10.1080/13642987.2018.1556904

Peshkopia, R., & Trahan, A. (2020). Support for the death penalty reinstatement as a protest attitude: The role of political trust. *International Criminal Justice Review*, 33(2), 1–19. https://doi.org/10.1177/1057567720963158

Peshkopia, R., Trahan, A. (2022). Does the EU message impact public attitudes toward the death penalty in EU membership-aspiring countries? Lessons from Albania. *Journal of Contemporary European Studies* Online first. https://doi.org/10.1080/14782804.2022.2031136

Peshkopia, R., & Voss, D. S. (2016). The role of ethnic divisions in people's attitudes toward the death penalty: The case of the Albanians. *Punishment and Society*, 18(5), 610–630. https://doi.org/10.1177/1462474516644678

Rom, M. C. (2015). Numbers, pictures, and politics: Teaching research methods through data visualizations. *Journal of Political Science Education*, 11(1), 11–27. https://doi.org/10.1080/15512169.2014.985108

Rozgonjuk, D., Kraav, T., Mikkor, K., Orav-Puurand, K., & Täht, K. (2020). Mathematics anxiety among STEM and social sciences students: The roles of mathematics self-efficacy, and deep and surface approach to learning. *International Journal of STEM Education, 7*(1), 46. https://doi.org/10.1186/s40594-020-00246-z

Slootmaeckers, K., Kerremans, B., & Adriaensen, J. (2014). Too afraid to learn: Attitudes towards statistics as a barrier to learning statistics and to acquiring quantitative skills. *Politics, 34*(2), 191–200. https://doi.org/10.1111/1467-9256.12042

Voss, D. S., & Peshkopia, R. (2012). *Attitudes toward clandestine migration in nations along the Balkan Route*. Paper presented at the annual meeting of the Midwest Political Science Association, Chicago, IL, April 11.

CHAPTER 17

Partnering with Master's Students on Policy Research and Practice

Laila Sorurbakhsh

INTRODUCTION

In higher education, the pedagogical convention for doctoral students is to develop a research agenda, while the focus for master's-level students tends to lie more in enriching their subject matter expertise and in practical skill development. However, with a well-defined and blended curriculum, master's-level students can simultaneously invest in a research agenda *and* in translatable skills, to the benefit of both academia and the fields they intend to serve. Moreover, faculty adopting this curriculum can collaborate with students on topics germane to their own interests as they mentor students in the science of scholarship.

In this chapter, I present a pedagogical framework for master's-level students and faculty that satisfies both intellectual curiosity and a desire to develop professional competence, achieved through mutual collaboration.

L. Sorurbakhsh (✉)
Elliott School of International Affairs, The George Washington University, Washington, DC, USA
e-mail: sorurbakhsh@email.gwu.edu

Using the case of students studying foreign and domestic policy, I outline how traditional, academic approaches in designing research questions can be useful to the practice of policymaking. By applying the principles of scientific inquiry, students of public and foreign policy can not only become better policymakers themselves, but also push policy toward a more evidence-based approach. Faculty, in turn, can push themselves to think outside the "peer-reviewed box" to partner on such publications as op-eds, web blogs, advocacy briefs, and think pieces.

Section I outlines a step-by-step guide to teaching a blended curriculum of policy and research, where students gain applicable skills rooted in theories of change. Section II describes the deliverables that students can expect from their coursework and highlights how these deliverables can not only add to the faculty's own portfolio, but also demonstrate an effective bridge between the gap between academia and practice. Finally, the conclusion section outlines the implications and recommendations for applying research-based approaches to practical applications.

Section I: Teaching Policy as Scientific Inquiry

While socializing graduate students to academic norms yields better engagement and productivity (Weidman & Stein, 2003), it requires a delicate balance for master's-level students, who may not pursue academic jobs post-graduation. In fact, graduate students in applied fields such as public policy or international affairs may be more practically minded in the sense that the pursuit of knowledge stems from a career-driven focus (Hayter & Parker, 2019). As such, traditional academic approaches, if not presented as valuable and translatable skills, may not attract or interest students enough to invest in their development. However, faculty should not dismiss these students as potential collaborators; on the contrary, these students are in the very unique position to be pivotal in bridging the gap between research and policy. Moreover, fostering scholarship from policy-focused and practically minded students can be embedded in more traditional teaching approaches, if a few developmental milestones are emphasized. Indeed, studies reinforce that collaboration and active engagement leads to a deeper learning overall (Harris, 2010). I outline a guided approach to working with students to think of policy projects as academic research and reconcile the nuances of each into a clear and workable framework.

Acknowledge Tensions + Bias Training + Literature Review + Policy Hypotheses

Fig. 17.1 Part I: Teaching policy as scientific inquiry

Figure 17.1 outlines the steps and learning activities associated with the end objective of producing a collaborative, research-based work. The framework above includes acknowledging the tensions between research and policy, an introduction to how bias can influence results, how to synthesize relevant research into new and interesting questions, and finally, how to articulate arguments for further exploration. Below, each step is discussed in greater detail:

Objective 1: Acknowledge the tension between evidence and values. Treating policy as a scientific enterprise is not without its caveats (Fischer, 2003; Stone, 2012). First, policy practitioners are often bound by ideological or values-based constraints, if not bound by constituents who elected them to office (Ryan, 2022). Second, the ethics surrounding policy, particularly experimental or innovative policy, remain fuzzy, as without prior research some implications are only understood once policies are implemented (MacKay, 2020; Moore, 2020). Third, the policy landscape, until very recently, tended to be less concerned with the recommendations derived from academic research, favoring instead lessons learned from more subjective evaluations of past practices and experiences (Ryan, 2022). Thus, the remedy of reconciling these two interests and approaches lies in the merging of policy and research design, while paying special attention to the tensions and nuances captured in each. The initial step is acknowledging these tensions; that on the one hand, policy must capture "hearts" in order to be adopted and implemented, while research aims to capture "minds," providing a rationale for why adoption and implementation is a good idea. By paying special attention to these nuances, and appreciating when and where the approaches are the most valuable, students are able to ascertain the best contexts for their use and application (details on which will be discussed later in the chapter).

Objective 2: Bias training. The next step requires students to confront their own biases. Extensive bias training allows for students to see where ideas originate, both in academia and in policy (Hagiwara et al., 2020). This type of training is beneficial to both future practitioners and future scholars for the same reason: students are allowed the opportunity to challenge long-held individual or collective assumptions. Indeed, the underlying goal of scientific inquiry rests on this very practice: of first laying out previous assumptions, then proposing challenges, opposing evidence, or alternative causal stories to test whether or not the assumptions hold (Letherby, 2013). Through this lens, students are then empowered to investigate policy in a way that moves away from preferences rooted in long-held beliefs and dichotomous choices toward new, undiscovered territory—the "grey areas" of policy. Traditional research is no different; in fact, the scientific method aims for objectivity in inquiry, or at the very least, the mitigation and awareness of the scholar's own subjectivity (Letherby, 2013). Only then can the lessons learned through the study be thought to be the best generalizable practice.

Objective 3: Read scholarship, write literature reviews. As students think through policy dilemmas through this lens, the third step is to teach them how to read scholarly materials and glean relevant information from them. Reading, interpreting, and reporting on scholarly research is not a skillset that is traditionally developed outside of academia, and thus, students must be introduced to this style of writing. In terms of "hard" skills, students learn how to produce literature reviews where key variables, ideas, and approaches are discussed. An added bonus is that as students acquaint themselves with the standing literature in the field, they are also inadvertently acquainting themselves with research design. Each test and application of inquiry, both qualitative and quantitative, offers new insight on how to approach their own questions.

Objective 4: Present proposals as hypotheses. The fourth and final task is for students, once they have extracted meaningful clues from the literature and from case study analysis, to present their proposals as hypotheses. Presenting hypotheses is a natural step for academics but rarely a formalized requirement for practitioners (Howlett, 2019; Shulock, 1999). However, introducing policy proposals as hypotheses yields that same benefit: instead of *imposing* policy recommendations, the student rather poses the policy in question as an experiment within which sufficient data should be gathered reliably and ethically. The hypothesis articulates the expected outcome of the policy without asserting that the outcome is a given, and leaves room for learning and redesign as necessary. In addition, the thought process encourages the student to think through the means by which data would be collected to test the hypothesis, and in turn the logistics of the policy's implementation. Should the policy proposal, for example, hypothesize as to whether an increase in hybrid vehicles reduces carbon emissions, then the nature of the inquiry demands that some test of the question proceed before decisions on the policy's viability are made and adopted. In short, through the scientific process of inquiry, suggestion, and confirmation, students are able to assess policy outcomes through a critical lens and offer their recommendations based on evidence rather than their own personal beliefs.

This section outlines an approach to blending real practice with the academic process of research. With the pedagogical value of this approach now outlined, the next section offers tangible deliverables that can be produced from this line of inquiry, benefiting both the student and the faculty mentor. Starting with the hypothesis developed in Section I, Section II presents various options and applications for students to pursue their work in tandem with faculty interests.

Section II: Blending Student and Faculty Research into Practical and Academic Deliverables

Once students achieve a foundational knowledge of structured inquiry, faculty can cultivate students' eagerness to apply and implement their new skill sets by working with them to produce a deliverable that best suits their career paths. Students of foreign and domestic policy will be evaluated in professional settings on the strength of their ideas, the clarity of their writing, and how they present evidence for their arguments (Fischer & Zigmond, 1998; Sorurbakhsh, 2022; Stevens, 2005). Thus, students focused on producing such polished, publishable writing samples can rely on faculty to provide clear and constructive feedback. The faculty, in turn, can provide essential mentorship by aiding the student in scoping their research to fit in line with their profession, and in line with their audience. However, just as students needed some initial training to advance to this step, faculty, too, require some professional (re-)training in successfully scoping the results of their faculty-student collaboration.

Faculty trained in traditional academic settings will undoubtedly recognize the "publish or perish" mindset that guides how those in their profession view their academic success. Beginning with their own graduate journey, publishing in peer-reviewed journals takes precedence over nearly all other facets of academic life, as success in this area often dictates whether or not students land coveted tenure-track positions. However, those in the policy world (both academic and professional) often regard publications with diverse, societal impact measures (for example, pieces published for think tanks, media briefs and op-eds, web blogs, and advocacy pieces) in the same esteem as peer-reviewed journal articles and book chapters (Adie & Roe, 2013; Asknes et al., 2019; Langfeldt et al., 2020). As such, should faculty themselves be open and willing to collaborate on a variety of projects, the likelihood of publication increases. While collaboration on academic papers is still an option, again, the tight timeline mandated by master's degrees makes this option slightly less tenable. Figure 17.2 outlines the variety of deliverables students can produce alongside faculty mentors based on their career trajectories and what will be most impactful and useful in their fields.

Figure 17.2 lists potential faculty-student partnerships resulting in academic papers, grant proposals, advocacy briefs, op-eds, and policy proposals. The first step in charting a path to collaboration requires the faculty to assess the end-goals of their students. For example, rising graduate students may have just completed their undergraduate degrees, while mid-career level students may seek additional training for career advancement, as others may look to retool and make a career switch altogether. The scope of the collaboration can be focused based on each student's career stage and preferred post-graduate professional sector.

Perhaps the easiest, most natural partnership is between a faculty member and a student who wishes to pursue a doctoral program, in which case collaborating on an academic paper yields the highest reward. The training outlined in Part I of this chapter introduces the student to the research design process, and culminates with a hypothesis that students can then pursue through analysis. As such, faculty and students

Fig. 17.2 Part II: Blending research into deliverables

pursuing this option will need to develop a plan for how best to proceed through such an analysis. Given the time constraint, the ideal approach is for students to (a) complement the faculty's research agenda, and (b) supplement the methodological skills that are needed to carry out the analysis. For example, when interests of the faculty and student align, faculty lend their expertise as students can drive new perspectives on research. Charting a preliminary research design points to whether the student's qualitative or quantitative skills need to be buttressed by additional coursework, and with special permission, whether focusing on the collaborative project can also simultaneously satisfy course requirements. Here, the balance of producing a high-quality analysis within a tightened timeframe relies on the resources and data available. Thus, the collection of new data (and any resulting submissions to institutional IRBs) is discouraged.

For students who wish to work for NGOs, think tanks, or other research-focused institutions, preparing a grant proposal or advocacy piece would be most feasible, and no less rewarding than an academic paper for both student and faculty. While in the previous case, students perform an analysis of either qualitative or quantitative data, the grant proposal or advocacy piece only requires production of conceptual-level design. Beginning with the policy hypothesis generated in Part I, students can assess what types of information can be gathered to answer the question.

Often, students will find that the data available to accurately study their hypotheses either may not exist, be subject to restricted access, or exists in a form that can be improved upon. Whatever the status of the available data, graduate students and faculty might consider two opportunities to capitalize on potential grant funding or advocacy. The first opportunity is in describing the data archetype that would need to be collected to answer the question posed, and how the data could, in fact, be collected. Defining target populations, questions, and logistics (such as funds and personnel needed) creates an outline to a grant proposal aimed to support achievement of this project, and in the collection of the new and relevant data. The second opportunity lies in specifying what gaps in policy such an oversight has produced and advocating for the pursuit of such information to better inform existing practices. For example, challenges in studying immigration in the discipline of political science mirror the obstacles (e.g. language barriers, documentation, self-selection, access, etc.) that government agencies and advocacy groups face when trying to collect such data. A well-founded grant proposal to pursue collection of such information, where faculty could serve as principal investigators and continue to oversee projects even as students graduate, could help jump-start a student's career while also filling a major gap in the delivery of a public good. Likewise, advocacy groups rely on such think pieces when submitting white papers and briefs to influence policy outcomes in line with their core missions (Collins, 2018; Sorurbakhsh, 2016), thereby the student and faculty can provide a real-world application of their research.

Finally, for students who may feel constrained in their level of influence both inside and outside their current or intended professions, scoping the projects to fit a wide or general audience can still breed impactful collaboration. In such cases, concentrating on media briefs, blog pieces, or op-eds brings visibility to the work being done on the issue, including the professor and student's own work. Media engagement of academic research piques the broader community's interest and can be distinguished on resumes as recruitment efforts, reflections of scholarly prominence, and collaborative achievements attributed to the university. Indeed, new metrics such as "number of Twitter followers," or "h-index" scores evolve to incorporate the far reaches of academic impact (Sugimoto et. al., 2017; Weller, 2015), and should be interpreted to the broadest extent possible. Faculty who rely on outside funding for their research, or who need to fulfill service requirements as part of their contracts, can utilize these types of non-peer-reviewed publications to these ends, with the added benefit of both a speedy and pressure-reduced process.[1] Students can, in turn, call attention to these types of publications easily through references to the pieces in their cover letters and other application materials, as evidence of their contributions to their respective fields. Ideally, both faculty and students can leverage their own professional networks within this field to introduce each other to a wider compatible audience, who may also serve as references or collaborators on future projects.

Combined with the training outlined in Part I, scoping projects to fit the needs of the students results in a diverse deliverable set that is mutually beneficial to both faculty and student partners. Figure 17.3 illustrates the full process and the variety of results produced.

---

[1] Faculty should, of course, confirm that these forms of writing are supported by their institutions or tenure and promotion committees.

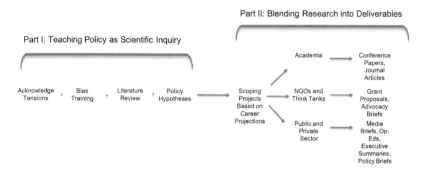

Fig. 17.3 Parts I and II combined: Training and scoping for optimal collaboration

Conclusion: Implications and Recommendations

The benefits of coupling the study of research and practice present themselves in numerous ways, both for faculty and for students. Students have the opportunity to design their own proposals, source funding, and institutional support, and shop their projects to audiences of their choice. For faculty, collaborating with students on their applied research can enhance the professor's own professional network, increase visibility of the professor's projects and affiliations, acquaint faculty with topics significant to their own research, and even result in conference participation, grant funding, and publications.

The key to such successful collaborations lies in (a) providing adequate but relevant training to students in the area of research, and (b) associating non-academic goals (such as policy influence or career motivation) with win-sets translatable across various facets of academic achievement. In these ways, students and faculty are rewarded for their efforts in mutually beneficial ways, while advancing a broader community of policymakers and academics alike. Indeed, such collaborations positively impact both the scholarly world and the policy landscape by addressing both theoretical and practical applications to research.

References

Adie, E., & Roe, W. (2013). Altmetric: Enriching scholarly content with article-level discussion and metrics. *Learned Publishing*, *26*(1), 11–17. https://doi.org/10.1087/20130103

Allen, H. K., Barrall, A. L., Vincent, K. B., & Arria, A. M. (2021). Stress and burnout among graduate students: Moderation by sleep duration and quality. *International Journal of Behavioral Medicine*, *28*(1), 21–28. https://doi.org/10.1007/s12529-020-09867-8

Aksnes, D. W., Langfeldt, L., & Wouters, P. (2019). Citations, citation indicators, and research quality: An overview of basic concepts and theories. *Sage Open*, *9*(1). https://doi.org/10.1177/2158244019829575

Collins, P. M., Jr. (2018). The use of amicus briefs. *Annual Review of Law and Social Science*, *14*(1), 219–237. https://doi.org/10.1146/annurev-lawsocsci-101317-031248

Fischer, B. A., & Zigmond, M. J. (1998). Survival skills for graduate school and beyond. *New Directions for Higher Education*, *1998*(101), 29–40. https://doi.org/10.1002/he.10103

Fischer, F. (2003). *Reframing public policy: Discursive politics and deliberative practices*. Oxford University Press.

Hagiwara, N., Kron, F. W., Scerbo, M. W., & Watson, G. S. (2020). A call for grounding implicit bias training in clinical and translational frameworks. *The Lancet*, *395*(10234), 1457–1460. https://doi.org/10.1016/S0140-6736(20)30846-1

Harris, M. (2010). Interdisciplinary strategy and collaboration: A case study of American research universities. *Journal of Research Administration*, *41*(1), 22–34.

Hayter, C. S., & Parker, M. A. (2019). Factors that influence the transition of university postdocs to non-academic scientific careers: An exploratory study. *Research Policy*, *48*(3), 556–570. https://doi.org/10.1016/j.respol.2018.09.009

Howlett, M. (2019). *Designing public policies: Principles and instruments*. Routledge.

Langfeldt, L., Nedeva, M., Sörlin, S., & Thomas, D. A. (2020). Co-existing notions of research quality: A framework to study context-specific understandings of good research. *Minerva*, *58*(1), 115–137. https://doi.org/10.1007/s11024-019-09385-2

Letherby, G. (2013). Theorised subjectivity. In G. Letherby, J. Scott & M. Williams (Eds.), *Objectivity and Subjectivity in Social Research* (59–78). SAGE Publications Ltd. https://doi.org/10.4135/9781473913929

MacKay, D. (2020). Government policy experiments and the ethics of randomization. *Philosophy & Public Affairs*, *48*(4), 319–352. https://doi.org/10.1111/papa.12174

Moore, G. J. (2020). *Niebuhrian international relations: The ethics of foreign policymaking.* Oxford University Press.

Nolan, R., & Rocco, T. (2009). Teaching graduate students in the social sciences writing for publication. *International Journal of Teaching and Learning in Higher Education, 20*(2), 267–273.

Ryan, P. (2022). *Facts, values and the policy world.* Policy Press.

Shulock, N. (1999). The paradox of policy analysis: If it is not used, why do we produce so much of it? *Journal of Policy Analysis and Management: The Journal of the Association for Public Policy Analysis and Management, 18*(2), 226–244. https://doi.org/10.1002/(SICI)1520-6688(199921)18:2%3c226::AID-PAM2%3e3.0.CO;2-J

Sorurbakhsh, L. (2016). Interest group coalitions and lobbying environments: Toward a new theoretical perspective. *Interest Groups & Advocacy, 5*(3), 200–223. https://doi.org/10.1057/s41309-016-0003-8

Sorurbakhsh, L. (2022). Translating social science skillsets for careers beyond academia. *Practicing Anthropology, 44*(3), 48–52. https://doi.org/10.17730/0888-4552.44.3.48

Stevens, B. (2005). What communication skills do employers want? Silicon Valley recruiters respond. *Journal of Employment Counseling, 42*(1), 2–9. https://doi.org/10.1002/j.2161-1920.2005.tb00893.x

Stone, D. (2012). Transfer and translation of policy. *Policy Studies, 33*(6), 483–499. https://doi.org/10.1080/01442872.2012.695933

Sugimoto, C. R., Work, S., Larivière, V., & Haustein, S. (2017). Scholarly use of social media and altmetrics: A review of the literature. *Journal of the Association for Information Science and Technology, 68*(9), 2037–2062. https://doi.org/10.1002/asi.23833

Weidman, J. C., & Stein, E. L. (2003). Socialization of doctoral students to academic norms. *Research in Higher Education, 44*(6), 641–656. https://doi.org/10.1023/A:1026123508335

Weller, K. (2015). Social media and altmetrics: An overview of current alternative approaches to measuring scholarly impact. *Incentives and Performance,* 261–276. https://doi.org/10.1007/978-3-319-09785-5_16

CHAPTER 18

Graduate Students and Learning How to Get Published

John Ishiyama

In this chapter, I discuss various approaches I employ in mentoring graduate students, particularly in terms of teaching them the research process and how to get published in academic journals. I focus on the stages of the mentoring process, from first-year students to developing a dissertation topic. Further, I emphasize how learning the research process not only helps graduate students progress in their theses and dissertations but helps them get published. In particular, I advocate the use of research groups of students that emerge from the scope and methods course, who I mentor as a group throughout their graduate careers. I focus on how I mentor students in getting published, first by observing how I write a published paper, then coauthoring, and then encouraging them to publish on their own. This is of mutual benefit to the students and the faculty member in as much as it helps the research productivity of all parties involved.

J. Ishiyama (✉)
Department of Political Science, University of North Texas, Denton, TX, USA
e-mail: john.ishiyama@unt.edu

© The Author(s), under exclusive license to Springer Nature Switzerland AG 2023
C. Butcher et al. (eds.), *The Palgrave Handbook of Teaching and Research in Political Science*, Political Pedagogies,
https://doi.org/10.1007/978-3-031-42887-6_18

A critical part of mentoring graduate students in political science and international relations is helping them understand the publishing process and especially how to get published for journal articles. There are several reasons for this. First, understanding the structure of an article helps graduate students understand a way of thinking regarding how to conduct scholarly research in political science. Becoming familiar with a "template" helps students organize their thoughts and understand the contributions of their research. Second, understanding the structure of an article helps students comprehend the writing of a dissertation. Indeed, many departments are moving toward an "article based" format for dissertations, where each individual chapter can be used as the basis for a journal article. This helps students get a head start in terms of getting pieces ready for publication (which helps them land an academic job and helps them get tenure and promotion). Third, understanding the journal publishing game helps them navigate the often-confusing journal publication process (and the seemingly unpredictable and arbitrary nature of editors' decisions). Knowing the game will help the students become more effective academic players and become more attuned to how to get published.

In the following sections, I first outline what I teach to graduate students in their first scope and methods class, which essentially outlines the basic features of a journal article and how to create an effective research design. This course helps start the process of helping to create scholarly thinking about topics. Second, I discuss how I help students cultivate a researchable project after the first year, which is then presented jointly at an academic conference. Third, I discuss the importance of graduate students having their work peer reviewed and the eventual moment when the student presents their own work and produces their own journal articles. I detail these steps below.

Getting Started: Using the Scope and Methods Course to Learn the Research Template

In most graduate programs in political science, there is a course dedicated to teaching students the fundamentals of the research process; this is often called "scope and methods" or "research design." It is in that course that the students learn what I call the "7 steps" of the research process. The course is designed based on the premise that the best way to learn how to conduct research is by doing it and gaining knowledge through successes and mistakes along the way. The focus of the course is on the production of a journal article by following a seven-step process:

- Step 1: Introduction/Problem statement
- Step 2: Literature review
- Step 3: The theory
- Step 4: The hypotheses
- Step 5: Project design

    a) variables, conceptualization, and operationalization
    b) data and methods

- Step 6: Results/analysis
- Step 7: Discussion/Conclusion

For the first step, students are asked to start with a general statement of research interest, which acts as the basis for the development of a research question. I ask each student to write down a topic they might find interesting to pursue, and then share that with other members of the class in our first meeting of the term. During the second seminar session, I randomly select students to tease out a researchable topic from the interest they expressed. This involves a series of questions posed to each student—what are they interested in generally? Are they interested in a particular country, and if so, what is it about that country that interests them? The fact they are a democracy? Or not? If they are interested in democracy, I ask them whether they are interested in why democracy emerges, or perhaps why there are different kinds of democracies? And then I ask them, what do you believe cause those differences? If they were to provide an explanation, I inquire what kinds of evidence they believe they would need to ascertain cause. This exercise has been quite effective in helping students begin to think of a researchable question.

Once the students have developed a research question, I ask them to think about how they might introduce this topic to a person who might read their paper. I ask them to write a short introduction in the form of a two-paragraph abstract, where they lay out what their project is about and most importantly, *why they are doing it*. I strongly discourage students from justifying their projects by saying they are "interested in the topic"— of course they are! So why restate the obvious? Rather, I encourage the students to think about a justification along the lines of (1) there is a gap in the existing literature; (2) there is a debate in the existing literature; (3) the existing work is flawed in some way; (4) they are extending the existing work to a new problem area. In essence, the course provides the students with a way of thinking about how to justify their work to a reader. This is a critical first step in the transformation of the student into a scholar.

After developing an introduction, we then turn to the development of the literature review (and its purpose to demonstrate to readers that the author is "up" on the literature, and that it helps set up the project). If they justify their project by saying there is a gap in the literature, the literature review should illustrate the gap; if the introduction includes a claim that there is a debate in the literature, then it should illustrate the contours of the debate. We then discuss the development of theory, hypotheses, as well as the design and methodology sections. Although we do cover the results and conclusion section, I emphasize the first five steps, because they constitute the features of a research design. By developing a research design in the scope and methods course, the student, hopefully, will have developed a project that could be completed if they chose to pursue it.

One way to illustrate the entirety of the process is to provide students with concrete guidance and an example that illustrates these steps, which students can emulate. For these purposes I employ a particularly useful textbook by Leanne Powner (2015), which provides step by step guidance for producing a research paper in political science. To "model" the research process, I go over a very well-written article (authored when he was a graduate student) by Bradley Epperly (2011). I use the article to illustrate each of the seven steps, and encourage the students to read the piece, less for content, and more for form. This has proven to be very effective in illustrating the "craft" of engaging in political science empirical research. Students identify the seven steps that appear in the article, and then we work through how the article addresses issues such as how to write an effective introduction; how to structure a literature review, how to construct a theory (and derive hypotheses), how to create measures (and walking them through some common measures we use in political science), how to present results, and how to interpret them. Finally, we discuss the elements of an effective conclusion.

Throughout the remaining part of the term, I use published articles to illustrate a variety of ways in which to collect data and engage in empirical research. These include papers that use experiments, field experiments, case studies, archival work, and a variety of quasi experimental statistical techniques. This helps illustrate the variety of ways one might conduct empirical research in political science.

Another purpose of the scope and methods class is to expose students to the variety of "tools" that are available to conduct empirical analysis, and talk about what tool is good for what "job." I introduce students to the "logic" of regression analysis (not doing it, but how it works conceptually, and how it allows controlling for alternative explanations for the dependent variable) and how we interpret results that are commonly reported in journal articles. This is because I think that the introductory scope and methods class should cultivate research literacy among first-year students. We also explore a variety of other models of regression, such as logit, multinomial logit, ordered logit, and hazard analyses (all conceptually) so that students will understand what these tools are for. However, we also explore qualitative techniques, such as process tracing (Collier, 2011), most similar systems and most different systems designs, case studies (Gerring, 2004; Lijphart, 1971), and Qualitative Comparative Analysis (Ragin, 2009).

Finally, given recent events involving the violation of research ethics in political science, another course discussion topic is research ethics. In this section, we cover issues of plagiarism and other examples of violating research ethics. We focus not only on general principles (Belmont Report, 1979) and discussing particular cases (Martinson et al., 2005; Singal, 2015; Van Norden, 2015), but also require students to undertake training sessions on plagiarism (offered by Indiana University online at https://www.indiana.edu/~academy/firstPrinciples/certificationTests/index.html) and complete a human subjects training course offered by my university. In this way, first-year graduate students receive instruction about how to engage in ethical research practices. By being aware of the need to engage in ethical conduct when engaging in political science research, particularly if they plan on using human subjects, this will forestall egregious violations of research ethics by students in the future.

From Students to Scholars—Learning the Craft of Presentation and Publication

Once the students have the basic tools to put together a research project, they are advised to approach a faculty member to help explore that topic further. Often times this initial project becomes the basis for their dissertation prospectus later. A few of them seek me out as their mentor, and once we agree on how to proceed with the project, I schedule weekly meetings with them. What results is the formation of a research group made up of usually 4–6 graduate students, which meets weekly over the course of at least one academic year, and often beyond. Although not all of our meetings are long (some are quite short), having regular meetings keeps the students on task and continually sharpens their skills.

I take students on as research mentees after their first year, i.e., after they have taken the battery of required methods and proseminar classes. Generally, I take on 4–6 students in their second year, and I meet with them individually to discuss what topics they would like to pursue. At first, we start with a paper, but generally, this paper forms the basis for a larger dissertation project. After meeting two or three times in the fall semester, I then schedule weekly group meetings that last about 90 minutes. During each group meeting, the student presents their paper to the group (at whatever stage of development it is in) and then the other students and I comment on their progress. I find that this continuous process of peer review helps students sharpen their thinking, which produces better projects. At about the same time, I add students to a research project that I or my coauthors will be doing in the fall, in preparation for a conference presentation. Although I am the lead author, I place the student as a coauthor, so they may attend the conference with me, experience the conference as an observer, and also get a line on their CV as a coauthor. The first time they appear on the paper, generally I write it up (they may have helped collect the data) and they are the secondary "observer-author" who largely free-rides. This way the author gently introduces the graduate student to the publishing process. It reduces the level of intimidation students feel when they first seek to get their work published. In many ways, this step is much like an apprenticeship, and a hand-holding exercise to first introduce students to publishing.

In addition to helping students produce research, the groups are also designed to help students navigate the program curriculum and also the profession. We often discuss issues that are part of the hidden curriculum and the unwritten rules of the profession, such as how to network with communities of scholars. For example, we provide guidance on how one can participate in organized sections and caucuses in our professional organizations, which is often a good way to make such connections.

After they have developed their paper projects over the course of their second year, we usually promote the presentation of the papers in departmental symposia, where other faculty and students can comment on their papers. In the fall of their third year, students write up their projects and present them at a professional conference. Usually, we target a smaller, more intimate, conference (such as the International Studies Association-Midwest conference, which has about 200 attendees, many of whom are graduate students). The student is now the first author, although I may "tag along" because I help the student with their methods and analysis. All the while, my research group continues to meet. The process of teaching the students how to conduct research not only benefits the students, but it helps me as a scholar. It promotes a synergy that links teaching research with doing research and is of mutual benefit to the student and the professor. It has resulted in many more publications for both the students and the faculty member.

In their fourth year, after the students have taken their comprehensive exams, they now are expected to present a paper in the Spring that is entirely their own (i.e., they "fly solo"). The paper project is designed to be one of the chapters of their dissertation, and once presented, they submit this piece for publication. I go over the process of submitting a piece to a journal with them, and what to expect after they submit. We use the journal submission process as a teachable moment, which they learn from regardless of whether their piece is accepted or not. If it is accepted, great! The first publication is usually a coauthored piece between the student and myself. The second publication, usually submitted by the end of their fourth year is a solo authored piece. This way by the time the student is ready to go on the job market, they have several entries on their CVs that make them very attractive job candidates.

It is important to remember that the entire process is like a pipeline. As one group of students matriculates out of the process, another group enters it. What is important is that each student receives continuous feedback from the faculty members and student peers. This does not involve harshly criticizing the student's work, but bringing up issues or questions that the student had not thought of originally. By putting the student on the spot, this also sharpens their ability to respond to questions extemporaneously, an important skill when making a research presentation, and especially a job talk.

Continuous feedback compels students to reflect on comments made and rethink their work—and through that process their work improves. In many ways, this is how I as a scholar learned how to improve my own work. Receiving feedback from my peers at conferences improved the quality of my manuscripts. My first drafts are generally horrible things. I am, however, a good rewriter, and after many revisions, the work becomes publishable.

But perhaps more important than faculty feedback is peer feedback. Feedback from peers does not fill the student with fear. Given the power asymmetries between faculty and students, students sometimes take faculty criticism as a signal that they did something wrong. On the other hand, feedback from peers is often viewed as less threatening and viewed as more constructive than critical. As a result, in my research groups, I encourage student presentations where fellow students provide feedback. I remain silent until after all the students have commented on the presentation. I may provide a few summary comments at the end, but the bulk of the discussion is carried out by the students themselves.

Although very intensive from the faculty member's perspective, mentoring a student project from conceptualization to publication is a great way to help students transform from students to scholars, from the ability to learn the process, to becoming a productive scholar.

Conclusions

In the above brief essay, I outline the mentoring practices I have adopted when showing my graduate students the process of publishing. As with all graduate programs, students must learn the basics of research design. However, the transformation process from student to scholar involves the early development of a project, followed by continuous peer review and feedback through ongoing research groups. This is the key to sharpening a paper into a publication. The group builds a support network of trusted colleagues, to whom the student listens for advice, not only about writing and research but about how to navigate the program and the profession. The mentor's role in this process is much like mentoring an apprentice; the faculty mentor takes the lead in the first projects, showing the student the craft of research. Only later does the student begin to fly solo, and that is when they complete their metamorphosis into a scholar. Over the years I have found this to be the most effective technique in mentoring graduate students who seek to become productive research scholars.

REFERENCES

Collier, D. (2011). Understanding process tracing. *PS: Political Science & Politics, 44*(4), 823–830. https://doi.org/10.1017/S1049096511001429

Epperly, B. (2011). Institutions and legacies: Electoral volatility in the postcommunist world. *Comparative Political Studies, 44*(7), 829–853. https://doi.org/10.1177/0010414011401226

Gerring, J. (2004). What is a case study and what is it good for? *American Political Science Review, 98*, 341–354. https://doi.org/10.1017/S0003055404001182

Lijphart, A. (1971). Comparative politics and the comparative method. *American Political Science Review, 65*(3), 682–693.

Martinson, B., Anderson, M., & De Vries, R. (2005). Scientists behaving badly. *Nature, 435*, 737–38. https://www.nature.com/articles/435737a

Powner, L. (2015). *Empirical research and writing*. Sage/CQ Press.

Ragin, C. (2009). What is qualitative comparative analysis (QCA)?. Retrieved September 15, 2021, from https://eprints.ncrm.ac.uk/id/eprint/250/1/What_is_QCA.pdf

Singal, J. (2015). The case of the amazing gay-marriage data: How a graduate student reluctantly uncovered a huge scientific fraud. *New York Magazine*.

U.S. Department of Health & Human Services, Office of Human Research Protection. (1979). *The Belmont Report: Ethical principles and guidelines for the protection of human subjects*. Department of HHS.

Van Noorden, R. (2015). Political science's problem with research ethics. *Nature*. https://doi.org/10.1038/nature.2015.17866

PART V

Research with Students: Experiential Learning and Civic Engagement

CHAPTER 19

Taking Community-Based Research Online: Benefits and Drawbacks for Researchers and Students

Rebecca A. Glazier

Community-Based Research (CBR) is a great way for busy scholars to engage in research that is helpful and meaningful to the communities with which they work (Bracic, 2018; Damon et al., 2017). CBR also presents an excellent learning opportunity for students, helping them grow personally and professionally (George et al., 2017), develop skills that are valued by employers (Bourner & Millican, 2011; Samura, 2018), and successfully graduate (Bringle et al., 2010; Yorio & Ye, 2012). The most impactful projects often involve direct engagement with the community and result in relevant and even actionable findings (e.g., Chow & Tiwari, 2020; Dawson, 2019; Ellis et al., 2022; Glazier et al., 2020). As CBR researchers share their findings with those they study, meet with

R. A. Glazier (✉)
School of Public Affairs, University of Arkansas, Little Rock, AR, USA
e-mail: raglazier@ualr.edu

© The Author(s), under exclusive license to Springer Nature Switzerland AG 2023
C. Butcher et al. (eds.), *The Palgrave Handbook of Teaching and Research in Political Science*, Political Pedagogies, https://doi.org/10.1007/978-3-031-42887-6_19

community leaders, and build relationships, many colleges and universities consider this work part of a faculty member's service load. Thus, CBR could potentially support the academic trifecta: research, teaching, and service.

Yet, most current CBR projects are conducted in person, leaving online students and online projects behind. As more students choose to take at least some online classes (Botsch & Botsch, 2012; Glazier et al., 2019; Seaman et al., 2018), having an online CBR option can expand access and make sure that online students have the same opportunities as students who take face-to-face classes, thus enabling online students to contribute as research assistants to CBR projects. Additionally, some CBR projects may want to incorporate online elements as a supplement to their in-person research efforts (Glazier & Topping, 2021), while other CBR projects may find moving online a necessity due to unforeseen circumstances, such as, for instance, a global pandemic.

What are the benefits and drawbacks of online CBR for researchers and students? How can busy faculty make CBR projects work best for them? We learned some valuable lessons when our longitudinal Community-Based Research project, the Little Rock Congregations Study (LRCS), was disrupted in 2020 by the COVID-19 pandemic, causing us to shift much of the project, and the corresponding research practicum course, online.

THE LITTLE ROCK CONGREGATIONS STUDY

Housed at the University of Arkansas at Little Rock, the Little Rock Congregations Study (LRCS) works with clergy and congregants in Little Rock, Arkansas to better understand the social, political, and religious impacts of faith-based community engagement on communities, congregations, and their members. CBR projects like the LRCS can be helpful for time-strapped faculty because they can support efforts in research, teaching, and service. In terms of teaching, courses designed to contribute to the project provide students with the opportunity to make connections between research and broader problems in their communities (Dawson, 2019). When this is done well, the resulting deliverables can inform policymakers, community organizers, and local leaders—and the creation and presentation of these materials is often considered service. Not only do students increasingly value these kinds of meaningful learning experiences that benefit society (Furco, 2010), they also often support university missions regarding broader social engagement (Nelson et al., 2019). Thus, CBR can have a "deep impact" on students, institutions, and communities, all while generating research findings that support publications for faculty tenure and promotion (Samura, 2018). With the right design and good oversight, an entire class of students working on a project for a semester can collect a large amount of data and make the kind of research progress that would be difficult for a Primary Investigator (PI) to make alone.

Since the LRCS project began in 2012, up until the 2020 data collection, over 180 undergraduate and graduate students conducted in-person research with clergy and congregants in Little Rock.[1] In preparation for 2020 data collection, we scheduled a research practicum course on religion and community for the fall of 2020. The onset of the pandemic in March 2020 made in-person contact unsafe and thus made it necessary to adjust our research plans, moving much of the project and the course online. Table 19.1 presents key differences across the different iterations of the LRCS, including in student researchers, data collected, and formats.

In prior iterations of data collection, students enrolled in similar courses attended worship services and community events, distributed paper surveys, and met with clergy face-to-face. The COVID-19 pandemic meant that being in the community in a physical sense was no longer an option for our students. Instead, we moved to electronic survey

Table 19.1 Comparative data from the Little Rock congregations study, 2012, 2016, and 2020

Study Year	Format	UALR Student Researcher N	Congregation N	Black Protestant Congregation N	Respondent N	Black Protestant Respondent N
2012	In Person	18	5	1	579	39
2016	In Person	16	17	5	1457	385
2020	Online	9	35	7	2293	102

[1] For more on the benefits of this specific CBR project to the students, faculty, university, and community, see Glazier and Bowman (2021).

distribution and sought to find creative ways for students to engage with the congregations and to foster community relationships online.

Doing Community-Based Research Online

Connecting online can be challenging. Humans are inherently social beings who connect more easily in person (Kock, 2005), where social and emotional cues are more readily available (Daft & Lengel, 1986; Marín-López et al., 2019). Knowing that doing community-based research, and building relationships with our community partners, online was going to be challenging, we adjusted our research design and course assignments to provide more opportunities to check in with students, return personalized deliverables to congregations, and increase oversight of student researchers.

Relationship-building with community partners needed to be more intentional as our interactions moved entirely online. Each student in the course was assigned to work with about four local congregations, which had been previously selected by the research team based on survey and interview responses from a population of 364 congregations in the city limits of Little Rock.[2] Thus, we were able to work with 35 congregations in 2020, a number the PI could never have coordinated alone. We designed an IRB-approved survey including religious, political, social, and community questions that clergy leaders in these congregations then distributed to their members.[3] At three key points in the semester, students provided written updates on their efforts to connect with the clergy and congregants at their assigned congregations through "congregation updates." They built connections electronically through attending virtual worship services, engaging with congregations' social media accounts, and offering help to clergy leaders via email. The students

---

[2] These congregations were selected to be both demographically and denominationally diverse, as well as representative of the city's religious population. They included 13 Mainline Protestant, 8 Evangelical Protestant, 7 Black Protestant, 2 Islamic, 2 Jewish, 2 Church of Jesus Christ of Latter-day Saint congregations, and 1 Catholic congregation.

[3] Our IRB approval covered congregation recruitment and promotion (Protocol #19–179-R1, approved December 19, 2019, with COVID modifications approved April 27, 2020), with survey distribution handled by individual congregations. Because congregations distributed surveys to their own members, we do not have denominators for the numbers of surveys distributed per congregation in order to calculate response rates.

also worked with faculty to design communication plans for the congregations, Frequently Asked Question (FAQ) sheets, timelines, and student researcher profiles. All of these resources were—and still are—housed on the project website (https://research.ualr.edu/lrcs/2020/09/22/congregation-resources/) and were distributed via email to congregation leaders.

These interactions provided great learning and professionalization opportunities for students, but how did moving online affect data collection? One way to assess the study's success in collecting data is the number of completed surveys: 2,293 across the 35 congregations. We can compare this to previous efforts in Table 19.1. Especially given the smaller number of student researchers and the new online format, this number of survey respondents is a strong signal in support of the research's success. More congregations were reached and more surveys were returned—yielding more data for the PI to analyze and publish from—than in previous iterations.

Another important assignment, and a deliverable to our participating congregations, was a personalized congregation report. Students used the information they learned about their congregations, together with survey data we collected, to help write a tailored report for each place of worship, which helped us connect with and strengthen our relationships with our community partners. An example report is available on the project website. We saw evidence of the value of these reports in the responses that we received from congregation leaders. As one leader wrote to us via email, "This is wonderful and a tremendous amount of work and information for us. Thank you for doing this and providing us with these reports. Lots of information for us to process!!" Another wrote, "This report looks so great, and has been so informative to read through, and I know it will give my leadership and me great help and direction in leading this congregation." The feedback from community leaders validates the quality of the research produced by the students and is one metric that shows how student researchers contributing to this online CBR project strengthened the project overall.

We also received specific feedback about the efforts the students made to build connections and relationships. As one congregation leader emailed to say, "Your students did an excellent job and were so helpful and conscientious during the process." Another one wrote, "I appreciate you and your team's work on this longitudinal study. It is valuable and will continue to be." When we distributed the final results via email, our community partners responded with comments like: "You're doing great work in our community!" and "I do trust that your good work will continue to bear fruit for our community." Thus, despite the challenges of making connections virtually during a pandemic, positive feedback from our community partners indicates that we often succeeded in strengthening these relationships. These external assessments of the researchers' efforts validate the benefits of online CBR and the contributions of the student researchers.

Additionally, moving online allowed us to collect new data we wouldn't have been able to get with paper surveys alone. Electronic surveys allowed for filter questions and skip logic, which made more advanced analysis possible once data collection was complete. And connecting with congregations via our project's social media page helped us gauge our reach into the community and growing impact (Glazier & Topping, 2021).

Recommendations for Online CBR Projects

The move online taught us a number of lessons, which we are using to inform the future of our LRCS project and which may be helpful to other CBR projects. Indeed, we previously found that supplementing our in-person outreach with digital connections improved credibility and response rates (Glazier & Topping, 2021), although our move completely online in 2020 had more mixed results. Following are recommendations for Community-Based Researchers who are considering online projects.

Humanize Electronic Interactions

Successful CBR projects prioritize building relationships with community partners, even for student researchers (Ryser et al., 2013), which is often easier to do face-to-face. Virtual interactions can serve as a good addition to in-person interactions, but when they are the only point of contact, it is even more critical that they be sincere and personal. Just as with online teaching, it is important that everyone get to know each other as real people (Glazier, 2021; Pacansky-Brock et al., 2020). For our project, that meant researchers attending virtual events with their cameras on, commenting on recorded sermons, and following up with a phone call when needed. Other researchers may want to hold virtual town halls, foster relationships on social media, or stay in close email contact.

Prioritize Clear Communication with Student Researchers

Some information is simply lost when relying on electronic communication alone. Student researchers may not understand key learning goals without the context that comes with body language, facial cues, and the opportunity to ask questions face-to-face (Daft & Lengel, 1986; Marín-López et al., 2019). Supervising researchers is important for any project that involves students, but it is perhaps even more critical when most of the research and the supervision is done online. Students need specific direction and opportunities to check back regularly and adjust. Assignments that require students to provide short updates on what they have been doing, how it is working, and what they plan to do to improve the relationship over the coming weeks can be quite useful. For us, periodic congregation updates helped accomplish this, as well as synchronous class meetings to discuss research progress. These check-in opportunities also gave the students ownership over the process as they made plans for how to continue to build relationships.

Sometimes There Is Just No Substitute for In-person Contact

In both 2012 and 2016, our surveys were distributed in person. By moving to electronic surveys in 2020, we were able to significantly reduce the logistical strain on our research team and to expand the number of congregations that we worked with (see Table 19.1). But we also noticed some decline in participation. Despite our best efforts, participation was significantly lower from Black Protestant congregations, compared to previous years of the study (see Table 19.1). We believe that the disproportionate decline in participation from Black Protestant congregations is at least partially due to our inability to foster relationships and build trust face-to-face; those relationships are especially important in communities of color where institutional trust is understandably lower (Hsu et al., 2014; Webb Hooper et al., 2019; Welch et al., 2007). For researchers studying online behaviors, like social media use or online health information seeking, digital relationships may yield more fruit (Lee et al., 2014).

Conclusion

Most Community-Based Research projects are conducted in person, but moving some or all of a CBR project online can expand research opportunities to new student populations and increase data collection. Doing so can be challenging, however. For our longitudinal CBR project, the Little Rock Congregations Study, which moved online by necessity as a result of the COVID-19 pandemic, we had mixed results. We met many of our goals as students participated in unique research, helped us recruit more congregations and respondents, and produced deliverables of value for the community. However, the limits of online relationship-building meant that participation by some congregations, particularly Black Protestant congregations, was lower than in previous iterations of the study. As one additional bright spot, using electronic surveys helped us produce personalized reports for each participating congregation, strengthening long-term relationships, and hopefully helping to improve future response rates.

While the LRCS is unique in its combination of longitudinal design, interdisciplinary content, and multimethod data collection, the challenges and considerations for moving a CBR project online are more broadly applicable. Although different projects may face their own unique trade-offs as they consider transitioning some or all of a CBR project online, thinking about how to best use online resources to facilitate CBR can be useful for many projects. Incorporating online elements can make CBR richer and potentially more successful as new community participants are brought in and more innovative communication platforms are utilized (Glazier & Topping, 2021). It can also make it possible for students who primarily take online classes to participate in CBR, which is a high-impact learning opportunity that can significantly improve their learning experience and chances for success. Online students can sometimes feel like "second class" students who don't have the same opportunities as students who take most of their classes face-to-face (Glazier, 2021). Providing some online CBR opportunities could help close that gap. As one student said in an anonymous course evaluation, "This course challenged me and I enjoyed it."

Although the COVID-19 pandemic disrupted our CBR project in Little Rock, Arkansas in 2020, it also provided us with the opportunity to incorporate online relationship-building into the project to a greater extent and streamline our data collection and management. In the end, students were able to contribute to and learn from the project, unique research findings were returned to participating congregations and the community as a whole, and the researchers collected more data than in previous iterations. Thus, this online CBR project supported all three areas of faculty workload—teaching, service, and research—making it an excellent investment of time for busy faculty.

IRB Statement

The research described in this manuscript was approved by the Institutional Review Board at the University of Arkansas at Little Rock: Protocol #19-179-R1, approved December 19, 2019, with COVID-19 modifications approved April 27, 2020.

COI Statement

The author has no conflicts of interest to declare.

Acknowledgements The author wishes to thank all of the student researchers who have contributed to the Little Rock Congregations Study over the years, as well as the community partners who have made the project a success.

References

Botsch, R. E., & Botsch, C. S. (2012). Audiences and outcomes in online and traditional american government classes revisited. *PS: Political Science & Politics, 45*(3), 493–500. doi:https://doi.org/10.1017/S104909651200042X

Bourner, T., & Millican, J. (2011). Student-community engagement and graduate employability. *Widening Participation and Lifelong Learning, 13*(2), 68–85. https://doi.org/10.5456/WPLL.13.2.68

Bracic, A. (2018). For better science: The benefits of community engagement in research. *PS: Political Science & Politics, 51*(3), 550–553. https://doi.org/10.1017/S1049096518000446

Bringle, R. G., Hatcher, J. A., & Muthiah, R. N. (2010). The role of service-learning on the retention of first-year students to second year. *Michigan Journal of Community Service Learning, 16*(2), 39–50.

Chow, E. H. Y., & Tiwari, A. (2020). Addressing the needs of abused Chinese women through a community-based participatory approach. *Journal of Nursing Scholarship, 52*(3), 242–249. https://doi.org/10.1111/jnu.12546

Daft, R. L., & Lengel, R. H. (1986). Organizational information requirements, media richness and structural design. *Management Science, 32*(5), 554–571. https://doi.org/10.1287/mnsc.32.5.554

Damon, W., Callon, C., Wiebe, L., Small, W., Kerr, T., & McNeil, R. (2017). Community-based participatory research in a heavily researched inner city neighbourhood: Perspectives of people who use drugs on their experiences as peer researchers. *Social Science & Medicine, 176*, 85–92. https://doi.org/10.1016/j.socscimed.2017.01.027

Dawson, R. S. (2019). Development of local geostories: Using data to improve community health and eenhance student learning about the social determinants of health. *Scholarship and Practice of Undergraduate Research, 2*(4), 43–44. https://doi.org/10.18833/spur/2/4/5

Ellis, B. H., Decker, S. H., Abdi, S. M., Miller, A. B., Barrett, C., & Lincoln, A. K. (2022). A qualitative examination of how somali young adults think about and understand violence in their communities. *Journal of Interpersonal Violence, 37*(1–2), NP803–NP829. https://doi.org/10.1177/0886260520918569

Furco, A. (2010). The engaged campus: Toward a comprehensive approach to public engagement. *British Journal of Educational Studies, 58*(4), 375–390.

George, C. L., Wood-Kanupka, J., & Oriel, K. N. (2017). Impact of participation in community-based research among undergraduate and graduate students. *Journal of Allied Health, 46*(1), 15E–24E.

Glazier, R. A. (2021). *Connecting in the online classroom: Building rapport between teachers and students.* Johns Hopkins University Press.

Glazier, R. A., & Bowman, W. M. (2021). Teaching through community-based research: Undergraduate and graduate collaboration on the 2016 little rock congregations study. *Journal of Political Science Education, 17*(2), 234–252. https://doi.org/10.1080/15512169.2019.1629299

Glazier, R. A., Driskill, G., & Leach, K. (2020). Connecting with community and facilitating learning through the Little Rock congregations study. *Metropolitan Universities, 31*(3), 22–43. https://doi.org/10.18060/23990

Glazier, R. A., Hamann, K., Pollock, P. H., & Wilson, B. M. (2019). Age, gender, and student success: Mixing face-to-face and online courses in political science. *Journal of Political Science Education, Published Online March 20, 2019*, 1–16. https://doi.org/10.1080/15512169.2018.1515636

Glazier, R. A., & Topping, M. P. (2021). Using social media to advance community-based research. *PS: Political Science & Politics, 54*(2), 254–258. https://doi.org/10.1017/S1049096520001705

Hsu, B., Hackett, C., & Hinkson, L. (2014). The importance of race and religion in social service providers. *Social Science Quarterly, 95*(2), 393–410. https://doi.org/10.1111/ssqu.12050

Kock, N. (2005). Media richness or media naturalness? The evolution of our biological communication apparatus and its influence on our behavior toward E-communication tools. *IEEE Transactions on Professional Communication*, 48(2), 117–130. https://doi.org/10.1109/TPC.2005.849649

Lee, Y. J., Boden-Albala, B., Larson, E., Wilcox, A., & Bakken, S. (2014). Online health information seeking behaviors of Hispanics in New York City: A community-based cross-sectional study. *Journal of Medical Internet Research*, 16(7), e3499.

Marín-López, I., Zych, I., Monks, C. P., & Ortega-Ruiz, R. (2019). Empathy, morality and social and emotional competencies in interpersonal interactions online. In M. Coetzee (Ed.), *Thriving in digital workspaces: Emerging ssues for research and practice* (pp. 217–233). Springer International Publishing.

Nelson, R. B., Yusef, K. M., & Cooper, A. (2019). Expanding minds through research: Juvenile justice and big data. *Scholarship and Practice of Undergraduate Research*, 2(4), 30–36. https://doi.org/10.18833/spur/2/4/10

Pacansky-Brock, M., Smedshammer, M., & Vincent-Layton, K. (2020). Humanizing online teaching to equitize higher education. *Current Issues in Education*, 12(2).

Ryser, L., Markey, S., & Halseth, G. (2013). Developing the next generation of community-based researchers: Tips for undergraduate students. *Journal of Geography in Higher Education*, 37(1), 11–27. https://doi.org/10.1080/03098265.2012.696596

Samura, M. (2018). Examining undergraduate student outcomes from a community-engaged and inquiry-oriented capstone experience. *Scholarship and Practice of Undergraduate Research*, 1(3), 40–47. https://doi.org/10.18833/spur/1/3/15

Seaman, J. E., Allen, I. E., & Seaman, J. (2018). *Grade increase: Tracking distance education in the United States.* https://onlinelearningsurvey.com/reports/gradeincrease.pdf

Webb Hooper, M., Mitchell, C., Marshall, V. J., Cheatham, C., Austin, K., Sanders, K., Krishnamurthi, S., Grafton, L. L. (2019). Understanding multilevel factors related to urban community trust in healthcare and research. *International Journal of Environmental Research and Public Health*, 16(18), 3280. https://doi.org/10.3390/ijerph16183280

Welch, M. R., Sikkink, D., & Loveland, M. T. (2007). The radius of trust: Religion, social embeddedness and trust in strangers. *Social Forces*, 86(1), 23–46. https://doi.org/10.1353/sof.2007.0116

Yorio, P. L., & Ye, F. (2012). A meta-analysis on the effects of service-learning on the social, personal, and cognitive outcomes of learning. *Academy of Management Learning & Education*, 11(1), 9–27. https://doi.org/10.5465/amle.2010.0072

CHAPTER 20

Combining Project-Based Learning and Service-Learning in Teaching Global Issues

Audrey Ruark Redmond

While preparing to teach a Global Issues course, I had an epiphany as I thumbed through the colorful pages of one of my daughter's books. It was a compendium of biographies that told the stories of remarkable women around the world. I couldn't stop thinking about how much information had to be synthesized and condensed to produce a single page that encapsulated the achievements of the women who filled the book. I began to wonder how I could recreate this research process in college courses. How could students use their time and effort to research current changemakers and inspire our local community with this novel approach?

I decided to employ a project-based, collaborative learning technique that required students to research and spotlight successes of modern

A. R. Redmond (✉)
Georgia Military College, Milledgeville, Georgia, USA
e-mail: aredmond@gmc.edu

© The Author(s), under exclusive license to Springer Nature Switzerland AG 2023
C. Butcher et al. (eds.), *The Palgrave Handbook of Teaching and Research in Political Science*, Political Pedagogies,
https://doi.org/10.1007/978-3-031-42887-6_20

women. Students worked in teams to explore a sub-topic that piqued their collective interest—women that lead, create, heal, innovate, and advocate. The teams condensed their research findings into a book—à la *Goodnight Stories for Rebel Girls* (Favilli & Cavallo, 2017) or *Herstory* (Halligan & Walsh, 2018). This student research was published and presented to local middle school students as a service-learning project. We know that active engagement leads to durable learning; i.e., when learning is deep and requires more effort the new knowledge we gain is grounded in the larger context, it sticks (Brown et al., 2014). Implementing collaborative project-based learning with a service-learning component requires just that of students—they are actively engaged in research and the service-learning is meaningful.

Collaborative Project-Based Learning

The American Association of Colleges and Universities (AACU) designates several evidence-based teaching and learning practices as "high-impact practices," or HIPs. One HIP, Collaborative Assignments and Projects (similarly known as Project Based Learning), gives students the opportunity to learn to work and solve problems in the company of others while sharpening their own understanding by listening seriously to the insights of others, especially those with different backgrounds and life experiences (American Association of Colleges and Universities, 2019). Additionally, the Buck Institute for Education (2021) details that "Project Based Learning (PBL) is a teaching method in which students learn by actively engaging in real-world and personally meaningful projects."

In my course, students worked in assigned teams to identify women currently making a difference in the world and to create a book that highlights their accomplishments and challenges. Women featured in this project are those who are fearlessly curious, don't hesitate to question the culture around them, and work to galvanize the path for women of the present and future. Each team produced a weekly two-page spread that included photographs, maps, and information on the individual featured. Students could not select well-known and researched individuals; they had to dig deep into current issues and organizations to identify women currently serving those around them. This task refined students' ability to research and compile information to be presented in a succinct manner. Teams had the responsibility of reporting on an individual improving the status of women each week during class. This collaborative assignment spanned the semester and had students creatively engage ideas about world culture and apply them to their local surroundings. Students were graded individually based on the work associated with their rotating roles and received an overall team grade on the final product. The end result was a printed compilation of the research that each team produced. This work was bound as a book and presented to a local middle school audience, to which they presented the printed class book and facilitated a workshop on the women and issues featured.

This collaborative approach to research placed authority in the hands of students to feature women who were not well known for their work. The purpose was to identify changemakers who had not yet received the spotlight for their work. The uncertainty of identifying good candidates for inclusion in this class book positions students well for making decisions in the real world. How do they decide (together) which individuals are important and doing good work, and how do they provide evidence? This approach pushes students away from the safety net of history books and into the wide-open world to determine how we identify those changemakers on our own terms (Hanstedt, 2018). Creating groups based on student interest was a critical element of success so that students connected course material to their long-term goals. Ensuring that students had a vested interest in the general area of their team research served as a conduit for community development among team members, a binding thread of sorts. The authors of *Learning That Matters* underscore that course design should motivate, challenge, and engage students. This field-guide for transformative cooperative learning offers solutions for common challenges to group work that were incorporated above (Zehnder et al., 2021, p. 127). The challenge of undertaking this collaborative project-based research project to benefit community stakeholders proved to be rigorous and fostered an environment to develop soft skills and deeper learning (Larmer, 2015).

Example of Assignment

Zehnder et al. demonstrate the importance of instructors designing group work to create "positive interdependence" so that students accomplish more working together than working independently (2021, p. 126). How can we do this well? By establishing clear expectations, abundant guidelines, and exemplary samples of past work. The assignment below details the project development timeline for a biweekly course that runs for 16 weeks.

Assignment Timeline

Week 5 Team Role Proposal Due.
Weeks 6–12 Weekly Project Development (by region).
Week 12 Final project due.
Week 16 Service-Learning Workshop.

Establishing Groups

The first step in creating positive interdependence was to cultivate a group environment with shared interests. In this particular course, I split students into five teams to complete the book project. Each team had a specific charge as to what types of individuals they would be identifying for the project. These team focus categories were based on the outline of *Herstory*:

Team 1: **Leaders**—Focus on Law, Governance, Conflict, and Politics
Team 2: **Creators**—Focus on Innovation, Technology, and Art
Team 3: **Healers**—Focus on Health and Environment
Team 4: **Innovators**—Focus on Education, Science, Sustainability, and Employment
Team 5: **Advocates**—Focus on Religion, Human Rights, and Family Dynamics

Figure 20.1, the team placement inventory, was distributed in the first week of class so that I could place students into appropriate groups. I created this document to aid in understanding student interests and to place them in groups accordingly. It was important to me to consider individual preferences and have students rank their preferred group so that the project felt meaningful to their goals and interests.

Establishing Expectations and Weekly Roles

Once the groups were established, students were tasked to complete a team contract and role rotation schedule. Figure 20.2 is the team role

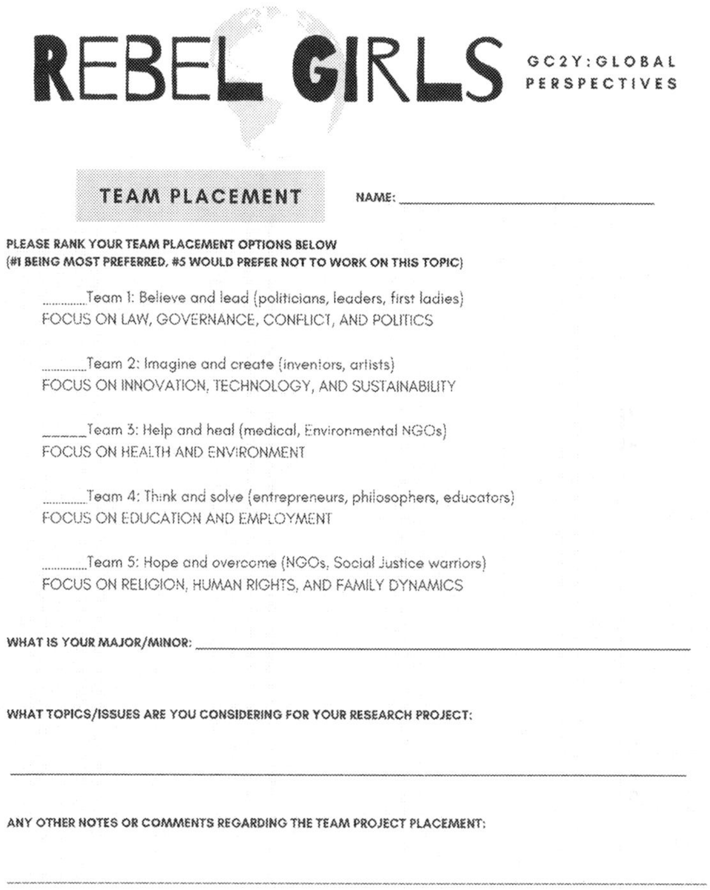

REBEL GIRLS
GC2Y: GLOBAL PERSPECTIVES

TEAM PLACEMENT   NAME: _____

PLEASE RANK YOUR TEAM PLACEMENT OPTIONS BELOW
(#1 BEING MOST PREFERRED, #5 WOULD PREFER NOT TO WORK ON THIS TOPIC)

............Team 1: Believe and lead (politicians, leaders, first ladies)
FOCUS ON LAW, GOVERNANCE, CONFLICT, AND POLITICS

............Team 2: Imagine and create (inventors, artists)
FOCUS ON INNOVATION, TECHNOLOGY, AND SUSTAINABILITY

_____Team 3: Help and heal (medical, Environmental NGOs)
FOCUS ON HEALTH AND ENVIRONMENT

............Team 4: Think and solve (entrepreneurs, philosophers, educators)
FOCUS ON EDUCATION AND EMPLOYMENT

............Team 5: Hope and overcome (NGOs, Social Justice warriors)
FOCUS ON RELIGION, HUMAN RIGHTS, AND FAMILY DYNAMICS

WHAT IS YOUR MAJOR/MINOR: _____

WHAT TOPICS/ISSUES ARE YOU CONSIDERING FOR YOUR RESEARCH PROJECT:

_____

ANY OTHER NOTES OR COMMENTS REGARDING THE TEAM PROJECT PLACEMENT:

_____

Fig. 20.1 Team placement inventory

proposal worksheet that I created to outline the basic details that needed to be decided: communication methods, information sharing platforms, procedures for additional meeting times, and specific role rotations.

Fig. 20.2 Team role proposal

Since the roles within each team were predetermined at the beginning of the semester and rotated weekly, students were able to discern the division of labor with less tension. Everyone on the team came prepared with an idea to pitch to the group at the first class meeting of the week. The team then decided on one influential person during that meeting for whom they were going to create a narrative. Teams referenced the role guide to determine who was responsible for each task to be brought to class on the second weekly class meeting. In determining the roles needed to create successful teams, Barkley et al., (2014, p. 86) served as an incredibly helpful resource. Their work thoroughly describes how labor is divided and suggests ideas for roles to be assigned. Each team was responsible for one entry each week (over the course of seven weeks), and the division of labor rotated so that each student had an opportunity to experience different elements of the production process. Team roles rotate weekly and include:

> **Fact Checker:** Finds resources, ensures accuracy, fact checks, ensures originality, sends bullet points to writer detailing resources used in weekly work
> **Writer:** Reviews fact checkers sources, writes the two-page narrative for the group, finds additional resources as needed
> **Editor:** Reviews writer's work for grammar and technical issues, reviews designer's work on Canva for formatting issues
> **Designer:** Finds or creates graphics, ensures copyright clearance, and formats the product on the class Canva template
> **Leader:** Keeps time, makes sure things are getting done, ensures communication among members, keeps other roles accountable, responsible for communicating needs/issues/questions to the instructor, presents the group's work at weekly check-ins, makes final decision in selecting featured individual, and ensures work is age appropriate for audience

Weekly Assignments

Once teams were established, they rotated the assigned roles throughout the duration of the collaborative project. One week was devoted to each continent of the world and students researched individuals in their topic area from that continent for inclusion in the course book. Groups completed seven total entries, each highlighting a different individual. After all four groups had completed their respective entries, all team pages were combined at the end of the semester into one document to form a complete course book. From this point forward, students devoted their energy into developing the service-learning program activities in which they showcased their collaborative research project.

So how, exactly, do you pull off the logistics of collaborative creative projects? Google Documents, or other shared document options, are a good place to start as students begin to compile and share research. Once the verbiage has been crafted, students will need to utilize a design and layout service to display their work. One option you might consider is Canva. Canva is a free tool to aid in graphic design. Though there are paid versions of Canva, the free option is sufficient for course use. Students can work in teams and synchronously edit the document, use templates to aid in cohesive formatting from team to team, and share easily with the instructor so that (if needed) the document version history can be accessed for assessment purposes. Utilizing a class book proved to be a successful and impactful learning assessment technique in gauging each group's weekly research (Barkley & Major, 2016, p. 248). Group submissions were graded weekly, based on contributions for each assigned role, and feedback was provided to aid with future iterations. Once the teams completed their chapter revisions, the document was downloaded as a PDF and compiled and edited with the assistance of an honors student who chose to take on additional work for honors college credit in the course. After researching options for having the books printed, Chatbooks was the most economical and expedient option for us to have a hard copy to distribute to students in the service-learning component of the course. We were graciously awarded grant funding by the university to cover the cost of the books which came out to around $20 per hardback book including shipping and processing fees.

Service-learning—Global Issues, Local Audience

Service-learning, also referred to as community-based engaged learning, provides field-based "experiential learning" with community partners as an instructional strategy. The AACU acknowledges that the key element of this approach is to give students direct experience with issues they are studying in the curriculum in conjunction with the opportunity to apply what they are learning in real-world settings and conclude by reflecting in a classroom setting on their service experiences (2019). Upon completion of the course book, students were left with a wonderful challenge—what purpose would this project serve if we didn't do anything with it? Students worked to develop and facilitate a community-based engaged learning partnership with 7th-grade students at Georgia College Early College (GCEC) to share the findings of their work and collaborate on how future changemakers might focus their efforts. By analyzing global issues in our local context, this project helped to build capacity for good among students and community partners alike.

One critical factor to consider when collaborating with community partners in service-learning endeavors is to ensure that the partnership is not burdensome for those it intends to serve. My students worked to handle scheduling, logistics, communication, preparing documents, and even visited classes before the workshop to introduce the topic. Student effort to detail was essential in avoiding undue burden on community partners (read: middle school teachers). Students developed Figs. 20.3 and 20.4 below to aid in the workshop as pre- and post-assessment worksheets. In the initial class visit, my university students asked the middle schoolers to think and respond to the following questions as a primer to the event.

1. What worries you the most when you think about issues happening around the world?
2. When you think about the people you look up to, what personality traits come to mind?
3. Think of two questions for the university students. What would you like to learn about?

These questions set out to get students thinking about leadership and issues that impact their world. Once they had reflected on these questions, they brought the worksheet with them to the event to complete. During the event, middle school students walked around to visit each college team and learn about their research. They completed the back of the worksheet to document what they learned during the event. After the event, the middle school students returned to their classes and completed the post-event reflection questions in a debrief with their teachers.

REBEL GIRLS

GC2Y/EARLY COLLEGE DAY

NAME: ______________________

TEACHER: ______________________

PRE-EVENT QUESTIONS

THINK ABOUT THE FOLLOWING QUESTIONS, AND RESPOND:

1. What worries you the most when you think about issues happening around the world?

____

____

2. When you think about the people you look up to, what personality traits come to mind?

____

____

3. Think of two questions for the GC2Y students (what would you like to learn about?):

____

____

____

WHAT TO EXPECT

The Georgia College GC2Y students are SO EXCITED to meet you! We will get together on December 3 from 11-Noon in the A&S Courtyard. You will see 5 tables where GC Sophomores are ready to teach you all about "Rebel Girls" (Women who are fearlessly curious, don't hesitate to question the culture around them, and work to galvanize the path for change - successful nonconformists).

You will walk around with this worksheet to hear about how these women overcame the odds to make the world a better place. **Take notes on the map** (be sure to write down the names and fun facts you find interesting from each area). Once you've made some notes, be sure to **ask any questions** you wrote down above, or any others that come to mind. Our time is short, and we would like for you to hear about 6 Rebel Girls, so **when you hear the bell be sure to rotate around to another group** (you will visit your favorite group twice).

POST-EVENT REFLECTION

THINK ABOUT THE FOLLOWING QUESTIONS, AND RESPOND:

1. What was the most interesting thing you learned?

____

____

____

2. What Rebel Girls stood out the most to you? Why?

____

____

____

3. What answers did the GC college students give to the questions you asked?

____

____

____

Fig. 20.3 Front page of service-learning pre-event handout for community partner

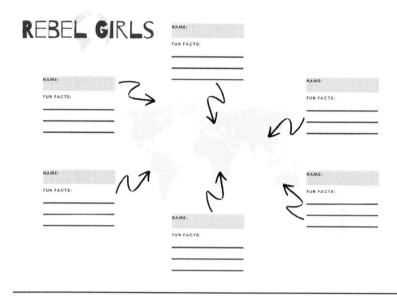

Fig. 20.4 Back Page of service-learning pre-event handout for community partner

Concluding Thoughts

I can remember sitting in classes as an undergraduate and lamenting over the material covered because I couldn't conceptualize the link between what we were learning and my "real life." As a result, one non-negotiable teaching practice that I exercise when executing this project is connecting students to the big picture of how skills developed through this work will benefit their long-term goals. I've noticed that when students develop a sense of purpose in classes, participation increases exponentially.

One of the best practices for in-class and out-of-class team time stemmed from supporting students through giving feedback and clear expectations. The Transparency in Learning and Teaching in Higher Education (TILT Higher Ed.) project is a national educational development and research project that helps faculty to implement a transparent teaching framework that promotes college students' success (Winkelmes, 2009). The TILT framework demonstrates that in courses where students perceived more transparency in assignment outcomes, significantly greater learning benefits were experienced (Winkelmes et al., 2016). I was strategic in my transparent design of the project by conveying the purpose of the project, explaining how the project linked back to our learning outcomes, identifying each required element of the project, creating a rubric to demonstrate how students would be evaluated, and including samples of past or aspirational work. Students knew from the beginning that roles would change regularly and had a clear picture of how their group assignment and the purpose of the project would benefit them in the long run. Research with undergraduate students can be exciting and impact their long-term trajectory when done purposefully.

While you don't need to teach a global issues course to use this framework of combining project-based learning and service-learning, my hope is that instructors will consider how the structure and reach of their pedagogy can shape student perceptions of course importance and will contribute to scholarly discussion about approaches to collaborative projects. It wouldn't be challenging to adopt a similar structure to any political science course and guide students to hone their research abilities, develop positive interdependence, and impact the local community in a positive manner.

This project also contributed to my own research agenda. Through researching effective evidence-based pedagogy, I was able to craft this assignment and contribute to the Scholarship of Teaching and Learning by offering best practices. My substantive research agenda examines the ways in which civic education and conflict converge. My work is interdisciplinary and integrates my academic background in political science, international affairs, and conflict studies with my interest in digital technology and global education. This teaching experience allowed me to connect my scholarly interests to the classroom environment while also offering an avenue for research and future publications of the outcome of this class project.

References

Barkley, E. F., & Major, C. H. (2016). *Learning assessment techniques: A handbook for college faculty.* Jossey-Bass.

Barkley, E. F., Major, C. H., & Cross, K. P. (2014). *Collaborative learning techniques: A handbook for college faculty.* John Wiley & Sons.

Brown, P. C., Roediger, H. L., & McDaniel, M. A. (2014). *Make it stick: The science of successful learning.* The Belknap Press of Harvard University Press.

Buck Institute for Education. *What is PBL?* PBLWorks. Retrieved January 2, 2022, from https://www.pblworks.org/what-is-pbl

Favilli, E., & Cavallo, F. (2017). *Goodnight stories for rebel girls*. Penguin Books Ltd.

Halligan, K., & Walsh, S. (2018). *Herstory: 50 women and girls who shook up the world*. Simon & Schuster Books for Young Readers.

Hanstedt, P. (2018). *Creating wicked students: Designing courses for a complex world*. Stylus Publishing, LLC.

High-Impact educational practices. American Association of Colleges and Universities (AACU). Retrieved September 28, 2019, from https://www.aacu.org/trending-topics/high-impact

Larmer, J., Mergendoller, J. R., & Boss, S. (2015). *Setting the standard for project based learning: A proven approach to rigorous classroom instruction*. ASCD.

Winkelmes, M. (2009). Transparency in teaching and learning in higher education project. Creative Commons License 3.0. https://tilthighered.com/

Winkelmes, M., Bernacki, M., Butler, J., Zochowski, M., Golanics, J., & Weavil, K. H. (2016). A teaching intervention that increases underserved college students' success. *Peer Review, 18*(1), 31–36. https://www.proquest.com/scholarly-journals/teaching-intervention-that-increases-underserved/docview/1805184428/se-2?accountid=11078

Zehnder, C., Alby, C., Kleine, K., & Metzker, J. (2021). *Learning that matters: A field guide to course design for transformative education*. Myers Education Press.

CHAPTER 21

Living Our Learning: Transformative Impacts of Study Abroad and Field Studies for Students and Faculty

Mark Hamilton and Katherine Almeida

Introduction

"Learning by doing" is an educational model celebrated around the globe and across centuries, with advocates ranging from Aristotle (2014) to John Dewey (1916) to Paolo Freire (1970). Prioritizing students' experience in teaching and learning allows them "to take ownership of the knowledge-acquisition process" (Glasgow, 2014, p. 526) and shift the faculty role to a facilitator or "trusted mentor" (Hamilton, 2019, p. 3).

M. Hamilton (✉)
Inter-American Defense College (IADC), Washington, DC, USA
e-mail: Mark.hamilton@iadc.edu

K. Almeida
William J. Perry Center, National Defense University (NDU), Washington, DC, USA
e-mail: Katherine.j.almeida-ramos.civ@ndu.edu

© The Author(s), under exclusive license to Springer Nature Switzerland AG 2023
C. Butcher et al. (eds.), *The Palgrave Handbook of Teaching and Research in Political Science*, Political Pedagogies,
https://doi.org/10.1007/978-3-031-42887-6_21

This chapter explores how a commitment to experiential learning—especially via academic field studies and study abroad—unlocks new forms of knowledge and expands learning and research opportunities for both faculty and students. The authors draw from shared experiences across multiple modalities in a unique academic program that includes extended study abroad, short-term field studies, and emergency "virtual" adaptations. Respectful interplay between teacher and student—and shared critical reflection on the desired outcomes—has enriched mutual learning and scholarship.

Differentiating Educational Experiences Abroad: The Long and the Short of It

Scholars of international education highlight the transformative impacts of student experiences based on the nature, time, and intensity of programs. In this chapter, focus is on "culture-based" programs (Engle & Engle, 2003, p. 4), developing students' cross-cultural relationships and multidimensional, socio-political appreciation rather than on "knowledge transfer" or "scientific exchange and the study of technological applications."

The same authors (Engle & Engle, 2003, p. 12) discuss five program typologies, ranked from least to most immersive: *(1) Study Tour, (2) Short-Term, (3) Cross-Cultural Contact, (4) Cross-Cultural Encounter, and (5) Immersion.* We consolidate these into two main categories based on the length of stay: *short-term field study* and *extended study abroad*.

Short-Term Field Studies as a Window to New Worlds

Short-term field studies open participants' eyes to new realities and create a window to alternative paradigms and ways of being. We refer here to trips lasting less than two months or as little as a week (Nguyen, 2017). Due to their relatively limited costs vis-à-vis more extended and immersive study abroad, these programs are popular among university students and comprise more than 50% of this international education sector (Engle & Engle, 2003; Iskhakova & Bradly, 2022; Sachau et al., 2010). Study abroad participation grew by more than 300% across the last three decades, but, in terms of scope, they still involve less than 2% of all university students (Bandyopadhyay & Bandyopadhyay, 2015; Institute of International Education—IIE, 2021).

Beyond the study abroad sector, educators discuss the value of historical/cultural "artifacts" in the classroom. This may include brandishing an ancient sword, handling a piece of pottery, or listening to a *samba* track, to facilitate student engagement and provide greater context (Citino, 2007; Hamilton & Jensen, 2021). A related methodology called "embodied learning" prioritizes physical movement to stimulate intellectual curiosity (Asher, 1969; Gardner, 2006; Hamilton, 2020; Kolb, 1984; etc.).

Field studies, among other learning benefits, integrate the value of both "artifacts" and "embodied learning." Transportation to new locations, even for a short time, allows students to experience a range of multisensory inputs, with exotic sights, sounds, and smells. Things "feel'" different as participants move and explore new "worlds."

Extended Study Abroad as a Tool to Engage New Identities and Narratives

Longer programs combine a key aspect of short-term field studies—engaging in a new setting as an outsider—with immersive elements of making a temporary "home." During a semester or yearlong program, students develop relationships in the host society and build lifestyle habits; finding favorite places to exercise, eat out, and meet with friends.

Regarding the impact of these programs, scholars highlight contributions to global citizenship (Tarrant et al., 2014) as well as multicultural awareness, language proficiency, leadership skills, and general academic performance (Hadis, 2005; Ingraham & Peterson, 2004; Zemach-Bersin, 2007). Still, measurement is a challenge, "Students returning from an overseas experience… report that it was a profound, even life-changing event. However, it seems to be difficult for students to articulate the ways in which they have changed" (Anderson & Lawton, 2011, p. 88).

Pagano and Roselle (2009, p. 229) employ the physics of light as a metaphor to explain knowledge development and personal growth among students: moving from simple "reflection" through a prism of "critical thinking" to produce the desired output of "refraction," which the authors refer to as "transformative knowledge." Immersive study abroad, particularly service-learning experiences, contribute to "refraction" in student learning. These experiences offer visibility to students' assumptions and incentivize their acknowledgment of relevant "knowledge gaps" (Murayama et al., 2019).

Case Analysis: Shared Experiences in a Unique Study Abroad Context

Reflecting (and hopefully "refracting") as co-authors, we acknowledge how short and long-term study abroad have contributed to our own professional trajectories, with enriching opportunities for personal and relational development, cultural competencies, and research innovations. We have played the roles of teacher and student in multiple countries and across varied institutions.[1]

One of our main shared experiences as co-authors is the educational partnership cultivated across several years at the Inter-American Defense College (IADC), evolving from roles of teacher-student to mentor-apprentice to professional colleagues, within an international, inter-cultural and inter-agency educational institution in Washington, DC.[2]

The IADC, operating under the umbrella of the Organization of American States (OAS) and Inter-American Defense Board (IADB), buzzes with diversity and foments daily conversations across four languages. Students from varied government sectors pursue graduate degree and build cooperative networks with future regional leaders (Hamilton, 2016, 2020; Taylor et al., 2020). This contributes to what Asada (2021) refers to as "knowledge diplomacy," creating relational bonds among diverse stakeholders.

---

[1] Prior to teaching at IADC, Dr. Hamilton studied at a semester study abroad program in Central America, based in Costa Rica. He returned years later as an intern and faculty member, building competencies in experiential education via service learning projects and short-term field studies with undergraduates. Critical reflections on a study trip to Cuba are explored in Hamilton (2001). Ms. Almeida's student-faculty narrative (on gender/field-studies) is discussed later in this article.

[2] Dr. Hamilton has served on the IADC faculty for more than ten years, and Ms. Almeida has played diverse roles: she was a student, nominated by the Dominican Republic as a diplomat. She graduated with distinction and then continued at the College as a staff member, supported by her country, serving as Assistant Faculty with increasing responsibilities across three years.

With the exception of a few students from the United States, IADC effectively operates as an extended study abroad program. Students in its one-year graduate program hail from up to fifteen countries, with an annual cohort of 50–70 participants. Approximately one quarter of graduates stay for a second year in a staff role, representing their countries and deepening their international experience. The College commits significant time to cultural exchanges by celebrating the national days of each student, organizing gatherings for spouses and families, and supporting participation in local sporting and cultural events. Time spent at IADC, in student or staff capacity, offers participants the opportunity to engage a wide range of American cultures, from the host nation where students "live" to deep engagement with peers from other states.

The IADC (2021, p. 50) prioritizes experiential learning in its curriculum via short-term field studies in the United States (US) and a multi-week study trip abroad to two or more other countries in the Western Hemisphere. These activities pair with a curricular commitment to working groups to support a pair of institutional learning outcomes, helping students "to develop professional relationships that reflect mutual trust and a spirit of inter-American integration" as well as build capacity for "collaborative responses to (shared) defense and security concerns" (IADC, 2021, p. 55).

In a recent survey of outgoing students (IADC, 2022, p. 11), 98% of them affirmed agreement with the former, and 100% with the latter learning outcome. This is consistent with broader trends in student feedback, faculty assessments, and employer and alumni surveys conducted at the IADC (2021). Reflecting on her own student experience at the College, one of this article's co-authors highlights the value of experiential learning activities in constructing faculty and student relationships that were "closer, more human, and in a sense, more real" than her prior classroom engagements (IADC, 2021, p. 56).

The Shock Wave of COVID-19 and Necessity to Develop Hybrid Responses

One of the most critical and unexpected challenges faced in recent years for higher education was the emergence of the coronavirus (COVID-19) pandemic, inducing limitations for all forms of presence-based classroom engagement and especially field studies and study abroad programming. The massive shock of COVID-19 more than halved the number of students involved in study abroad (IIE, 2021), and the sector is still in recovery.

At the IADC, local health precautions forced a rapid move to virtual modalities of instruction, and faculty worked to develop these capabilities and adapt course delivery. This is consistent with the experiences on other campuses and study abroad programs (Gaitanidis, 2020; Krishnan et al., 2021; Liu & Shirley, 2021).

When an international field study planned for execution in April 2020 was canceled due to strict quarantine restrictions in the US, faculty developed a group-based project for students to explore how a sampling of regional countries responded in the immediate aftermath of the pandemic. In lieu of a presence-based field study, we arranged targeted student meetings with global experts, IADC alumni, and action officers from each country, leveraging available online platforms to simulate a "normal" field study experience. Outcomes were quite positive for student learning amid adverse circumstances, as documented in Almeida et al. (2020) and Hamilton and Almeida (2020). Still, we concurred with the need to return to in-person instruction and presence-based field studies as soon as possible.

Planning a new academic year in the shadow of the pandemic, IADC prioritized in-person programming through major technology and infrastructure upgrades. Hybrid instruction served as a bridge until the entire student cohort could integrate with the class in Washington, DC, and, even then, students were required to wear masks in virtually connected auditoriums and seminar rooms to maintain social distancing.

These precautions and protocols allowed a study abroad experience to continue at IADC, even as most university campuses around the country moved 100% virtual. The unique learning outcomes of the College, its focus on international engagement, and the continued personnel investments by regional nations allowed for a rich, if altered, student experience. Short-term field studies remained virtual, with a few local exceptions, but surveys highlighted the value-added of any attempts for in-person field experiences.

The most recent cohorts to graduate IADC enjoyed a more "normal" experience, sharing one auditorium and working in more natural group settings, eventually without mask requirements and health checks. Some of the field studies and academic activities remained virtual; however, students were able to participate in a field study abroad, enjoying interactions with one another in both formal and informal settings.

The challenges of COVID-19 remain in play, evolving into an endemic issue to manage by higher education students, faculty, and administrators. Thus, the IADC and other institutions must seek an appropriate balance in the use of virtual, hybrid, and presence-based modalities, prioritizing the safety of campus stakeholders, while also leveraging the experiential learning value of study abroad and field study programming (IIE, 2021). This value includes the often under-studied benefit of these types of international activities: their catalyzing effect for faculty and student research.

Linking Study Abroad and Research Innovation: Lessons from Experience

For both of us as co-authors, the insights culled via field studies and study abroad experiences have been critical to our research initiatives and publication efforts, to include this chapter. The "window to other worlds" previously described for short-term trips and the "new identities and narratives" engaged for immersive experiences lend themselves to deepened critical reflection and openness to collaborative work and research.

In terms of collaborative work, the cross-cultural and interactive dynamic of study abroad programs feature oft-untapped potential in terms of research. Many education scholars have highlighted the role of engaged faculty for the success of these programs (Coryell et al., 2010; Paus & Robinson, 2008; Vande Berg, 2007; etc.). Others discuss the collaborative value of service-learning projects (Ducate, 2009; Pagano & Roselle, 2009; Tarrant et al., 2014). What is less discussed by many scholars are the possibilities of collaborative research as an output for faculty and students alike (Moseley, 2009; Shostya & Morreale, 2017).

Study abroad and field studies offer the physical and cultural space for faculty and student participants to challenge biases "through reflection, active learning, and placing ourselves in uncomfortable situations" (Strange & Gibson, 2017, p. 86). We develop new relationships, build new concepts, and feel new emotions amid the discomfort of cognitive dissonance. Drawing on the light metaphor of Pagano and Roselle (2009), a key challenge for faculty is helping students to move from "reflection" (sharing or mirroring their experiences) to "refraction" (creating transformative knowledge via critical thinking).

Returning to the IADC case study, we see significant collaboration and mentoring of students in research, but mainly after graduation. Students are not encouraged to focus on academic publishing during the intensive year shared on campus, in the community with families, and traveling with peers for field studies. Writing efforts focus on "reflective essays"—connecting academic content with students' experiences—along with group-based analyses of defense and security challenges/collaboration at the regional level.

After IADC students graduate, though, faculty prioritize research collaboration and mentoring for alumni. Many remain for another year at the College to serve on the staff, in direct contact with the faculty, as in the case of one of the co-authors. This offers a conducive environment for ongoing academic engagement and application of knowledge gained across the prior year. Other students head back to their countries to take on leadership roles, sometimes serving in academic roles at national war colleges, centers of strategic studies, or similar institutions. The IADC incentivizes alumni and staff research with an annual *Aureom Scriptor* writing contest, assessed by faculty members via blind review, and a growing Research and Publications division works with alumni (in-residence and abroad) as it builds up institutional partnerships across the Americas.

The permanent faculty works closely with alumni to support their writing efforts, encouraging them formally and informally in a continuing learning process and providing feedback for publications in regional outlets, including IADC's own *Hemisferio* journal. Faculty also collaborate with alumni as co-authors on book chapters, journal articles, and policy documents. Time together at the College provides a helpful base for such products, and virtual tools honed during the pandemic expand these possibilities. Co-authoring with alumni catalyzes a unique mentoring relationship and builds upon the mutual respect and experiences already cultivated in field studies and study abroad. Most recent faculty publications include contributions from former students, including the current article.

Conclusions and Lessons for Other Contexts

To recap, we have analyzed how short-term academic field studies and extended study abroad programs contribute to student learning and facilitate innovative research opportunities. Co-authors explored the unique institutional case of the IADC, which serves as a yearlong study abroad program, while also providing short-term field studies in the US and abroad. We also engaged the effects of the pandemic, in terms of an emergency shift to virtual learning and the impacts for international education. The main body closed with a discussion of how student engagement abroad helps to catalyze critical thinking, expression of new ideas, and potential for research collaboration among faculty and students (or alumni).

In terms of lessons applicable to other contexts, including undergraduate settings, here are four closing reflections (or "refractions") related to research collaboration:

1. *Experiential learning often plants a seed of interest, and faculty can water it:* Students who participate in field studies and study abroad often show more academic interest than their peers in areas related to their recent experiences. Faculty who are open to mentoring can help grow the buds of future research, for students and faculty alike (Giedt et al., 2015).
2. *Relationships matter, not only for positive student attitudes during the program, but also to set the stage for future research:* Those faculty who cultivate a safe space for students in study abroad programs—carefully balancing levels of comfort and discomfort—are also the most likely to be rewarded with students' critical engagement. Students who feel cared for by faculty members show far greater openness and expression about their learning experiences (Engle & Engle, 2003; Hamilton, 2001, 2020; O'Malley et al., 2019). They are more likely to step into the unknown, to "try on" new ideas, and eventually write about it, including conducting research with or without the assistance of their professors.
3. *Faculty engagement with students should not stop when the program ends:* Rexeisen (2013) observes a "boomerang effect" for many students upon study abroad completion: "The positive gains achieved while abroad may be lost, at least temporarily, after returning home" (Rexeisen, 2013, p. 178). This speaks to the critical importance of re-entry orientation, but also to the value of ongoing institutional and faculty contact with alumni after graduation from an experiential learning program. Cultivating alumni networks, developing internships, and incentivizing specific outlets for research collaboration, like those discussed for the IADC case,

create lasting bonds as well as interesting faculty-alumni publications.
4. *Contacts established by faculty through study abroad programming can open new avenues for their own research.* In addition to supporting students' and alumni research, faculty can leverage their own participation in academic programs abroad to build relationships with diverse subject matter experts, conduct field interviews, and deliver professional presentations, all away from one's home campus. Faculty can seek collaborative research opportunities with other professionals working in these areas, integrating students or alumni along the way.

To conclude, this chapter has explored how a commitment to experiential learning—especially via field studies and study abroad—unlocks new forms of knowledge and greatly expands learning and research opportunities for interested faculty and students.

REFERENCES

Almeida, K., Hamilton, M., & Pereyra Bordón, R. (2020). Un abordaje académico creativo a una situación compleja, llamada COVID-19. *Revista Guarnición: Ejército Nacional-Republica Dominicana, 22*, 84–85.

Anderson, P. H., & Lawton, L. (2011). Intercultural development: Study abroad vs. on-campus study. *Frontiers: The Interdisciplinary Journal of Study Abroad, 21*(1), 86–108.

Aristotle. (2014). *Cambridge texts in the history of philosophy: Aristotle: Nicomachean ethics* (R. Crisp, Ed.; 2nd ed.). Cambridge University Press.

Asada, S. (2021). Study abroad and knowledge diplomacy: Increasing awareness and connectivity to the host country, host region, and world. *Compare: A Journal of Comparative and International Education, 51*(4), 580–595.

Asher, J. (1969). The Total Physical Response approach to second language learning. *The Modern Language Journal, 53*(1), 3–17.

Bandyopadhyay, S., & Bandyopadhyay, K. (2015). Factors influencing student participation in college study abroad programs. *Journal of International Education, 11*(2), 87–94.

Citino, R. (2007). Military histories old and new: A reintroduction. *The American Historical Review, 112*(4), 1070–1090.

Coryell, J., Durodoye, B., Wright, R., Pate, E., & Nguyen, S. (2010). Case studies of Internationalization in adult and higher education: Inside the processes of four universities in the United States and the United Kingdom. *Journal of Studies in Higher Education, 16*(1), 76–98.

Dewey, J. (1916). *Democracy and education: An introduction to the philosophy of education*. Macmillan.

Ducate, L. (2009). Service learning in Germany: A four-week summer teaching Program in Saxony-Anhalt. *Die Unterrichtspraxis/Teaching German, 42*, 32–40.

Engle, L., & Engle, J. (2003). Study abroad levels: Toward a classification of program types. *Frontiers: The Interdisciplinary Journal of Study Abroad, 9*(1), 1–20.

Freire, P. (1970). *Pedagogy of the oppressed*. Seabury Press.

Gaitanidis, I. (2020). Studying abroad at home: The meaning of education abroad during the pandemic. *Portal: Journal of Multidisciplinary International Studies, 17*(1/2), 67–72.

Gardner, H. (2006). *Multiple intelligences: New horizons*. Basic Books.

Giedt, T., Gokcek, G., & Ghosh, J. (2015). International education in the 21st century: The importance of faculty in developing study abroad research opportunities. *Frontiers: The Interdisciplinary Journal of Study Abroad, 26*(1), 167–186.

Glasgow, S. (2014). Stimulating learning by simulating politics: Teaching simulation design in the undergraduate context. *International Studies Perspectives, 15*(4), 525–537.

Hadis, B. (2005). Why are they better students when they come back? Determinants of academic focusing gains in the study abroad experience. *Frontiers: The Interdisciplinary Journal of Study Abroad, 11*, 57–70.

Hamilton, M. (2001). Independence daze: Coming face to face with America's foes. *Re:Generation Quarterly, 7*(4), 22–23.

Hamilton, M. (2016). Juggling defense and security studies in the Americas: Challenges for international professional education and the case of the Inter American Defense College. *Hemisferio, 2*, 114–148.

Hamilton, M. (2019). Prioritizing active learning in the classroom: Reflections for professional military education. *Journal of Military Learning, 3*(2), 3–17.

Hamilton, M. (2020). Networks of power: A simulation to teach about durable inequality. *Journal of Political Science Education., 16*(1), 79–90.

Hamilton, M., & Almeida, K. (2020). Conclusion. In A. Colombo (Ed.), *Virtual OCONUS field study proceedings* (pp. 62–64). Inter-American Defense College.

Hamilton, M., & Jensen, B. (2021). Power of metaphor: Linking ideas to experience via story, symbol and simulation. *Journal of Military Learning, 5*(1), 57–68.

Ingraham, E., & Peterson, D. (2004). Assessing the impact of study abroad on student learning at Michigan State University. *Frontiers: The Interdisciplinary Journal of Study Abroad, 10*, 83–100.

Institute of International Education (IIE). (2021). *Open Doors report, 2021.* http://opendoors.iienetwork.org

Inter-American Defense College (IADC). (2021). *Self study report.* Prepared for the Inter-American Defense College (IADC) and Middle States Council for Higher Education (MSCHE), Washington DC.

Inter-American Defense College (IADC). (2022). *Class 61—End of year assessment report.*

Iskhakova, M., & Bradly, A. (2022). Short-term study abroad research: A systematic review 2000–2019. *Journal of Management Education, 46*(2), 383–427.

Kolb, D. (1984). *Experiential learning.* Prentice Hall.

Krishnan, L., Sreekumar, S., Sundaram, S., Subrahmanian, M., & Davis, P. (2021). Virtual 'study abroad': Promoting intercultural competence amid the pandemic. *The Hearing Journal, 74*(4), 38–39.

Liu, Y., & Shirley, T. (2021). Without crossing a border: Exploring the impact of shifting study abroad online on students' learning and intercultural competence development during the COVID-19 pandemic. *Online Learning, 25*(1), 182–194.

Moseley, W. (2009). Making study abroad a win-win opportunity for pre-tenure faculty. *Frontiers: The Interdisciplinary Journal of Study Abroad, 18*, 231–240.

Murayama, K., FitzGibbon, L., & Sakaki, M. (2019). Process account of curiosity and interest: A reward-learning perspective. *Educational Psychology Review, 31*(4), 875–895.

Nguyen, A. (2017). Intercultural competence in short-term study abroad. *Frontiers: The Interdisciplinary Journal of Study Abroad, 29*(2), 109–127.

O'Malley, A., Roberts, R., Stair, K., & Blackburn, J. (2019). The forms of dissonance experienced by US university agriculture students during a study abroad to Nicaragua. *Journal of Agricultural Education, 60*(3), 191–205.

Pagano, M., & Roselle, L. (2009). Beyond reflection through an academic lens: Refraction and international experiential education. *Frontiers: The Interdisciplinary Journal of Study Abroad, 15*, 217–229.

Paus, E., & Robinson, M. (2008). Increasing study abroad participation: The faculty makes the difference. *Frontiers: The Interdisciplinary Journal of Study Abroad, 17*, 33–49.

Rexeisen, R. (2013). Study abroad and the boomerang effect: The end is only the beginning. *Frontiers: The Interdisciplinary Journal of Study Abroad, 33*, 166–181.

Sachau, D., Brasher, N., & Fee, S. (2010). Three models for short-term study abroad. *Journal of Management Education, 34*(5), 645–670.

Shostya, A., & Morreale, J. C. (2017). Fostering undergraduate research through a faculty-led study abroad experience. *International Journal of Teaching and Learning in Higher Education, 29*(2), 300–308.

Strange, H., & Gibson, H. (2017). An investigation of experiential and transformative learning in study abroad programs. *Frontiers: The Interdisciplinary Journal of Study Abroad, 24*(1), 85–100.

Tarrant, M., Rubin, D., & Stoner, L. (2014). The added value of study abroad: Fostering a global citizenry. *Journal of Studies in International Education, 18*(2), 141–161.

Taylor, J., Pereyra Bordón, R., Hamilton, M., Garma, S., & Almeida, K. (2020). Evolución histórica/académica del Colegio Interamericano de Defensa. In A. Colombo (Ed.), *Simposio académico hemisférico: Prioridades para el diseño curricular en defensa y seguridad*. Washington, DC: Inter-American Defense College.

Vande Berg, M. (2007, Fall/Winter). Intervening in the learning of U.S. students abroad. *Journal of Studies in International Education, 11*(4), 392–399.

Zemach-Bersin, T. (2007). Global citizenship and study abroad: It's all about US. *Critical Literacy: Theories and Practices, 1*(2), 16–28.

CHAPTER 22

Using Exit Polls to Teach Students and Sustain a Scholarly Agenda

Matthew P. Thornburg and Robert E. Botsch

Political science faculty, especially those working at teaching-oriented institutions, face financial and practical obstacles to publishing peer-reviewed research. Faculty using quantitative methods to study American public opinion need datasets with sufficient statistical power to reach robust conclusions. Costs have risen dramatically with a public increasingly unwilling to answer surveys. While excellent survey datasets such as the American National Election Studies or Cooperative Election Study

---

We invite readers to email us at matthewth@usca.edu for more details of our own exit polling methods, datasets, and analysis.

M. P. Thornburg (✉) · R. E. Botsch
University of South Carolina Aiken, Aiken, SC, USA
e-mail: matthewth@usca.edu

R. E. Botsch
e-mail: bobb@usca.edu

© The Author(s), under exclusive license to Springer Nature Switzerland AG 2023
C. Butcher et al. (eds.), *The Palgrave Handbook of Teaching and Research in Political Science*, Political Pedagogies,
https://doi.org/10.1007/978-3-031-42887-6_22

are freely available, the standardized bank of questions restricts the populations and ideas researchers may explore.

For many such faculty, this dilemma is even more acute as they teach the data collection process to their undergraduate students in research methods courses. Research is a dynamic, messy process, and conveying the excitement and reality of social scientific analysis is a challenge for any instructor. Many undergrads experience the methods course more as a hazing ritual than the keystone of their political science major program. Sadly, the end result is all too often low teaching evaluations from students bored by lectures on the details of this analytical process.

We suggest that student-administered exit polling offers both a source of high-quality data to sustain a peer-reviewed faculty research agenda as well as an effective pedagogical tool to teach political science research methods. The authors have taught at a southeastern public regional university for a total of more than four decades, during which they have conducted exit polls every two years starting in 1992, save 2020 and 2022 when the pandemic intervened. Those fourteen polls averaged well over 600 completed interviews each. During the most recent exit poll, conducted in 2018, 29 student volunteers administered over 900 surveys in Aiken County, South Carolina, creating a dataset used for both public scholarship and peer-reviewed publication. While several useful guides exist for faculty members directing student-administered exit polls,[1] we focus on the benefits of local exit polling for both research and pedagogy and offer a few tips and suggestions for faculty on administering local exit polls in this fraught and polarized time.

Methodology of Student-Administered Exit Polling

The most well-known exit polls in American politics are the National Election Pool surveys conducted every federal election, which aid the media in its calls on election night. To measure the preferences of voters casting a ballot in person, these surveys use a combination of cluster sampling on representative polling places with systematic sampling of individuals leaving the polling places at the surveyed precincts. Many

---

[1] See Berry and Robinson (2012), Bracic et al. (2017), Cole (2003), Croco et al. (2019), Grimshaw et al. (2004), Lelieveldt and Rossen (2009).

academic political scientists replicate this basic methodology to conduct their own exit polls (Berry & Robinson, 2012; Grimshaw et al., 2004).

It is important to carefully select the polling places your students will survey. The methodology to do so is fairly standard. Polling places in the electorate are weighted by their expected number of voters. Researchers choose the sampled polling places such that their weighted average on various characteristics matches the overall electorate. Large exit polls may stratify the polling places on partisanship (e.g. strongly Republican, lean Republican, etc.) and randomly sample polling place locations from these strata so that the weighted average of the sampled polling places matches the overall partisan vote of the electorate (Grimshaw et al., 2004). In states (primarily in the South) where race and ethnicity of voters is available in the voter file, selecting polling places representative of the electorate's racial composition, as well as partisanship, is possible. Finally, geographic distribution of the polling places is an important consideration. The sampled polling places should account for the diversity of location in the electorate. In Aiken County, South Carolina, for example, the population is broadly divided into the cities of Aiken, North Augusta, a region known as Midland Valley, and outlying rural areas. We sample all of these areas in rough proportion to their relative size.

To some extent, the selection of polling places is as much an art as a science. For a survey of a smaller political entity such as a county (about 80 polling places in our county that is almost as large as the state of Rhode Island), the number of possible polling place combinations that balance on the needed characteristics has to be small (in our case about ten) because of the number of students in our research methods classes. In such a case it may make more sense to select the combination of polling places by trial and error since so few random combinations actually balance on the measured characteristics. The critical determinant is whether the precincts chosen successfully represented the electorate in previous presidential or gubernatorial elections. Physical factors are also important. Where possible, the researcher should choose polling places that have one entrance/exit for voters, offer shelter from the weather outside, such as an overhang, and have sufficient space where filling out questionnaires will not disrupt the precinct operations.

We train student pollsters in systematic sampling to minimize the bias of the sample collected. Rather than sample voters who ask to take the poll, or look "friendly," it is critical that students approach voters at regular intervals to ensure a representative sample within each precinct. In our surveys, we typically assign each student at a polling place to survey one gender of respondent. Students rigorously train to follow a script. After a voter fills out the questionnaire, the student must approach the next voter of their assigned gender leaving the polling place. For inevitable voter questions about why some individuals were asked but others were not, students carry scripts and our contact information.

College students, particularly individuals majoring in social sciences or statistics, can be quickly trained to follow directions. The certainty of a continuing relationship with the college or university after Election Day minimizes shirking of duties. At our institution, students participate in the exit poll as part of their class requirements for political science research methods. They are compensated with an experience of important educational value. Over nearly three decades, almost all our students successfully complete the polling work on Election Day.

Questionnaire design should follow standard survey methodology practice.[2] We would suggest that the questionnaire be limited to no more than both sides of a legal-sized sheet (falloff on the second side has not been significant). We caution researchers not to ask any questions they are not prepared to defend to an inquisitive local reporter in search of a story. Exit polls are an important opportunity to interact with the public, which may prove a double-edged sword. Though we have had a few problems, faculty sometimes have stoked controversy with exit poll questions perceived to be insensitive (Querry, 2014).

Exit Polls in Peer-Reviewed Research

Many student-administered exit polls generate peer-reviewed political science research (Abramowitz, 1989; Bishop & Fisher, 1995; Bracic et al., 2017; Claassen et al., 2008; Druckman, 2004; Thornburg, 2020). The advantages of this approach are many, but we highlight here our high response rates, cost-effectiveness, and customization.

Falling response rates to surveys are a well-known phenomenon in the field of public opinion research. In a time where many survey modes suffer response rates in the single digits, exit polls continue to enjoy relatively high rates of cooperation and completion. The National Election Pool's exit poll response rate was 45% in 2016 (DeSilver, 2016). We find that

---

[2] E.g., Atkeson and Alvarez (2018), Bradburn et al. (2004).

using local college students employing the methods discussed here does far better with an average around 70%. Our 2018 exit poll response rate was 75%.

A principle of quantitative research which we strive to impart on our research methods students is that high response rates not only reduce survey costs but also result in a more representative sample. That is certainly the case here. Researchers debate the degree to which lower response rates affect the quality and representativeness of samples collected. While studies find the relationship between nonresponse rate and bias of the survey is moderated by a number of factors (Groves & Peytcheva, 2008), more recent evidence indicates that nonresponse bias on factors which researchers cannot stratify upon, such as support for Donald Trump or political interest, distort current pictures of the American electorate (Cavari & Freedman, 2022).

Exit polls are not immune to nonresponse bias in terms of party identification (Clinton et al., 2022) or demographics (Kuriwaki & Yamaya, 2019). Even our exit polls with their high response rates are affected by some nonresponse bias. Most academic researchers using exit polls for peer-reviewed research benefit from the fact they are not trying to report the results on election night. Instead, researchers looking to construct a representative picture of the electorate have the time to eventually obtain accurate population parameters in terms of the aggregate vote for various offices, as well as turnout data from voter files. Kuriwaki and Yamaya (2019) utilize a two-step procedure, with rake weights for partisanship and education followed by entropy balancing (Hainmueller, 2012) using the voter file. This accounts for any nonresponse bias in overall partisanship as well as demographic nonresponse bias.

Costs for student-administered exit polls are low compared to commercial polling firms. Initial costs are mainly clipboards and perhaps small tables (though most students bring their own tables or some kind of folding platform). Our major annual costs are printing and data entry, which can be done either by paying highly competent upper-level students (done in most years prior to 2018) or employing a professional firm. The bottom line is that our costs at worst were about two dollars per completed interview. The excitement of voters leaving the polling place after participating in an election and their eagerness to express their political views combine with the goodwill of the university in the community to drive up response rates, which effectively subsidizes the cost of the survey over other polling methods.

Our exit polls are also amenable to a number of sophisticated survey techniques such as randomized experiments (Yamaya, 2019). In 2018, to study state legislative races, our students sampled extra precincts in two State House districts to create representative pictures of these districts (Thornburg, 2020). We customized questionnaires for each polling place to correspond to these overlapping geographies and the races taking place in each. Through this approach we surveyed a representative sample of the overall county as well as the two State House districts.

Exit Polls in Teaching

Among the core courses of the political science major, the methods course has an anecdotal reputation as particularly challenging to teach. Political science majors often choose the major because of an "interest in practical politics and a propensity for following current events" (Bergbower, 2017). While this motivation serves them well in subject-matter courses of the major, it fares poorly in the research methods classroom. Many students fail to see the relevance of methods to understanding the politics they enjoy reading about in the media (Parker et al., 2008). This lack of perceived relevance is a formidable obstacle to success in research methods (Hewitt, 2001; Parker et al., 2008).

Quantitative, large-N approaches to understanding political phenomena rely on abstract concepts involving probability and randomness, such as the law of large numbers and statistical significance. Students who enter a research methods class already anxious and skeptical of its utility (Slocum-Schaffer & Bohrer, 2021) struggle to master these ideas, let alone connect them to the politics that motivated their original love of the major. When instructors fail to engage and excite students in active learning, the class may move into "survival mode" as the students refocus their efforts from understanding the material to simply passing the course.

A robust literature prescribes active learning to aid the political science research methods classroom (Currin-Percival & Johnson, 2010; DeWitt, 2010; Druckman, 2015; Hewitt, 2001; Hubbell, 1994; McBride, 1994, 1996). More generally, active learning increases student interest and self-efficacy (Hendrickson, 2021) as well as overall learning (Duchatelet et al., 2020; Shellman & Turan, 2006) in political science courses.

Notably, for teaching research methods, literature suggests exit polling as an active learning practice (Berry & Robinson, 2012; Bracic et al.,

2017; Cole, 2003; Emery et al., 2014). Our experience supports this suggestion. We find that exit polls provide a memorable experience, provide team-building cooperative skills, motivate student interest, elucidate abstract concepts, and show the messy and exciting reality of research firsthand to political science majors.

Students remember the exit poll experience throughout their undergraduate career, and many tell us later that it was one of their most memorable experiences as a political science major. Several have gone on to graduate school for survey methodology or careers in public opinion research. While the experience of interacting with the public via exit polling is intimidating, and while we ask a lot of the student pollsters, nearly all of our students successfully complete the methods class. The post-election debrief is inevitably lively and boosts the energy in the course during the stretch between our fall break and Thanksgiving holiday.

We also find students better understand abstract principles of quantitative research after exit polling. As they engage voters throughout the day, they observe the law of large numbers at work as the precinct sample gradually approaches the precinct population parameters on various demographic characteristics. And as they hand out surveys and are forced to turn away voters wanting to volunteer, they grasp why systematic sampling is necessary rather than taking self-selected respondents to gather a representative sample.

Finally, students gain an appreciation for the dynamics of research. They take genuine pride in their contribution and eagerly await results. But perhaps most importantly, they see that research design is imperfect; it only approximates an ideal. For example, during the 2016 exit poll we found that samples in precincts with African-American student interviewers showed more pro-Democratic error from the actual precinct vote compared to precincts with only white students. This was despite comparable response rates with students doing equally well in following procedures. This impromptu mystery led to an informative lesson in race-of-interviewer effects and discussions on how we might deal with this problem in future exit polling.

Suggestions and the Future of Exit Polling

While the advantages of exit polling are many, researchers have reasons to pause in performing student-administered surveys right now. Currently, the field of public opinion struggles with falling response rates and questions of systematic bias in polling. Willingness to answer surveys has become asymmetric on the political spectrum (Clinton et al., 2022). At the same time, affective political polarization has reached new heights. More Americans are voting before Election Day. And the conduct of elections is increasingly politicized. Nevertheless, we think student-administered exit polls face fewer problems than other forms of public opinion research. We offer some practical suggestions for how to perform a successful exit poll with students and how to address some of these issues.

Above all, exploit your "home court advantage." Make sure prospective respondents know that the person asking them to complete the survey is a local university student. The name tag should prominently display the school name and logo and even colors, as well as the student's name. The greeting should include "I'm a student at ____" in the first sentence.

If you can get a local media outlet to sponsor the survey so as to allow the name of the outlet to be on the name tag as we did for many years with our local newspaper, that reinforces the local identity and adds credibility and gravitas. We routinely ran a few questions of local interest on surveys and gave the paper exclusive stories on the findings at no financial cost to them. Even when the local paper was not a sponsor, we issued press releases that created stories in the paper.

Employ a "plea for pity" in the form of asking a personal favor to help the student interviewer to get their assignment done and/or get a good grade. "Good morning/afternoon (with eye contact and a big smile). My name is ____ and I am a student at ____ helping to do a survey as a class assignment. I really appreciate your giving me a few minutes to help me get my assignment done." The student interviewers are taught to make the request a command with voice inflection down at the end rather than a question with voice inflection up. This takes a lot of training and practice sessions to get right.

Each precinct should have one of your most reliable and confident students assigned to it, though we should add that predicting who will be the best interviewers is often surprising. That student should have all the materials (envelopes with the morning and afternoon surveys to be completed, clipboards, pencils with extras and a pencil sharpener, a "ballot box" into which respondents fold and place their completed survey, which helps ensure anonymity, and perhaps a tv table on which to place the box). That student is responsible for getting these materials to the precinct location before the polls open. We always try to mix gender and ethnicity at precinct locations. Students must visit their locations prior to election day so that they know how to get there and exactly where to set up. You also need to account for transportation for all the student interviewers.

Because you cannot get to all locations and cover emergencies yourself, you will need at least one or two floaters who can act as trouble-shooters if problems arise. We employ seniors who have done this before and pay them approximately $50 for the day. They should have clipboards, a ballot box, and pencils in case a "no show" happens. All individuals in the field (floaters and students) should have a sheet listing all locations, who is working each location, quotas for each time slot and location, and cell phone numbers for everyone, including the floaters and yourself. Because we have a geographically large county, we are usually able to get to only about three locations in the morning and in the afternoon just to check on how things are going and to give encouragement—usually more than 100 miles of driving. We take pictures of the students at work that we later post on the course website. The floaters cover the locations we are unable to get to, so we plan ahead on the locations floaters will check, though plans often get changed when problems arise.

Building a relationship with local election officials is critical. Visit the head of your local elections office and explain what you want to do and enlist their help. Stress that you will follow all rules pertaining to exit polling so that you do not interfere with the voting process. This needs to be done well ahead of time so that the local officials can let the precinct workers know at their training sessions that local college students will be exit polling at their location. Go over where you will set up at each location. Find out whom the precinct workers should call to confirm that students have permission to do the survey. Our student interviewers were instructed to check in with the precinct workers before setting up and to stress that they would be following all the rules laid out by the election officials. Encouraging other students to work as poll workers will help cement this relationship and build civic responsibility.

Finally, we submit our exit poll projects for IRB review. Due to the less than minimal risk to participants, these projects invariably receive an IRB exemption. We find this presents a learning experience when teaching research methods. The preparation of the research protocol for IRB submission by the instructor coincides with our unit on research ethics, and students see an actual project wind its way through the institutional safeguards for human subjects research.

Conclusion

While all faculty deal with the competing demands of their job differently, we attest to the benefits over the last three decades from melding teaching and research through exit polling. At its best, this endeavor synergizes these two aspects of the job, allowing a researcher to ask original questions and employ active learning practices. Exit polls are one of a dwindling number of survey modalities enjoying high response rates, low cost per completed interview, and customization by the researcher. At the same time, they allow faculty to tackle one of the most difficult courses to teach in undergraduate political science using effective pedagogy. We encourage other faculty to take advantage of this unique opportunity.

References

Abramowitz, A. I. (1989). Viability, electability, and candidate choice in a presidential primary election: A test of competing models. *The Journal of Politics, 51*(4), 977–992. https://doi.org/10.2307/2131544

Atkeson, L. R., & Alvarez, R. M. (Eds.). (2018). *The Oxford handbook of polling and survey methods*. Oxford University Press.

Bergbower, M. L. (2017). When are students ready for research methods? A curriculum mapping argument for the political science major. *Journal of Political Science Education, 13*(2), 200–210. https://doi.org/10.1080/15512169.2017.1292917

Berry, M. J., & Robinson, T. (2012). An entrance to exit polling: Strategies for using exit polls as experiential learning projects. *PS: Political Science & Politics, 45*(3), 501–505.

Bishop, G. F., & Fisher, B. S. (1995). "Secret ballots" and self-reports in an exit-poll experiment. *Public Opinion Quarterly, 59*(4), 568–588. https://doi.org/10.1017/S1049096512000431

Bracic, A., Israel-Trummel, M. L., & Shortle, A. F. (2017). Exit polling: Field research and pedagogical benefits of community engagement. *Oklahoma Politics, 27*. https://ojs.library.okstate.edu/osu/index.php/OKPolitics/article/view/8270

Bradburn, N. M., Sudman, S., & Wansink, B. (2004). *Asking questions: The definitive guide to questionnaire design—for market research, political polls, and social and health questionnaires.* Wiley.

Cavari, A., & Freedman, G. (2022). Survey nonresponse and mass polarization: The consequences of declining contact and cooperation rates. *American Political Science Review*, 1–8. https://doi.org/10.1017/S0003055422000399

Claassen, R. L., Magleby, D. B., Monson, J. Q., & Patterson, K. D. (2008). "At your service": Voter evaluations of poll worker performance. *American Politics Research*, 36(4), 612–634. https://doi.org/10.1177/1532673X08319006

Clinton, J. D., Lapinski, J. S., & Trussler, M. J. (2022). Reluctant republicans, eager democrats? Partisan nonresponse and the accuracy of 2020 presidential pre-election telephone polls. *Public Opinion Quarterly*, 86(2), 247–269. https://doi.org/10.1093/poq/nfac011

Cole, A. (2003). To survey or not to survey: The use of exit polling as a teaching tool. *PS: Political Science & Politics*, 36(2), 245–252. https://www.jstor.org/stable/3649317

Croco, S. E., Suhay, E., Blum, R., Mason, L., Noel, H., Ladd, J., & Bailey, M. A. (2019). Student-run exit polls 101. *PS: Political Science & Politics*, 52(2), 361–366. https://doi.org/10.1017/S1049096518002330

Currin-Percival, M., & Johnson, M. (2010). Understanding sample surveys: Selective learning about social science research methods. *PS: Political Science & Politics*, 43(3), 533–540. https://doi.org/10.1017/S1049096510000776

Desilver, D. (2016). *Just how does the general election exit poll work, anyway?* Pew Research Center. https://www.pewresearch.org/short-reads/2016/11/02/just-how-does-the-general-election-exit-poll-work-anyway/

DeWitt, J. R. (2010). Using collaborative research projects to facilitate active learning in methods courses. *The Journal of Faculty Development*, 24(1), 19. https://www.proquest.com/openview/1e26da7b574ed25e11edae9add70df28/1?pq-origsite=gscholar&cbl=39886

Druckman, J. N. (2004). Priming the vote: Campaign effects in a US Senate election. *Political Psychology*, 25(4), 577–594. https://doi.org/10.1111/j.1467-9221.2004.00388.x

Druckman, J. N. (2015). Research and undergraduate teaching: A false divide?: Introduction. *PS: Political Science & Politics*, 48(1), 35–38. https://doi.org/10.1017/S1049096514001565

Duchatelet, D., Bursens, P., Usherwood, S., & Oberle, M. (2020). Beyond descriptions and good practices: Empirical effects on students' learning outcomes of active learning environments in political science curricula. *European Political Science*, 19(3), 327–335. https://doi.org/10.1057/s41304-020-00259-w

Emery, J. K., Howard, A., & Evans, J. (2014). Teaching better, teaching together: A coordinated student exit poll across the states. *Journal of Political Science Education*, *10*(4), 471–486. https://doi.org/10.1080/15512169.2014.947419

Grimshaw, S. D., Christensen, H. B., Magleby, D. B., & Patterson, K. D. (2004). Twenty years of the Utah Colleges exit poll: Learning by doing. *Chance*, *17*(2), 32–38. https://doi.org/10.1080/09332480.2004.10554898

Groves, R. M., & Peytcheva, E. (2008). The impact of nonresponse rates on nonresponse bias: A meta-analysis. *Public Opinion Quarterly*, *72*(2), 167–189. https://doi.org/10.1093/poq/nfn011

Hainmueller, J. (2012). Entropy balancing for causal effects: A multivariate reweighting method to produce balanced samples in observational studies. *Political Analysis*, *20*(1), 25–46. https://doi.org/10.1093/pan/mpr025

Hendrickson, P. (2021). Effect of active learning techniques on student excitement, interest, and self-efficacy. *Journal of Political Science Education*, *17*(2), 311–325. https://doi.org/10.1080/15512169.2019.1629946

Hewitt, J. J. (2001). Engaging international data in the classroom: Using the ICB Interactive Data Library to teach conflict and crisis analysis. *International Studies Perspectives*, *2*(4), 371–383. https://doi.org/10.1111/1528-3577.00066

Hubbell, L. (1994). Teaching research methods: An experiential and heterodoxical approach. *PS: Political Science & Politics*, *27*(1), 60–64. https://doi.org/10.2307/420460

Kuriwaki, S. & Yamaya, S. (2019). *Charleston exit poll technical report*. Harvard University. Retrieved January 10, 2023, from https://caps.gov.harvard.edu/files/caps/files/charleston-poll.pdf

Lelieveldt, H., & Rossen, G. (2009). Why exit polls make good teaching tools. *European Political Science*, *8*(1), 113–122. https://doi.org/10.1057/eps.2008.46

McBride, A. (1994). Teaching research methods using appropriate technology. *PS: Political Science & Politics*, *27*(3), 553–557. https://doi.org/10.2307/420226

McBride, A. B. (1996). Creating a critical thinking learning environment: Teaching statistics to social science undergraduates. *PS: Political Science & Politics*, *29*(3), 517–521. https://doi.org/10.2307/420835

Parker, J., Scott, S., Dobson A., & Wyman, M. (2008). *International benchmarking review of best practice in the provision of undergraduate teaching in quantitative methods in the social sciences*. Economic and Social Research Council.

Querry, K. (2014, November 8). *Polling problems: Exit poll asks whether 'blacks are getting too demanding' in push for equal rights*. KFOR. https://kfor.com/news/polling-problems-exit-poll-asks-whether-blacks-are-getting-too-demanding-in-push-for-equal-rights

Shellman, S. M., & Turan, K. (2006). Do simulations enhance student learning? An empirical evaluation of an IR simulation. *Journal of Political Science Education, 2*(1), 19–32. https://doi.org/10.1080/15512160500484168

Slocum-Schaffer, S. A., & Bohrer, R. E. (2021). Information literacy for everyone: Using practical strategies to overcome 'fear and loathing' in the undergraduate research methods course. *Journal of Political Science Education, 17*(sup1), 363–379. https://doi.org/10.1080/15512169.2019.1694935

Thornburg, M. P. (2020). Anatomy of a one-party region: The primacy of race and white partisanship in southern state legislative elections. *Journal of Political Science, 48*. https://digitalcommons.coastal.edu/jops/vol48/iss1/2/

Yamaya, S. (2019). *Voting across the government: An exit poll experiment in South Carolina* (Master's thesis). Princeton University. http://arks.princeton.edu/ark:/88435/dsp0102870z683

CHAPTER 23

An Experiential Approach to Teaching the Importance of the Iowa Caucuses

Jay Wendland

Working in a small, liberal arts environment brings with it several rewards, but poses serious challenges to the ability to complete research projects given the heavier teaching and service load. When I saw the opportunity to combine my research interest in campaign strategy in presidential nominating contests with an experiential course for students, I could not pass it up. In an effort to convey the importance and uniqueness of the Iowa Caucuses in the presidential nominating process, from January 16–21, 2020 (roughly two weeks prior to the caucuses and just two months prior to the nationwide COVID-19 shutdown) I was able to travel with five students from Daemen University near Buffalo, NY to Des Moines, IA to attend political events, talk with grassroots volunteers and organizers, and absorb as much of the unique campaign environment as Iowa had to offer.

J. Wendland (✉)
Department of History and Political Science, Daemen University, Amherst, NY, USA
e-mail: jwendlan@daemen.edu

© The Author(s), under exclusive license to Springer Nature Switzerland AG 2023
C. Butcher et al. (eds.), *The Palgrave Handbook of Teaching and Research in Political Science*, Political Pedagogies,
https://doi.org/10.1007/978-3-031-42887-6_23

The uniqueness of Iowa and the other early states—those that hold their primary or caucus prior to Super Tuesday—is the prominence of retail politics found in the run-up to the contest. Retail politics are something most of us are familiar with when it comes to our local and state officials, but rarely experience from our presidential candidates. This type of political campaigning involves attending local events in an effort to target and connect with voters on issues of importance to them on a small-scale (or potentially even individual) level. Attending county fairs, holding town hall meetings with public question and answer sessions, and eating at popular local restaurants are all common ways in which presidential contenders engage in retail politics across the state of Iowa that few Americans get to experience. In Iowa, we were able to tour the Capitol building in Des Moines, during which time my students were able to talk with a couple of Iowa state legislators, learning a brief history of Iowa and its politics. We also attended four rallies/town hall meetings and a democracy forum, which was attended by several of the Democratic candidates running for the nomination, providing these students the opportunity to see several of these candidates up close and personal (getting "selfies" with four top-tier Democratic candidates), an opportunity unavailable to them in New York.

Iowa's first-in-the-nation status in the American presidential nominating process is one that often causes confusion and consternation to students. This small, Midwestern, predominantly White state also caught the ire of some of the Democratic contenders in the 2020 race (Scott, 2019). Despite the concerns surrounding Iowa's representativeness (see Lewis-Beck and Squire (2009) for a counterargument), Iowa's ability to "set the agenda" for the remainder of the nomination season requires students to understand the prominent position Iowa holds in the primary calendar. As this trip was conducted in conjunction with an independent study course on the presidential nominating process, understanding Iowa's prominent role was an important component of the course.

The Importance of Experience

Kolb (1984) tells us that "Learning is the process whereby knowledge is created through the transformation of experience" (p. 38). Kolb's argument can be applied to a variety of disciplines, but ultimately advises that students, regardless of discipline, need to engage in their education through action. This generally suggests that students need to be actively participating in their instruction (Hawtrey, 2007) or demonstrating knowledge from something they have done (Weiland, 1981). Experiential learning allows students to actively engage in their education, helping them to better solidify the knowledge they gain in the classroom.

By traveling to Iowa to observe retail politics, students were able to obtain firsthand observations of what candidates do in order to appeal to Iowa voters. In addition to seeing what the candidates themselves do, they were able to see the vast amount of work done by the grassroots volunteers as well as the organization that goes into the Iowa caucuses. We attended a variety of campaign events with candidates in Iowa, where students not only learned about the candidates running for office, but were also able to learn from others who attended the events. They were able to speak with Iowans about how they were deciding which candidate to vote for, how many events they had been to, and whether or not they had yet gotten involved with other campaigns.

In addition to the trip, throughout the following spring semester, the students were enrolled in an Independent Study course with me entitled, "Iowa 2020: The Importance of Retail Politics in Presidential Nominating Contests." Throughout the semester, the students learned the history of the presidential nomination process, the importance of the early states and the rules of the nomination process, the dynamics of the nominating contests, as well as the strategies employed by the candidates running for nomination. To demonstrate their knowledge of the nominating process, students were expected to write several papers throughout the semester, reflecting on what they learned both from the course itself and its experiential component. The course culminated with a co-authored manuscript approximately the length of a journal article, in which the students analyzed their experience in Iowa and placed it within the scholarly context conveyed by the materials assigned in the classroom. This paper was then archived through the University's Office of Academic Affairs.

Why Focus on Campaign Visits?

One of my research interests is candidate strategy in presidential nominating contests—specifically the role candidate visits play in mobilizing voters and expanding their vote share (Wendland, 2017, 2019). These visits consist of campaign rallies, town hall meetings, community events, among others. Ultimately, a visit allows a candidate to speak to voters about their goals, vision, and top priorities in more detail than voters are able to glean from an advertisement. Ads generally provide brief 30 or 60 second snapshots into a candidate's background, biography, or policy positions whereas a campaign visit allows the candidate to expand on these for much longer. The candidates are not paying for airtime, but instead are offering voters an opportunity to come to an event, learn about their policy positions, and their vision for their potential presidency. It also allows voters to see a candidate in a less scripted environment. With campaign ads there is always a potential for a "re-shoot," a script rewrite, or editing after the ad has been recorded. With a campaign visit, the candidate can prepare remarks, but they cannot control the questions that might get asked (if incorporating audience questions) or the level of applause received. Worse yet is the potential for political gaffes. The classic example of a campaign gaffe during a visit is President Gerald Ford's ignorance of how to properly shuck a tamale prior to eating it—a noticeable faux pas in the Southwest (Popkin, 1994). In the 2016 Republican nominating contests, Jeb Bush was recorded (and instantly "memed" and "gifed") upon asking his audience to "please clap" after discussing how different he would be than Donald Trump in the White House (Benen, 2016).

In order to understand candidate strategy in presidential nominations, there are four key elements to pay attention to: visits, advertisements, momentum, and endorsements. Understanding campaign momentum largely includes understanding the other dynamics as well—as ads, visits, and endorsements (along with primary and caucus wins later in the contest) all impact a candidate's momentum (Bartels, 1988). Candidates can try to build momentum by increasing a sense of viability, electability, and inevitability around their campaign, but momentum is also greatly impacted by media narratives in addition to the actions taken by a candidate. Endorsements, too, are largely outside of a candidate's direct control. Endorsements from party leaders and other political elites are clearly an important component of the nomination process (Cohen et al., 2008) and candidates have some control over how the announcement of an important endorsement is handled, but candidates have little control over who gives them endorsements. In contrast, candidates have a great deal of control over advertisements (at least official campaign ads) and visits. They make decisions about where to run ads, where to conduct visits, and the focus of the message.

What I wanted my students to gain from this opportunity was an understanding of the importance of connecting with the voters—something candidates have a great deal of control over. Iowa presents a unique opportunity for such learning to occur, as it has historically held "first in the nation" status since the McGovern-Fraser reforms of 1972. For a detailed accounting of these reforms see Jewitt's (2019) work on the importance of the rules that govern the process. Candidates flock to Iowa in order to interact with voters all in an effort to win the first contest of the season, which nets them better fundraising numbers, increased media coverage, and a big boost of momentum—especially if that candidate exceeds expectations on caucus night (Aldrich, 1980; Bartels, 1988). Candidates hope to use this boost to propel themselves to victory in more early primaries and ultimately the nomination—referred to as the bandwagon effect by Kenney and Rice (1994)—where they will become their Party's standard bearer and go on to compete in the general election.

In an effort to do so, candidates spend an inordinate amount of time in Iowa. They hold rallies, attend local fairs and festivals, conduct town hall meetings where they take questions from those in the audience, and of course, shake a lot of hands. In fact, Iowa regularly receives hundreds of visits from candidates throughout the nomination process. Many might assume larger, more populous states might receive more attention from the prospective nominees, but Iowa consistently receives a great deal of attention during the nomination season (Kamarck, 2009). Looking at the visits Iowa has received since 2008, as shown in Table 23.1, this is true of both major political parties. Importantly, almost all of these visits involved some ability for voters to interact with the candidates running for office—a unique phenomenon reserved mostly for states that are slated to hold their contests early in the nomination calendar. While the number of Democratic visits in 2016 and 2020 look very different (with visits in 2020 surpassing the number of visits in 2016 by 800!), 2016 saw only two viable candidates seeking the Democratic nomination while 2020 saw dozens. The Iowa caucuses were held before any government action was taken in response to the COVID-19 pandemic, so visits were held throughout the run-up to the Iowa caucuses without any COVID-19 restrictions.

Table 23.1 Iowa visits from major party candidates

	Democratic	Republican
2008	444	272
2012	–	387
2016	74	268
2020	887	–

Note Obama sought reelection in 2012 and Trump sought reelection in 2020 without major opposition, so no data were collected

Source Data from 2008 compiled from *Washington Post* Events Tracker; Data from 2012 compiled from *Politico* Candidate Tracker; Data from 2016 compiled from *National Journal* Travel Tracker, 2020 data compiled from *Des Moines Register*, *New England Cable News*, *Nevada Independent* and *Post and Courier* in Charleston, SC

STUDENT-FACULTY COLLABORATION

Upon returning to New York, the students completed a course with me focused on the presidential nominating process. Throughout the course the students were asked to read about and discuss the history of the nomination process to better understand the evolution of how involved the parties and voters were in the process. We also discussed the importance of the rules in the nomination process as well as the campaign strategies normally employed while running for the nomination. Finally, the students were asked to write a journal article-length paper focused on the importance of retail politics in presidential nominating contests, using their observations and experiences in Iowa as the data for their empirical evidence. This was a co-authored piece, with each student participating in the writing of the paper under my guidance. Daemen University's Office of Academic Affairs offers "Think Tank Grants" for faculty who embark on research projects with students. I was fortunate enough to receive such a grant and was able to significantly defray the cost of participation to students. Think Tank projects and/or papers are then archived through the Provost's Office and are available for download via their website. So, while this paper was not published in the traditional sense, it was made publicly available. I hope to continue to offer this experience to students during future presidential nomination cycles, with funding opportunities constantly being sought in order to continue to offer this opportunity at an affordable cost.

Due to the final archiving of this paper, students were instructed to craft it as though they were going to submit it for publication, mirroring the standard structure of a published article: introduction, literature review, hypotheses, data, findings, and conclusions. Throughout the literature review, they briefly summarized the history and rules of the presidential nomination process and discussed the typical strategies employed in a nominating contest. They also discussed the importance of campaign visits in nominating contests as well as the actual definition of a visit, hypothesizing that visits are a good avenue by which to learn about the candidates running for office. Then, the students summarized their experience in Iowa, traveling around the state to attend various rallies and town hall meetings hosted by different candidates in an effort to learn and observe the type of information the typical Iowan has access to during the run-up to the Iowa caucuses. Finally, they reported their findings. Their conclusions were mainly focused on the importance of retail politics as well as how different Iowans behaved in comparison with New York voters.

Lessons Learned

One of the biggest lessons the students learned, as reported in their reflection papers, was the seriousness with which Iowans take their "first in the nation" responsibilities. Students were impressed by the vast number of yard signs found throughout the state (practically one in every yard), which they argued highlighted the diversity in opinion across the state as well as the level of involvement with which Iowans were willing to engage. All of these students came from electorally "safe" states, so were not familiar with how competitive some of these races can get.

Students were able to regularly interact with Iowans at these campaign events and were impressed with the level of engagement among Iowan voters. They did not formally interview anyone, but would talk with others in attendance at some of the rallies we attended. Many people acknowledged having attended several candidates' rallies, some of whom they saw multiple times in person, confirming that many Iowans take seriously their ability to properly vet each candidate. Additionally, many people traveled from neighboring states to attend several of the campaign events, knowing that Iowa would present them with a better opportunity to see the candidate(s) than waiting for the candidate to travel to Nebraska, for example. So, given that some voters will travel from outside

Iowa to attend an event, event attendance does not exactly translate into votes for that candidate.

Yet, traveling across state lines to attend a political rally does, arguably, exemplify excitement. By attending a campaign event, it becomes clear which candidate is generating more excitement among voters in the state. My students agreed that of the four candidates' rallies we were able to attend (Biden, Buttigieg, Sanders, and Warren) and other candidates we were able to see speak at a democracy forum (John Delaney, Amy Klobuchar, Deval Patrick, and Andrew Yang), the candidates that were able to generate the most excitement were Buttigieg, Sanders, and Warren. And, after all of the dust cleared in the final tallying of Iowa's caucus votes—and there was A LOT of dust in 2020—that was the order in which the candidates finished, though Buttigieg and Sanders were a very close one-two finish.

While pundits and the press talk about excitement, without attending a rally firsthand, excitement is a difficult concept for which to account. Conceptualizing excitement became a topic of discussion in class and the students and I agreed that one potential measurement for excitement would be distance traveled to attend a political event. Those events which attracted mostly local attendees might signal less excitement than those where attendees traveled significant distances to hear from a candidate—especially those who could not participate in Iowa's Caucuses. We met several attendees from neighboring states that wanted to see the candidates and knew they would not be holding many events in Nebraska, Illinois, or Minnesota. Another potential measurement could be crowd size, as 1,000 attendees could signal higher levels of excitement than 100 attendees. Overall, this discussion has produced the beginnings of a new paper I plan on writing on the topic of conceptualizing excitement—potentially in collaboration with former students.

Based on their final co-authored paper, and course reflections, it was clear that students learned a lot about the presidential nomination process and were able to apply what they experienced in Iowa to our classroom discussions about campaign dynamics (see Fig. 23.1 for photo of student participants). Taking into account the evidence presented by Weiland (1981) and Kolb (1984), it is clear that experiential learning is important for students, as it helps reinforce classroom learning, allowing them to draw connections between what happens in the classroom and what happens during the experiential component. While not all courses lend themselves to a trip as described in this chapter, I have endeavored to incorporate as many experiential components to my courses as possible. Sometimes it is offering extra credit for attending a museum exhibit or attending a local talk (e.g. I offered extra credit to students for attending a talk given by Margaret Atwood a few weeks before we discussed *The Handmaid's Tale*). No matter the experience, it will help cement classroom lessons in a student's mind. By supplementing a course on the presidential nominating process with the experience of traveling to Iowa to observe various campaign events, I was able to successfully convey the importance of the Iowa Caucuses—and retail politics more broadly—both academically and experientially.

Fig. 23.1 Photo of students in front of the Capitol building in Des Moines, IA (From left to right: Tysai Washington, Ricardo Marquez, Sam Williams, Lindsey Hornung, Carlos McKnight. *Source* Jay Wendland)

REFERENCES

2020 New Hampshire candidate tracker: See which presidential primary hopefuls have visited. (2020). *New England Cable News*. https://www.necn.com/news/politics/2020-presidential-primaries-which-candidates-visited-new-hampshire/222478/

Aldrich, J. H. (1980). *Before the convention: Strategies and choices in presidential nomination campaigns*. University of Chicago Press.

Bartels, L. M. (1988). *Presidential primaries and the dynamics of public choice*. Princeton University Press.

Benen, S. (2016, February 3). Jeb Bush urges audience, "Please clap." MSNBC.Com. https://www.msnbc.com/rachel-maddow-show/jeb-bush-urges-audience-please-clap-msna787916

Cohen, M., Karol, D., Noel, H., & Zaller, J. (2008). *The party decides: Presidential nominations before and after reform*. The University of Chicago Press.

Election 2020: Presidential candidate tracker. (n.d.). *The Nevada Independent*. Retrieved May 31, 2022, from https://thenevadaindependent.com/election/2020/candidate-tracker

Hawtrey, K. (2007). Using experiential learning techniques. *The Journal of Economic Education, 38*(2), 143–152. https://doi.org/10.3200/JECE.38.2.143-152

Iowa caucuses candidate tracker. (2020). *Des Moine Register*. https://data.desmoinesregister.com/iowa-caucus/candidate-tracker/index.php

Isenstein, L., McGill, A., Railey, K., & Wollner, A. (2016). 2016 travel tracker. *National Journal*. http://nj-travel-tracker.herokuapp.com/

Jewitt, C. E. (2019). *The primary rules*. University of Michigan Press. https://www.press.umich.edu/10020994/primary_rules

Kamarck, E. C. (2009). The fight to be first: Why Iowa and New Hampshire dominate presidential nominating politics. In *Primary politics: How presidential candidates have shaped the modern nominating system* (pp. 51–80). Brookings Institution Press. http://www.jstor.org/stable/10.7864/j.ctt6wpgb7.7

Kenney, P. J., & Rice, T. W. (1994). The psychology of political momentum. *Political Research Quarterly, 47*(4), 923–938. https://doi.org/10.1177/106591299404700409

Kolb, D. A. (1984). *Experiential learning: Experience as the source of learning and development* (1st ed.). Pearson Education.

Lewis-Beck, M. S., & Squire, P. (2009). Iowa: The most representative state? *PS: Political Science & Politics, 42*(1), 39–44.

Parker, J. E., & Lovegrove, J. (2020). 2020 SC presidential candidate tracker. *Post and Courier*. https://www.postandcourier.com/2020-sc-presidential-candidate-tracker/article_754233ac-8160-11e9-b945-fb18f39c077c.html

Politico. (2012). *2012 presidential election—Candidate tracker.* Politico. http://www.politico.com/2012-election/candidate-map/

Popkin, S. L. (1994). *The reasoning voter: Communication and persuasion in presidential campaigns* (2nd ed.). University of Chicago Press.

Scott, E. (2019, November 13). Castro argues that Iowa does not reflect America's diversity enough to lead the primaries. *Washington Post.* https://www.washingtonpost.com/politics/2019/11/13/castro-argues-that-iowa-does-not-reflect-americas-diversity-enough-lead-primaries/

Washington Post. (2008). Election 2008: Events tracker. *Washington Post.*

Weiland, S. (1981). Emerson, experience, and experiential learning. *Peabody Journal of Education, 58*(3), 161–167. https://doi.org/10.1080/01619568109538329

Wendland, J. (2017). *Campaigns that matter: The importance of campaign visits in presidential nominating contests.* Lexington Press.

Wendland, J. (2019). Rallying votes? A multilevel approach to understanding voter decision-making in the 2016 presidential nominating contests. *Journal of Political Marketing, 18*(1–2), 92–118. https://doi.org/10.1080/15377857.2018.1478659

CHAPTER 24

Triple the Benefits Without Tripling the Work: Combining Teaching and Research in Service to the Community

Elizabeth A. Bennion

Successfully integrating teaching, research, and service is a strategic and rewarding way to achieve the public purpose of higher education: educating citizens for democracy. Civically engaged teacher-scholars integrate teaching, research, and service in ways that benefit the community at large.

This chapter begins by briefly outlining a variety of ways to successfully combine teaching, research, and service, emphasizing the advantages of grounding this work in a commitment to civic engagement and drawing upon examples from my own career. I then provide detailed examples of two community-engaged projects that combined teaching, research, and service in ways that benefited me, my students, and the local community.

E. A. Bennion (✉)
Department of Political Science, Indiana University South Bend, South Bend, IN, USA
e-mail: ebennion@iusb.edu

© The Author(s), under exclusive license to Springer Nature Switzerland AG 2023
C. Butcher et al. (eds.), *The Palgrave Handbook of Teaching and Research in Political Science*, Political Pedagogies,
https://doi.org/10.1007/978-3-031-42887-6_24

The purpose of sharing these examples is to help readers conceptualize similarly rich and integrated projects of their own.

Double Your Impact: Combining Teaching and Research to Produce Informed and Engaged Citizens

Two useful ways to combine teaching and research are scholarly teaching and the scholarship of teaching and learning. Scholarly teaching is an intentional practice informed by evidence, research on teaching and learning, well-reasoned theory, and critical reflection; its main goal is to maximize learning (Potter & Kustra, 2011). A scholarly approach to teaching might involve reading about new teaching methodologies, reflecting on teaching practices, attending teaching conferences and workshops, or asking for peer feedback, including summative peer reviews. In contrast, the scholarship of teaching and learning (SoTL) is a systematic analysis of research questions related to student learning that are shared publicly to advance the field of teaching and learning. As with other forms in scholarship, such works are designed for others to critique, develop, use, and refine over time.

In my view, scholarly teaching should include teaching from and about original scholarship, including one's own original research. It is important for students to understand where knowledge comes from. Students studying political science should understand, and engage in, the scientific process, including developing research questions, formulating and testing hypotheses, and answering these questions using appropriate research designs and methods. Talking about the methodology and research used in extant scholarship, rather than merely sharing the findings of such work as established facts, is an important part of teaching students to understand—and prepare to engage in—academic research. Using one's own research can be particularly instructive as students can ask their instructors about decisions they made—including the appropriateness and ethics of the research design.

Selecting topics that are relevant to students' lives and/or demonstrating the real-world community impact of such research can be particularly interesting and engaging for students. For example, when teaching about U.S. voter turnout and the youth vote, I share my published field experiments testing the effectiveness of classroom-based voter registration drives on our campus (Bennion, 2009) and nationally (Bennion & Nickerson, 2016), along with my experiments demonstrating the limitations of email-based get-out-the-vote (GOTV) messages (Bennion & Nickerson, 2011), and the importance of linking emails urging students to register directly to a state's online voter registration system (Bennion & Nickerson, 2022). Each of these projects included students from our campus—and other campuses—as subjects, making the research particularly relevant and relatable to students. Students complete worksheets that require them to answer questions about their instructor's research hypotheses, methods, and findings, and the implications of these findings, while also asking questions and proposing follow-up research of their own. This approach teaches students about voting behavior, while also teaching them about research methods, and creates space for discussing the importance of young voters. Students discuss their own commitment, or lack of commitment, to political engagement and ponder the importance of, barriers to, and best ways to incentivize student voters to get engaged.

Students who show a keen interest in research can also become research assistants (RAs). Even under-resourced regional public universities without graduate students can leverage work-study funding to hire undergraduate RAs.[1] My undergraduate and graduate student RAs have co-authored conference papers, professional newsletter essays, encyclopedia entries, and book chapters with me, in addition to serving as copy editors, database managers, and more. Students have helped me share best practices in teaching civic engagement by conducting thorough literature reviews of how political science educators assess civic learning outcomes (Bennion & Dill, 2013) and key findings about civic learning outcomes appearing in the *Journal of Political Science Education* (e.g., Bennion & Laughlin, 2018). They have written about how to engage in local issues to benefit the community while enhancing student learning outcomes (Hurley et al., 2022a), how to use simulations to promote active learning about government (Hurley et al., 2022b), and how to cultivate civil and productive political discourse (Isenbletter et al., 2022). Like other forms

---

[1] Students who qualify for federal financial aid usually qualify for work-study. The employer pays only 25% of the hourly wage of a work-study student, while the federal government pays the remaining 75%.

of experiential learning, faculty-student research is a high-impact learning practice that promotes learning and increases retention (Bennion, 2015a).

When thinking about fruitful ways to combine teaching and research, faculty should also consider all the ways they teach and mentor students. As a student club advisor, I wanted to know the best ways to use registered student organizations to develop students' civic skills and identity. With the help of an undergraduate RA, J. Cherie Strachan and I conducted a National Survey of Student Leaders (NSSL) to assess democratic engagement and civic learning on college campuses and develop recommendations for structuring organizations' activities, structures, and leadership to promote democratic outcomes (Strachan & Bennion, 2016; Robiadek et al., 2019). Working with students to conduct research about how to best promote student learning is an ideal way to identify evidence-based best practices to facilitate student learning and engagement.

The Triple-Play: Integrating Teaching, Research, and Service to Engage Learners and Strengthen Democracy

Figure 24.1 highlights ways to combine teaching, research, and service to enhance student learning experiences and enrich life as a faculty member by maximizing the creativity, efficiency, and effectiveness of faculty work.

At the intersection of teaching and research is scholarly teaching and the scholarship of teaching and learning. At the intersection of teaching and service is service learning and related forms of community-based learning. At the intersection of research and service is the scholarship of engagement and other forms of community-based research designed to promote the public good (Barker, 2004). At the center of the diagram, represented by the star, are projects that combine teaching, research, and service to enhance student learning and promote the common good. As a civically engaged teacher-scholar, these are the opportunities I value most. Faculty members highlight such projects when building a case for reappointment, promotion, and/or tenure and when applying for teaching awards, research grants, and community service awards. Such projects strengthen all sections of a faculty member's dossier, allowing faculty to focus their efforts on a single project rather than splitting their time on separate, less coherent, often unrelated projects. Instead of worrying about how to "make time" for research (or service, or teaching prep), the

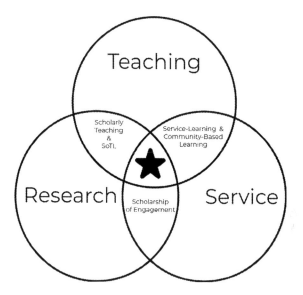

Fig. 24.1 The integration of teaching, research, and service

faculty member can focus on a single project that checks all these boxes; this saves time, enhances focus, and provides a richer and more meaningful experience for the faculty member while also providing significant benefits for students and the community at large (Bennion, 2015b). The remainder of this brief chapter provides two specific examples of such synergy.

Mobilizing Voters During a Competitive Congressional Election

As part of my U.S. politics and elections courses, I engaged students as fieldworkers, going door-to-door to mobilize voters as part of a randomized field experiment testing the effectiveness of different messages on voter turnout.

The non-partisan voter registration drive provided a service to the community, increasing voter knowledge and participation. The training and incorporation of students as fieldworkers enhanced my teaching, providing students with experiential learning about campaigns, elections, voter attitudes, and social science fieldwork. Meanwhile, the fact that

I designed the experiment as a research project, using random assignment and a solid experimental design allowed me to publish the results of the field experiment—documenting a significant boost in turnout rates among young voters contacted by the student canvassers (Bennion, 2005). The fact that campaign managers for the partisan campaigns admitted to cutting young voters with a lower propensity to vote and unknown party loyalties off their walk lists provides a compelling explanation for the substantively and statistically significant gap in the treatment effect on younger voters versus older voters (see Bennion [2005] for a detailed analysis of treatment results). In short, the student canvassers did, in fact, make a difference in the turnout rate of young voters. But did students feel like the experience was worthwhile? Did they feel like they made a positive difference in the community, and did participating in the fieldwork deepen their knowledge or teach them something they had not learned in the classroom?

I studied the effects of the experience on student knowledge and attitudes using student reaction papers and pre- and post-canvassing surveys, allowing students to reflect on the learning process while enhancing my assessment of my teaching strategies through the scholarship of teaching and learning (Bennion, 2006). Students identified several educational and personal benefits of the field experiment including getting involved with the community, renewing their faith in democracy, strengthening their commitment to voting, gaining a new appreciation for candidates, and improving the image of young people (Bennion, 2006).

Preparing Students to Engage
To prepare students, I discussed the mobilization campaign on the first day of class during the syllabus review, encouraging students to select the canvassing date that worked best for them and to mark their calendars during the second week of classes. The following week, before students signed up for a training session and canvassing time, I explained the process and the nature of the experimental design and stressed the reasons why I believed this learning experience would benefit the students. I also verbally acknowledged that many students might be feeling nervous about participating in the activity and assured them that previous student canvassers felt the same way but were pleasantly surprised by the experience. Throughout the course, I discussed topics directly related to students' upcoming fieldwork, including: voter turnout rates in the

United States, structural factors influencing voter turnout, the relationship between turnout and various demographic characteristics (including education and age), American attitudes toward politics, the quality of U.S. election campaigns, the difference between labor intensive and capital intensive campaigning, the effectiveness of grassroots voter mobilization campaigns, and the resurgence of political science field experiments. The goal was to help students acquire the background knowledge and theoretical framework required to contextualize their experiences in the field and to reflect on the connections—and gaps—between what they were learning in class and what they experienced first-hand while canvassing a local neighborhood.

In addition to in-class preparations throughout the semester, I also worked with trained peer mentors/supervisors to host a one-hour weekend training session with students immediately before sending them out into the field. This allowed me to assign partners, distribute the walk lists, explain each column of the list, remind students about the procedure for contacting voters, and give students time to role play and practice the canvassing script and to talk with their partners about how to distribute the work. I gave each pair of students a walk list, a pencil or pen, the correct amount of campaign literature, and a map (with their walk route highlighted). I also provided students with pizza and refreshments upon their return to the training site, allowing time for a post-canvassing debriefing while the student supervisors audited the completed walklists.[2]

Get-Out-the-Vote Project Details and the Student Experience
A total of 71 students participated in a three-day, nonpartisan, door-to-door, voter mobilization campaign during a competitive congressional election. This mobilization campaign was designed as a randomized field experiment. Students were provided with specific names and addresses

---

[2] More details about how to incorporate a randomized field experiment into a traditional political science course are provided in an article published in the *Journal of Political Science Education* (Bennion 2006, Appendix B). This includes a discussion of how to: (1) incorporate the assignment into your syllabus, (2) obtain the list of registered voters, (3) randomize the list of registered voters, (4) create walk lists and call lists for the student canvassers, (5) prepare students in the classroom, (6) host training sessions, (7) supervise the mobilization campaign, and (8) analyze the data to measure the effectiveness of the mobilization campaign. It also contains details about how to get students to the start of their walk route, ensure that students l complete the canvassing, and support students in the field.

of people to contact. The students targeted a randomly selected group of registered voters in three precincts adjacent to the university. Each student canvassed for three hours and carefully recorded their contacts. After the experience, students wrote about the most positive and negative aspects of the experience. Participants in the voter mobilization campaign included students in two sections of an Introduction to American Politics course as well as students in an upper-division course entitled Public Opinion and Political Participation. Select members of the Political Science Club and student interns served as precinct captains charged with supervising and encouraging the canvassers.

In their open-ended reflection papers, students identified nine educational and personal benefits of the field experiment. From the students' perspective, the most positive aspects of the field experiment were getting involved with the community, renewing their faith in democracy, strengthening their commitment to voting, gaining a new appreciation for candidates, and improving the image of young people (see Bennion [2006], Fig. 24.1, for a complete list of student responses). Students' responses about the most negative aspects of their experience were also quite uniform. In students' open-ended reaction papers, the most frequent responses included: the cold weather, rude citizens, the negative political attitudes displayed by some citizens, residents who refused to answer the door, and multiple trips to the same house without a successful contact. However, these experiences were not universal, and students balanced comments about rude voters with the excitement of those who seemed pleased to see them mobilizing voters. They stressed that the difficulty reaching some registered voters, despite long walks in the cold, made them appreciate the difficulties faced by political campaigns and the heavy reliance on mass media. In short, students recognized that even the least pleasant parts of their canvassing experiences increased their empathy for candidates and campaign volunteers and provided valuable lessons about political mobilization and grassroots democracy (Bennion, 2006).

The following year, 67 students participated in a three-day, nonpartisan, door-to-door voter mobilization campaign while 20 additional students participated in a telephone-based mobilization campaign. Participants in this campaign included students in two sections of an Introduction to American Politics course as well as students in a 100-level American political controversies course. Again, specially trained members of the Political Science Club served as precinct captains charged with supervising and encouraging the student canvassers. The second field experiment took place during an uncompetitive mayoral election. Each of these students completed an anonymous survey containing closed-ended questions designed to reflect the themes that emerged from students' written comments about the previous year's field experiment.

Responses to this survey indicated that most students were glad to have participated in the mobilization campaign (69%). This was particularly true of students who met with voters face-to-face (73%). The follow-up survey demonstrates the reasons most students were pleased with their out-of-class learning experience. A majority felt that the mobilization project allowed them to interact with other students in an enjoyable way (91%), to get involved with the community in a positive way (85%), to help improve the image of college students (71%), and to do something important—something that might make a difference in the lives of others (70%). Students also reported that the project gave them a new appreciation for the hard work of candidates (84%), reinforced key concepts discussed in class (79%), reinforced their own belief that voting is important (75%), and made them feel that they needed to vote on Election Day (73%). Overall, students were pleased by citizens' responses to their efforts. Few reported negative attitudes among citizens (33%), whereas many reported positive attitudes among citizens (95%) and citizens appreciation of their efforts (85%). Students did face some difficulties including refusals (83%), outdated voter lists (79%), fatigue (69%), and voter rudeness (60%). Like the previous semester, students explained that these difficulties helped them to better understand political attitudes in the U.S. (63%).

This required student field experience is one example of a Triple-Play (or "hat trick") for teacher scholars. A single project enhanced the quality, quantity, and coherence of my work. Published political science and SoTL scholarship, innovative teaching, and documented student learning are all products of this effort which also, and importantly, strengthened local democracy, mobilized new voters, and enhanced students' commitment to voting and community engagement.

Partnering with Public Television to Educate the Community

As a political scientist, I am often called upon to teach beyond my own classroom by teaching the public about politics through solicited lectures, presentations, and media interviews. I use my skills as a researcher to prepare for such appearances and my skills as a teacher to communicate information in a way people can understand. Based on this skill set, our local PBS station invited me to host a weekly public affairs TV program, Politically Speaking, that features interviews with public officials, academics, and activists discussing important political issues shaping our state, region, and nation (www.wnit.org/ps).

Before accepting the invitation, I asked my department chair if I could create a seminar designed to engage students in producing a weekly public affairs program for our local PBS affiliate WNIT. In addition to screening live callers, students would serve as research assistants, producing street videos capturing people's opinions on controversial issues, compile relevant "fast facts" to show on screen, and develop program ideas and host notes based on their research of weekly policy topics. The idea was approved instantly, and students' research was featured every week on a program broadcasted to an area with 1.2 million viewers in 22 counties.

Preparing Students to Engage
Before working in the TV studio, students watched the program, took a tour of the station and studio, and met key station personnel. The syllabus provided students with a set of specific learning objectives and a task list so that they knew what to expect and what was expected of them. They discussed the call-screening sheet they had created with the producer and engaged in a role play activity before taking live calls. I provided a basic overview of the policymaking process in Michigan and Indiana and showed students how to track legislation and research local legislators. We discussed good sources to use when studying local political developments and students also met with an expert from instructional media services to get tips on producing street videos for the show. Most importantly, the entire course was treated like a workshop where students' research-based facts, ideas, and feedback were taken seriously, subjected to frequent peer and instructor review, and used to shape a live public affairs program televised to the region. This format prioritized teamwork and a growth mindset while creating a strong incentive for students to fact-check themselves, and each other, to ensure the accuracy of the broadcast.

Politically Speaking Project Details and the Student Experience
This course included many learning objectives. Students were expected to: demonstrate Internet-based research skills, explain how the policymaking process works in Indiana and Michigan state governments, identify state and local officials for the region (including party identification and key issue priorities), create relevant on-screen facts pertaining to each episode's policy topic, describe the direction and diversity of public opinion surrounding controversial policy proposals, analyze a policy discussion by identifying strengths and weaknesses in guest arguments and performance, and identify content and production strengths and weaknesses of the program from a viewer perspective. To gain these skills, students conducted background research on episode guests, state politics, and local political issues. They used their research-based knowledge to propose questions for guests, conduct on-location interviews with local residents, screen calls at the TV studio during live call-in programs, and develop materials for the program's social media platforms. Students interested in TV production had the option of operating a (largely stationary) host camera or helping in the control room, and all students shared ideas regarding program content, design, and production value by providing written and verbal feedback on every episode (see Bennion [2015b] for assignment details and point values).

Students cited political science and other relevant literature, tracked state and national legislation, and followed current events. They developed their knowledge and research skills while serving the community. In reflecting on their experiences in the course, students reported an increase in self-confidence and interpersonal communication skills and in their ability to confront and discuss opposing viewpoints, think critically about public policies, and engage in respectful civic dialogue with people offering diverse opinions and perspectives. Students' post-course reflections focused on the growth they experienced in skills and knowledge but also stressed a transformative effect their hands-on work as researchers and production assistants had on their attitude about politics and their own role in the community. While they appreciated the ability to meet political leaders and see their names in the credits that roll at the end of each episode, the benefits of the seminar went far beyond this. Students reported that they followed politics more closely and felt a greater sense of political efficacy, willingness to contact their elected officials, and interest in political engagement than before they took the course.

> ... I would like to be elected to some form of office. I now watch most political debates on TV and listen to them on radio. I consider myself a political enthusiast, something that was not true before taking the course.—Seminar Participant

> I was able to meet many politicians since coming into the class. I know almost 100% more than I did before the class. During this class, I learned more about the American public and how it views politics. The class also offered insights and front row looks at policy creation and procedures. I have gained vital policy researching skills in the class that I feel would otherwise take years to learn how to accomplish. I gained a personal and business connection to a policy-maker because I was connected with the class ... and information about how to contact policymakers [which] allows me and the people in my fraternity to make our voices heard.—Seminar Participant

Using a scholar's insights to teach beyond the classroom in service to the community is a powerful way to strengthen and defend democracy. Engaging students as researchers adds additional layers of impact as students also become teachers and scholars whose work promotes an informed citizenry and serves the public at large. As in the case of the voter mobilization projects, students dug into the literature before engaging with the public, and we shared the results of our research with a public audience.

Such synergy is consistent with Earnest Boyer's model of scholarship that includes the scholarship of discovery, the scholarship of integration, the scholarship of application (engagement), and the scholarship of teaching and learning (Boyer, 1990). In fact, all four forms are scholarship are required, and were utilized as part of this project. Hosting the television show is part of my work as a public intellectual. It involves the scholarship of application—which uses disciplinary expertise requested by a community partner (the TV station) that is reviewed by peers (the producers) and shared with a larger audience. It draws upon the scholarship of discovery (including original research) and requires the scholarship of integration which requires the synthesis of information across disciplines, topics, and time. Students engaged in all these forms of scholarship with me, and the results of this approach were assessed through the scholarship of teaching and learning.

Students enjoyed the hands-on research experience and reported both an increased knowledge of state and local politics and a strong sense of comradery and accomplishment in having their work featured on air (Bennion, 2015b).

Conclusion: Work Smarter, Not Harder

Getting students involved in your research can have benefits for you and your students. You become more productive as a scholar, while students gain a deeper understanding of the course material and the research process. Engaging students in community-based research provides additional real-world experiences that are useful for resume-building, skill development, citizenship training, and networking. Training students as researchers, fieldworkers, and teachers for innovative programs designed to educate and engage the broader community is an excellent way to inject enthusiasm into your teaching and increase the productivity and impact of your research, teaching, and service. Whether engaging students in neighborhood canvassing or in TV production, the key to success is to focus on your learning objectives and to focus on developing skills—such as original research, political messaging, networking, and oral communication—that students can use in their lives beyond college.

References

Barker, D. (2004). The scholarship of engagement: A taxonomy of five emerging practices. *Journal of Higher Education Outreach and Engagement, 9*(2), 123–137.

Bennion, E. A. (2005, September). Caught in the ground wars: Mobilizing voters during a competitive congressional campaign. *The Annals of the American Academy of Political & Social Science, 601*, 123–141.

Bennion, E. A. (2006). Civic education and citizen engagement: Mobilizing voters as a required field Experiment. *Journal of Political Science Education, 2*(2), 205–227.

Bennion, E. A. (2009, Winter). I'll register to vote if you teach me how: Results of a classroom-based field experiment. *The Indiana Journal of Political Science, 11*, 20–27.

Bennion, E. A. (2015a). Experiential education in political science and international relations. In J. Ishiyama, W. J. Miller, & E. Simon (Eds.), *Handbook on teaching and learning in political science and international relations* (pp. 351–368). Edward Elgar.

Bennion, E. A. (2015b). Partnering with your local PBS station to promote civic and political engagement. In M. T. Rogers & D. M. Gooch (Eds.), *Civic education in the twenty-first century* (pp. 433–454). Lexington Books.

Bennion, E. A., & Dill, H. M. (2013). Civic engagement research in political science journals: An overview of assessment techniques. In A. R. M. McCartney, E. A. Bennion, & D. Simpson (Eds.), *Teaching civic engagement: From student to active citizen* (pp. 423–436). American Political Science Association.

Bennion, E. A., & Laughlin, X. E. (2018). Best practices in civic education: Lessons from the Journal of Political Science Education. *Journal of Political Science Education, 14*(3), 287–330.

Bennion, E. A., & Nickerson, D. W. (2011). The cost of convenience: An experiment showing e-mail outreach decreases voter registration. *Political Research Quarterly, 42*(3), 858–869.

Bennion, E. A., & Nickerson, D. W. (2016). I will register and vote if you show me how: A field experiment testing voter registration in college classrooms. *PS: Political Science & Politics, 49*(4), 867–871.

Bennion, E. A., & Nickerson, D. W. (2022). Decreasing hurdles and increasing registration rates: An online voter registration systems field experiment. *Political Behavior, 44*(4), 1337–1358.

Boyer, E. L. (1990). *Scholarship reconsidered: Priorities of the professoriate.* Carnegie Foundation for the Advancement of Teaching.

Hurley, D. J., Isenbletter, K. C., & Bennion. E. A. (2022a). Engaging in local issues to benefit the community and enhance student learning. *Civix, 1*(1). Retrieved March 1, 2023, from https://sites.google.com/view/apsacivic/publications/civix-essays

Hurley, D. J., Isenbletter, K. C., & Bennion. E. A. (2022b). Using simulations to promote active learning about local, state, and national government. *Civix, 1*(1), 24–27.

Isenbletter, K. C., Hurley, D. J., & Bennion, E. A. (2022). Cultivating civil discourse for our democratic future. *The Political Science Educator, 25*(2), 20–23.

Potter, M. K., & Kustra, E. D. H. (2011). The relationship between scholarly teaching and SoTL: Models, distinctions, and clarifications. *International Journal for the Scholarship of Teaching and Learning, 5*(1). Retrieved March 1, 2023, from https://doi.org/10.20429/ijsotl.2011.050123

Robiadek, K. M., Bennion, E. A., & Strachan, J. C. (2019). Assessing democratic engagement through student organizations. *Journal of Student Affairs Research and Practice, 56*(5), 595–607.

Strachan, J. C., & Bennion, E. A. (2016). Extending assessment beyond our own programs and campuses: The national survey of student leaders and the inter-campus consortium for SoTL research. *PS: Political Science & Politics, 49*(1), 111–115.

CHAPTER 25

Thriving Together: Connecting Civic Engagement, International Relations Pedagogy, and Undergraduate Research as Workload

Alison Rios Millett McCartney

With so many demands on a professor's time and energy from obligatory workload commitments, to promotion, tenure, merit requirements, one should rightly ask: how can a professor successfully pursue their career goals while also supporting undergraduates in their research interests? In this model, based on my upper-level class "Civic Engagement and International Relations" taught at a regional comprehensive public university, undergraduate research has been integrated into the instructor's

A. R. M. McCartney (✉)
Department of Political Science, Towson University, Towson, MD, USA
e-mail: amccartney@towson.edu

© The Author(s), under exclusive license to Springer Nature Switzerland AG 2023
C. Butcher et al. (eds.), *The Palgrave Handbook of Teaching and Research in Political Science*, Political Pedagogies,
https://doi.org/10.1007/978-3-031-42887-6_25

three workload areas of scholarship, teaching, and service.[1] Significant outcomes include over 100 undergraduate research presentations based on work in this class at local, regional, national, and international conferences, both co-publishing and co-presenting by students and instructor at major national and international disciplinary conferences, development and receipt of several grants and awards for students and instructor, and new, recognized service opportunities for the instructor. Learning through the development of this model also has contributed to campus-wide initiatives which have improved access to, options for, and recognition of undergraduate research across disciplines. This chapter begins with a review of this model and its student and instructor outcomes and then explains how a university-wide faculty committee, two civic engagement offices, and connections made across campus via this model, such as with the Honors College, improved the pursuit of undergraduate research for students and professors while also advancing workload integration and promotion, tenure, and merit opportunities. Overall, this model's lessons for instructors and students resulted from integrating undergraduate research into all instructor workload areas while connecting with larger campus undergraduate research and civic engagement initiatives.

We know from many studies that participation in undergraduate research yields a greater likelihood of graduate school enrollment, job placement connected to the field, and general satisfaction with their college careers. In addition to showing how a civic engagement service-learning course can spawn productive undergraduate research outcomes, this chapter explains how this connection can also yield fruitful outcomes for the instructor in scholarship, teaching, service, and workload. While not measurable for one person, this path also has brought much job satisfaction, which many attribute to positive mentoring experiences (Temple et al., 2010; Vandermass-Peeler et al., 2018). The key has been learning to integrate undergraduate research into all aspects of my career—an ongoing process.

---

[1] #2077, "TU Alumni: Impacts on Participation in TU-BCPS Model United Nations program (PI: McCartney, Alison M)" was Exempt approved by the Towson University IRB Committee. See also Alison Rios Millett McCartney and Sivan Chaban, "Bringing the World Home: Effectively Connecting Civic Engagement and International Relations," in Teaching Civic Engagement: From Student to Active Citizen, eds. Alison Rios Millett McCartney, Elizabeth A. Bennion, and Dick Simpson. Washington, D.C.: American political Science Association, 2013: 259–277.

STARTING WITH ONE CLASS

The building of this model started with one class, "Civic Engagement and International Affairs," which I created to work with a new department civic engagement initiative, the Towson University-Baltimore County Public Schools Model United Nations (TU-BCPS MUN), an inclusive, equity-based Model United Nations conference. This fall semester service-learning class, an elective in the Political Science major, includes written and oral components meant to connect traditional international relations knowledge and analysis with civic engagement-service-learning (CESL) experiential learning skill development (for details see McCartney, 2006).

One assignment entails a 20-page research paper on one organ or association agency of the United Nations (ex: UNICEF). Students are required to research and evaluate the agency's success in fulfilling its mission globally and to explore its local connections. Pitched to a junior level, most students are major/minors in Political Science, International Studies, or our Law and American Civilization program (also counts as an Experiential Learning elective in the Honors College). It is rarely the first upper-level class that they have taken, but the only official pre-requisite is that they have taken an introductory class in international relations or comparative politics. Thus, while preferred, I cannot rely on political science methods training or writing training beyond the University-required freshman English course and freshman research seminar (which introduces basic research skills, such as formulating and defending a thesis statement). Students also present their agency, with learning exercises, in a local high school social studies class that is associated with the civic engagement activity connected to the class, and they do a first-run presentation before college classmates in my course to get feedback. However, this presentation's goal is not to present and defend the same argument of the paper; rather, its goals are to inform high schoolers about the agency, its activities, and the local connections to its work. These presentations nonetheless provide experience with conveying ideas and concepts to others beyond the classroom and an introduction to dissemination and are a way of connecting service with global and local learning that is accessible to all students regardless of their financial or family circumstances. Students who earn a grade of B or higher in the course are invited to continue working with the conference and their research for the spring semester.

While the fall class immediately was integrated into my teaching workload and running the TU-BCPS MUN is my service load, a student years ago asked how she could continue to work with the Model UN conference and if this work could be connected to her graduate school aspirations. In the spring 2004 semester, I tested a CESL independent study plan with her to develop her fall course research paper into a more advanced undergraduate research project. She and I even went to a national undergraduate research conference together following the work, which led me to develop this option for all future classes. Students can earn between 1 and 3 credits in a civic engagement independent study class in political science, which counts toward the Political Science major/minor, the International Studies major/minor, and/or Honors College Experiential Learning requirements. Those who earn one credit serve as after-school coaches for the Model UN teams, help prepare for and work the actual conference weekend, and help other students with their conference presentations; thus, they do not undertake advanced undergraduate research. Students who earn three credits do the above, plus revise and expand their research papers from the fall. These students must also apply to present their work at a local, regional, and/or national undergraduate research conference. The local, on-campus option ensures that all students get to present and allows the inclusion of students with family or work obligations that limit travel.

One of the challenges in facilitating this type of student learning is how to integrate independent studies into one's workload, as they often do not "count" in the same way as traditional classes. At one point, my institution counted 21 credits of independent study/internship/thesis within an academic year as one traditional course. However, it is hard to plan such outcomes given students' changing interests, and at times I have earned no workload credit. At other times, an instructor could get paid for off-load teaching. Currently, an instructor can earn a maximum stipend of $800 for a maximum of eight credits per semester if they do not take workload anothercredit, so I often am operating beyond workload requirements for teaching. Yet, in addition to helping me maintain a stable of workers for my service project, their research has contributed to my scholarship.

When I began my academic career, I did not intend to research the effects of civic engagement pedagogy on undergraduate learning. However, I began to integrate their CESL work with my own scholarship in ways that I had not originally planned for my career. As I delved into the literature on civic engagement education, began teaching my courses, and attended the American Political Science Association (APSA) yearly Teaching and Learning Conference (TLC), I sought to better understand the long-term impacts of their CESL work for their civic engagement outcomes and career outcomes. My students wanted these answers too, so I brought one into the research process starting with some survey work that appeared in a book chapter in 2013, which was supported by an on-campus faculty development grant (McCartney & Chaban, 2013; McCartney in Matto et al 2017; Blair and McCartney in Matto et al 2021). While that chapter could only show preliminary data given the short time, it started me on a path of incorporating students into this work. In 2017, I conducted survey with the previous student, who was by then an alumnus, and another then-current student, and we presented the work at the 2018 TLC. (McCartney, Rice, and Chaban, 2018). Since 2019 with the help of a grant from BTU (Baltimore-Towson University), a campus-based entity that supports civic engagement efforts, I have been working with a former graduate student and two undergraduates (now alumni) on further research, and we have presented work thus far at one international conference and two national conferences, with another pending. For 2022–2023, I have another faculty development grant for longitudinal research on both civic engagement and undergraduate research outcomes and have brought in a new undergraduate to assist. We plan to use all of this data for a forthcoming book project on our model of combining civic engagement education in and with the community with undergraduate research.

I have reaped numerous benefits from my teaching and mentoring in the area of civic engagement. Not only have the students earned scholarships and grants and had the opportunities to co-publish, but I have been able to incorporate their research projects into my own scholarly work. More specifically, I have leveraged these experiences into several journal articles, book chapters, and three co-edited books in addition to over 20 international, national, and regional conference presentations, 16 workshops, 15 speeches and panels, and five on-campus presentations. Further, my civic engagement program has led to 24 international, national, and local grants for my travel and associated programs, ranging from $500-$129,000, eight teaching and scholarship awards, and a system-wide award from the University of Maryland for mentoring. In sum, this work with the students, connected to my civic engagement program, has yielded substantial career outcomes, while also advancing their futures.

Student Outcomes

The students whom I have worked with have had significant outcomes. Collectively they have presented their research at two international conferences, 13 national conferences (plus 2 more canceled due to COVID-19 and one more canceled due to funding), 35 regional conferences, and 55 local undergraduate research event presentations. The national and regional conferences include a mix of high-level professional association conferences such as APSA and APSA TLC and undergraduate-focused research conferences such as the National Conference on Undergraduate Research (NCUR), the National Collegiate Honors Council conference (NCHC), the Northeast Regional Honors Council (NRHC), and the Virginia Commonwealth University Undergraduate Political Science Research Conference. Local presentations have been part of a yearly university-wide Undergraduate Research and Creative Inquiry Forum and an Honors College experiential learning presentation event, which are useful options for students who cannot travel due to family or job commitments. They have written nine honors theses directly from this work and eight more indirectly from this work (topic morphed). They have earned over 50 travel grants, 13 locally-competitive research grants ranging from $500–$5000 (instituted in Fall 2017), and a Fulbright.

Table 25.1 shows some basic demographic data on the number of students who have taken the fall class, and Table 25.2 shows those who then pursued the independent study option for credit, which totals 38.4% of students who took the fall class (note that a few students graduated in the fall semesters and thus were not eligible to continue). These projects have led to significant direct and associated student outcomes. Direct outcomes, those attributable to this undergraduate research project, include conference presentations (105), research grants received (13 since 2017, the first year that such opportunities were available), publications, University-level awards, graduation roles such as commencement speaker (20 since 2015), and leadership opportunities, and development of additional research projects and theses. Associated outcomes, which are definitely related to the undergraduate research experience but may also be the result of multiple experiences, include other awards, other publishing, and graduate school enrollment, as noted in Table 25.3. Careers that I could track based on LinkedIn profiles for those now beyond graduate school are shown in Table 25.4.

Table 25.1 Enrollment in fall course (n = 238) 2004–2008; 2009–2015; 2017–2021[a]

Gender	Non-binary	0
	Female	149 = 62.6%
	Male	89 = 37.4%
Race/ethnicity	Black	31 = 13%
	Latinx/Hispanic	18 = 7.6%
	Asian	11 = 4.6%
	International	17 = 7.1%
	Mixed	5 = 2.1%
	White	156 = 65.5%

Note [a]Gaps are due to instructor sabbaticals

Table 25.2 Enrollment in spring independent study (n = 89) 2004–2022

Gender	Non-binary	0
	Female	60 = 67.4%
	Male	29 = 32.6%
Ethnicity	Black	6
	Latinx/Hispanic	5
	Asian	5
	International	8
	Mixed	3
	White	62 = 69.7%
	Non-white/intl.	27 = 30.3%

Table 25.3 Graduate school outcomes

Fall class	Spring indep. study
Total eligible = 224 (14 still enrolled)	Total eligible: 85 (4 still enrolled)
No data = 52 = 23.2%	No data = 6 (7%)
Attended/in grad school = 101 = 45.1%	Attended/in grad school: 42 = 49.4%
Type of school:	Type of school:
MA Education = 8	MA Education = 4
MPA/MA IR/Global Studies/Security Studies = 39	MPA/MA IR/Global Studies/Security Studies = 16
Law = 30	Law: 11
MA/MS—Other = 24	MA/MS Other: 11

Overall, the data demonstrates that for this group, participation in undergraduate research correlates to a very strong likelihood of acceptance to graduate school, especially in fields in or related to political

Table 25.4 Trackable career outcomes

Fall course	Spring indep. study
Total eligible = 224 (14 still enrolled)	Total eligible: 85 (4 still enrolled)
No data = 57 = 24%	No data = 8 = 9.4%
Education = 9	Education = 2
Private enterprise = 62	Private Enterprise = 23 = 27.1%
Law = 26	Law = 12 = 14.1%
Research/think tank = 3	Research/think tank = 3
Govt/public service = 24	Govt/public service = 13 = 15.3%
Military = 5	Military = 4
Healthcare = 3	Healthcare = 1
Higher ed admin/research = 4	Higher ed admin/research = 0
Non-profits = 17	Non-profits = 11 = 13%
Fulbright now = 1	Fulbright now = 1
In PhD program now = 2	In PhD program now = 2
In MA/Law program now = 11	In MA/Law program now = 5
In undergrad now = 14	In undergrad now = 4

science such as security studies and law. This group likely has been more interested in graduate school even before the fall class, but the results for both classes remain striking. Nationally, 39% of graduates from four-year institutions attended some graduate school within four years of finishing their undergraduate degrees in 2017, with a large majority in business, education, and health care (Baum & Steele, 2017). As encouraging students to attend graduate school has been one of my primary goals from the beginning in offering the independent study class, this outcome bolsters the argument that pursuing undergraduate research leads to more advanced education. These projects also correlate to jobs in the public and private sectors, with over 60% in jobs/graduate school fields in political science or related fields, such as law, high school social studies, military service, research, and non-profits in education and public policy.

University-Wide Innovations

As encouraging students to attend graduate school has been one of my primary goals from the beginning in offering the independent study option, I saw that my university lacked support for both instructors and students pursuing undergraduate research. I have used this work to argue for changes at the university level, including increased recognition of this work in promotion, tenure, and merit (PTRM) documents, increased financial support of students and faculty, and for publishing opportunities and new service opportunities that feed back into supporting students and faculty. First, when I started on this path, there simply was no place in our PTRM forms and documents to account for undergraduate research outcomes. One could only count the number of supervised credits. Wanting all of my work with students to count, I created new categories in our documents for "Innovative Teaching," "Undergraduate Research Conference Presentations," and "Undergraduate Grants," all of which are now generally accepted categories across the university, and presented these options at university-wide PTRM meetings. I also discussed undergraduate awards in my teaching narrative as they emerged. Through example and continual explanation of what these outcomes meant in terms of my workload and student career outcomes, I and others doing similar work in STEM were able to persuade PTRM committees at all levels, my department chair, dean, and eventually the provost that undergraduate research was valuable to the University's mission of undergraduate education and should be counted. For example, I discussed in my required yearly narrative on teaching the number of hours that I spent mentoring students to learn about, apply for, prepare for, and attend undergraduate research conferences. Doing so was and is not required or expected as part of a standard independent study, nor has it been warranted in every independent study which I have led. When possible, I have attended undergraduate research conferences such as NCUR with students. While adding to my time commitment, these conference experiences have furthered mentoring relationships and increased my own knowledge about the undergraduate research process and how to better mentor students in that process, such as the many resources offered by the Council on Undergraduate Research (CUR) and other models of developing undergraduate research programs (Hakim, 2000; Kinkead & Blockus, 2012).

Second, resource support was thin. With other colleagues on campus who are part of our Undergraduate Research and Creative Inquiry Faculty Committee, I used this knowledge plus my own experience and student outcomes to successfully show that my institution should be doing more to support students and faculty in undergraduate research. At that point, the committee had developed a university-wide yearly showcase, and it only offered meager travel grants which did not cover travel beyond the immediate area. When a new provost came, we were able to leverage examples from other institutions, our own experiences, and the national data which showed how undergraduate research increased retention and graduation rates to increase funding (Hensel, 2012), which had been flat for nearly 20 years, to show that more resources were warranted investments in our students.

Third, in order to increase attention and support for undergraduate research beyond STEM fields we took a multi-pronged approach. We began by developing new, very competitive yearlong grants for undergraduate research projects, generally given to 10–15 students across the university. We also increased student travel grant amounts. Next, we allowed faculty who were traveling with students to an undergraduate research conference to apply for this separate pool of grant money outside of their regular conference travel grant, which encouraged additional mentoring and collaboration. Given the success of that program, we then argued successfully for more funds to develop competitive summer research grants starting in summer 2020, which seek to pay for the equivalent of a part-time job in the summer ($5000) for about 10 students and provide a $500 stipend for each supervising faculty member.

Since the inaugural 2017–2018 group, I have had at least one student per year earn one of the yearlong grants and have had 1–2 students per summer win one of these grants. I noted all in my own annual workload reports and PTRM materials, and this mentorship was highlighted in both my department's letter and the dean's letter in favor of promotion to full professor as an example of outstanding teaching.

In pursuing these resources, this independent study work made me an appealing candidate to work with our most advanced students on campus in the Honors College. Appointed by the provost in 2014 as Faculty Director, I revamped Honors requirements for Experiential Learning and began to emphasize and promote undergraduate research. This led to my appointment on the URCI committee, where I began to lobby for and then helped to create the grants mentioned above.

As I started to work with Honors College students across disciplines, I realized that there was no one place for students to get peer support, much as they do in our Writing Center and Tutoring Center. Working with one particularly ambitious student in 2017 who shared this same concern, an assistant provost, and an Honors College staff member, we established a Student Government Association-approved club, the Undergraduate Research Club (URC). This interdisciplinary club brings students across campus for biweekly meetings which include information and advice on starting projects, finding mentors, applying for and getting grants to attend conferences, finding publishing opportunities, meeting alumni who did undergraduate research, integrating undergraduate research into career objectives and applications, connecting undergraduate research to competitive national scholarships such as the Fulbright and the Truman, and practicing presentations before one another.

As an official club, we also had to start fundraising. Our biggest event is Research Grams, where anyone on campus can order a Gram from our research menu and get an in-person or Zoom-based 5-minute research presentation by ordering from a menu listing our club members' projects (see McCartney et al., 2020). URC got over 80 orders in our first year (our goal was 20) and won the campus-wide award for best new student club from the Vice President of Student Affairs. Of course, some faculty and staff teamed up to send Grams to all top administrators. This activity showed high-level administrators that students across disciplines were very interested in more undergraduate research support. Together with the continual pleading of the faculty committee, we leveraged URC's work into a position for Faculty Director of Undergraduate Research, and this person now co-directs URC, which eases my time commitment.

While the URC's ultimate goal was supporting student researchers, it also strategically affected my own workload. For example, I could count my position as a URC faculty adviser as a component of my professional service commitment. Further, the role eased my advising load because rather than engaging in time-consuming and repetitive one-on-one sessions with undergraduate researchers, I can send students to club events and meetings for this information and support. These students now have developed a community, and the peer support aspect is adding leadership skills to their development (Hensel, 2012; Vandermass-Peeler et al., 2018).

Lessons Learned and Recommendations for Success

Of the greatest lessons that I have learned in pursuing undergraduate research, the three biggest are developing effective mentoring, building across the campus, and promoting connections to my career. For mentoring, I always start by learning about and connecting with students' existing interests and skills in another class. This way, I can gauge their level of interest and whether or not they are capable of completing an undergraduate research project. Further, by starting with other coursework which includes a 20-page research paper, they build upon background knowledge and experience in constructing and defending an argument, disseminating basic knowledge orally, and writing and organizing a substantial paper. I schedule regular meetings with them as a group and individually throughout the spring semester, and we set research goals and draft deadlines individually depending on what each student needs and the conferences to which they apply. Having local conference options is a plus for students with other commitments while having University-supported travel options is an exciting draw for other students. Often, students pursue both options.

If I break out my data by years, the data are skewed to more measurable mentoring outcomes as time progresses because I got better at identifying conferences, grant, and award options for students and directing students to them. I now actively seek to develop a mentoring relationship with these students, a known marker of better student outcomes (Hensel, 2012; Vandermass-Peeler et al., 2018). Our Office of Civic Engagement facilitated the development of this option in 2008 through its Service-Learning Faculty Fellows program (Surak et al., 2017), which included a stipend and some program funding.

I learned more about existing University resources through this program and made connections in it, which then helped me to better connect my students to resources. This second lesson is to build connections across the University to learn about existing resources on campus to support students and instructors. When these supports are limited or non-existent, a persistent instructor with a small cadre of engaged students, a network of colleagues, and research on what other institutions are doing can show the value of undergraduate research and gain more resources to fix these problems. Prime materials include samples of PTRM documents, workload criteria, grant support for students and instructors, and outcomes for students. I suggest developing a strong LinkedIn profile or finding another way to keep in touch with alumni apart from the official Alumni Office to maintain connections and have access to mentoring success stories. As competition for undergraduates increases, never discount the impact factor when speaking to administrators.

Regarding workload, mentoring undergraduate research was not a problem when I had one or two students, but in most spring semesters I usually have four or more, which becomes a challenge. Integrating undergraduate research work in all areas of our jobs is the final key to success. In research, I have taken on some students as co-researchers, a relationship that is extended into their alumni years. For example, they know my civic engagement program from the inside and can contribute materials and ideas developed from their participation. They have made substantial contributions to survey instruments, and their social connections are helping me to complete longitudinal data on outcomes. We are now co-presenting at professional conferences and writing a book. These students also volunteer for my service project, the TU-BCPS MUN, sometimes even long after graduating. This alumni network kept the project afloat—even thriving—during the COVID-19 pandemic, which helped it to maintain resources after the pandemic closures ended.

Finally, in teaching, while I have not always gotten paid or course load credit for every student, undergraduate research has made me a better teacher and mentor. In the classroom, I have sharpened my research paper assignments and feedback with an eye to identifying the most talented students, some of whom may not readily stand out because they are short on family-grown college skills such as confidence and self-efficacy. Outside of the classroom, I actively seek conversations about students' interests and ambitions and try to connect them to university resources such as the URC, the Honors College, and other leadership opportunities. The lesson is to approach one's teaching, research, and service much like a weaving project, integrating and connecting as one builds one's career rather than assuming that the pillars of teaching, research, and service stand separately.

References

Baum, S., & Steele, P. (2017). *Who goes to graduate school and who succeeds?* Post-Secondary National Policy Institute. https://pnpi.org/who-goes-to-graduate-school-and-who-succeeds/

Blair, A., & McCartney, A. R. M. (2021). "Introduction Section I; Global Civic Engagement Education." In E. C. Matto, A. R. M. McCartney, E. A. Bennion, A. Blair, T. Sun & D. Whitehead (Eds.), *Teaching Civic Engagement Globally*, (pp. 3–16). American Political Science Association.

Hakim, T. M. (2000). *How to develop and administer institutional undergraduate research programs.* Council on Undergraduate Research.

Hensel, N. (Ed.). (2012). *Characteristics of excellence in undergraduate research.* Council on Undergraduate Research.

Kinkead, J., & Blockus, L. (Eds.) (2012). *Undergraduate research offices & programs: Models & practices*. Washington, DC: Council on Undergraduate Research.

Matto, E., McCartney, A. R. M., Bennion, E., & Simpson, D. W. (Eds.). (2017). *Teaching civic engagement across the disciplines*. American Political Science Association.

Matto, E., McCartney, A. R. M., Bennion, E. A., Sun, T., Blair, A., & Whitehead, D. (Eds.). (2021). *Teaching civic engagement globally*. American Political Science Association.

McCartney, A. R. M. (2006). Making the world real: Using a civic engagement course to bring home our global connections. *Journal of Political Science Education, 2*(1), 113–128.

McCartney, A. R. M. (2013, February). Teaching civic engagement: Debates, definitions, benefits, and challenges. In A. R. M. McCartney, E. Bennion, & D. W. Simpson (Eds.), *Teaching civic engagement* (pp. 9–20). American Political Science Association.

McCartney, A. R. M., Bennion, E., & Simpson, D.W. (Eds.). (2013). *Teaching civic engagement: From student to active citizen*. American Political Science Association.

McCartney, A. R. M., & Chaban, S. (2013). Bringing the world home: Effectively connecting civic engagement and international relations. In A. R. M. McCartney, E. Bennion, & D. W. Simpson (Eds.), *Teaching civic engagement* (pp. 259–277). American Political Science Association.

McCartney, A. R. M. (2017). "Introduction," In E. C. Matto, A. R. M. McCartney, E. A. Bennion, & D. Simpson (Eds.), *Teaching Civic Engagement Across the Disciplines*. Washington, D.C. American Political Science Association.

McCartney, A. R .M., Mackenzie, R., & Sivan, C. (February, 2018). "Does Civic Education Last? A Lomgitudinal Case Study." Paper presented at American Political Science Association Teaching and Learning Conference, Baltimore, MD, 2–4.

McCartney, A. R. M., Napoli, R., Johnson, K., Cahalan, L., & Pace, B. (2020). Building undergraduate research across the disciplines: New ideas outside of the classroom with an interdisciplinary undergraduate research club. *Scholarship of Practice of Undergraduate Research, 3*(3), 1–9. https://www.proquest.com/openview/1127294607746143af61b1bef0167b6e/1.pdf?pq-origsite=gscholar&cbl=3882659

Surak, S., Jensen, C., McCartney, A. R. M., & Pope, A. (2017). Teaching faculty to teach civic engagement: Interdisciplinary models to facilitate pedagogical success. In E. Matto, A. R. M. McCartney, E. Bennion, & D. W. Simpson (Eds.), *Teaching civic engagement across the disciplines*. American Political Science Association.

Temple, L., Sibley, T. Q., & Orr, A. J. (2010). *How to mentor undergraduate researchers*. Council on Undergraduate Research.

Vandermass-Peeler, M., Miller, P. C., & Moore, J. L. (2018). *Excellence in mentoring undergraduate research*. Council on Undergraduate Research.

CHAPTER 26

Connection Over Content: How Civically Engaged Research Can Improve Teaching, Research, and Service

Kirstie Lynn Dobbs

Political science is a cornerstone discipline for defining and implementing civic engagement in the classroom and beyond (Matto et al., 2017; McCartney et al., 2013). Political science has even coined its own term for research where scholars work with communities to solve issues of governance, which directly parallels civic engagement. This form of inquiry is called civically engaged research (CER) (Bullock & Hess, 2021). However, the value of this work in the classroom and research in the tenure and promotion process is still a major obstacle for colleges and universities (Changfoot et al., 2020; Moffett & Rice, 2022). This obstacle is partly due to the difficulties in creating a narrative that connects

K. L. Dobbs (✉)
Department of Political Science and Public Policy, Merrimack University, North Andover, MA, USA
e-mail: dobbsk@merrimack.edu

© The Author(s), under exclusive license to Springer Nature Switzerland AG 2023
C. Butcher et al. (eds.), *The Palgrave Handbook of Teaching and Research in Political Science*, Political Pedagogies,
https://doi.org/10.1007/978-3-031-42887-6_26

engaged research with all aspects of scholarship, especially when university policies tend to reward this form of work only in terms of a faculty's service role—ignoring its value in both the areas of teaching and research. Others struggle to commit to this work on campuses where supportive resources are relatively scant (Alperin et al., 2019). Given these challenges, scholars might avoid engaging in public scholarship until they have received tenure and promotion.

Although frameworks that address these challenges have been discussed (Franz, 2009; Moffett & Rice, 2022), literature that helps scholars identify available resources for engaged work is lacking. This chapter seeks to fill this gap by providing a practical guide for faculty that builds a research agenda connected to the community and their teaching. I further argue that connecting with those around us, especially with community partners and colleagues across departments *before* leaning on our content areas, creates new avenues for building all areas of scholarship in mutually reinforcing ways that allow us to work smarter, not harder.

This practical guide is modeled through my experiences creating an interdisciplinary summer civic engagement program called Youth Voice. Youth Voice represents a community and interdisciplinary collaboration in which a political scientist effectively mentored students, provided service to the community, secured internal and external grant funding, and built out a research agenda that simultaneously resulted in tools used in the classroom. The program was co-facilitated with undergraduate students and ran for four weeks during July 2021. Youth aged 11–14 learn about their local community, how to express their voice, and how to develop tools for activism through writing, speaking art, and digital media. Research outcomes of this work included successfully submitting conference proposals and academic papers for publication. For assessing community outcomes, we found in our research that the youth who participated in the program developed a stronger sense of community and became more likely to engage with local actors in promoting social justice. We also provided a safe space for youth during the summer to explore their unique talents and grow academically. I use many of the activities and resources we developed for the Youth Voice program in the political science classroom, thereby effectively bridging my research, teaching, and community-engagement efforts.

Presenting a Case Study Through Guided Reflection

Reflecting on the "Self"

As you begin your journey with a civically engaged research project, self-reflect on your unique skills and talents that could serve as a contribution to a community. For example, I tutored middle schoolers during graduate school, which enabled me to comfortably engage with 11–14-year-olds in an academic setting, which is much different than teaching undergraduates on my college campus. These experiences could help combat a local problem exacerbated during the COVID-19 pandemic. In the United States, significant inequity persists in our educational system in terms of equipping students with the necessary tools for effective engagement in civic and political life, including reading, writing, and discerning fact from fiction via online media (Einhorn, 2020; Kuhfeld & Lewis, 2021; Kuhfeld et al., 2020). This issue was relevant to my research agenda and is also a significant concern for folks working in the youth development and educational sectors. Reflect on the questions below to start identifying how your unique talents might make a positive contribution.

First, what major ideas, issues, priorities, and community needs would either you or your students like to raise awareness about? Second, what unique gifts/experiences do you bring to the community? These gifts could go beyond your academic work and reflect who you are outside of political science.

Reflecting on Relationships

Next, connections on and off campus are vital to creating a scholarly agenda that serves many "buckets" of our academic work. Given my position as a professor teaching in the Early College Program at Merrimack College, which is housed in the School of Education, I have connections with professors and administrators outside the School of Liberal Arts. In the spring of 2021, I along with colleagues in the School of Education and Social Policy saw an opportunity to create a program that supported our research agenda and served a community need. The opportunity arose through a local grant calling for projects centered on closing opportunity and achievement gaps among youth in our area. As a result, we created the Youth Voice program.

A colleague who serves as the Special Assistant to the President for Civic and Community Affairs introduced us to a Merrimack College community partner, the Merrimack Valley YMCA. The YMCA was interested in collaborating with us on this project because they sought new programs to host during the summer. Ultimately, we were awarded $4,000 from internal and external funding to run the program. This funding was mostly used for stipends for undergraduate students, with a smaller portion allocated to art supplies. Without the campus and off-campus connections, developing the program would have been incredibly challenging. Other connections included a biology professor, who hosted a podcast on COVID-19 with the youth participants, and a contact from the Youth Development Organization in Lawrence, Massachusetts, who hosted a workshop on youth leadership during the program. I also relied on former students to discuss their path to leadership in their local community with the middle schoolers. To start identifying connections in your academic and non-academic life, reflect on the questions below.

Brainstorm your connections/relationships with individuals, groups, and organizations engaged in community work on and off campus. Is there a connection between those actors and your course content or research? How might those connections be strengthened by having students and established sources interact?

Reflecting on Student Involvement

For Youth Voice, we also brainstormed ways our undergraduate students at Merrimack might be involved. On top of the $4,000 to run the Youth Voice program, we also applied for internal funds through the Sakowich Center for Undergraduate Research (SCURCA). These SCURCA funds are used to pay students to work as undergraduate research assistants during the summer, and students were selected through an application with the intention of choosing one student from each school at Merrimack. Ultimately, our students represented the fields of political science/history, health sciences, biology, and criminal justice. Through SCURCA, Merrimack College awarded us $8,500 to mentor four students on research projects related to youth civic engagement and to train them as co-facilitators of the Youth Voice program. The students researched youth civic engagement programs throughout the world to gain an understanding of how we might apply global models to the development of Youth Voice. The SCURCA funds were dispersed to students in May–June 2021 prior to facilitating Youth Voice.

Our research design included running pre- and post-surveys with both the undergraduate facilitators and the Youth Voice participants and qualitative focus groups with both sets of students after completion of the program. The pre-surveys focused on assessing participants' baseline levels of civic engagement before completing the program. The post-survey asked the same questions but assessed their likelihood of engaging civically after completing the program. The qualitative interviews focused on how participants felt about the program increasing their understanding of the community and how young people can serve as effective leaders to make positive contributions to society. The research from this study resulted in a peer-reviewed publication co-authored with the undergraduate students, three conference presentations, a working paper, and of course this book chapter. Youth Voice will also serve as a case study in my working book project that analyzes the impact of the COVID-19 pandemic on Gen Z.

Youth Voice also represents an interactive partnership in which we seek to run the program throughout multiple summers. We will gather new data and new grant money with each New Year. As of the writing of this chapter, Merrimack College has invited our research team to submit a full proposal that would grant us $50,000. This money would fund Youth Voice for two years, increase the number of undergraduate co-facilitators, and give the faculty members course releases to focus on developing the curriculum into a publicly accessible "tool kit" for educators and practitioners running civics programs. The intent is to also incorporate the program into graduate programming at Merrimack to have more sustainable and institutionalized opportunities for students to help run the program. To start investigating your potential collaborations across campus and student involvement, reflect on the questions below.

How are you currently collaborating with non-academic partners in your research, teaching, or service? In what capacities could students be incorporated into those collaborations in mutually beneficial ways?

Reflecting on Pedagogy

Finally, through creating Youth Voice, I learned new pedagogical strategies from my colleagues in Education and Human Development and Human Services that I had not come across in my training as a political scientist. The central theme that bridges all aspects of my scholarly work is "connection over content," a phrase I heard when conducting participant observation research at a community workshop in Newport, Rhode Island. To achieve our goals collectively, we must first connect as individuals before diving into the content. My colleagues in the education and human development fields stressed an important theme: identity. They firmly believed in encouraging students to connect their identity with the content they were learning in the classroom. This is not a foreign concept to political scientists (McCartney et al., 2013), but I believe I gained a more grounded understanding of how political scientists could be more intentional about this aspect of our work.

The learning goal of connecting identity and civic engagement was incorporated into several activities during Youth Voice, three of which I adapted for my undergraduate classroom in the introduction to U.S. Politics course, which heavily emphasizes political participation and civic engagement. I chose to discuss these three activities because they apply to numerous classroom settings and can be adapted to fit any content area. The first activity is called "the identity tree." Students drew with markers or created with construction paper a tree that emphasized different parts of their identity (significant elements of their past, present, hopes and dreams, mentors, etc.). I use this activity as a first-week icebreaker in the undergraduate classroom to get to know my students while connecting my students to each other. A second activity was the "social identity wheel," a circle broken up like a piece of pie that displays different identity components within each "slice." These identity markers include age, ethnicity/race, income, religion, sexual orientation, gender identity, and ableism. Students are asked to mark the "slices of pie" most important to them. This leads us to discuss how different identity markers are activated in various people, which often shapes how we view ourselves, the community, and the world. The "values continuum" was a third activity in which students moved about the room under signs that displayed "strongly agree, agree, indifferent, disagree, and strongly disagree" after reading various phrases, such as "The government should always side with the majority, even if it's wrong" or "The reason people are poor is because of an unfair and unjust economy." The movement about the room showed the variation among students in how they felt about these often divisive topics.

Another area where I have connected my engaged research and the classroom is through "place-based learning." During Youth Voice, we took the students on a walking tour of the city of Lawrence to learn about various social justice murals painted by youth activists from the area. I also use this walking tour as a field trip in my State and Local Politics class and in a first-year exploration course called Rebels, Riots, and Revolutions. We connect concepts we are learning in class about economic development, activism, and the "creative class" with what they observe as they walk around downtown Lawrence. This walking tour served as a great activity during the Youth Voice program. Many participants told us that the walking tour was their favorite part of the program. They loved getting out of the "classroom setting" at the YMCA by engaging directly with their community. It also impacted my undergraduate students—without me having to develop any new content for class on the day of the field trip. This activity also fulfilled a university-driven, diversity, equity, and inclusion learning objective. Some undergraduate students develop negative stereotypes about Lawrence, given its high crime rate. Students remarked how walking around the city and seeing the beauty of the social justice murals depicting pride for their city with its history of immigration and diversity changed their perspective on the people who live there. The students realized that despite the economic hardships Lawrence has faced in the past, the city has many assets, including diversity, a strong sense of identity and community, and an entrepreneurial spirit. In sum, connection with places can be as fruitful as connecting with people. Reflect on the questions below to investigate how you might bridge your research and service with teaching.

Finally, I want you to reflect on what you want your students to gain from your experience engaging with community stakeholders. Is there a real-life story that would give students practical insight into politics, governance, and society? Is there an activity you completed that could be replicated in the classroom? Is the research that you gathered connected to class topics?

A Project to Take With You

If you are interested in building an activity that lends itself to civic and community engagement, I suggest implementing a civic engagement portfolio project in your classroom. Regardless of the course content area, you likely have an issue, priority, or problem that students could raise awareness about or attempt to redress. Have students focus on that issue (or allow them to choose one of their own) and guide them through a project that has five steps. First, I have students think about their own lived experiences and reflect on the various communities they belong to and how they might make a positive contribution to these spaces and/or locations. The students research an article that is related to their chosen community and a specific priority they are passionate about. They present these articles to each other in class and write a half-page reflection on how their lived experiences motivated them to choose their article. Second, students research their issues. They write a 3–5-page paper with at least eight legitimate sources about their topic. They are encouraged to include in their paper data that explains their problem, different policy proposals or actions taken to redress this problem, and strategies for how folks are raising awareness about this issue. Third, students identify short-term, intermediate, and long-term goals for resolving this issue. The short-term and intermediate goals often involve creating a campaign for raising awareness either in digital spaces or in real life. Long-term goals typically include redressing the issue, like organizing a clean-up of the city or pushing for more legislation to be passed. Fourth, students identify resources on and off campus to help them achieve their goals. Fifth, they complete either their short-term or intermediate-term goal and present the outcome in class. They are graded based on their ability to articulate a clear rationale for goals, as well as creativity and professionalism.

As a research tool, this project helps illuminate the issues that young people care about, an integral part of my research agenda. As a pedagogical tool, this activity helped students feel empowered to make positive changes in their community and helped me develop new activities and goals for future courses. A student in my U.S. Politics class focused their civic engagement project on promoting gender-neutral housing on Merrimack's campus. This student presented their proposal to the administration. I had another student present their proposal to the local police department on how to improve police response to domestic abuse cases. Another student used their project to support their internship in lobbying for a high-speed rail transport system across the United States.

Bridging Disciplinary and Institutional Divides

Overall, this case study demonstrates how civically engaged research can answer the call within political science to connect our research with community problems while meeting college and university expectations for faculty to pursue interdisciplinary collaborations. Embracing these pressures through community-driven research yields opportunities for political scientists to engage in research projects that attract undergraduate research assistants from fields across disciplines while also increasing access to institutional resources, especially internal funding. These collaborations also fulfill service and community-engagement mission priorities and enhance pedagogical methods. The key is bridging institutional resources with community priorities and non-academic partners. When executed effectively, this "bridge" increases efficiency without compromising quality in either research, teaching, or service. A final conclusion rests on the idea of connection over content. This case study showcases how connecting genuinely with our unique skills, talents, and relationships creates opportunities for learning that span our disciplinary boundaries—without overburdening our bandwidth when creating content.

References

Alperin, J. P., Muñoz Nieves, C., Schimanski, L. A., Fischman, G. E., Niles, M. T., & McKiernan, E. C. (2019). How significant are the public dimensions of faculty work in review, promotion and tenure documents? *ELife*, *8*, e42254.

Bullock, G., & Hess, D. R. (2021). Defining civically engaged research as scholarship in political science. *PS: Political Science & Politics*, *54*(4), 716–720. https://doi.org/10.1017/S1049096521000676

Changfoot, N., Andree, P., Levkoe, C., Nilson, M. A., & Goemans, M. (2020). Engaged scholarship in tenure and promotion: Autoethnographic insights from the fault lines of a shifting landscape. *Michigan Journal of Community Service Learning*, *26*(1), 239–263. https://doi.org/10.3998/mjcsloa.3239521.0026.114

Einhorn, E. (2020, December 15). COVID is having a devastating impact on children - and the vaccine won't fix everything. *NBC News*. https://www.nbcnews.com/news/education/COVID-having-devastating-impact-children-vaccine-won-t-fix-everything-n1251172

Franz, N. (2009). A holistic model of engaged scholarship: Telling the story across higher education's missions. *Journal of Higher Education: Outreach and Engagement*, *13*(4), 31–50. https://openjournals.libs.uga.edu/jheoe/article/view/1268/1265

Kuhfeld, M., & Lewis, K. (2021). Technical appendix for: Learning during COVID-19: An update on student achievement and growth at the start of the 2021–22 school year. NWEA. https://www.Learning-During-COVID-19-An-update-on-student-achievement-and-growth-at-the-start-of-the-2021–2022-school-year.pdf

Kuhfeld, M., Tarasawa, B., Johnson, A., Ruzek, E., & Lewis, K. (2020). Learning during COVID-19: Initial findings on students' reading and math achievement and growth. NWEA. https://www.nwea.org/content/uploads/2020/11/Collaborative-brief-Learning-during-COVID-19.NOV2020.pdf

Matto, E. C., McCartney, A. R. M., Bennion, E. A., & Simpson, D. W. (2017, July). *Teaching civic engagement across the disciplines*. American Political Science Association.

McCartney, A. R. M., Bennion, E. A., & Simpson, D. (2013). *Teaching civic engagement across the disciplines*. American Political Science Association.

Moffett, K., & Rice, L. (2022). Creditable civic engagement? Aligning work on civic activity with faculty incentives. *PS: Political Science & Politics, 55*(2), 401–403. - https://doi.org/10.1017/S1049096521001712

CHAPTER 27

Campus & Community Engagement of Student Research: The Evolution of a Senior Capstone Project

Carrie Humphreys

Working at a regional comprehensive university, teaching is expected to account for 70% of my position with scholarship and service equally split among the remaining 30%. While my research expectations are lower than they would be at a research-intensive university, they are still present, and it is stressful carving out sufficient time to draft abstracts, apply for conferences, prepare papers or presentations, and edit those papers into journal-worthy articles. It makes sense, given these circumstances, to look more at how my teaching can translate into research. There are many ways we can leverage our teaching and turn it into research via curriculum and course designs, assignments, assessment, etc. Even small activities and classroom "experiments" can inspire research ideas. Along these lines of

C. Humphreys (✉)
College of Business and Global Affairs, University of Tennessee at Martin, Martin, TN, USA
e-mail: Chumph16@utm.edu

© The Author(s), under exclusive license to Springer Nature Switzerland AG 2023
C. Butcher et al. (eds.), *The Palgrave Handbook of Teaching and Research in Political Science*, Political Pedagogies,
https://doi.org/10.1007/978-3-031-42887-6_27

tiptoeing into a research project, this chapter will offer insights based on an evolving senior capstone assignment for international studies majors that inspired a research project on campus and community engagement and offer suggestions for how others can similarly use their teaching to generate new research.

Before describing my project, it is important to acknowledge that the idea of research based on teaching is well-established. SoTL is a continuously growing field across grade levels and disciplines, including political science. In surveying the literature, however, the articles often read as well-crafted and pre-planned activities or assignments or intimidatingly extensive undertakings, which may deter faculty from replicating these tactics in their own classrooms or may convince them that their own classroom experiences are somehow lesser than those published in SoTL journals. For example, the extensive literature on simulations and games is based on detailed, elaborate, and pre-planned assignments (Baumann & FitzGibbon, 2021; Bursens et al., 2018; Hellstrom, 2017; Kammerer & Higashi, 2021; Leib & Ruppel, 2020; Lovell & Khatri, 2021; Williams & Chergosky, 2019). Moreover, many of these SoTL articles also feature an assessment mechanism like pre-/post-surveys of students' understanding of the topics and interest in the activity (Hasturkoglu, 2019; Stapleton, 2020). This trend is part of the growing call for assessment and an empirical-based approach to SoTL which is an important development in the field but can contribute to the faculty feeling even less prepared to take on such a research project (Burcu, 2020; Clark & Scherpereel, 2023; Craig, 2014; Duchatelet et al., 2020; Hamann & Hamenstadt, 2021; Hutchings et al., 2011; Murphy et al., 2023). Simulations and games, while worthwhile active learning exercises, require extensive planning by instructors and time for students to prepare. While these SoTL-oriented teaching activities are laudable, not everyone thinks ahead enough to build a simulation into a course, and even if they do, they might not have time to prepare a survey or otherwise assess the impact of a new activity or assignment, not to mention submit an IRB proposal, with the intent to publish their findings, before the course begins. Teaching, and the research it can inspire, does not always come with this initial level of advanced preparation. Sometimes the changes we make or assignments we experiment with are developed the same week as the unit is taught. This does not mean our teaching interventions cannot be leveraged for a research project; they still might provide the basis or inspiration for a project!

Other streams of SoTL research involve extensive course changes like utilizing a flipped classroom design or developing an online course (Betti et al., 2020; Bowers, 2019; Divjak et al., 2022; Hamann et al., 2021; Touchton, 2015; Whitman Cobb, 2016). While most of us were forced to move classes online in the spring of 2020 due to the COVID-19 pandemic, an unusual circumstance worthy of study and research, my main thought at the moment was not "how can I use this for research?" but more "how do I get the bare necessities ready for a new modality in three days?" Assuming course design changes can only occur before a semester begins can mislead us into thinking that we have missed possible research opportunities and must wait until future semesters. This is simply not true! The smaller ways we innovate in the classroom can also be sources of inspiration for research.

In sum, my intent in this chapter is not to discount the impressive SoTL work that already exists across a number of modalities. However, thinking you need to start new research by having a highly developed SoTL project in mind can be intimidating and overwhelming for many instructors. The focus of this chapter, therefore, is how we can leverage our teaching for research on a more regular basis and at any point during a semester. The sections that follow explore how we can more frequently utilize teaching to work smarter, not harder, by finding ways to generate research ideas even with less initial forethought and limited time commitment.

The Constant Cycle of Teaching Innovation

I constantly try new things in my classes. In teaching a 4–4 course load, with multiple sections of the same class each semester and a regular rotation of classes, it can be painfully clear where assignments fall flat in their objectives, topics fail to pique the interest of students, and when the timing of assignments across classes creates an overwhelming crush of grading. Some changes I incorporate when I write the syllabus, like moving up the date of presentations to ease the grading load or switching out assignments, and others are done while I am prepping for tomorrow's class, like changing the case study on human security from the Rohingyas fleeing Myanmar to Ukrainians fleeing the Russian invasion. I have not always considered these types of changes as worthy of research, but I am getting more in the habit of considering anything related to my classes as having research potential thanks to a project inspired by my senior capstone class for international studies majors.

International studies is a relatively small major at my institution and is closely allied with political science. The international studies side had been neglected and was in decline prior to my appointment as program director. While the number of majors was growing prior to the COVID-19 pandemic, the senior capstone has been consistently small, under 10 students. In this class, seniors undertake a multi-step research project that, quite traditionally, includes a literature review, paper draft, revisions, and, at least initially, a final class presentation. However, after two years of relatively uninspired class presentations to a small audience of their peers, I was interested in trying something new. I solicited input from my colleagues and consulted existing literature on capstone classes and projects (Fernandez et al., 2018; Hinckley et al., 2021; Houck, 2021; McClellan et al., 2021).

As a first step, I replaced the final presentation with a research poster in my syllabus while saving the question of where to display the posters for later in the semester. The two initial ideas were to feature the students' posters either in our classroom or displayed in the college, but instead, I heard about a new interactive classroom space in the university library. After contacting our information literacy librarian, we agreed to co-host an *International Studies Gallery* where we could invite everyone from the campus, faculty, and other students, to come and circulate the room of digital posters displayed on touchscreen TVs. Students stood next to their posters, offering insights, and answering questions for the two-hour open house-style event. During this first event in the fall of 2019, I was not yet thinking of this as my own research project. Instead, my thoughts leading up to the gallery were more "I hope people come" and "I hope this is a good experience for students." More out of curiosity than a fully conceptualized research project, the librarian and I kept a rough count of how many people came through the event. We also offered visitors a chance to vote for the "people's choice" poster, and the students and I reflected after the fact on what they liked and what we should change next year. I put all these notes in a folder and did not think about them again until the following fall when I taught the class again. As I prepared for the next capstone and reviewed my notes, my focus was still on improving and sustaining the poster assignment rather than seeing how it could be leveraged as research.

From Forced Adaptation to Research Project

Most of us are painfully aware of how much teaching changed in 2020 and my senior capstone was no different. My momentum for the *International Studies Gallery* dissipated—students were not on campus and instruction was remote, so what could we do? The librarian and I both agreed that we wanted to host the event again, so we transitioned to a virtual format. After surveying our options, we settled on using a Wix website to host the event. We uploaded three key pieces—the posters, student bios, and short videos of the students explaining their posters or offering highlights. Students were tasked to monitor and respond to comments and questions over the course of a week. This was a very different event in its second year—a longer event with more indirect encounters. We feared that online fatigue would dampen interest and participation in the event, so the relatively high level of engagement we achieved was surprising. After the first day of the event, the site "broke" due to a volume of comments exceeding what is permitted by the free version of the website. The librarian, the students and I were all amazed by the high level of participation. Not only were we getting a steady stream of visitors and comments, but my librarian colleague and I also had several faculty members email us directly with interest in doing something similar with their students. Compared with the in-person event the previous year, the virtual format reached a much larger audience of alumni, friends, and family from across the United States and globally, in addition to faculty across campus. We more than quadrupled our engagement with over 230 unique visitors in 2020, including members of the local community who had no official affiliation with the campus.

This was the moment for me when I saw how this poster assignment, introduced as part of my regular course routine to cut underperforming assignments and innovate, had potential as a SoTL research project. I did not start with the idea of researching how to engage the campus and community in student research, but in seeing the engagement flourish, I was inspired. I started brainstorming the many ways this could expand into a fully-fledged research project by looking into assumptions about engagement, including different types of engagement (faculty to student, student to student, community to student), and tracking the effectiveness of different tactics to increase engagement.

This path of teaching to research was more inductive than how I had assumed SoTL scholarship unfolded. I started with what I did in the classroom and later paired it with broader educational and SoTL topics like student research and engagement. More specifically, as I have continued to work on this project, it is coalescing around this research question: Undergraduate student research (papers, presentations, and posters) is mostly contained within a limited classroom or discipline setting. With very few students afforded opportunities to present at conferences, how can we make opportunities to showcase student research more accessible across campus and engage the community in student research projects and presentations?

This is an ongoing project, and I am still approaching the project from several avenues by collecting more comprehensive data, with IRB approval, and deciding what aspect to submit to a conference.[1] The first aspect is in terms of format and engagement levels. The poster gallery has run for three years now and in three different formats—2019 only in person, 2020 only virtual, and 2021 a hybrid (both in person and virtual). Especially as we continue to move past the pandemic, will there be sustained interest in the virtual format, or will we continue to reach our highest levels of engagement using a hybrid format? We are continuing to track the number of visitors across years and formats. Another aspect involves the spread of similar poster events on campus as more disciplines seek ways to highlight students' research across campus. There were at least three poster-related events on campus in the fall of 2021, all near the end of the semester. I have been reaching out to these faculty to learn more about how their disciplines approach the use of posters, what is similar or different across our event experiences, and what levels of engagement they are achieving (i.e., are the events competing?). Lastly, there is also the student aspect—their interest in the assignment, the value of their interactions with campus and community members, and whether this experience builds their confidence in applying to present at conferences.

---

[1] Short of a full-fledged SoTL project route, or as a stop along the way, instructors could consider sharing their early-stage work via professional newsletters, relevant blogs, "reflection" sections in some academic journals, or APSA Educate.

Recommendations

Reflecting on this experience, what are my top tips for continuing to use teaching as inspiration for research? I'll offer three. First, as teachers, we are surrounded by material that could be translated into research. From more substantive topics covered in classes to assignments and assessments to experiential learning, we have a pantry full of options to choose from. As university budgets continue to feel the squeeze and research funds become more elusive and competitive, we should increasingly draw inspiration from what we regularly do—teach!

Second, it is important to keep notes and record details as you teach. We do not always know if and what could inspire research from our classes and teaching. Changing or introducing a new topic or assignment often does not feel research-worthy on its own or in the moment, but it might eventually inspire a project. I am trying to be more conscientious about noting what I change, why, and how it went. For example, I borrowed a basic foreign policy simulation from the *Active Learning in Political Science* blog in which students make choices about war or peace in pursuit of their state's goals (Sears, 2018). Students lock in their choices on scraps of paper. The first few classes I tried this with said it was one of their favorite activities of the semester, so I have continued to use it. However, in those first few iterations, I never kept the scraps of paper with the student choices and outcomes; they immediately went into the recycle bin after class. However, I started to wonder if the end results, which often varied significantly between sections, were shaped by gender distributions or the different majors of students within these classes. Now that my curiosity is piqued, I am exploring this as a future research project as well. While I am in the process of recruiting my colleague who also teaches this class and completing the IRB, I can continue to make personal notes from class observations and begin anchoring my project in the vast simulation literature. There is a lot of research potential in what we frequently do as teachers.

Finally, do not shy away from approaching potential research more inductively. Planning and foresight are great if you already have an idea in mind and the time, but those projects can also feel overwhelming for those with heavy teaching loads or those who are well into the semester. Instead, much like the evolution of my senior capstone project, the puzzle, question, or observation may come at the end of a semester or a year later. It is equally valid to work backwards—from an observation (wow, look at how many visitors we had at the online event!) to find the relevant connections to existing research (engagement) to drafting a research question and then submitting a relevant IRB, collecting data for testing, etc.

In conclusion, teaching is the bulk of my position, but research is still required. Finding ways to align teaching and research can aid in efficiency and productivity. In some cases, I more carefully organize research to assess the effectiveness of a new activity with a pre/post survey, but not all my research starts out as purposefully. In other cases, I note and keep track of what I am changing or doing in my classes for when inspiration may strike like it did with my international studies senior capstone and research on engaging the campus and community in student research. It may be a month, semester, or year later when you realize how and what you are doing could translate to research, but it is all around us—be patient and learn to recognize the value in all that you do as a teacher.

References

Baumann, E., & FitzGibbon, J. (2021). Developing simulations for the politics and international relations classroom. *Journal of Political Science Education, 17*(1), 285–298. https://doi.org/10.1080/15512169.2019.1623047

Betti, A., Garcia Domonte, A., & Biderbost, P. (2020). Flipping the classroom in political science: Student achievement and perceptions. *Revista De Ciencia Politica, 40*(3), 589–616. https://doi.org/10.4067/S0718-090X2020005000102

Bowers, M. (2019). Show me what you're thinking: Using student-generated photography to flip the political science classroom. *Journal of Political Science Education, 15*(4), 498–506. https://doi.org/10.1080/15512169.2018.1509007

Burcu, O. (2020). Refocusing group work on collaborative learning and diversifying assessments in political science departments. *European Political Science, 19*(1), 140–157. https://doi.org/10.1057/s41304-019-00212-6

Bursens, P., Donche, V., Gijbels, D., & Spooren, P. (2018). *Simulations of decision-making as active learning tools: Design and effects of political science simulations*. Springer.

Clark, N., & Scherpereel, J. A. (2023). Do political science simulations promote knowledge, engagement, skills, and empathy? *Journal of Political Science Education*. https://doi.org/10.1080/15512169.2023.2204236

Craig, J. (2014). What have we been writing about?: Patterns and trends in the scholarship of teaching and learning in political science. *Journal of Political Science Education, 10*(1), 23–36.

Divjak, B., Rienties, B., Iniesto, F., Vondra, P., & Zizak, M. (2022). Flipped classrooms in higher education during the COVID-19 pandemic: Findings and future research recommendations. *International Journal of Education Technology in Higher Education, 19*(1), 1–24.

Duchatelet, D., Bursens, P., Usherwood, S., & Oberle, M. (2020). Beyond descriptions and good practices: Empirical effects on students' learning outcomes of active learning environments in political science curricula. *European Political Science, 19*(3), 327–335.

Fernandez, O., Lundell, D., & Kerrigan, S. (2018). Taking high-impact practices to scale in capstone and peer mentor programs, and revision university studies' diversity learning goals. *The Journal of General Education, 67*(3–4), 269–289.

Hamann, K., & Hamenstadt, U. (2021). Empirical approaches to understanding student learning outcomes and teaching effectiveness in political science. *European Political Science, 20*(3), 393–396. https://doi.org/10.1057/s41304-020-00278-7

Hamann, K., Glazier, R., Wilson, B., & Pollock, P. (2021). Online teaching, student success, and retention in political science courses. *European Political Science, 20*(3), 427–439. https://doi.org/10.1057/s41304-020-00282-x

Hasturkoglu, G. (2019). Situated learning in translator and interpreter training: Model United Nations simulations. *Journal of Language and Linguistic Studies, 15*(3), 914–925. https://doi.org/10.17263/jlls.631533

Hellstrom, M. (2017). Gaming the classroom: The transformative experience of redesigning the delivery of a political science class. *Issues and Trends in Educational Technology, 5*(2), 60–81. https://doi.org/10.2458/azu_itet_v5i2_hellstrom

Hinckley, R. A., McGuire, J., & Danforth, T. L. (2021). Improving student success in the capstone seminar: The importance of prior research intensive experience. *Journal of Political Science Education, 17*(1), 20–31. https://doi.org/10.1080/15512169.2019.1608831

Houck, A. M. (2021). Failure to launch: False starts in designing the political science capstone as a true ending to the major. *Journal of Political Science Education, 17*(1), 79–100. https://doi.org/10.1080/15512169.2019.1598873

Hutchings, P., Taylor Huber, M., & Ciccone, A. (2011). *The Scholarship of teaching and learning reconsidered: Institutional integration and impact.* Jossey-Bass.

Kammerer, E., Jr., & Higashi, B. (2021). Simulations research in political science pedagogy: Where is everyone? *Journal of Political Science Education, 17*(1), 142–147. https://doi.org/10.1080/15512169.2021.1920420

Leib, J., & Ruppel, S. (2020). The learning effects of United Nations simulations in political science classrooms. *European Political Science, 19*(3), 336–351. https://doi.org/10.1057/s41304-020-00260-3

Lovell, D., & Khatri, C. (2021). Do early simulations work? Simulations in gateway political science courses at community colleges. *Journal of Political Science Education, 17*(1), 139–148. https://doi.org/10.1080/15512169.2019.1705164

McClellan, F., Kopko, K. C., & Gruber, K. L. (2021). High-impact practices and their effects: Implications for the undergraduate political science curriculum. *Journal of Political Science Education, 17*(S1), 674–692. https://doi.org/10.1080/15512169.2020.1867562

Murphy, M. P., Heffernan, A., Dunton, C., & Arsenault, A. C. (2023). The disciplinary scholarship of teaching and learning in political science and international relations: Methods, topics, and impact. *International Politics*. https://doi.org/10.1057/s41311-022-00425-5

Sears, N. (2018). Simulating war and peace in IR theory with a classroom game. *Active Learning in Political Science*. Retrieved July 1, 2022, from https://activelearningps.com/2018/08/20/simulating-war-and-peace-in-ir-theory-with-a-classroom-game/

Stapleton, P. (2020). Knowledge surveys as an assessment tool of simulation course outcomes. *Journal of Political Science Education, 16*(4), 413–429. https://doi.org/10.1080/15512169.2018.1526089

Touchton, M. (2015). Flipping the classroom and student performance in advanced statistics: Evidence from a quasi-experiment. *Journal of Political Science Education, 11*(1), 28–44. https://doi.org/10.1080/15512169.2014.985105

Whitman Cobb, W. (2016). Turning the classroom upside down: Experimenting with the flipped classroom in America government. *Journal of Political Science Education, 12*(1), 1–14. https://doi.org/10.1080/15512169.2015.106343

Williams, R. J., & Chergosky, A. (2019). Teaching judicial politics through a Supreme Court simulation. *Journal of Political Science Education, 15*(1), 17–36. https://doi.org/10.1080/15512169.2018.1493997

PART VI

Embedding Research in Teaching and Generating Research Ideas from Teaching

CHAPTER 28

In Unity There Is Strength: How to Incorporate Your Research into Teaching

Wei-Ting Yen

INTRODUCTION

Often time when academics talk about incorporating research in teaching, we refer to either training PhD students to do their original work or including students in your research as assistants or collaborators. However, most degree-granting postsecondary institutions in the United States are not research universities with high or very high levels of research activities,[1] and most academics' jobs do not focus on training PhD students. When teaching involves professional-track master students or undergraduates, our job centers more on helping students learn about a subject systematically. As such, our research and teaching become more disconnected and go their separate ways. Integrating research and

---

[1] https://nces.ed.gov/programs/digest/d20/tables/dt20_317.20.asp (Accessed on June 21, 2022).

W.-T. Yen (✉)
Government Department, Franklin and Marshall College, Lancaster, PA, USA
e-mail: wyen@fandm.edu

© The Author(s), under exclusive license to Springer Nature Switzerland AG 2023
C. Butcher et al. (eds.), *The Palgrave Handbook of Teaching and Research in Political Science*, Political Pedagogies,
https://doi.org/10.1007/978-3-031-42887-6_28

teaching activities becomes increasingly challenging when teaching undergraduate or professional-track master students who have limited exposure to conducting original research.

This chapter is about how to actively and effectively integrate our research and teaching for academics teaching non-PhD students. There are three immediate benefits in closing the gap between our research and teaching. First, we already spend a lot of time and energy thinking about our research, which is what we are passionate about. Finding ways to connect our research and teaching allows us to channel the passion and connect it with our students. Students get motivated when they feel our enthusiasm for the subject, and motivated students achieve better learning outcomes (Ambrose et al., 2010). Second, embedding our research in our teaching also gives us a way to approach our research differently, and sometimes it helps improve our research, especially in terms of how to frame and communicate our research with a broader audience. Last, in the long run, it simply saves us time and mental energy to transit between research and teaching.

When teaching non-PhD students, it requires more conscious decisions and course designs to connect research and teaching, and this is what this chapter is about. This chapter examines a variety of ways our research can facilitate our teaching and offers tips to identify opportunities in our research process that can be turned into teaching moments to improve student engagement. To this end, the chapter is divided into two parts. The first part identifies teaching opportunities in the research process. I organize different strategies based on the level of preparation or adaptation needed in the process of turning those research steps into teaching opportunities. The second part provides concrete tips on how to actively embed your research in your teaching. This section can be particularly useful for instructors at Primarily Undergraduate Institutions (PUIs) where research resources are more limited and teaching and service loadings can be more demanding. I use one introductory undergraduate course as a running example to demonstrate concrete steps of how to actively incorporate research into undergraduate teaching. I conclude the chapter with a brief discussion on how your research can motivate your students toward more effective learning.

Because of my experiences working in a PUI setting, this chapter is written with three types of academics in mind. It would certainly be most useful for instructors working in the PUI setting. Besides, the chapter may also be useful for novice instructors or teacher-scholars who are trying to integrate their teaching and research more. My overall goal is to help academics with more demanding teaching obligations to find ways to channel their research passion into more effective teaching.

TEACHING OPPORTUNITIES IN THE RESEARCH PROCESS

How to identify teachable moments in your research process? In this section, I list some steps in our research process that can become good teaching opportunities. I organize the strategies based on the needed adaptation efforts. I start with the strategy with a minimum level of preparation to the one with a maximum level.

Teach What You Want to Read for Your Research

The most straightforward way is to assign readings that you are going to read for your research. This strategy requires almost zero to minimum preparation and is most suitable for undergraduate upper-level seminars or graduate-level courses. This strategy is particularly useful for researchers who are in the process of writing a book manuscript. The literature review section in a book manuscript is usually more extensive regarding the breadth and depth of the works reviewed. Each strand of research can easily become a week's reading list. The literature review section can easily become the skeleton schedule for your syllabus. You can also use teaching as an opportunity to help you organize and summarize your understanding of a research topic or your literature review section. For instance, you can assign what you plan to read to your students and have them summarize and evaluate the literature. During seminar discussions, you may use the opportunity to deepen your thoughts and analyses of the literature. If you happen to be writing the book when you are teaching the course, the benefit can be immediate and multiplying.

Use the Theoretical Debates in Your Research

Another useful strategy is to turn the conceptual/theoretical debates happening in your research area into an assignment or a discussion/debate topic in the classroom. Compared to the previous strategy, it takes more preparation to turn the theoretical debates into teaching opportunities and the focus of preparation is on how to tailor the theoretical discussion to fit the level of your course, which will be discussed more extensively in the next section. The gist of this strategy is to use existing debates in the field and turn them directly into assignments or class activities.

For example, in comparative politics, one major debate is about what democracy is and is not and how to measure democracy. Another major debate is about what causes and sustains democracy. In my undergraduate-level research method class, I directly turn the debate on different conceptualizations of democracy into a series of assignments. I first have students compare and contrast how major comparative datasets (e.g., Freedom House, POLITY IV, V-Dem, etc.) conceptualize and operationalize democracy. I then have them use varied democracy proxies to study one country's democratization process.[2] In the research method class, students are then asked to use the case study to evaluate pros and cons of different conceptualizations. If it is a comparative politics course, I then ask students to apply theories of democratization and evaluate which argument explains the case better.

The "Background Learning" Strategy

When academics start a new research topic, we often need time to do some preliminary research. The preliminary research can of itself become teaching materials. The "background learning" strategy is useful especially when one is trying to start a new project/topic. Teaching obligations can motivate (or force) you to put in the time to do the initial research with concrete deadlines. Because it is also a new topic for you, the amount of preparation time needed can vary quite a lot. Depending on the course level and your energy level, there are two routes to adopt this strategy. First, one can choose the lecture route (which definitely requires more preparation). For instance, when COVID-19 started in 2020, I was curious about how regime types and state capacity impacted government variations in their COVID-19 responses. I did preliminary research and made it a lecture in my Asian Politics course, which students also highly appreciated given the timeliness of the topic was. The lecture also helped me organize my initial thoughts which ultimately led to several related publications (Yen, 2020; Yen & Liu, 2022; Yen et al., 2022). The second

---

[2] This part varies from class to class and depends on my research focus at the time. I usually ask students to focus on specific countries I want to know more about or keep track of.

route one can choose is to directly turn background information research into assignments for students. The caveat is that quality may vary quite a bit depending on students' levels. If you are to turn background information research into an assignment, I suggest two additional points: (1) still do some preliminary research yourself and point students toward the direction you want. For example, you can provide resources they should read and research; (2) limit the research scope for students. For instance, you may have different group's research different aspects of the background. In a nutshell, when you need more background information for your research, it can become a teaching opportunity as well.

Leveraging Community Engagement and Empirical Evidence

When it comes to finding teaching opportunities in research, what counts as research also matters. In many academic institutions (especially PUIs), scholarly activities are counted more broadly and there are research opportunities through community outreach. If community outreach is something you do, there are multiple ways in which we can combine "researching our community" with "teaching about our community." For instance, you can directly invite community partners to your classes, which requires minimum preparation. Another strategy is to have students analyze the data you collected (either qualitative or quantitative). For example, if you are teaching political participation and working on civic engagement in the community, it would be a great opportunity to have students look at the data and summarize what drives civic engagement in the neighborhood. In general, students get more motivated when researching the environment surrounding them. More broadly, you can modify the empirical data for your research, tailor them to fit the course levels, and have students summarize descriptive statistics and identify trends. Nevertheless, it may take longer than you think to prepare your empirical data for your students, so adopt this strategy only when you see a great fit between your empirical data and what you are teaching.

How to Integrate Research into Teaching

The previous section touches on where and how your research process can inform your teaching. This section addresses the same topic in a slightly different fashion: if you already know what you are teaching, how can you actively incorporate more of your research into your teaching? Below

I provide concrete step-by-step tips to guide you through the process. To illustrate the step-by-step tips more vividly, I use one course I am currently teaching as a running example. The course is *Introduction to Comparative Politics*.

In a nutshell, a more productive process is to employ the strategy of backward design. That is, to start with the expected learning outcomes and the cognitive process students may have to go through to achieve the learning goals. Then, work backward to think through the assessment tools you want to use to evaluate students' success. Assessment tool design is a good place where you can actively incorporate your research. The next step is to organize the content into weekly lectures, discussion questions, and class activities. This is the second place where you can use your research to help you design your course content.

Why is it a more productive process to adopt a backward design approach? Because there are some fundamental differences between research and teaching. First, the end goal is different. Research is to produce systematic knowledge to enhance our understanding of the world around us. It is to use what we already know to explain what we do not know. As such, the end goal of research is to push for an explanation of the new phenomenon or the unknown. In contrast, teaching is to organize and "translate" the knowledge we already know so that students can understand the world around us through analytical frameworks, and this is especially true when teaching undergraduates, so the end goal is knowledge dissemination. Second, the audience is different. The audience of research is mostly peers in the field, who already have deep background knowledge of the subject. Students are the audience of your teaching. The further away students are from conducting original research, the bigger the gap is between research and teaching, and the more adaptation you would need from research to teaching. Due to the differences in the end goal as well as the audience, research should be tailored and incorporated differently depending on the levels of a course. Therefore, it is more productive to start from the endpoint, which is the learning objectives upon completion of a course, and design backward.

Step 1: Identify and Align Learning Objectives with Learning Typologies

To incorporate your research into teaching more effectively, the first and foremost is to identify what the learning objectives are. The learning outcomes you set have direct implications on what and how your research should be incorporated. When identifying learning objectives, try using specific and measurable outcomes. Bloom's taxonomy provides a useful starting point. There are six levels of cognitive process in learning, including knowledge, comprehension, application, analysis, synthesis, and evaluation.[3] Each of these levels represents one essential aspect of the learning process. Try to match the dimensions of the learning process with the objectives. Needless to say, your learning objectives should be closely related to the course levels.

Example: Introduction to Comparative Politics
Because it is an introductory course for the major as well as a general education course, the main objective is to lay the foundation for advanced courses and motivate undeclared students to get interested in political science. As a result, I focus on the cognitive domains of remembering and understanding fundamental political science concepts and the ability to apply these concepts in different contexts. My other goal is to introduce students to how social scientists study and measure political institutions. To this end, the learning objectives are (I bolded the verbs related to Bloom's learning taxonomy):

- **Recognize** and **explain** how political institutions at different levels affect people's lives and can **apply the knowledge** to different contexts and to real-world events.
- **Gain familiarity with** the resources available (**i.e., know where to find what data**) for studying politics in the developing world.

Step 2: Incorporate Your Research into Assessment Tools

Once you identify the learning objectives for a course and match the learning objectives with Bloom's learning typology, the second step is to think thoroughly about the assessment tools you want to use to evaluate your students' progress. This is where you can include some of the teaching opportunities discussed in the previous section. Background learning and theoretical debates are usually two ways I incorporate my research into assessment tools.

---

[3] https://bloomstaxonomy.net/ (Accessed on June 21, 2022).

Example: Introduction to Comparative Politics
To achieve the above-mentioned learning objectives, I need to design assessment tools to evaluate whether students can define and explain political concepts and apply those concepts in various contexts. Meanwhile, I also aim to familiarize students with existing datasets political scientists use to study the world.

Last time when I re-designed the course, one of my research projects was to study how state capacity shapes governmental variation in crisis response (Yen, et al., 2022). I turned to the dataset I was using at the time, the Quality of Government (QoG[4,5]) Students then were asked to compare the two measures and how political scientists develop two different measures to study state capacity. Because I was already comparing different measures of state capacity for my research, I did not do much extra work to turn it into an assignment.

Step 3: Incorporate Research into Course Content

After you plan your assessment tools, the next step is to plan weekly lectures and class activities. Here, again, how your research can contribute to your course content is contingent upon the course level. If you are teaching an upper-level seminar, assigning students what you intend to read for your research would be a good strategy. If you are teaching a lower-level course, applying background learning to your research can be more useful. Sometimes, I also turn theoretical debates in the field into classroom debates.

Example: Introduction to Comparative Politics
For this introductory level course, I teach basic concepts such as modern state, regime types, and regime change. Given that there is constant development in regime change around the world, I always pick a new case to focus on when I teach regime change. For instance, in 2019, I wanted to keep track of Venezuela's presidential crisis. I turned the event first into my lecture material and then assignment content. Another example would be the 2021 regime change in Myanmar. I adopted the same strategy to stay informed about cases of democratic backsliding. On ongoing world

---

[4] https://qog.pol.gu.se/data/data-portal (Accessed June 8th 2022).
[5] https://fragilestatesindex.org/, (Accessed June 8th 2022).

events, Monkey Cage at The Washington Post often has good background readings for undergraduate students too, which makes teaching real-time events easier.[6]

Motivation: The Secret Source

Behind all the tips and strategies in better aligning our teaching with our ongoing research lies another fundamental factor for more effective learning: motivation. Research has shown that students' motivation has a direct impact on their learning behaviors and learning outcomes (Ambrose et al., 2010). Authentic and real-world applications can motivate students, and political science research often can be directly linked to ongoing real-world events. We political scientists are also often motivated by ongoing world events to continue our research. Try to channel what motivates you to do your research to your students. Help connect the dots for your students between the ongoing issues happening in the world and how our theoretical framework has relevance and offers useful perspectives. Your students will get motivated too. Moreover, we all have to pitch our research to the general audience, finding the right way to motivate students provides an opportunity for us as researchers to approach our research topics from different angles. The iterative process often helps us as researchers to frame our research better. In sum, higher levels of integration help channel one's passion for research into teaching and motivate students, which can become reciprocal stimulation for your ongoing research.

In a time when faculty burnout is a real problem in higher education (Gewin, 2021), it is of vital importance to find ways to work smarter but not harder to have a fulfilling career in academia. In this article, I discuss various ways research can inform teaching in political science. I identify opportunities in your research that can be transformed into teaching moments. The chapter also offers concrete tips on finding ways to incorporate research into your teaching. The primary suggestion is to start from the level of cognitive understanding we hope our students can achieve in the course before deciding how to incorporate research into

---

[6] https://www.washingtonpost.com/monkey-cage/ (Accessed June 8th 2022).

teaching. Once the learning objectives have been identified, work backward to pick and choose which part of your research can be tailored and included in teaching.

This chapter provides a skeleton structure and tips on how to actively incorporate your research into your teaching because the benefit is immense. Even though the suggestions are by no means exhaustive and need to be tailored according to the specific academic setting one is in, the chapter provides a starting point for academics working in teaching-oriented institutions to think about ways to bring their research closer to their teaching.

References

Ambrose, S. A., Bridges, M. W., DiPietro, M., Lovett, M. C., & Norman, M. K. (2010). *How learning works: Seven research-based principles for smart teaching*. John Wiley & Sons.

Gewin, V. (2021). "Pandemic Burnout Is Rampant in Academia." *Nature, 591* (7850), 489–491.

Yen, W. (2020). Taiwan's COVID-19 management: Developmental state, digital governance, and state-society synergy. *Asian Politics & Policy, 12*(3), 455–468. https://doi.org/10.1111/aspp.12541

Yen, W., & Liu, L. (2022). When democracy meets the COVID-19 pandemic. In John Fu-Sheng Hsieh & Robert Cox (Eds.), *Democratic Governance in Taiwan*, Chapter 8. Routledge Studies on Comparative Asian Politics. Routledge.

Yen, W., Liu, L., & Testriono, E. W. (2022). The imperative of state capacity in public health crisis: Asia's early COVID-19 policy responses. *Governance, 35*(3), 777–798. https://doi.org/10.1111/gove.12695

CHAPTER 29

Creating Positive Feedback Cycles Between Teaching and Research

Eric Loepp

Many instructors in higher education surely empathize with the White House aide in the film *The American President* who, in response to a fellow advisor proposing that the president focus on one thing at a time, quipped, "We don't have time to do one thing at a time." Though the film is fictional, the sentiment is not. Instructors in higher education—particularly those at teaching-intensive-universities—are tasked with teaching, research, and service expectations that can be intimidating, especially for early-career faculty. Although long hours will always be part of academic life, there are steps we can take to make the challenge less daunting. This chapter proposes reframing the traditional conceptualization of the classic teaching-research-service paradigm as distinct sets of duties by instead treating them as mutually reinforcing beams. In particular, research and teaching should be viewed as activities that can

E. Loepp (✉)
University of Wisconsin-Whitewater, Whitewater, WI, USA
e-mail: loeppe@uww.edu

© The Author(s), under exclusive license to Springer Nature Switzerland AG 2023
C. Butcher et al. (eds.), *The Palgrave Handbook of Teaching and Research in Political Science*, Political Pedagogies,
https://doi.org/10.1007/978-3-031-42887-6_29

sustain and enhance each other; that is, they can create a positive feedback cycle wherein progress in one area promotes progress in another. Establishing this cycle not only saves time, but can *improve* the quality of both the teaching and the research we produce. In this chapter, I describe sample strategies from my experiences as a faculty member who aspires to produce quality research while working at an institution where a 4–4 teaching load is standard. My goal is to model a strategic mindset that may help instructors economize their energy output. I hope what follows may be useful to instructors as they think about how they might weave multiple applications out of the same creative thread.

Integrating Research into Teaching

Including materials from the research enterprise into course preparation is not a new phenomenon. Instructors in higher education are, by definition, experts in narrow bands of knowledge; *of course* they will teach classes in those areas.[1] In many cases, products of research expanding that knowledge—namely high-quality books, articles, or other artifacts (e.g., blog posts, media interviews)—regularly make their way onto course syllabi. (That point needs not to be iterated here except in passing).

Yet there are other opportunities to incorporate research in the classroom that do not require substantial materials such as published volumes. Research products—even working drafts or preliminary formulations—can be used as fodder for service and elective courses. Perhaps the simplest example can be found in research methods courses. Products from our research efforts can inform activities we deploy in the classroom. For instance, when I teach students about conducting literature reviews and crafting theories that push the frontier of our collective knowledge of a subject, I will assign students the first few pages of a peer-reviewed article that I have (co-)written. They are then charged with interrogating the opening sections of the article to identify the theory and the extant knowledge that informed it.[2] When we talk about independent and dependent

---

[1] Of course, instructors are often called upon to teach service courses beyond their disciplinary expertise, as well, especially at teaching-intensive institutions.

[2] I have found students (usually!) enjoy a joke that no, I am not paid every time the article is downloaded, so the reason I'm assigning them my own work is simply because I know it well. Incidentally, this crack has on more than one occasion inspired questions from students genuinely curious to know more about the publication process.

variables, I have students read the next few sections of the same paper, scouring the pages until they find the specific variables I used. When I instruct on the logic of the experimental method, I ask students to read deeper into the manuscript and identify the factorial design I employed. To be sure, instructors should utilize a variety of examples from multiple authors to showcase the breadth of the political science discipline and the many voices within it; however, there is no reason not to utilize the case studies with which we are most familiar—our own.

This model is not limited to research methods classes. Instructors can utilize research-related productions in all manner of courses. For instance, scholars are often invited to pen op-eds or join radio shows or podcasts to share expertise generated and informed by their research. These endeavors can serve as the foundation for phenomenal learning experiences if translated into properly calibrated course activities. For example, I was recently invited to draft a short article about the nature and evolution of polarization in the American electorate. In crafting a document that aims to make political science accessible to a non-academic audience, I realized that this exercise generated precisely the sort of deliverable I would expect from advanced undergraduate students in my *Public Opinion and Political Behavior* course. So, I made it one. As part of their final exam, I invited students to create an encyclopedia entry that addressed one of several fundamental questions we explored in the course. Figure 29.1 presents the instructions. After students selected their question, they reviewed a few project parameters, and, critically, they had access to a sample encyclopedia entry that clearly demonstrated what the deliverable should look like.[3] The sample was simply a (modified) version of the article I wrote. Creating a sample entry purely for supporting students in their final exam would have been a nice—but labor-intensive—instructional touch. However, by repurposing an article drawing on my substantive disciplinary knowledge into a sample deliverable to guide student work, the labor served multiple ends: I produced a publication that went in my dossier, I saved time preparing an assessment for class, and students

---

[3] The embedded link did not direct students to the website hosting the article. Instead, I created a copy of the article without logos, names, etc. in a .PDF and placed it in a Google Drive. This file also included exam-specific instructions and information that was not included in the original article. The link in the final exam document opened the .PDF, ensuring students wouldn't be distracted by ads or attempt to mimic formatting decisions by the website that published the article.

Option 1. Encyclopedia Entry

This option tasks you with writing an entry for an encyclopedia of political behavior. First, select the title of your entry from this list:[1]

- What's the Deal With Political Independents?
- Political Reasoning: An Oxymoron?
- Is Politics About Issues or Identity?
- The Perils of Studying Public Opinion

Your entry should be approximately 1,000 words long, providing the reader with a succinct but thorough examination of the question. As appropriate, break your essay into relevant subsections. Be sure to incorporate and cite at least three relevant pieces of empirical/scholarly work from our course as you make your case. To help you get started, Dr. L created an example encyclopedia entry responding to the question: "Polarization: Is It Getting Worse?" Feel free to copy the same template if you would like. A bonus point will be awarded if you include a relevant quote from *The West Wing* like Dr. L did!

Fig. 29.1 Modifying research activities for classroom use

enjoyed a high-quality example that serves as a model for their own work.[4]

In addition to integrating research-related productions into courses, instructors should view their courses as opportunities to further develop their disciplinary knowledge. Political phenomena emerge and evolve long after we complete our graduate training, so it is crucial to stay up to speed on developments in our field. This can be difficult when preparing multiple courses and developing material for double digits worth of student contact hours each week. Look for ways to use that preparation time to sharpen knowledge in your subfield. One great way to do this is to request that you be assigned particular courses that will allow you to brush up on developments in your research area. An example from my experience: I completed my graduate training in political behavior when terms like "affective polarization" were beginning to circulate more frequently in the political science lexicon. I jumped at the opportunity to teach the public opinion course referenced above because preparing it would allow me to examine the affective polarization literature that would serve both my immediate instructional needs as well as my longer-term

---

[4] Of course, individuals should consult their departmental standards when selecting publication opportunities to ensure that energies expended in writing efforts will be worthwhile as far as performance evaluations are concerned. Indeed, articles like these are not necessary going to make or break a tenure case, but it is worth noting that teaching-intensive universities are often willing to recognize these types of works as qualified publications.

research interests.[5] If your research area does not align with a particular course on your department's books, inquire about creating it! Even if you cannot get a permanent course added to the roster (or if the process will take a while) propose a special topics course in the interim. In the spring of 2020, I was fortunate to teach a course called *Picking a President* that centered on the presidential nomination process. Preparing for this course gave me an opportunity to refresh my understanding of topics such as delegate allocation formulas and rule changes from the prior election that would inform my preparation for my next research project related to political primaries.

I hasten to caution that our courses should not *merely* be vessels to support research. Course learning objectives should not take a back seat to research interests. We need to offer courses that meet the goals and needs of the department and institution. We must be deliberate and selective when repurposing research materials into class activities. Yet, in many cases, our research activities can also serve our pedagogical interests.

Producing Research Through Teaching

When we think about the role of students in the research process, we often think of undergraduates as subjects in academic studies. Yet *our own* students may serve as useful sounding boards for preliminary theoretical or design-related research ideas. In my research methods course, I often use early drafts of my own research designs as examples students can critique via large-group discussion as well as in graded assignments. For example, after learning the fundamental rules of social science survey writing, students are asked to apply the lessons they learned to survey instruments I am in the process of developing. Although undergraduates may not (yet) have the skills to offer a comprehensive review of some survey elements, they are well-positioned to provide a crucial piece of feedback: how do ordinary survey takers interact with the instrument?

---

[5] It is important to be strategic about course selection, especially as a newer faculty member. For instance, if an instructor were initially assigned three unique class preparations (preps) spread over four separate courses, it may not be in the new faculty member's best interest to propose a *fourth* unique prep that semester to replace a section of one of the others. In addition, some institutions will assign introductory courses to new hires in order to help them develop their pedagogical style or simply to lighten their load, so it is important to consult with senior colleagues and/or the department chair about expectations and opportunities related to research-relevant course offerings.

Are instructions unclear? Is it too long? More advanced students may offer substantive feedback, as well. Is there another way one might specify a dependent variable? Is the experimental manipulation strong enough? Undergraduate reviewers will rarely fundamentally alter our theories and inspire us to reformulate our regression models. Yet students can be a valuable set of eyes that help us understand how participants will receive our work.[6] Moreover, students often express more enthusiasm for opportunities to serve as consultants on actual research endeavors as opposed to hypothetical scenarios drawn from textbooks.[7]

Teaching activities may also produce research as an end in and of itself. Many institutions encourage instructors to pursue scholarship related to teaching and learning as part of their larger research agenda. Indeed, such publications are often factored into tenure and promotion decisions. The lessons learned from that research can of course serve our instructional enterprise, as well. We may uncover effective strategies for conveying certain information, or develop fruitful methods to encourage thoughtful, spirited, and civil conversations about controversial topics in online discussion boards.

One research production that emerged from my teaching grew out of a desire to promote active learning in the classroom. One day early in my career, I was walking around the room gathering notecards marked with student responses to a straw poll. *This is a waste of time*, I thought, *It's only a multiple-choice question.* I began questioning both the administration and substance of the exercise. *There must be a quicker way to collect these data. And surely there are richer data out there than simple poll questions.* I was shaking my head when I returned to my office. *I'm an experimentalist. Why am I not using experiments in the classroom to demonstrate causality related to important phenomena that students should know?*

---

[6] Incidentally, inviting students to review surveys or other documents that will be viewed by research participants also helps identify typos, grammatical missteps, and, in the case of digital surveys, logic/programming errors. Indeed, students take good-hearted but very real pleasure in catching their instructors' mistakes!

[7] This observation also informed my decision to have students design and field their own survey experiments as part of our course.

I set about designing a series of simple experiments embedded in an online survey that students completed as a course activity. Over the rest of the term, I revealed the experimental results in class, question by question, as we reached the relevant segment of our American politics and government course. For example, when we explored media and politics, I displayed for students the results of an experiment in which I randomly assigned participants to read an online news story that included one of two media logos (MSNBC or Fox News) and evaluated the story for accuracy, fairness, and political tone. In class, I showed students how they perceive the exact same story to be more politically liberal or conservative in tone based on which outlet they think wrote it. Figure 29.2 presents part of the graphical output I shared with students during our segment explore media stereotypes and bias.[8]

Later in the same week, I presented students with the results of another experiment in which they were asked to interpret a data graph containing information on government spending on welfare programs. Their task was to decide if they thought the increase in spending in this area over time was minimal, significant, or something in between. The experimental conditions and results are presented in Fig. 29.3. The data revealed that

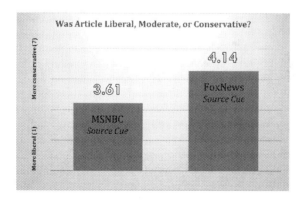

Fig. 29.2 Results of media source cue experiment shared in class

---

[8] Note that since this was an introductory course, I simplified the graphic to exclude certain statistics like the margin of error and confidence level. The goal here was to illustrate source cue effects conceptually, rather than statistical elements like average treatment effects. Those come later in our research methods sequence.

manipulating the y-axis in a data chart can severely impact how viewers make snap judgments about the nature of the trend it contains. In this case, a truncated y-axis (Panel B) led students to perceive a much greater welfare spending increase than a non-truncated y-axis (Panel A). The grand finale of the exercise was my reveal that the example in question came from an actual graphic used by a news channel that truncated the y-axis (Panel C). In the short term, the data inspired a rich conversation about how we identify and define media bias. In the longer term, the data inspired conference presentations, workshops, and peer-reviewed publications demonstrating and advocating for a data-driven classroom (Loepp, 2018, 2019). Meanwhile, students were extremely positive about this pedagogical effort, reporting that it makes the class more interesting and helps them connect with and grasp the course material.

Finally, classroom activities and discussions can also inspire future research projects. On more than one occasion, students have made a provocative comment or observation that struck me as worth investigating. For instance, a student recently shared something they observed while driving in northern Wisconsin: "Trump/Pence" signs with bullet holes through the "Pence" portion. These macabre displays—which I only know about because this student brought it up—motivated a lot of thinking as well as several few research ideas to explore the nature of intra-party feuds. Students need not be highly experienced or methods-trained to produce insights that may be a wonderful source of curious research questions. Further, experiences like these could easily form the foundation of either an independent study course or an undergraduate research experience.

Creating a Positive Feedback Cycle

Teaching and research need not be considered wholly distinct features of a job description. Rather, they should be considered mutually reinforcing pillars of an academic career. Research can inform multiple facets of teaching, and our classes can serve as laboratories and test kitchens for both disciplinary research and scholarship on teaching and learning. Figure 29.4 presents a model for how we might conceptualize a relationship between teaching activities and scholarly initiatives as a positive feedback loop.

29 CREATING POSITIVE FEEDBACK CYCLES BETWEEN ... 357

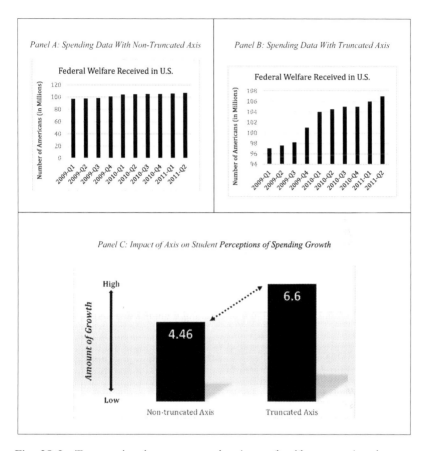

Fig. 29.3 Truncated and non-truncated variants of welfare expansion data

To be sure, there will always be unique needs related to the teaching, research, and service requirements of academic work.[9] Yet time spent working on a research project may be adapted to serve teaching activities and vice versa. Incidentally, this same logic also applies to the service portion of higher education. A set of lecture slides can serve as the foundation of a community speaking engagement. Service on an inclusive

---

[9] Grading papers is one example of a teaching activity that may not offer much in the way of research or service applications.

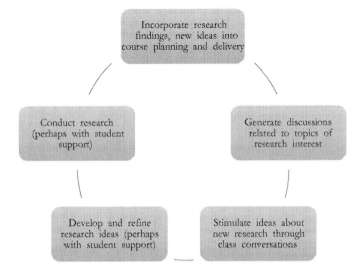

Fig. 29.4 The positive feedback cycle between teaching and research

excellence committee assisting with program planning may result in on-campus experiences in which students can participate as part of a course on race and politics. Chairing a committee to promote voter participation on campus may establish contacts with local election officials who later visit the class to talk about voting laws.

Instructional positions in higher education demand considerable time and effort. One way to promote a healthy work–life balance is to evaluate the potential for a particular task to produce multiple applications. Doing so will not necessarily eliminate long days or reduce the number of items on our to-do list, but it can be one piece of a larger ecosystem of activities that allow us to serve our students well, maintain a robust research agenda, and enjoy the pleasures of academic life.

REFERENCES

Loepp, E. (2019). Data-based teaching: An introduction and call for collaboration. *PS: Political Science & Politics, 52*(4), 743–748. https://doi.org/10.1017/S1049096519000568

Loepp, E. (2018). Beyond polls: Using student data to stimulate learning. *Journal of Political Science Education, 14*(1), 17–41. https://doi.org/10.1080/15512169.2017.1359094

CHAPTER 30

Using Review Sessions to Jumpstart Research Projects in Methods Coursework

Wesley Wehde

Many, though not all, political science undergraduate programs require students to take a course on research methods. While the content of these courses can vary drastically, an emphasis on research design and analysis is common. Many, if not most, of these courses focus primarily on quantitative, statistical methods. Given these courses are not bound to a substantive content area, they may be particularly suited to the incorporation of an instructor's research agenda with their teaching responsibilities. A variety of techniques exist to integrate teaching and research into research methods curricula, including student–teacher semester-long collaborative projects (see Currin-Percival & Gulahmad, 2021, for an example) or having students in the course participate as content analysts and coders (Fisher & Justwan, 2018). However, this chapter focuses on a simpler, potentially less work- and time-intensive method of integrating research and teaching. Specifically, I demonstrate how review sessions near the end

W. Wehde (✉)
Texas Tech University, Lubbock, TX, USA
e-mail: wwehde@ttu.edu

of the semester can provide instructors an opportunity to jumpstart a research project.

The chapter proceeds as follows. First, I briefly describe the structure of the research methods course that I teach, which provides important context for how the review session(s) can be used to initiate a research project. I then describe, in detail, the process of creating a review session that can be relatively quickly and easily transitioned into a research manuscript. In so doing, I emphasize the kinds of research projects amenable to this approach. Next, I briefly describe my experience transitioning a review session into a manuscript. This step will, naturally, have high variance across authors but it may be useful for instructors to read about how I did so successfully (Wehde & Choi, 2021). Finally, I conclude with thoughts on the potential for the use of this process in other courses as well as how it might relate to other methods for teaching quantitative research methods courses in political science.

RESEARCH METHODS IN POLITICAL SCIENCE

Research methods courses in the undergraduate political science curricula are somewhat typical though not ubiquitous in the United States and elsewhere. Research suggests between a quarter and two-thirds of American undergraduate political science programs include a methods requirement (Parker, 2010; Thies & Hogan, 2005). Related research finds some variance in topics covered in undergraduate methods courses; however, measurement, research design, survey methods, and quantitative data analysis are covered in most courses described by those surveyed (Turner & Thies, 2009). Thus, while instructors have significant leeway in how they teach a research methods course, these common topics ease the success of the following proposal for the integration of teaching and research.

These four topics identified by Turner and Thies (2009) also form the structure of the research methods course in which I used an end-of-semester review session to initiate a research project. Importantly, this focus on quantitative data analysis requires teacher-scholars to also choose a software or program to teach. Scholarship on teaching and learning within political science reveals widely varying approaches to this choice as well. Those who focus on ease of use often teach SPSS. Others focus on the availability of the software and employer preferences, which often leads to teaching options such as Excel or R (see Li, 2021 for more on comparing software choices). For my course, I teach R and RStudio as tools for conducting basic quantitative data analysis because they are open-source and therefore free to students (see Scheller, 2022 for more on cost and an example in public affairs). As such, I also rely on an open-access text for teaching R and quantitative analysis in political science. This text, which I helped co-author, follows a structure common to quantitative methods textbooks, proceeding from the basics of measurement and research design to descriptive and inferential statistics through basic linear regression (for undergraduates, see Wehde et al., 2020a, 2020b; for more depth on the underlying math and expanded topics for graduate students see Jenkins-Smith et al., 2017). This content provides the structure for a review session that I have used successfully to begin a research project, although any tool and text that covers these general topics can be adapted to this purpose.

How to Use Review Sessions to Jumpstart Research

Before considering this approach, teacher-scholars should reflect on how long it typically takes them to do the analysis for a rough first draft of a manuscript. If you know that creating summary statistics tables and figures as well as model output tables and figures takes five hours of focused work, then you should plan accordingly. Undertaking this endeavor with more data cleaning and preparation work would call for a different plan and more time set aside. Additionally, if you don't yet have the beginnings of a research question and hypotheses, then you will need to start working on this project earlier. In general, I recommend teacher-scholars begin working on the review session one or two weeks before the class session(s) for which they will need the material and slides, so they will have enough time to think through the project and to create the materials.

Assuming a course structure and text choice like that detailed above, I will now describe how a review session or sessions can be useful for teacher-scholars in jumpstarting a research project. The most crucial prerequisite for this technique to work is an already-collected dataset. Data in political science can come in many forms, from qualitative in-depth interviews to administrative and budgetary data to quantitative surveys, survey experiments, and more. Given the focus on quantitative analytical methods, a dataset ready for quantitative analysis is also necessary. Teacher-scholars can choose any type of quantitative data that they have familiarity with and that would be accessible to their students. One way to increase accessibility for students is to use examples of the teacher-scholar's research agenda and the types of data they work with throughout the course. Thus, by the end of the term when review sessions are necessary, students will already have the background information required to understand the data being used.

The review session should also cover initial units on research design and measurement. In a research methods course, review sessions can take a myriad of forms. For the purpose of integrating research and teaching, this review session contains both traditional lecture slides as well as more interactive code and analysis-based time. Thus, the first section on research design would incorporate a set of slides describing the study's design. This should include information about the study as observational or experimental, a key learning outcome in most quantitative research methods courses. This can then transition into data collection, design, and the specifics of conceptual and variable measurements.

For measurement, the teacher-scholar should then review key concepts such as units and levels of analysis as well as different types or levels of measurement. Measurement levels and their conceptual differences should transition the teacher-scholar into the analysis and coding-based sections. Specifically, these concepts can and should be used to demonstrate the different kinds of descriptive statistics and associated figures appropriate across levels of measurement. At this stage, the teacher-scholar should create a table of descriptive statistics for most variables they think they will use in their research project. This allows the teacher-scholar to first review these relevant concepts, (re)familiarize themselves with the appropriate data, and have a ready-to-go "Table One" for their manuscript. For reviewing the appropriate visualization techniques, the dependent variables should most likely be used since understanding the full distribution of these variables is vital to any quantitative analysis relying on regression techniques. These visualizations thus serve as a review for the students as well as potential figures for the resulting manuscript. At this stage, the slides will likely exceed what would be necessary for a typical manuscript; reviewing the many different types of visualizations, students should learn will require far more figures than a manuscript does.

Once you have created these visualizations, the review session(s) slides should include the visualizations themselves, information about the pros and cons of the different types, and information on how to create them. In R and RStudio, this can be facilitated through RMarkdown slides which allow the creator to easily display the code and the code's output on the same or adjacent slides. For other software, the teacher-scholar will proceed as needed; for Stata, the commands and output can be shown. In Excel, the teacher-scholar can include a screen capture of the process or a step-by-step guide to visualization production. An example of the slides produced for the review session described below can be found on the author's website.[1] These slides, and the associated visualizations and analyses, are the primary output or product of this process. They can then be used to provide the initial elements of a manuscript data and methods section as well as preliminary analyses that can inform theory building and hypothesis development and testing.

In general, quantitative research methods courses include an introduction to inferential statistics. As such, the review materials should remind students of most, if not all, of the methods taught throughout the course, proceeding from simplest to most complex. Unsurprisingly, the final stage in this process, in my experience, is an introduction to multiple linear regression. Review sessions can take multiple approaches to this content. In research methods classes, regression diagnostics are often taught and emphasized; however, for the purposes of published research, these are often assumed or ignored. As such, for the purpose of integrating research and teaching, a greater emphasis in the review session may be placed on creating and interpreting regression outputs. This approach allows the teacher-scholar to focus on the use of quantitative methods in building theory and testing hypotheses, a key outcome for a quantitative research methods course. This also follows the structure of most typical political science research manuscripts.

What Kinds of Projects Can You Jumpstart?

Projects for which this method is most appropriate will have a few common characteristics. First, they will generally be quantitative and likely descriptive, though causal projects can also work. Additionally, these projects should use data already familiar to students, which allows the instructor to primarily focus on issues of analysis in the review session. The more ready the dataset the better as this requires less front-end work for

---

[1] https://wwwehde.com/wp-content/uploads/2022/06/Review-Lecture.pdf.

the instructor. These projects should also be ones in which linear regression is either the main or a supplemental form of analysis. Projects where the data require more complex analytical methods such as hierarchical, discrete choice, or non-linear models will be more difficult to adapt to this technique. If there is an interesting measurement choice that will also be beneficial to the success of the project, because understanding measurement issues is a key learning outcome of most research methods courses. Co-authored projects may also be especially amenable to the use of this technique as one author, or authors, can focus on the other parts of the manuscript while the teacher-scholar focuses on the initial analyses produced for the review session.

My experience with this technique involved a project examining the determinants of policy preferences among the public in the US. In particular, we focused on understanding the balance of preferences across state and federal levels and across different environmental and natural hazard domains. This project fits well with the ongoing example of understanding climate change beliefs that the class had been structured around. Thus, students were already somewhat familiar with the key independent variables of interest such as ideology, demographics, and environmental beliefs and experiences. This highlights again that the instructor can focus on any area of research most useful to them and interesting to students, since research methods courses are usually not domain specific. Regarding measurement, I used a subtractive index for measuring my dependent variable which reminded students of how combinations of variables and measures can result in interesting outcomes.

My Experience

As described above, I began to prepare for the week of reviews about two weeks beforehand. The actual work of analyzing the data and creating the slides took approximately five to ten hours to create and prepare for class. For a course that meets twice weekly for 75 minutes each class, I chose to dedicate one whole session to this endeavor and the other session of the week to answer students' questions about coding and their projects. In this case, I already had the inklings of an idea for a project based on previous research I had done with a co-author (Choi & Wehde, 2019). My co-author agreed to let me start the next step in this line of research with this review session. Thus, the main work of the preceding weeks was creating the visualizations, conducting the analyses, and creating the slides.

This process requires a variable amount of time, of course, depending on the data and project complexity. In this case, the project was well suited to a review session due to its reliance on survey data as well as the need for some variable recoding and management, a sometimes-overlooked component of quantitative research methods courses. Once created, the slides with the analysis were used in the class review session to walk students through the process from data management to inferential analysis. In the two times I have used this technique, students seemed to enjoy the content. In particular, the slides served as a resource for them; having one document that covered the main analytical and visualization techniques covered throughout the entire course was useful. This singular document served as a functional how-to guide for their final projects in one version of the course.

I have used this technique for a version of the class with a final paper and one with a final exam. For the paper, the review is useful as it reminds students of the expected structure and order of their analyses and papers. It also can help them clarify the analytical and descriptive techniques most useful for their data, since some necessary topics would have been covered first much earlier in the semester. When the course included a final take-home exam instead of a paper, students were required to analyze the provided data and produce a short report based on that data. This report was intended as a decision aid for a hypothetical state agency boss who wanted to know more about implementing a program comparing schools with e-book libraries to those with traditional libraries. The exam allowed students to creatively consider different outcomes of interest provided in the hypothetical data. They were also tested on their ability to identify and use methods appropriate for the question and data. The exam functions similarly to a paper but with a much more narrowly defined agenda and set of expectations. For the version with a final paper, the students' homework assignments throughout the semester are intended to provide them with the structure to have much of the paper already written. Of course, in practice, students may change topics or may not use the scaffolding assignments as intended; thus, the function of the review session becomes effectively the same as for a final exam.

The bulk of the work on the research project will, of course, come after the review session. However, this review session is, as the title states, intended to get a specific project going. I found it useful to force me to create tables and figures and run analyses that I otherwise might have avoided in the absence of a particular deadline, such as a conference. Incorporating them into the course material created a deadline and merged my teaching and research responsibilities. After the research methods review session, the teacher-scholar can proceed as necessary to complete the process. In my case, I met with my co-author, and we began fleshing out the literature review and theory based on the preliminary findings from my review session. As stated previously, this resulted in a manuscript we submitted and eventually published (Wehde & Choi, 2021). The review session analysis became the skeleton on which we built the manuscript's theory as well as the slightly more advanced methods which we ultimately used. As I created these analytical materials, my co-author began working on the accompanying theory and literature based on our previous conversation.

Ultimately, we submitted the paper less than 5 months after the Spring semester in which we began the project for this review session. Strategically one could use the review sessions technique each semester the course is taught; however, that might lead to overextension on the teacher-scholar's part. Rather I would suggest that this technique be used once a year, as teaching schedules permit. In the Fall, it would be a great way to prepare a paper for Spring conferences while in the Spring, this approach can help teacher-scholars segue into summer, when they may have slightly more time to focus on research.

Conclusions

While it is unlikely this method can be applied to all courses, I believe the idea of using review sessions to jumpstart a research project could work in certain other settings. The first is probably obvious: any methods class, including qualitative ones, or those focused more extensively on design. The general structure of these courses is often quite similar to that of an introductory quantitative methods course; therefore, these courses would lend themselves to the review session approach, reproducing the first steps of a manuscript analysis process. The other course type that might lend itself to this process is a highly focused upper-level undergraduate class or a specific graduate research seminar (though not a field seminar). This type of course may be more useful for drafting a theory or literature review section that is comprehensive and analytical; however, one can imagine a review slide deck for a focused seminar (say, on the politics of climate change) that could help build a research manuscript.

In addition, the proposed process could possibly be used in conjunction with other innovative ways of teaching research methods. One commonly documented course strategy in research methods is community-based partnership or client-focused research (Bachner, 2020; Pudlo et al., 2022; Solop et al., 2022). These courses focus on the unique relationship between research methods and the job market. The proposed research-teaching integration technique could be used in this sort of class as an example of how a slide deck can be built. It could also be used in conjunction with data from the community partner or client and produce future collaborative efforts between the teacher-scholar and their chosen partners. This project would also work well in classes that follow the Fisher and Justwan (2018) scaffolding approach. In fact, the scaffolded structure is similar, in some respects, to the course described previously. Finally, this technique might also be useful in a research methods course such as the one described by Currin-Percival and Gulahmad (2021) in which students and instructors collaborate on a semester-long research project. The described review session could be used to facilitate a manuscript collaboration between students and teachers on their collected data and provide a review for a final exam.

Ultimately, this chapter provides useful ideas to those interested in integrating research and teaching in quantitative research methods courses. I have found success in the past with this review session method and believe the review session is an often under-utilized teaching session for both the teacher and the student. In quantitative research methods courses, carefully designed review sessions and slides can and should be used, if possible, to jumpstart a new (or new-ish) research project or manuscript.

References

Bachner, J. (2020). Refocusing methods courses on workplace applications. *Journal of Political Science Education*, 16(2), 257–261. https://doi.org/10.1080/15512169.2020.1727748

Choi, J., & Wehde, W. (2019). Venue preference and earthquake mitigation policy: Expanding the micro-model of policy choice. *Review of Policy Research*, 36(5), 683–701. https://doi.org/10.1111/ropr.12354

Currin-Percival, M., & Gulahmad, S. (2021). Adapting experiential learning opportunities: A political science research methods course case study. *Journal of Political Science Education*, *17*(sup1), 311–325. https://doi.org/10.1080/15512169.2020.1713800

Fisher, S., & Justwan, F. (2018). Scaffolding assignments and activities for undergraduate research methods. *Journal of Political Science Education*, *14*(1), 63–71. https://doi.org/10.1080/15512169.2017.1367301

Jenkins-Smith, H. C., Ripberger, J. T., Copeland, G., Nowlin, M. C., Hughes, T., Fister, A. L., & Wehde, W. (2017). *Quantitative research methods for political science, public policy and public administration (with applications in R)*. https://shareok.org/handle/11244/52244. https://doi.org/10.15763/11244/52244

Li, R. (2021). Teaching undergraduates R in an introductory research methods course: A step-by-step approach. *Journal of Political Science Education*, *17*(4), 653–671. https://doi.org/10.1080/15512169.2019.1667811

Parker, J. (2010). Undergraduate research-methods training in political science: A comparative perspective. *PS: Political Science & Politics*, *43*(1), 121–125.

Pudlo, J. M., Ellis, W. C., & Cole, J. M. (2022). Coproduction as pedagogy: Harnessing community data partnerships for the classroom. *PS: Political Science & Politics*, *55*(1), 182–187.

Scheller, D. S. (2022). A case study of R in public affairs education: Effective use in hybrid and asynchronous online statistics courses. *Journal of Public Affairs Education*, *28*(3), 302–323.

Solop, F. I., Anderson, H. N., Barsky, C., Schnurr, E., & Witlacil, M. (2022). Introducing Client-Focused Research (CFR) projects into the research methods curriculum: Key considerations for political science instructors. *Journal of Political Science Education*, *18*(3), 1–17. https://doi.org/10.1080/15512169.2022.2058518

Thies, C. G., & Hogan, R. E. (2005). The state of undergraduate research methods training in political science. *PS: Political Science & Politics*, *38*(2), 293–297.

Turner, C. C., & Thies, C. G. (2009). What we mean by scope and methods: A survey of undergraduate scope and methods courses. *PS: Political Science & Politics*, *42*(2), 367–373.

Wehde, W., & Choi, J. (2021). Public preferences for disaster federalism: Comparing public risk management preferences across levels of government and hazards. *Public Administration Review*, *82*(4), 733–746. https://doi.org/10.1111/puar.13432

Wehde, W., Bark, T., Jenkins-Smith, H., Ripberger, J., Copeland, G., Nowlin, M., Hughes, T., Fister, A., & Davis, J. (2020a). *Quantitative research methods for political science, public policy and public administration for undergraduates: With applications in Excel*. East Tennessee State University. https://dc.etsu.edu/etsu-oer/4/

Wehde, W., Jenkins-Smith, H., Ripberger, J., Copeland, G., Nowlin, M., Hughes, T., Fister, A., & Davis, J., (2020b). *Quantitative research methods for political science, public policy and public administration for undergraduates: With applications in R.* East Tennessee State University. https://dc.etsu.edu/etsu-oer/5/

CHAPTER 31

"Doing" Political Theory in the Classroom

E. Stefan Kehlenbach

INTRODUCTION

I begin every semester of my introductory political theory class by pointing out to my students that in political theory "learning" and "doing" are synonymous. One learns about political theory only by doing political theory. In this piece, I will argue that by framing the act of teaching political theory as a collaborative act of "doing" political theory, both the students and the instructor have a more collaborative learning experience. This experience is enhanced when the instructor brings their own research into the classroom and can even lead to new ideas and avenues of study for the instructor. When the instructor views the class as "doing" political theory collaboratively, rather than an authoritative act of "telling," it creates a more rewarding learning environment and opens the class up to forms of critical pedagogy that de-hierarchize the classroom. It also allows the instructor to bring their own research and expertise into the classroom. Doing this creates a generative process of learning that may lead to additional original research as a result.

E. S. Kehlenbach (✉)
University at Albany, Albany, NY, USA
e-mail: skehlenbach@albany.edu

© The Author(s), under exclusive license to Springer Nature Switzerland AG 2023
C. Butcher et al. (eds.), *The Palgrave Handbook of Teaching and Research in Political Science*, Political Pedagogies,
https://doi.org/10.1007/978-3-031-42887-6_31

In this chapter, I will first briefly explore what it means to do political theory research. Then, I will frame my conception of "doing" political theory and place it within a larger interpretive and pedagogical tradition, focused both on the definitional qualities of political theory, as described by scholars like Wendy Brown and John Gunnell. I will then use the pedagogical tradition of Paulo Freire and others to show how this act of "doing" political theory is necessary for critical pedagogy. Finally, I will show how political theory is ideally situated to bring the instructor's scholarship into the classroom and what the benefits are for teachers and students. Because political theory is an interpretive discipline, mainly focused on the reading and interpreting of texts, allowing students to develop their own interpretations and present their ideas in class is a natural part of instruction. This allows for a more free-flowing exchange of ideas, often stimulating new research ideas in the instructor.

The flexibility of the political theory canon and the breadth of material available to the political theory instructor means that bringing in current, even incomplete research into the classroom is easy and rewarding. Overall, I advise political theory instructors to be bold in their rejection of classroom hierarchies and to exercise similar boldness in the assignment of texts. With proper encouragement, even the most introductory students can read and grapple with incredibly difficult material, leading to expansive conversations and novel insights. Additionally, political theorists should not shy away from teaching their research directly, while also being mindful of the pitfalls that may occur from presenting one's own research as a settled truth. Overall, focusing on the material that underlies research is uniquely beneficial, as the passion and interest that an instructor shows in their own research easily translates to student enthusiasm, and students appreciate the chance to work on answers to meaningful questions. Political theory teaching should be understood as a collaborative act of "doing" political theory together with students, rather than an unequivocal exercise of passing knowledge down to willing, but passive, minds. Approaching the teaching of political theory in this way has several advantages both for the students seeking to learn political theory and the instructors who have to balance the twin responsibilities of teaching and research.

What Is Political Theory Research?

Political theory research can be many things, from the deep study of canonical texts, using any number of differing methodologies and interpretive strategies, to new engagements with modern problems using a wide variety of source material, including art, music, and other forms of expression not traditionally considered either political or a part of formal political science. Indeed, both the substance and value of political theory have been a subject of long and contentious debate within the field itself. Many scholars have attempted to sketch out the scope and limits of political theory as a discipline, resulting in a long series of debates stretching across the twentieth century (Brown, 2010; Gunnell, 1993, 2011; Kaufman-Osborn, 2010; Strauss, 1988; Wolin, 1969).[1] Most usefully for the scope of this chapter, Bhikhu Parekh sketches a view of political theory as a range, spanning from questions aimed at understanding essential truths or deep experiences of the political, as presented by canonical texts, to postmodern deconstructions of the very idea of the political. (Parekh, 2013) The varying, contradictory, and occasionally outright hostile interactions among different scholars on this issue seem to belie a deep confusion within the work of political theory. One solution is to resort to the attitude of Justice Potter Stewart and merely claim that "we know it when we see it." Another is to perhaps take a broader view and see that this conflict helps us develop working definitions to reasonably discuss the main subject, the act of teaching political theory.

A definition of political theory that is broad enough to be relatively uncontroversial but still useful enough to operationalize for pedagogical purposes may be as follows: political theory is the study of the ways that people (including ourselves) experience the politics and understand our political existences. In this way, it might be seen to be a toolbox for understanding. We read texts, contemplate ideas, and examine the world around us as a way to fill our toolbox to better understand our present. This is true whether we are undertaking a deep textual analysis of Plato or doing contemporary critical theory. This is what, in a broad sense, constitutes political theory research, the reading of text and examination of ideas as a way to better understand our present.

---

[1] A full accounting of the different positions is beyond the scope of this paper, but it is worth noting that there is not a single idea about what constitutes political theory or political theory research.

The purpose of this brief diversion through the history of meta-thought about political theory is an initial attempt to pin down what it is that we do when we undertake political theory research. Research in political theory is different from research in other subfields of political science, instead of proposing hypotheses or defending scientific ideas, we engage deeply with ideas, usually mediated through texts. Our papers, books, and discussions reflect this engagement.

How Do We Teach Theory?

Traditionally, teaching political theory, especially to undergraduate students, takes a standard form. In the first, students are exposed to the "great works" of the political theory canon, a set of Western texts that is argued to make up the totality of political thought. These texts are mostly presented as excerpts, with students reading concentrated sections of these texts, while accompanied by an interpretive text, like Michael Sandel's *Justice* or another secondary textbook (Sandel, 2010). On the surface, there is nothing wrong with this course structure, especially paired with a competent instructor. Students will leave the course having received an interesting engagement with the types of ideas and works that have shaped our world and might even be inspired to think deeply about their own lives as a result. However, such instruction does not provide much edification for the instructor and certainly doesn't support the goal of integrating teaching and research. This is true even if the instructor's own research is on a canonical text, as students will only spend a week or so on that text. In this model, instructors are encouraged to develop lectures where they disseminate knowledge from the lectern and then subject students to "objective" exams where they are quizzed on the minutiae of specific thinkers.

This represents what might be described as the "traditional method" of teaching political theory with its focus on delivering course content through lectures and focusing narrowly on the "great works." However, as the move toward critical pedagogy has become popular, there is an increasing desire to move away from this particular style of teaching and embrace a more discursive, open-ended structure aimed less at imposing a tradition of intellectual understandings on students and more at embracing the diversity of views at play in the modern classroom (Stommel et al., 2020). As Paulo Freire argues, this traditional model is an example of the "banking" form of education, which sees students as "'receptacles' to be 'filled' by the teacher" (Freire, 2018, p. 72). This form creates a specific power structure within the classroom, what Michel Foucault terms "hierarchical observation," where the purpose of teaching is to have students create a specific form of knowledge about themselves, designed exclusively for the instructor, who then uses this knowledge to pass judgment on the students (Foucault, 1995).

This "banking" model of education, with its inbuilt power structures, makes it more difficult to teach collaboratively. It becomes impossible to see students as fellow travelers on the intellectual journey. It also becomes much more difficult to use one's own political theory research in the classroom, as the instructor becomes tied to these traditional forms and standard texts.

To break out of this mold and both embrace a more open, collaborative form of teaching political theory and focus on "doing" political theory. Bell Hooks provides an example of this, showing us that "as a classroom community, our capacity to generate excitement is deeply affected by our interest in one another, in hearing one another's voices, in recognizing one another's presence" (hooks, 2014, p. 8). This focus on generating excitement through shared interest makes up the core of "doing" political theory in the classroom. By building a classroom community, we can focus on doing what Kevin Gannon calls "radical hope," where we can look forward and imagine a better future, through the act of teaching (Gannon, 2020).

Overall, the traditional method of teaching political theory is problematic for those interested in disrupting these older forms and is ineffective for combining teaching and research. Luckily, these two elements are tied together, as combining teaching and research is easier when critical pedagogy is embraced. The solution is to embrace a political theory pedagogy focused on "doing" political theory. This pedagogical strategy opens up the classroom for more critical and engaged discourse around the course material. It also lets the instructor bring more of themselves into the classroom, meeting what Bell Hooks calls the "self-actualization" of teaching, which makes the act of teaching so enjoyable (hooks, 2014).

"Doing" Political Theory in the Classroom

But what does it mean to be "doing" political theory in the classroom? Put simply, it is teaching texts in an interpretive way. Instead of relying on the "banking" model to inform students that, as an example, Plato intended a specific, objective meaning of the parable of the cave, we allow students to engage with their text on their own terms. We validate their interpretations and allow them to bring their own experiences to the table. The canon of political theory lends itself to a wide range of interpretations, with little that is established as "objective" or "settled" interpretation, especially in the details of specific texts. The research work of political theory is found in both the contestation of these interpretations as well as the broader project of taking these interpretations and using them to bring meaning to our everyday lives. There is no reason why this approach could not be opened up to even the most introductory students as well. If we work to treat the canon of political theory as a toolbox for understanding modern life, even when we apply it to the ancient and classical philosophers commonly found in the lower-level introductory courses, we allow students to engage with the texts on their own terms. We then work to train them not just to read old books, but to also become political theorists, even if just for a semester.

This approach can take several forms, but in my classroom, it begins with the syllabus. Instead of skimming through several excerpts from multiple authors in one week, I assign large chunks of a single author, even whole books when appropriate.[2] Assigning a large number of consecutive pages allows students to engage with the wider scope of the author and pick up on nuances of the text that might be missed with shorter excerpts. This is especially useful in introductory-level courses, where small excerpts require students to adjust to the different languages and styles of many different authors in one sitting. Then, at the beginning of class, I start by asking a broad, open-ended question for the students to discuss in small groups. As an example, I might ask students if Hobbes' *Leviathan* is a descriptive text or a normative text. This isn't a formal assignment, and there are no points attached.[3] Instead, the goal is to foster discussion and get students used to the idea of presenting their own interpretations of the text. I then began the formal class by asking for a quick report on the discussion that happened in the small groups, requiring them to justify their answers with evidence and reference to the text. This easily and naturally transitions into a focused discussion of

---

[2] The entirety of Machiavelli's *The Prince* can be assigned for one week of class, as an example.

[3] Many of my courses are also ungraded, so students do not receive quantitative grades at all. I have written about this strategy elsewhere (Kehlenbach, 2022).

the text for that week. At this point, students become more invested in the class and the discussion because they have already had a chance to engage with the text in a low-stake way. Focusing the discussion around having students take positions about an interpretation and then defend it by referring to the text itself both makes the class more student-driven and allows them to take ownership of their own views and develop their own arguments about the text, thus "doing" political theory.

In addition to the many advantages that taking such an approach to pedagogy has for student learning, it also has many advantages for the instructor, who wants to engage in a critical pedagogy while also supporting their own research agenda. One of the major advantages that comes out of a focus on "doing" is freedom from the canon of political theory. Often the canon of political theory can feel like a prison, trapping us into assumptions about what undergraduates "must" know before they can consider themselves educated in political theory. But the very existence of the canon comes under significant fire (Mills, 1999). We can begin moving beyond the canon when teaching all levels of political theory. The focus on "doing" can help facilitate this. Once you start thinking of students as fellow thinkers, you can open up the class to other views and more expansive definitions of political theory. It allows instructors the opportunity to focus less on what students must learn and allows the instructor to think more about the ways in which their independent research can be applied to the classroom.

One potential worry here is that moving beyond the canon might involve teaching texts that are exceptionally difficult, thus alienating students who are unable to keep up. However, in my experience, focusing on "doing" political theory mitigates this problem substantially. By reassuring students that the reading is indeed difficult, and they are not inadequate if they didn't understand the reading on the first try, students can begin to focus on the process rather than on any outcome. I share my own reading process with students and encourage them to see the text as a puzzle to figure out. For especially tricky texts, I then translate this to the classroom, diagramming the text collectively and working to display the arguments visually while walking through students' own views and interpretations. When doing this, I emphasize both that there is no "correct" answer and that we are all engaged in a collaborative act of "doing" political theory. This turns the classroom into an active scholarly environment that allows both the instructor and students to collectively build toward a full interpretation of the text.

What Do You Gain?

A classroom focused on "doing" political theory allows the instructor to teach their own research ideas. A personal example serves to illustrate this case. When teaching an upper-level modern political theory course, I decided that I was going to lean into the structure of "doing" political theory and create a more open-ended course, focused on my own research into technology and politics. Instead of a traditional course focused on canonical thinkers from the mid-nineteenth and twentieth centuries, I developed a new course based on my research agenda and designed the class around the texts that I was engaging with, reaching beyond what might strictly be seen as political theory to include historical, sociological, and ethnographic work in this class. I admit that this was facilitated by a number of structural factors that may not be true in every circumstance. First, the course description on file was intentionally written broadly to allow for a wide variety of course material. Second, this was an upper-level course for political science majors; a lower-level or introductory course may be more difficult. In the opening sessions of the class, I encouraged students to think about the role that technology plays in their own lives and how these questions might be framed as political. I also emphasized that this class was based on work in progress and that their contributions would be seen as well-intentioned and valid, regardless of my own interpretations of the texts. To encourage this, I set up the class, which met twice a week, into a lecture/discussion format. During the first meeting of the week, I prepared a lecture on the texts, using this time to help walk students through major arguments, diagramming difficult passages and presenting what I admitted was my own interpretation. Then at the second meeting, we had an unstructured discussion where students brought up questions and presented their own views and observations. Setting up the class this way allowed me to think through my own research by teaching my own foundational texts while also engaging students directly. Students expressed excitement for a class that represented cutting-edge political theory work and were happy to see that their contributions were taken seriously. Beyond additional student engagement, this course also provided a number of material benefits for my own research.

I have always found that presenting work that is in progress to be beneficial. Presenting work, either at conferences or to peers, is useful in clarifying arguments and generating ideas. Bringing my own research into the political theory classroom essentially allowed me to present my work twice a week to a sympathetic audience. It was amazing to see how engaged students were when they could see the process of research happen before their eyes. I also found that the prepared lectures were useful for the writing process. If recorded, or well prepared, it is possible to mine these lectures for material, using the arguments developed in class to support the work being done in the more professional scholarship. Bringing students into the act of "doing" political theory allows the instructor to gain immediate feedback on the work they are producing, in the form of lectures or prepared material, while also providing a focused outlet for this developing scholarship. In this way, an instructor can test out ideas before a sympathetic audience and see how the concepts work before subjecting their ideas to the rigors of peer review. Additionally, students have good ideas. They are engaging with the same material, and focusing on the task of "doing" political theory means they are empowered to present their ideas, which may be innovative and spark new perspectives for scholarship in progress. In my class, the discussions, spurred by student questions and observations, opened up new ways of thinking about my central research question and led me to unexpected investigations.

However, bringing one's own political theory research into the classroom leads to the tricky question of assigning your own writing. On the one hand, this seems like a simple and easy way to support political theory research and teaching at the same time. However, on the other, this might affect the hierarchical relationship in the classroom that the focus on "doing" political theory seeks to contest. Presenting work that the instructor has written, even work in progress, should be done with great care as it may intimidate students into abandoning their original views and interpretations in favor of supporting the instructor or telling them what they want to hear. Presenting your own work as a required reading, rather than one interpretation in a community of thinkers, works to establish the strict authority of the instructor, something we try to avoid through critical pedagogy.

Conclusion

Overall, the focus on "doing" political science in the classroom is a critical pedagogical strategy that empowers students to take their own views seriously and think about their contributions as part of the long historical and scholarly tradition of doing political theory. Doing this avoids the banking model of education and allows for student self-empowerment through the discussion of meaningful topics and engagement with important texts. This also has beneficial effects for the instructor who is looking to integrate their teaching and research. An emphasis on students "doing" political theory opens up the political theory classroom to new ideas and new course materials, thus allowing instructors to engage in expansive conversations with students about their own research agendas and to even use the classroom as a space to investigate the questions that arise within this research. Students can be an asset to research, as their perspectives and interpretations provide a constant form of feedback to the instructor engaged in scholarly work. Embracing a form of "doing" political theory in the classroom pays dividends to the student and the instructor while resisting the hierarchical, dominating approaches of traditional political theory classrooms.

References

Brown, W. (2010). Political theory is not a luxury: A response to Timothy Kaufman-Osborn's 'Political theory as a profession.' *Political Research Quarterly, 63*(3), 680–685. https://doi.org/10.1177/1065912910369843

Foucault, M. (1995). *Discipline & punish: The birth of the prison* (A. Sheridan, Trans., 2nd ed.). Vintage Books.

Freire, P. (2018). *Pedagogy of the oppressed* (50th anniversary). Bloomsbury Publishing\.

Gannon, K. M. (2020). *Radical hope: A teaching manifesto.* West Virginia University Press.

Gunnell, J. (2011). *Political theory and social science: Cutting against the grain.* Palgrave Macmillan.

Gunnell, J. G. (1993). *The descent of political theory: The genealogy of an American vocation.* University of Chicago Press.

hooks, b. (2014). *Teaching to transgress.* Routledge.

Kaufman-Osborn, T. V. (2010). Political theory as profession and as subfield? *Political Research Quarterly, 63*(3), 655–673. https://doi.org/10.1177/1065912910367495

Kehlenbach, E. S. (2022, December). A study of ungrading in upper-level political theory courses. *Journal of Political Science Education*, 19(3), 397–407. https://doi.org/10.1080/15512169.2022.2160336

Mills, C. (1999). *The racial contract* (1st ed.). Cornell University Press.

Parekh, B. (2013). Theorizing political theory. In N. O'Sullivan (Ed.), *Political theory in transition*. Routledge.

Sandel, M. J. (2010). *Justice: What's the right thing to do?* Farrar, Straus and Giroux.

Stommel, J., Friend, C., & Morris, S.M. (2020). *Critical digital pedagogy: A collection* [Online]. Hybrid Pedagogy Incorporated.

Strauss, L. (1988). *What is political philosophy? And other studies*. University of Chicago Press.

Wolin, S. S. (1969). Political theory as a vocation. *The American Political Science Review*, 63(4), 1062–1082. https://doi.org/10.2307/1955072

CHAPTER 32

Picturing Connections Between Hunger and International Relations: Using Images to Improve Learning and Research

Thiago Lima

Despite the capacity to produce healthy food and feed everyone, about one-third of the global population lacked access to adequate food in 2020, a situation worsened by the COVID-19 pandemic, but not created by it (Dias et al., 2021; Moseley & Clapp, 2020). As a teacher and researcher in Brazil, one of my main challenges is to help international relations students understand that there are international and domestic structures that perpetuate or worsen hunger and malnutrition not only in Brazil but in many other countries worldwide. Another challenge is to get students interested in researching the connections between hunger and international relations.

In my experience, using images in assessments was useful to cope with both challenges. It not only improved their learning process but also

T. Lima (✉)
Federal University of Paraíba (UFPB), João Pessoa, Brazil
e-mail: tlima@ccsa.ufpb.br

© The Author(s), under exclusive license to Springer Nature Switzerland AG 2023
C. Butcher et al. (eds.), *The Palgrave Handbook of Teaching and Research in Political Science*, Political Pedagogies,
https://doi.org/10.1007/978-3-031-42887-6_32

helped me to build new research projects and to have better research assistants and co-authors. In this sense, it was very important for the activities of the Research Group on Hunger and International Relations (FomeRI, an acronym in Portuguese) that I have been coordinating at the Federal University of Paraíba (UFPB) since 2012. In the last 11 years, I have published 26 articles in this field, 15 of which were co-authored with FomeRI's students.

In 2014, after two years of conducting reading cycles through FomeRI, I felt that the students had difficulty connecting with the issue of hunger, resulting in a lack of personal interest in the subject. Studying and discussing economic data, statistical tables, and texts were not sufficient to create the empathy that I expected from them. To tackle this issue, I started teaching undergraduate courses on agri-food systems, hunger, and international relations in 2016 and experimented with various active learning strategies involving images to promote more commitment and empathy. Essentially, I asked students, individually or in groups, to choose and present images (photos, paintings, HQs, small videos, engravings, etc.) related to the texts they were studying. They were required to explain the image's context and explain why it represented their reflections on the course's assigned readings. I used this activity in different ways in four different years, and the results were very satisfactory in terms of my personal impressions. Although I did not collect any systematic data, my experience as a teacher and research coordinator improved. In the following sections, I explain how I came up with the idea of using images in assessments and how I executed it. I also summarize how this strategy brought benefits to the students' learning process, my teaching practice, and the research agenda that I developed along with UFPB's students.

From Reading Groups to an Elective Course

Historically, hunger has been a neglected theme in the field of international relations in Brazil (Lima, 2014). Even today, few international relations courses have research areas or disciplines dedicated to the issue of hunger, and the situation was no different at UFPB. Recognizing this gap, I started the FomeRI Group in 2012, with two fundamental tasks.

The first task was to host extra class reading cycles on the connections between hunger and international relations. Each cycle had up to 10 students, including veterans from previous cycles. The cycles comprised an average of seven meetings, each lasting two hours, per academic period (four months). The second task was to conduct research. Often, research projects were elaborated after the reading cycles, or the cycles were used to spark interest in students who would later become my assistants or co-authors.

The contact with the students in these activities from 2012 to 2014 left me with the impression that they had a very distant view of the problem of hunger in Brazil and elsewhere. In fact, Brazil had been very successful in fighting against hunger from 2003 to 2014, and the strong national economic performance had reduced misery in the country during that period. When I asked students, usually aged 17 to 22, if they remembered seeing large numbers of hungry people in the streets, begging, picking garbage, or migrating to escape hunger—all things that I had seen with my own eyes since childhood—they usually said that they did not have that memory. Hunger, as a social problem, was not a concrete experience for most of them.

In 2015, I decided to transform the reading cycles into an elective course at the undergraduate level, with the goal of gathering more students around the theme. The first course was offered in 2016 and explored "Hunger, Food Security, and International Relations." The second course occurred in 2017 and focused on "International Governance of Agri-Food Relations." The third and fourth courses were titled "International Relations and Agri-Food Systems" and were taught in 2019 and 2021. Together, these courses received an average of approximately 30 students and were structured with four-hour classes per week and a total workload of 60 hours per period, which meant 15 encounters per academic period. In this format, I was required to carry out at least three assessments.

In all versions of the course, I kept a basic line that goes from the historical creation of hunger under capitalism and as a consequence of the expansion of the international system from Europe to the world, and closed with a reflection on what can be done to eliminate hunger in Brazil and the world. For this last part to be developed to satisfaction, students needed to engage in the course and develop empathy with hungry populations. In this way, the sense of urgency needs to dialogue with academic knowledge that sees hunger as a complex problem. That is, there are no simple solutions, but this should not prevent efforts from being made to change the situation immediately.

Integrating Images into the Learning Process

In my 2016 course, I informed my students that two out of three evaluations would be around a photo exhibition. I was inspired by a colleague who was studying photography as a hobby. He liked to take pictures of day-to-day urban scenes and explain why they were meaningful to him. So I required the students to choose a photo on the internet that depicted connections between hunger and IR and present their reflections on it in relation to the texts studied in the course. They were also required to submit a three-page essay that reflected on the chosen photo. During the research process, some students requested permission to present paintings instead of photos, which I allowed as I considered it to be a positive sign of interest and engagement. The exhibition day saw around 15 presentations, with each student allotted 10 minutes to present followed by five minutes for comments from the class. The images were shown using a data projector. Some images were more commonplace or selected with less care, while others were chosen with great interest, as in the case of paintings. Three widely recognized images were "Migrant Mother"[1] under a tent in the United States, "The Vulture and the Little Girl"[2] in South Sudan, and the painting "Os Retirantes" (Internally displaced migrants—free translation),[3] which depicted the refugees of drought and famine in Brazil. Even though some images were familiar to some, discussing their contexts in relation to the course texts generated productive debates during the exhibition and in the subsequent classes. One photo that garnered everyone's attention was that of the concentration camps for famine refugees in the Brazilian state of Ceará in 1932.[4] I had to verify the sources used by the students to believe what I was seeing.

The "Migrant Mother" and the picture of the Brazilian Concentration Camp inspired research projects within FomeRI, with the first one still ongoing with the assistance of undergraduate students. The goal is to

---

[1] "Migrant Mother" by Dorothea Lange, 1936, Nipomo, California, is available at https://www.moma.org/collection/works/50989.

[2] "The vulture and the little girl", by Kevin Carter, 1993, Ayod, Sudan (now South Sudan) is available at https://en.wikipedia.org/wiki/The_Vulture_and_the_Little_Girl.

[3] "Os Retirantes", by Cândido Portinari, 1934, Brazil is available at https://masp.org.br/busca?search=retirantes.

[4] Available at Rios (2014).

understand the crisis that made U.S. citizens go through a hunger and famine process very much like those of Brazil in the 1930s, as well as the government responses and the probable international causes. The latter image not only opened a research agenda that resulted in a published paper (Lima, 2023) but also allowed me to write about it in the media and to be invited for interviews and lectures on this topic.

In 2017, I modified the assessment method. I was inspired by a colleague's presentation at a seminar in Zimbabwe. My Mexican colleague, insecure of her English skills, decided to write and read her presentation. To make the moment more ludic—and to divert some attention from herself—she prepared an automatic presentation of photos and engravings on the Zapatistas, the subject of her communication. It was very charming, not only because the Zapatistas make very beautiful and meaningful pieces of art[5] but also because she was able to lock everyone's attention.

Since I had approximately 40 students, individual presentations were no longer feasible. I divided the class into groups, and each group was responsible for writing a speech to be read in the classroom as if they were at the United Nations. The speech should be accompanied by an automatic presentation of images, and an illustrated speech. The speeches should be 12–15 minutes long, and they had to submit a written version of it on which I could see them using the course's text as references. All speeches had to address the general theme "Seed and Sovereignty," inspired by the book organized by Shiva (2016). Students were free to choose any type of image, and they used photographs, drawings, paintings, magazine covers, advertising videos, or short footage prepared by the groups themselves, as this one.[6]

Most of the discourse was very combative, highlighting what the groups perceived as food injustices tied to the dynamics of international relations. Themes included the standardization of eating habits and the loss of cultural diversity; the oligopolization of the international agri-food system; science and technology as power resources; and the unequal distribution of natural and food resources mediated by the international market and currencies. It was evident that the images were chosen with care,

---

[5] One example is available at Martí i Puig, S. (2022). El muralismo zapatista: Una revuelta estética. *Latin American Research Review*, 57(1), 19–41. https://doi.org/10.1017/lar.2022.2.

[6] https://www.fomeri.org/post/teatro-pol%C3%ADtico-e-a-reforma-agr%C3%A1ria

and some were very creative. While some presentations were better than others, the whole activity was very moving. Some students were brought to tears by their classmates' speeches, and some presentations received real ovations. It was a splendid way to conclude the course.

In 2019, I had approximately 40 students and used the evaluation method again, but with a significant modification. Instead of using Shiva's book or any other book as a basis, I only provided the main theme for the speeches, "Food Sovereignty," and instructed the students to defend, defy, or constructively criticize the concept from the perspective of international relations. Although the results were satisfactory, they were not as good as in 2017. Several factors may have contributed to this, including the students being shyer than the previous year, many of them already having participated in FomeRI study cycles, so the theme was not new to them, and many being in their last year, which made their approach to the course more pragmatic. While the images were acceptable, they were not very inspiring. Another possible factor was that I focused too much on the speeches and less on the images when explaining the activity to the class.

In 2021, I had 25 students, and the course was online due to the COVID-19 pandemic. In this scenario, reading a speech would not have the same impact because it would not be possible to witness the real reaction of the audience. Initially, I considered requesting videos with illustrated speeches, but I noticed that students were already overwhelmed with "digital tasks" in a remote learning context. Therefore, I asked the groups to prepare a five-page photo-essay in which they had to explain why a particular photo of their choice illustrated the problem of hunger and its connections to international relations. They had to support their arguments with texts from the course and present them to the virtual class.

The results were excellent, and the class was very committed to the choice of photographs and the development of their arguments. Unlike previous years, hunger had become an urgent problem during the pandemic (Rede PENSSAN, 2021), and I believe this motivated the students. Meanwhile, Brazil was setting continuous records in food exports. The themes of the photographs were diverse, including the expansion of soybeans in Brazil, childhood obesity in Mexico during the pandemic, food aid to Zimbabwe, food diversity in Andean countries, and food insecurity in families headed by women, among others. However, I believe the most striking image was the one showing people disputing the remains of bones.[7] The group that presented the essay, composed of White students, made an argument about why Black people were the ones disputing the bones. They mobilized arguments around colonialism and the transformation of food into commodities, reflecting on how White people have more access to sources of income and food. They debated how this situation, in the case of Brazil, stems from the historical formation of the country as a colony.

Final Remarks: How Images Have Impacted My Teaching and Research

The use of images in my course assessments has made a significant impact on my teaching and research experience. In terms of teaching, challenging students to find the best image to illustrate their thoughts while considering the course's texts was a productive way to capture their attention and mobilize their efforts. Presenting their work to the class was useful in provoking discussions, and the cases represented by the images themselves became natural examples that helped to situate IR dynamics and theories. Moreover, in the context of UFPB, this type of assessment was markedly different from what the students were doing in other courses, making it an exciting novelty for them.

I also learned new tools from these experiences. First, illustrated speech. Many students had never prepared a text to read in public, and in Brazil, it is common to consider this type of presentation boring or an escape strategy for those who do not dominate the subject. However, illustrated speech was an exercise that created incentives for students to develop the ability to write discourses and read them to an audience. These are skills that many international relations professionals perform and develop throughout their careers. Second, I started using the strategy of contextualizing iconic images to start my classes. This works as a great icebreaker as it stimulates student participation from their cultural, and not necessarily academic, knowledge. I often use the painting Retirantes, photos of the Concentration Camps, and the Migrant Mother series, as well as music videoclips. Underlying all of them are questions such as: What is that person in that image doing there? How did she get there?

[7] Domingos Peixoto, 2021, Rio de Janeiro, Brazil: https://www1.folha.uol.com.br/mercado/2021/09/caminhao-de-ossos-no-rio-e-disputado-por-populacao-com-fome.shtml.

What are the processes, in terms of international relations, that placed that person there? Third, I believe that, overall, I got more commitment and empathy from the students than if I had not used the image strategy. It seems that they were motivated when they found that they could use their studies to analyze historical or day-to-day situations that were not, at first glance, themes of international relations.

Finally, I believe that these assessments contributed to the renewal of FomeRI's members by sparking interest in the group's research agenda. After ten years of this connection between reading cycles, teaching, and research, much of my academic production is co-authored with FomeRI's students. Students who participated in reading cycles or took classes with me performed better as research assistants and members of the group. Some of FomeRI's students have concluded their postgraduate studies at UFPB or in other universities, published their own papers, and become university teachers, carrying out the theme of hunger and IR through their research and teachings.

References

Dias, A., Amorim, L. S., Barbosa, I. P., & Lima, T. (2021). COVID-19 e (in)segurança alimentar: Os efeitos da pandemia na cadeia mundial de suprimento de alimentos. *Carta Internacional, 16*(2), e1151. https://doi.org/10.21530/ci.v16n2.2021.1151

Lima, T. (2014). Fome e Relações Internacionais: Uma agenda oportuna para o Brasil. *Carta Internacional, 9*(1), 94–104. https://cartainternacional.abri.org.br/Carta/article/view/111

Lima, T. (2023). The concentration camps for famine victims in Brazil and the struggle for their public memorialisation. *Third World Quarterly*. Advance online publication. https://doi.org/10.1080/01436597.2023.2190506

Moseley, W. G., & Clapp, J. (2020). This food crisis is different: COVID-19 and the fragility of the neoliberal food security order. *The Journal of Peasant Studies, 47*(7), 1393–1417. https://doi.org/10.1080/03066150.2020.1823838

Rede PENSSAN. (2021). *National survey of food insecurity in the context of the COVID19 pandemic in Brazil*. Retrieved April 24, 2023, from http://olhepararaafome.com.br/VIGISAN_AF_National_Survey_of_Food_Insecurity.pdf

Rios, K. S. (2014). *Isolamento e poder: Fortaleza e os campos de concentração de Seca de 1932*. Imprensa Universitária.

Shiva, V. (2016). *Seed sovereignty, food security: Women in the vanguard of the fight against GMOs and corporate agriculture*. North Atlantic Books.

CHAPTER 33

Knowledge Production and Student Learning in Political Science: Bhutan and The Politics of Happiness

Sarina Theys

INTRODUCTION

The maxim 'publish or perish' is a well-known phenomenon to academics from all ranks as the pressure to publish has long been considered a key fact within academic disciplines (Caplow & McGee, 1958; Lucas, 2006). Academic career paths are shaped by our publications as they are key elements in getting an academic job, standing out among peers, and career progression. Furthermore, publications in prestigious journals signal academic talent and enhance the reputation of academics as well as universities. However, the pressure to publish has far-reaching consequences such as heightened stress levels, the marginalization of teaching, and research that may lack relevance, creativity, or innovation

S. Theys (✉)
School of Law and Social Sciences, The University of the South Pacific, Suva, Fiji Islands
e-mail: Sarina.theys@usp.ac.fj

© The Author(s), under exclusive license to Springer Nature Switzerland AG 2023
C. Butcher et al. (eds.), *The Palgrave Handbook of Teaching and Research in Political Science*, Political Pedagogies,
https://doi.org/10.1007/978-3-031-42887-6_33

(Kinman & Jones, 2008; Miller et al., 2011). In addition to this, the pressure to publish takes time and energy away from teaching activities such as curriculum development, course preparation, lectures, seminars, grading, and advising. Consequently, academics with higher teaching loads tend to publish less. One way to deal with the publishing pressure and its consequences is to work smarter by integrating teaching and research.

This chapter is an example of research-led teaching which involves structuring the curriculum around subject content that is based on the research of teaching staff (Griffiths, 2004). More specifically, the chapter will illustrate how I have embedded my research on Bhutan and its development philosophy, Gross National Happiness (GNH), in an upper-year course on 'The Politics of Happiness', which has been embedded into the curriculum as a compulsory part of the Politics undergraduate degree programs. I elaborate on two approaches in detail. First, I used photos to discuss my research experience, the research methods that I have used during the field research in Bhutan, and the research findings. Second, I invited guest speakers who shared their expert knowledge on happiness with the students.

The chapter proceeds as follows. The next section discusses my research on Bhutan and GNH and how I have incorporated it into a course on The Politics of Happiness. Two approaches are discussed in detail: visual methods and guest speakers. The chapter concludes by highlighting the importance of embedding research into teaching and providing examples of how my approach might be applied to more generic courses.

Bhutan and The Politics of Happiness

Bhutan is a Buddhist kingdom situated in South Asia. It is landlocked between two Asian hegemons, China to the north and India to the south. The country is known for its development philosophy GNH, which promotes a holistic and sustainable approach to development by giving equal importance to economic and non-economic aspects of wellbeing (Royal Government of Bhutan, 2013; Theys, 2017; Theys & Rietig, 2020).

My research on Bhutan and GNH was a catalyst for the development of an upper-year course on 'The Politics of Happiness' in the field of Politics. I co-developed the course when I was teaching at a Russell Group University in the United Kingdom. The Russell Group is an association of twenty-four universities in the United Kingdom that are considered to be world-class, research-intensive universities. Furthermore, the university I was based at is consistently ranked among the top five in student satisfaction for research-intensive universities in the United Kingdom.

The Politics of Happiness is a compulsory course—requiring second-year undergraduate students to follow the course in order to progress to their third year. The course was divided into two parts. The first part covered philosophical approaches to happiness in the Ancient World (e.g., Socrates) and in the Modern World (e.g., John Stuart Mill), economics of happiness (e.g., economic growth), psychology of happiness (e.g., Maslow's Hierarchy of Needs), politics of happiness (e.g., democracy), and happiness and political ideologies (e.g., liberalism). The second part focused on the meaning and measurement of happiness (e.g., pleasure and satisfaction with life scale), GNH in Bhutan, happiness in other countries (e.g., the United States and India), international approaches to happiness (e.g., the United Nations), local approaches to happiness (e.g., happiness walk), and criticisms and alternatives to happiness (e.g., Ubuntu).

These topics were taught through the traditional lectures-based instructional approach and further discussed during small classes. In the lectures, I used visual methods, including photos taken during the field research, and invited experts to talk on some of the topics covered in the course. I will elaborate on these methods in the next section.

Photographs

I used photographs to illustrate and explain my research experience in Bhutan, the research methods used during my field research, and my research findings. For instance, at the start of the course, I explained that I conducted field research in Bhutan in 2009, 2011, and 2014. During this time, I examined whether and how GNH was implemented in government policies, and how GNH was developed, projected, and interpreted at a national and international level. One of the photos that I used showed Bhutanese men wearing a *gho*, the national dress of Bhutan, and playing archery, the national sport of Bhutan. Other photos that I showed depicted traditional houses and buildings in Bhutan, and monasteries and monks as Bhutan is a Buddhist country and GNH is influenced by Buddhist philosophy. These photos enabled students to form an image of the country that we were discussing and provided background information on GNH.

I also used photos to discuss the nature of the research and the research methods that I used in Bhutan. Specifically, I explained that the field research enabled me to observe and interact with Bhutanese state and non-state actors and that my research aim was to understand how these actors perceive, project, implement, and practice GNH. I further explained that I conducted original research which generated first-hand knowledge on topics discussed in the course. I collected qualitative data in a natural environment and the methods that I used included semi-structured interviews and (non) participant observation. To illustrate this, I showed a photo of research in action. The photo that I showed was taken at the end of one of the interviews that I conducted with Jigme Y. Thinley, the Prime Minister of the first democratically elected government of Bhutan.

I also used a photo of myself with Jigme Y. Thinley, the Prime Minister of the first democratically elected government of Bhutan, to discuss some of the findings of my research. For instance, through semi-structured interviews, I learned that Jigme Y. Thinley played a key role in developing GNH into today's concept, and in mobilizing GNH on a national and international level. He challenged fundamental ideas about what constitutes development and placed happiness on the global agenda. For example, the United Nations General Assembly (UNGA) adopted Resolution 65/309 *Happiness: towards a holistic approach to development* and declared 20 March each year the International Day of Happiness. Following this, other states adopted happiness in their policies and organizations and individuals engaged with the happiness policy. For instance, Venezuela created a Ministry of Supreme Social Happiness in 2013, there are annual World Happiness Reports, and UNESCO launched a Happy Schools Project. These findings were also published in a top international relations journal which was ranked 4th in the discipline ranking (See Theys & Rietig, 2020).

Furthermore, using photos in lectures is a powerful tool to engage students (Hallewell & Lackovic, 2017; Roberts, 2018) as they not only prompt a response from students (Horne, 2015) but also help them to grasp the content of the course, memorize it, and stimulate their thinking and creativity (Ulusoy, 2019). Research has also shown that most students today are visually oriented who expect and need visuals rather than verbal text content in their learning (Oblinger, 2003). These claims are corroborated by students who have stated that they learn better when visuals are involved in the class material as they 'bring another way to hear/see the information', 'provide a different perspective on the topic', and 'prove points that are explained in class' (Ulusoy, 2019).

Besides photos, I also invited guest speakers who are experts working on GNH or happiness more broadly. The guests were recruited through the networks that I have built through my research on Bhutan and GNH. The section below further elaborates on this.

Guest Speakers

Guest speakers are experts who share their knowledge, expertise, and real-life experiences with students (Lang, 2008). At the start of the course, I discussed the importance of networking for connecting to and working with other experts as well as the exchange of ideas. I selected guest speakers who are working on topics covered in the course. They delivered a talk online, via Skype, as they were based in different countries, and there was no budget to bring them over.

I had several Skype meetings with each guest speaker prior to their talk. During these meetings, I discussed my research in and on Bhutan, including GNH, and the course that I co-developed on The Politics of Happiness. I shared the course outline with the guests and asked them to prepare a talk on their expertise on happiness or GNH. I attended each session, which started with a brief introduction of the guests, including their work and expertise. The guests were free to choose the format of their talk, handouts, or a PowerPoint presentation. Each guest had about 40 minutes to talk after which a 20-minute question-and-answer discussion took place. I asked students to prepare questions prior to the talk and to email them to me.

One guest speaker was John De Graaf, an American activist, author, and filmmaker whose mission is 'to help create a happy, healthy, and sustainable quality of life for America' (de Graaf, 2022). John discussed his book—*What's the Economy For, Anyway?: Why It's Time to Stop Chasing Growth and Start Pursuing Happiness* (de Graaf & Batker, 2011)—and linked it to the concept of GNH. John challenged the students to reconsider the goal of the economy, including the importance given to GDP. He highlighted that a good economy should produce a better standard of living, and not simply accumulation of things. This perspective resonates with several topics discussed during the course such as GNH, as it is focused on collective happiness; the economics of happiness with a focus on GDP; and political philosophical approaches to happiness such as egalitarianism.

Another guest, Dutch diplomat, and researcher Dorine van Norren (2017, 2020) discussed Global South perspectives on happiness, including GNH, and highlighted the need to incorporate these perspectives in Western discussions on development, wellbeing, and happiness. Perspectives discussed by Dorine included the African philosophy of *Ubuntu* (a collective way of looking at the world—I am because we are) and native American Buen Vivir (the right way of living in harmony with nature and others). Dorine's talk provided in-depth knowledge of alternatives to happiness and how other countries understand and interpret happiness.

The guest talks were well received by the students who used the 20 minutes timeslot to ask a variety of questions. The nature of the questions ranged from more clarification on how we can change our approach to economic development to how applicable Global South perspectives on happiness are for people in the United Kingdom and the West more broadly. One student exchanged contact details with Dorine as he was planning to write a thesis on Ubuntu and wanted to discuss it in more detail with her. Student feedback was very positive ranging from exciting, interesting, and fascinating to inspirational, eye-opening, and thought-provoking. Students also highlighted that the guest lectures were a unique experience that enabled them to learn from experts in the field about important things in the real world. They confided that the guest speakers motivated them to learn more about the topics that were discussed. This became visible when some students decided to write a dissertation on happiness whereas others wanted to visit Bhutan.

Conclusion

The aim of this chapter is to provide an example of how political science faculty can work smarter by integrating their research into their teaching. I have used one of my research areas to illustrate how I have embedded my research on Bhutan and GNH in a second-year undergraduate course on The Politics of Happiness. Although critics might argue that The Politics of Happiness is a specialized course and thus, easier to embed research into teaching, the approach discussed in this chapter can also be applied to generic courses., such as an international relations or global politics course. Potential guest lecturers might be academic experts working on an international relations theory or a diplomat who discusses foreign policy and the importance of diplomacy for sustaining the current world order. Academic experts can be approached at conferences whereas diplomats can be reached via social media or email. As such, the approach discussed in this chapter is broadly applicable.

My research on Bhutan and GNH has significantly improved my teaching in a time and resource-efficient way, thereby enabling me to connect detailed real-world data with existing academic literature and debates on political economy, development, and happiness. Furthermore, the guest speakers supplemented my teaching by exposing students to their expert knowledge and recent developments in the field by bridging practice and theory. By incorporating my research into the heart of the student experience, I was able to broaden their knowledge on the topic, share my enthusiasm for research, and inform students about the knowledge production process.

REFERENCES

Caplow, T., & McGee, R. J. (1958). *The academic marketplace*. Basic Books.

de Graaf, J., & Batker, D. K. (2011). *What's the economy for, anyway?: Why it's time to stop chasing growth and start pursuing happiness*. Bloomsbury Publishing.

de Graaf, J. (2022). *John de Graaf*. Retrieved March 1, 2022 from https://www.johndegraaf.com/

Griffiths, R. (2004). Knowledge production and the research–teaching nexus: The case of the built environment disciplines. *Studies in Higher Education, 29*(6), 709–726.

Hallewell, M. J., & Lackovic, N. (2017). Do pictures 'tell' a thousand words in lectures? How lecturers vocalise photographs in their presentations. *Higher Education Research & Development, 6*, 1166–1180.

Horne, A. (2015, May 19). Using Photos in the classroom #1—The 'surprise factor. *Cambridge World of Better Learning*. https://www.cambridge.org/elt/blog/2015/05/19/using-photos-classroom-1-surprise-factor/#:~:text=Photographs%20offer%20a%20powerful%20way,language%20they've%20been%20learning

Kinman, G., & Jones, F. (2008). A life beyond work? Job demands, work-life balance, and wellbeing in UK academics. *Journal of Human Behavior in the Social Environment, 17*(1–2), 41–60.

Lang, J. M. (2008). Guest speakers. *The Chronicle of Higher Education, 54*(31). http://chronicle.com/article/Guest-Speakers/45746/

Lucas, C.J. (2006). *American higher education: A history*. Palgrave Macmillan.

Miller, A. N., Taylor, S. G., & Bedeian, A. G. (2011). Publish or perish: Academic life as management faculty live it. *Career Development International, 16*(5), 422–445.

van Norren, D. E. (2017). Development as service. *A happiness, Ubuntu and Buen Vivir interdisciplinary view of the Sustainable Development Goals* [Doctoral dissertation, Tilburg University].

van Norren, D. E. (2020). The sustainable development goals viewed through gross national happiness, Ubuntu, and Buen Vivir. *International Environmental Agreements: Politics, Law and Economics, 20*(3), 431–458.

Oblinger, D. (2003). Boomers, gen-xers, and millennials: Understanding the 'New Students.' *EDUCAUSE Review, 38*(4), 37–47.

Roberts, D. (2018). The engagement agenda, multimedia learning and the use of images in higher education lecturing: Or, how to end death by PowerPoint. *Journal of Further and Higher Education, 7*, 969–985.

Royal Government of Bhutan. (2013). *Happiness: Towards a new development paradigm.* Thimphu.

Theys, S. (2017). Constructivism. In S. McGlinchey, R. Walte, & C. Scheinpflug (Eds.), *International relations theory* (pp. 63–41). E-International Relations.

Theys, S., & Rietig, K. (2020). The influence of small states: How Bhutan succeeds in influencing global sustainability. *International Affairs, 96*(6), 1603–1622.

Ulusoy, E. (2019). *Importance of visuals in class discussions.* Faculty Resource Network. Retrieved March 10, 2022 from https://facultyresourcenetwork.org/publications/critical-conversations-and-the-academy/importance-of-visuals-in-class-discussions/.

PART VII

Conclusion

CHAPTER 34

Conclusion

Elizabeth Gordon, Tavishi Bhasin, Maia Carter Hallward, and Charity Butcher

We set out with the goal of creating an edited volume replete with ideas, approaches, and strategies for integrating teaching and research. The chapters in this book are particularly well positioned to aid political science faculty affiliated with teaching-focused institutions, though faculty at research-intensive universities will also find numerous tips for aligning their research and teaching. This concluding chapter draws out important themes from the book's six main sections, highlights ethical

---

M. C. Hallward · C. Butcher (✉)
School of Conflict Management, Peacebuilding and Development, Kennesaw State University, Kennesaw, GA, USA
e-mail: cbutche2@kennesaw.edu

M. C. Hallward
e-mail: mhallwar@kennesaw.edu

E. Gordon · T. Bhasin
School of Government and International Affairs, Kennesaw State University, Kennesaw, GA, USA
e-mail: egordon@kennesaw.edu

© The Author(s), under exclusive license to Springer Nature Switzerland AG 2023
C. Butcher et al. (eds.), *The Palgrave Handbook of Teaching and Research in Political Science*, Political Pedagogies,
https://doi.org/10.1007/978-3-031-42887-6_34

403

considerations related to undertaking the approaches described herein, and provides an overview of how professors can better align their teaching and research activities to improve the quality and impact of both.

This project emerged from numerous conversations over the years with political science colleagues at diverse institutions, all struggling with the challenges we ourselves face as faculty members at an institution with heavy teaching loads and increasing research and service expectations. Given these competing demands on our time, we wanted to collectively document ways that faculty could work smarter, not harder, to successfully address these various essential job duties while retaining our humanity. We are so pleased with the resulting volume, the diversity of voices within it, and the creativity of our contributors in devising and sharing a myriad of strategies for integrating teaching, research, and service to fulfill our roles more efficiently, to better serve our own needs at different points in our careers, and to simultaneously provide our students with engaging learning experiences both inside and outside the classroom.

A Philosophical Approach to Teaching and Scholarship

Several themes emerged as part of this book regarding approaches, strategies, and examples of how to best integrate the three essential areas of our academic lives. Among these is creating a philosophical approach to our work as teacher-scholars that critically reflects on the synergy between these often artificially separated areas of our academic lives before we enter the classroom. Whether, like Murphy, we engage in writing and rewriting our teaching philosophy statements to reflect our approaches at different stages of our careers, or whether this manifests in our discussion of our roles as teacher-scholars and university citizens in our annual reviews and tenure and promotion portfolios, a thoughtful, philosophical approach reminds us to prioritize integration of our teaching and research however and wherever we can. Just as importantly, this approach also sends a clear message to those reading these statements and narratives that our teaching and research roles are complementary, encouraging them to see

---

T. Bhasin
e-mail: tbhasin@kennesaw.edu

the value in processes and outcomes that integrate these areas, such as SoTL publications resulting from class activities or classroom assignments based on our research. Critically, such activities should be valued intrinsically, as they are often more creative and enriching for faculty, students, and the larger university community, with a broader reach than purely empirical or theoretical scholarship. However, as various chapters in this volume demonstrate, many institutions still lack resources for supporting teacher-scholars; we hope the contributions in this volume help raise awareness regarding the impact that teaching and learning centers, as well as career centers (as noted by Mallinson), can have on student learning and faculty productivity.

ETHICS AND THE SCHOLARSHIP OF TEACHING AND LEARNING

A second theme prevalent across contributions in this volume is that of SoTL ethics, particularly how to engage ethically in research that involves our students. As we increase collaboration with students, staff, and faculty at our institutions, we are likely to produce more SoTL publications, and many journals, including the *Journal of Political Science Education*, require authors to demonstrate institutional review board (IRB) approval for studies involving human subjects (i.e. students) or to provide a discussion of ethical research practices (if in a country without a formal IRB process). While many institutions have strong institutional review boards that guide such research, this is certainly not universal, and therefore it is important to discuss the ethical considerations involved in conducting research involving students in the classroom, as well as to outline the key steps involved in planning and designing such research. First, in keeping with many of the authors in this volume, we encourage faculty members to consider SoTL publications as a potential venue for sharing your own classroom interventions and their impact on student learning. If you are considering introducing an innovative assignment or assessment or collaborating with students on a classroom or extra-curricular activity, think proactively about how you might assess their learning and intellectual growth through the project. Some of the steps involved in conducting SoTL research include thinking through the ethical considerations early in conducting research on our students. These include student agency (giving students the option to opt out of surveys or from their work being used as samples for our publications), protections for students in the aggregate in our publications (protecting anonymity), and submitting the project for IRB approval so that our institutions can provide ethical oversight and legitimacy. Increasingly, scholars at institutions without institutional review boards are also being asked to include ethics statements in their SoTL submissions to journals to demonstrate they have conducted their research in keeping with broader ethical standards of the discipline, even if there is no such requirement at their home institutions. Even if you do not apply for IRB approval or create assessment tools the first time you innovate in the classroom, however, you can use what you learned in your trial run as the basis for crafting your IRB submission before the next time you experiment with that same assignment or teaching activity, as demonstrated in the chapter by Humphreys.

IRB applications can indeed take time, and may require revisions, so as noted by many of the authors in this volume, it is useful to plan ahead; it has also served us well to do additional advance work in the lead up to these projects such as drafting clear rubrics and instructions for students to make our lives easier in the implementation and analysis stages. Having such tools also can improve the quality of our research outputs by allowing us to have adequate sample sizes across different sections of courses, and even different semesters, without changing other parameters of the quasi-experimental research design. And, of course, designing surveys is just one way of assessing student learning. As illustrated in chapters such as Oztas and Redmond, students can demonstrate their learning through other avenues, such as metacognitive exercises or transferring their knowledge to other audiences.

Creating Strong Collaborations

Broader considerations include collaborating well with students and other partners. This may include informing them and educating them about the research process and the ethical challenges involved in such work. It also includes providing collaborators with early and adequate training so that they may fulfill their roles to the best of their abilities but also so they can take away the most learning from these experiences. Several contributors in this volume lay out different types of student–faculty collaboration as well as what level of intervention and mentoring is needed for the various types. Managing faculty and student expectations regarding patterns of communication, oversight, and deliverables is essential for success. Finally, part of our growth as teacher-scholars is learning our own strengths and limitations. Working smarter, not harder, involves planning research and classroom activities that not only complement each other, but that have reasonable, achievable goals and make the most of your available resources, including collaboration with students and other partners.

Importance of Student Agency in Learning

Another theme found in most of the chapters is the importance of student agency and having students be active participants in their own learning. For example, Kehlenbach emphasizes having students "do" political theory in the classroom, enhancing the collaborative learning experience. Other chapters focus on having students create assignments, including simulations and games (Allendoerfer; Butcher, Hallward and Tillman). Wendlend had students participate in exit polling for the Iowa caucuses, and Redmond discusses student-led service-learning projects. Oztas suggests having students craft their own learning objectives. In each of these examples, students have agency in their learning, and faculty and students work collaboratively to create a learning environment that benefits both the students and faculty. While faculty provide the scaffolding for the learning experience, by engaging students as partners in the learning process, faculty are freed up to help support and observe the impact of such learning activities on the students, creating an opportunity to document and write up the findings of such learning activities on student growth.

Varied Approaches for Integrating Teaching and Research

A primary goal of this book is to document innovative approaches to integrating teaching and research. Our authors provide examples varied in direction and type of integration (teaching influencing research and incorporating our research into our teaching) but also at varying levels of commitment. One of the key takeaways from this book, we hope, is that there is no one-size-fits-all approach when it comes to integrating our varied roles as faculty members. For some, it may work best to proceed with lower levels of student collaboration where students can help with data collection whereas for others it may involve co-authorship, involving a much higher investment of time and effort training students and overseeing their work. The pros and cons of these various approaches are captured neatly in Henshaw's chapter on making contingency work, and Bijsmans also provides concrete advice on considering types of research partnerships with students. Chapters in this volume show many possible combinations of teaching and research integrations, as well as how faculty have evolved in their approaches over the years and at different institutions; there is something for everyone, whatever your current motivations and limitations. Our authors also demonstrate that sometimes the possible synergy between our teaching, scholarship, and service may not appear for several years (Humphreys), and show the capacity for developing new campus institutions through documenting our efforts (McCartney). We hope these various case studies encourage faculty to continually reflect on how we can find synergy between our teaching, research, and service to improve our efficiency.

Chapters in this volume not only demonstrate a range of approaches to integrate teaching and research but also provide a range of research outputs. While colleges and universities traditionally emphasize research products such as journal articles or book chapters, authors show various ways that these outputs can also be venues for highlighting teaching, such as by evaluating student learning in a SoTL piece, or by having student researchers serve as co-authors in an apprenticeship model (Ishiyama). As noted by Blair, textbook writing is another way to integrate teaching and research, and, in the process, potentially attract new students to the field. Many different approaches to incorporating students into a research project, from data collectors to in-class reviewers of anonymized manuscripts, to full research partners, are discussed across a number of different chapters, along with the pros and cons of the various approaches. Across the board, contributors are self-reflective, noting that different career paths, institutional contexts, and environmental factors (such as the COVID-19 pandemic) shape the choices faculty can and should make in designing their desired research outputs and their path to achieve them.

Several chapters encourage faculty to think of students as collaborators in different types of research outputs. For example, contingent faculty may not have multiple years at the same institution to see a writing project through with students, nor might they have research recognized or expected as part of their workload (Henshaw). Fortunately, fully realized peer-reviewed research pieces are not the only kind of valuable output from student research collaboration. For example, data entry work completed by students can represent research progress for the faculty member and a learning experience for the students even in shorter timeframes, allowing students who lack the time to commit to a larger research project the opportunity to develop skills and reap other benefits. Students, when properly trained, can also help collect survey data, contribute to community partnerships, or conduct exit polling interviews. As detailed in several chapters in this volume, students can also help produce pedagogical materials such as simulations, textbooks, and other instructional materials. This kind of research experience leverages students' unique perspective as peers of the end product's consumers, i.e. they bring a sense of what they and their classmates would find useful and enjoyable, which faculty may lack.

ENRICHED FACULTY–STUDENT AND STUDENT–STUDENT INTERACTIONS

An added benefit to connecting teaching and research is the enrichment of faculty/student and student/student relationships. In most of the approaches described here, faculty describe working closely with students outside the classroom and/or interacting with them in different and potentially more effective ways in the classroom compared to traditional lecture formats and their attendant barriers. Several chapters in this volume describe the benefits of traveling with students to further research, e.g. to present joint work at conferences (Reilly), to engage in study abroad opportunities (Hamilton and Almeida), or to collect data (Wendland). Such travel creates unique mentoring opportunities as students observe their professors at work outside of the classroom and can competently engage in similar work alongside them. Additionally, students are likely to enhance their relationships with each other when taking their projects off campus. Integrating research and teaching can even enhance relationships between faculty and prospective students, by incorporating student research into pitches used in new student recruitment (Reilly).

While research collaboration can build partnerships, pre-existing faculty/student relationships can also drive collaboration. As explained in "The Benefits and Challenges of Faculty/Students Research Partnerships" (Bijsmans) and "Teamwork Makes the (Research) Dream Work" (Hellwege, et al.), as well as several other chapters, selecting the right students to work with makes a big difference to the ease and success of a research effort. Most faculty members are likely to select students who have made a favorable impression on them as being eager, bright, hardworking, and skilled in relevant ways (e.g. strong writing skills, methodological skills). If the goal is to create access to research experiences for a diverse group of students, though, several caveats should be considered. First, faculty may have less opportunity to get to know students in online and hybrid modalities, compared to those in regular face-to-face classes. Therefore, online students may enjoy fewer research opportunities or may have to be more assertive to attain them. However, Glazier's chapter does provide some good advice on how to engage online students in research despite the many challenges. Second, if faculty are selecting students with whom they have a rapport, unconscious bias can creep into the selection process. People generally create rapport more easily with others who are like them in relevant ways, so faculty should take care not to primarily recruit students who resemble their own backgrounds in terms of race, gender, class, religion, political outlook, etc.

Overloaded and Undercompensated Faculty

One limitation to innovative teaching/research ventures is the problem of uncompensated faculty time and effort. Setting realistic expectations of oneself (as well as one's students) is key to minimizing the risk of overload. Another key to managing the load is to carefully select research topics (Henshaw and Mallinson). While accommodating pedagogical goals and student interests, faculty should keep in mind that projects falling outside their own expertise are likely to demand more time and more intense faculty input. Furthermore, not all research-oriented student/faculty collaborations will fall neatly under a faculty member's teaching or research obligations, and some may fit but exceed expected workload. However, as we have seen in this volume, it may be possible to perform a hat trick by using these collaborations to enhance a faculty member's professional service. Some of the most obvious examples would be research involving community partners (Dobbs, Redmond, and Glazier).

Creating research products of value to community groups should fall squarely within many political science departments' service expectations. Faculty might also pursue projects that straddle the research/service boundary and could count for either or possibly both, such as contributing to in-house downloadable repositories (Wendland) or writing textbooks and other instructional material (Blair and Strachan). Other service-oriented approaches might include enhancing student

34 CONCLUSION 411

recruitment and advisement efforts by highlighting student research experiences and outputs (Reilly) or arranging on-campus presentations or workshops based on student research collaborations.

We leave you with this collection of ideas, approaches, and strategies and a myriad of examples of faculty members across varied institutions around the world, finding creative ways to maximize the impact of their efforts across their scholarship, teaching, and service while conserving time, energy, and intellectual resources in the process. We hope you find a continuous source of inspiration but also clear examples and blueprints for how to integrate your teaching, scholarship, and service at a pace and level that suits your needs and the demands of your institution. This book does not seek to provide comprehensive coverage of all the ways in which faculty members may combine their efforts across work areas. We only hope our book brings this important conversation to more faculty interested in finding and implementing similar interventions where there exist synergies between their roles.

Index

A
Adjunct(s), 103, 172
Affective polarization, 352
American Government, 24, 51, 104, 142
American politics, 106, 260, 292, 355
APSA Educate, 92, 108, 332
APSA TLC, 306
Assessment, 18, 25, 36, 53, 64–69, 80, 83, 143, 155, 224, 238, 249, 290, 327, 328, 333, 344–346, 385–387, 391, 392, 406

B
Biographies, 231, 276
Blended curriculum, 195, 196
Bloom's taxonomy/Bloom's learning taxonomy, 62, 345
Boyer's model of scholarship, 296

C
Canva, 237, 238
Capstone, 9, 27, 28, 130, 150, 187, 328, 330, 333, 334
Civically engaged, 285, 288
Civically engaged research (CER), 9, 317, 319, 324
Civic engagement, 8, 9, 50, 104, 110, 142, 285, 287, 301–305, 312, 317, 320–322, 324, 343
Civic engagement-service-learning (CESL), 303–305
Clergy, 220–222
CNN, 355
Co-author(s), 56, 66, 68, 96, 118, 121, 123, 131, 153, 176, 177, 212, 248, 249, 251, 252, 363, 366, 368, 386, 387, 408
Cognitive analysis, 156
Collaborative learning exercises, 40
Community-based partnership(s), 369
Community-based research (CBR), 8, 219–221, 223, 224, 226, 227, 288, 297
Community college, 93, 103

Comparative politics, 9, 50–53, 55, 303, 342, 344–346
Conceptualization, 209, 214, 342, 349
Congregations, 220–223, 225–227
Constitution Day, 26
Contingency, 171, 173, 179, 407
Contingent faculty, 7, 172, 173, 175, 176, 178, 179, 408
Course designs, 18, 25, 233, 327, 329, 340
COVID/COVID-19, 8, 65, 68, 91, 145, 157, 220–222, 226, 227, 249, 251, 273, 277, 306, 313, 319–321, 329, 330, 342, 385, 390, 408
Critical pedagogy, 373, 374, 376, 377, 379, 381
Critical thinking, 8, 51, 61, 69, 76, 80, 140, 183, 247, 251, 253
Cultural exchange programs, 8
Curriculum, 8, 18, 52, 53, 92, 115, 128–130, 139, 151, 182, 183, 185–188, 190, 191, 195, 212, 249, 321, 394

D
Debriefing, 53, 54, 58, 70, 80, 83, 85, 291
Democracy, 41, 54, 83, 91, 209, 274, 280, 290, 292, 293, 342, 395
Directed research, 62, 64
Doctoral students, 29, 30, 195

E
Early career scholars, 171
Educational experiences abroad, 246
Embodied learning, 247
Engaged citizens, 286
Evidence-based pedagogy, 242
Excel, 164, 362, 365

Exit polls, 9, 260–268
Experiential learning, 8, 9, 63, 130, 238, 246, 249, 251, 253, 254, 275, 280, 288, 289, 303, 304, 310, 333
Experimental, 51, 109, 153, 154, 197, 211, 290, 351, 354, 355, 364
Experimentation, 17, 154–156, 186
Experiment(s), 155, 184, 190, 198, 210, 264, 287, 289–293, 327, 328, 355, 406

F
Faculty engagement, 253
Faculty-student research, 116–118, 120–122, 288
Field studies, 8, 246, 247, 249–253
First-generation students, 167, 168
Flipped classroom, 329
FomeRI, 386, 388, 390, 392
Food aid, 390
Food diversity, 390
Food exports, 390
Food injustice(s), 389
Food security, 387
Forced adaptation, 331
Fox News, 355
Freedom House, 91, 342
Funding, 2, 3, 7, 9, 92, 131, 138–140, 142–146, 157, 175, 178, 183, 202, 203, 278, 306, 312, 320, 325

G
Games, 6, 61–71, 77, 80–83, 85, 208, 328, 407
Geneva Convention, 66
Get-out-the-vote (GOTV), 287, 291
Global governance, 94
Global issues, 10, 231, 239, 242

Global North, 102, 103
Global South, 103, 398
Google Documents (Google Doc), 238
Graduate programs, 133, 134, 141, 208, 214, 249
Graduate students, 3, 7, 15, 24, 50, 117, 140, 144, 165, 166, 172, 196, 201, 207, 208, 211–213, 215, 221, 287, 305, 363
Grants, 9, 138, 142–146, 151, 153, 164, 168, 179, 200, 201, 203, 278, 302, 305, 306, 309, 310, 312, 318, 321
Great Contraction, 138–140, 146
Gross national happiness (GNH), 10, 394–399

H
Happiness, 394–399
Higher Education (HE), 5, 79
High Impact Practices (HIPs), 150, 232
Honors College, 238, 302–304, 306, 310, 313
Humanities, 78, 145, 146, 152, 404
Human rights, 61–68, 70, 234
Hunger, 10, 385–388, 390, 392
Hypotheses, 79, 198, 201, 210, 279, 286, 287, 363, 365

I
iClickers, 24, 25
ICONS, 50
Information literacy librarian, 330
Institutional review board (IRB), 53, 62, 76, 143, 149, 182, 201, 222, 227, 267, 328, 334, 405, 406
International affairs, 68, 196, 242, 303
Internationalisation, 92

International relations, 19, 50, 51, 62, 63, 65, 68, 104, 208, 301, 303, 385–387, 389, 390, 392, 398, 399
International Relations in Action, 50
International Studies, 76, 103, 104, 108, 213, 303, 304, 328, 330, 331, 334
Iowa caucus(es), 9, 273, 275, 277, 279, 281, 407
iziSurvey, 185, 186

J
Job market, 14, 20, 172, 179, 213, 369

L
Lab, 7, 133, 134, 150, 152, 164, 169
Learner-centered, 37
Learner-centered teaching, 40, 62
Learning objectives, 5, 36, 38, 52–55, 57, 70, 80, 122, 294, 297, 323, 344, 345, 348, 407
Learning typologies, 344, 345
Lecture capture, 24
Liberal arts (college), 3, 36, 103, 172, 174, 175
Literature review, 175, 198, 209, 210, 279, 287, 330, 341, 350, 368

M
Mafia, 6, 75–77, 80–83, 85
Masters-level students, 195, 196
Media, 94, 108, 109, 199, 202, 222, 224, 225, 260, 264, 266, 276, 277, 292–295, 318, 319, 350, 355, 389, 399
Media bias, 356
Mentoring, 23, 29, 30, 117, 127, 128, 133, 150, 154, 161, 164, 169, 173, 175, 207, 208, 214,

215, 252, 302, 305, 309, 311, 312, 406, 409
Metacognition, 38
Metacognitive exercises, 5, 35, 41, 44, 406
Metacognitive knowledge, 38
Metacognitive model, 44
Metacognitive skills, 41, 43
Metacognitive strategies, 36, 39, 43, 44
Methods, 7, 8, 43, 63, 77, 93, 118, 129, 140, 143, 152, 181–183, 186, 188, 198, 207, 208, 210–213, 232, 235, 259, 260, 263–265, 287, 303, 354, 355, 361–363, 365, 366, 368, 369, 377, 390, 394–396
Migrant Mother, 388, 391
Minority-serving institutions, 103
Mock trial, 26
Model UN (MUN), 26, 56, 302–304
Monkey Cage, 347

N
National Conference on Undergraduate Research (NCUR), 306, 309
National Election Pool survey, 260
Nearpod, 25

O
Online, 8, 26, 63, 68, 70, 92, 116, 220–227, 250, 319, 329, 331, 334, 355, 397, 409, 410
Operationalization, 10, 209
Organized crime, 75, 77, 80, 83
Os Retirantes, 388

P
Party identification, 263, 295

Photographs/photo(s), 232, 280, 386, 388–391, 394–397
Policymakers, 94, 95, 196, 203, 220
Political Behavior, 185, 186, 188, 351, 352
Political economy, 399
Political elites, 276
Political participation, 292, 322, 343
Political Science Club, 292
Political theory, 63, 373–382, 407
POLITY IV, 342
Pollsters, 261, 265
Portfolio, 15, 16, 128, 130, 132, 196, 323, 404
Positive feedback cycle, 350, 356, 358
Post-doctoral researchers, 172
Poster gallery, 332
Practical applications, 183, 196, 203
Primarily Undergraduate Institutions (PUIs), 340, 343
Primary Investigator (PI), 221–223
Project-based learning, 232, 242
Public opinion, 36, 129, 156, 186, 259, 262, 265, 266, 292, 294, 295, 352
Public service, 25

Q
Quality of Government (QoG), 346
Quantitative, 43, 64, 181, 183, 187, 198, 201, 259, 263–265, 343, 361–365, 367, 369, 378

R
R, 362–364
R1 (university/institution), 172, 176
Random digital dialing (RDD), 185, 186
Real-world application, 174, 202, 347
Reflection, 5, 14, 17, 20, 23, 38, 41–43, 49, 51, 62, 65, 66, 70,

83, 92, 93, 95, 172, 202, 239, 246–248, 251, 253, 279, 280, 286, 292, 295, 324, 332, 386–388
Reflection prompts, 42
Reflective essays, 36, 44, 252
Regional comprehensive (university), 1, 127, 172, 327
Regional public university, 103, 287
Regional university, 3, 260
Research assistants (RA), 7, 30, 138–140, 142, 144–146, 151, 162, 164, 165, 167, 168, 175, 179, 287, 386, 392
Research-based learning, 183, 184, 187, 190
Research methods, 10, 153, 154, 190, 260–264, 268, 287, 342, 350, 351, 353, 361, 362, 364–367, 369, 394–396
Research-oriented teaching, 7, 183–185, 188, 190
Research team, 7, 116, 162, 164, 166–170, 222, 321
Role-play(s), 6, 51, 77–80, 82, 84, 85, 291, 294
RStudio, 363, 364

S
Scholarship of Teaching and Learning (SoTL), 2, 4, 5, 14, 16–18, 24, 44, 50, 53, 104, 182, 242, 286, 290, 296
Science, Technology, Engineering and Mathematics (STEM), 116, 138, 140, 145, 146, 309, 310
Self-assessment(s), 36
Self Determination Theory (SDT), 79
Self-reflection activities, 38
Service-learning, 8, 26, 134, 232, 238, 240–242, 251, 288, 302, 303, 407

Simulation(s), 6, 25, 26, 41, 49–58, 61, 63–65, 80, 328, 333, 407, 409
SMART goals, 39
SPSS, 362
Statecraft, 50, 55
Statistical methods, 361
Structured inquiry, 199
Student-centered, 6, 62, 76, 77, 139
Student research assistant, 145, 161–163, 165, 167
Study abroad programs, 249–253
Super Tuesday, 274
Survey, 24, 25, 76, 83, 84, 92, 129, 164, 184–188, 221–226, 249, 259–268, 290, 293, 305, 313, 321, 328, 334, 353, 355, 367, 405, 406
Survey experiments, 186, 354, 363
Survey methods, 187, 362
Survey research, 8, 182, 184–187

T
Teacher-scholar model, 4, 5, 7, 44, 137–139, 141
Teacher-scholar(s), 5, 6, 102, 103, 138, 143, 144, 146, 362–366, 368, 369, 404–406
Teaching philosophy statements, 13–20, 404
Teaching portfolios, 14–16, 129
Teaching-research-service paradigm, 349
Team building, 162, 170, 265
Teamwork, 6, 27, 85, 162, 167, 294, 409
Textbooks, 6, 93–98, 101–110, 210, 354, 376, 409, 410
The Vulture and the Little Girl, 388
Think-pair-share, 38
Transformative knowledge, 247, 251

Transparency in Learning and
  Teaching in Higher Education
  (TILT), 241

U
Undergraduate Research Club
  (URC), 9, 310, 311, 313
Undergraduate research experience,
  149–151, 156, 306, 356
Undergraduate research (UR), 65,
  127, 128, 130, 134, 139, 149,
  157, 165, 167, 301, 302,
  304–313, 320, 325
Undergraduate students, 6, 7, 9, 24,
  28, 50, 52, 57, 62, 64, 65, 69,
  121, 128, 135, 145, 150, 153,
  156, 162, 166, 176, 242, 260,
  318, 320, 321, 323, 347, 376,
  395
United Nations (UN), 303, 389, 395
UN Security Council, 63

U.S. politics, 289, 322, 324

V
Variables, 51, 56, 198, 209, 211,
  351, 364, 366, 367
V-Dem, 342
Visiting professors, 172, 173
Voter registration, 9, 287, 289

W
Walklists, 291
Wix, 331
World politics, 37, 38, 41–44

Y
Youth Voice, 9, 318–323

Z
Zapatistas, 389